VILMA VUKELIĆ

A PAST RESCUED
FROM OBLIVION

A self-portrait of a young woman
defying the conventions of her time

FriesenPress

Suite 300 - 990 Fort St
Victoria, BC, V8V 3K2
Canada

www.friesenpress.com

Copyright © 2020 by Ivana Caccia
First Edition — 2020

Translator Ivana Caccia
Editing consultant Susan Buchanan

ISBN
978-1-5255-5628-9 (Hardcover)
978-1-5255-5629-6 (Paperback)
978-1-5255-5630-2 (eBook)

1. Biography & Autobiography, Historical

Distributed to the trade by The Ingram Book Company

VILMA VUKELIĆ

A PAST RESCUED
FROM OBLIVION

Translated from the German original by

Ivana Caccia

Ottawa 2020

PREFACE

We all have at home a drawer or a box full of photographs, odd documents, and old letters that we keep as mementos of our passage through life. At the bottom of my drawer lay for many years a thick folder containing my grandmother's memoirs, which she had admittedly written with her grandchildren in mind a couple of years before her death in 1956. It was a messy bundle of yellowed pages covered from top to bottom with typewritten text and a myriad of hardly readable handwritten corrections and additions—all in German. Some forty years ago, I made a heroic short-lived attempt to translate it. The twenty-odd pages that I did translate at the time into Croatian (my mother tongue) were shown to a literary expert in Croatia who immediately realized that my grandmother was an excellent writer and an astute observer of her surroundings. Vlado Obad translated the bulk of the manuscript from German into Croatian, gave it a title, *Tragovi prošlosti* (Traces of the Past), and it was published in Zagreb in 1994. She has been ever since a recognized literary figure in Croatia.

I forgot all about my copy of the manuscript until one day I happened to rummage through that deep drawer and, on an impulse, pulled out the folder. I decided to read it. The memoirs covered the events of my grandmother's life from her earliest childhood (she was born in 1880) to 15 August 1904, the day her first child, Branko, was born. It was a vividly and intelligently told story of the intellectual awakening at the turn of the twentieth century of a young woman born into a well-off Jewish family in a small provincial town called Osijek, at the outskirts of the Austro-Hungarian Empire. I decided that I would not falter this time in translating the manuscript myself, to its last page, this time into English, and hopefully give it the wider audience it deserves.

It is a remarkable contribution to women's history in the form of a self-portrait of an intelligent and audacious young woman and a burgeoning feminist, who resisted the pressures by her family and friends to follow the social norms imposed on women of her generation. It is a contribution to the history of central and southeastern Europe, with its detailed and spirited descriptions of the bourgeois life in a provincial town on the shores of the River Drava, close to the Hungarian-Croatian border.

At the same time, it is a contribution to Jewish history, with its specific emphasis on life in small Jewish settlements in central and eastern Europe (today's Croatia, Hungary, Austria, The Czech Republic, Slovakia, Romania). It is also an account of the optimistic, late nineteenth-century, Jewish endeavours towards social integration and full acceptance by the surrounding society—hopes and expectations tragically shattered soon after.

Most of all, it is a lively and charming account of a happy childhood full of colourful descriptions of a little girl's discoveries of the wonderful as well as bleak aspects of life. There is also an account of life in an elite boarding school in Vienna and a romantic love story, including chance meetings, an overprotective and unsympathetic father, house confinements, daily secret exchanges of love letters, and a happy ending (or so it appeared at the time!).

My grandmother was a keen observer and an avid reader. Her reading was extensive, and she talks frequently in her memoirs of authors and poets who had a major impact on her intellectual maturing. This translated version is annotated to provide readers with basic information on people—writers, visual artists, theatre performers, historical and political personalities—whose names she mentions in the text, and to situate various geographic places in their present-day geopolitical space.

I invite you to meet my remarkable grandmother and read her story.

Ivana Caccia

Ottawa, March 2020

PART I

A CHILDHOOD IN A SMALL TOWN BY THE RIVER

et me begin by saying something about my hometown—Osijek. It is situated on one of the most fertile plains in Europe, on the shores of the navigable River Drava, which throws itself into the Danube a short distance downstream. One of the most important European trade roads, running from Vienna all the way to Constantinople, passes nearby. Throughout its past—most significantly after 1848—the area thrived on the export of raw materials typical of this region such as wood, leather, cereals, and wine, as well as on the manufacture of various goods. There was a definite potential to make easy money, which attracted numerous able merchants from Moravia, Bohemia, Hungary, and Slovakia to settle here. Their customs and linguistic diversity gave the town a unique character, distinguishing it from others in Croatia.

In its early days, Osijek consisted of several independent town districts, which differed so much among themselves in their customs and ways of life that they even formed separate municipalities in Empress Maria Theresa's time.[1] Due to the number of its inhabitants and its wealth, the Lower Town was for a long time most prominent. During the reign of Maria Theresa, the Upper Town had only 378 households and altogether four shops, whereas 539 families lived in the Lower Town. The majority of those living in the Lower Town were of Croatian origin, but there were also 137 Serbian, 43 German, and two Jewish families. At that time, and for a long time afterwards, Jews and Serbs were not allowed to settle in either the area around the military controlled Tvrđa (the Fortress) or the Catholic Upper Town.

One of the reasons the three municipal units were not unified administratively was the fact that the roads that connected them were almost impassable, especially in winter, when whole neighbourhoods would literally sink into the swampy ground. The same town magistrate was simply not able to attend to his business in all three units at the same time.

But it was not only the difficulties caused by the terrain that divided those municipal communities. There was also a mutual antagonism and an uneven rate of progress. By the beginning of the nineteenth century, the Upper Town had clearly overtaken the Lower Town in its development. The antagonism and competition prevailed and deepened so that by the end of that century, the town was still divided into two distinct parts with one thing in common—the inhabitants of both parts were equally proud of their *Esseker*[2] identity. While the Upper Town Essekers were enjoying a rapid advancement in their way of life and exhibited all the flaws and advantages of the *nouveaux riches*, the economic status of the people of the Lower Town saw no improvement, and it could even be said that it had regressed. Motivated by materialistic interests, those from the Upper Town embraced utilitarian modernism and blindly copied everything that came from large cultural centres such as Vienna and Budapest. Those from down under considered them reckless and big-mouthed. They vigorously objected to their advanced ideas (presented to the town council in the form of various and expensive projects) and found it difficult to accept the fact that the Upper Town citizens, despite their flaws, were not only much better off but also had a far greater influence on the town council.

As for the origins of the city and its three communities, there exist only assumptions and legends, none of which confirms with historical certainty the various claims regarding the time and circumstances of their establishment. One such legend has it that the Lower Town was founded by the inhabitants of a small village on the other, left side of the River Drava, when they decided to relocate and escape regular floods taking place every year along the lower left bank of the river, which endangered their homes and property. The Fortress was originally built by the Turks as defence against Christian military advances from the north, and its inhabitants were forced to pay an annual tribute to the pasha in Nagykanizsa.[3] Close to the Fortress was a seven-kilometre-long wooden bridge heading towards the village of Darda. It was built over the spreading arms of the River Drava and the surrounding marshlands. In its time, the bridge was considered to be an eighth Wonder of the World. During their final retreat from the area, the Turks burned it down. The Upper Town was, in its early stages, most likely a fishing village. That changed with the arrival of German craftsmen, who settled in the shelter of the citadel walls. It was the favourable geographical position at the crossroads of many trade routes—considered an important economic factor before the arrival of railroads—that has played a crucial role in making these three disparate communities merge and form over the course of two centuries the urban agglomerate as it stands today.

While nothing new had been built in the Lower Town for a long time, a new street named Comitatsgasse, or Županijska Street (County Street), emerged in the Upper Town in the 1860s. The street soon became the town's commercial and social centre of gravity. It was a wide road running from the main square in the Upper Town down to Tržna Street (Market Street) and from there through the nearby villages of Čepin and Tenje, all the way to the towns of Đakovo and Vinkovci. Furthermore, it provided a direct connection with Bosnia and was recognized as fully passable and the shortest way inland throughout the year. Even after the introduction of the railroads in the area, Osijek served as the terminal of a single railway line that connected it to Budapest. When travelling to Zagreb, one had to make a detour by first stopping at Dombóvár, taking the connection from Kaposvár to Zákány, and after yet another crossing over the River Drava, returning to Croatia and heading for Zagreb.

Županijska Street was quickly settled by wealthy merchants, who built their houses and opened their shops across the street from the parish church and the County Palace. The one-storeyed houses had neatly plastered facades decorated with stucco ornaments in the form of festoons of flowers, shells, and winged angels, and white and green window shutters. Well-stocked warehouses were in the backyards. Big horse-driven carts could be seen daily going through wide-open carriage gates delivering heavy loads of various goods and merchandise.

The most elegant building in town at the time was the Grand Hotel, next to which was an equally elegantly outfitted gentlemen's club called Casino. This was a place where the town dignitaries read their newspapers, played a few card games, and exchanged their opinions on politics. In the Casino building itself was a small but cozy theatre where every year a different German theatre company, of variable artistic quality, staged its performances. Often the actors were first timers who used this stage to test their performing skills. More often, they were out-of-favour or unsuccessful old actors who had already been on all provincial stages in the Austro-Hungarian Empire. Here they would once again impersonate young lovers in curly white wigs, older ladies would star as ingénues, and singers who had already lost their voices would once more attempt to reach high C major.

As late as 1885, the only public transportation between the Upper Town and the Lower Town was an old omnibus in the shape of a big chest pulled by an old skinny horse along a cobbled path full of potholes. It took a whole hour to get from one main square to the other, although the distance between them was only four kilometres. That omnibus and that ride from one part of the city to the other form one of my earliest childhood memories.

Changing homes is disturbing for a child and to me it happened every summer as my mother was sickly for a long time after my birth and used to go on health trips to Karlsbad,[4] Ischl,[5] or other sanatoriums. On the eve of her departure, my grandmother would fetch me from home and ride with me to the Lower Town by omnibus. My grandparents owned a house a close distance from the omnibus station. Those changes in my surroundings must have had undoubtedly a disturbing effect on me. A child cannot observe with indifference that the bedroom walls have suddenly changed, that different arms and hands put her to bed, and the bed itself is not the same familiar crib. A child notices when the air smells different, when the night consists of different sounds and some other cockerel is crowing under the window at the break of dawn, when another kitten is mewing in the front yard, and when the breakfast coffee with the bread bun tastes different from at home.

All these various fragments of memory have, however, something in common. Who can after sixty years claim with certainty that something in the past was experienced in precisely this way, and not some other way? The past is intertwined with the present and it is hard to recover the memory of an event in the distant past without stumbling over more recent layers of consciousness that indirectly influence our original impressions. Many things have, in the meantime, accumulated in our minds from other sources—photographs, other people's accounts, and explanations. One must break through these heterogeneous layers of consciousness and extract the original memory underneath the subsequent additions—even when it sometimes appears impossible—and differentiate between what one actually saw and experienced at the time and what has later been added by means of hindsight.

My grandparents' house was a one-storeyed building resembling all the other houses encircling the large grass-covered main square of the Lower Town. At the front of the house was a retail shop specializing in textiles and sewing accessories, which my grandfather first opened himself in 1852 and later managed in partnership with David Hermann.[6] The store itself was some thirty-six square metres in size and had a narrow shop window with colourful ribbons, sewing accessories, fustian, and Katun cloth on display. The two owners managed the shop in a strictly puritan way. They were honest and serious, neatly calculating everything, even the tiniest details. At the start, such a method makes any large profit practically impossible, but it does ensure success in the long run. At five in the morning, the whole household would be already up and running. The shop stayed open throughout lunchtime and closed late in the evening, when small paraffin lamps were lit and the entire neighbourhood began to slip into darkness. In the early days, regardless of the weather, my grandparents would go to country fairs to showcase their goods. By the 1880s, that was no longer necessary. The shop was doing well. They established good relationships with their regular customers, whose tastes and needs they learned to know well and to whom they were able, from time to time, to offer advantageous price reductions. The relationship between the two owners was not based on a specific formal agreement, or on constant mutual supervision, but rather on complete trust. Each of them took from the till only the amount of money they needed to cover the necessities of life. Although the two partners invested their capital and labour in equal shares into the venture, my grandparents, who had only one child, did not in any way consider it inappropriate that their share of the profit was almost three times lower than that of their partner's, who had a big family. The same was true with regard to the merchandise. Everybody took from the store what they needed, whether linen, fustian, cloth, thread, wool, soutache, or buttons, always according to the number of people who required clothing. Here three, there nine. Even the workload distribution was done according to the same principle. My grandmother helped the partner's wife whenever there was a need. She helped with numerous births, took care of the older children during their mother's absence, attended to them when they were ill, and knitted, mended, and sewed for them. She did not mind living in the small apartment on the courtyard side and gladly let the other family have the larger one overlooking the street with more room and light. And there was never an exact settlement of accounts between the partners, be it from the moral or material point of view. Not even when they were forced to go their separate ways as partners some years later, after my grandfather fell seriously ill.

Both apartments were located behind the shop but there was no particular wall dividing them. A short staircase led directly from the shop into my grandmother's bedroom. It was actually a small windowless room with two beds, two night tables, and a washstand. Next to it was a slightly more spacious and more comfortable living room with windows overlooking an open porch. It was modestly decorated but there were also a few fine pieces of furniture, including two wardrobes made of walnut and decorated with rosewood marquetry, which my grandmother had received as a wedding present from her older sister Veronika and had therefore held in high esteem.[7] In fact, there was a family story to be told in connection with each piece of furniture she possessed. She used to retell me those stories as she carefully dusted the precious objects. I remember almost all of them because most of these objects and pieces of furniture are now in my possession. I believe that I inherited through them my grandmother's understanding of life and the entire family tradition, which bypassed my parent's home. I feel a deep inherent connection with my grandmother's world, which comprised the entire nineteenth century and stretched even further back into the past. That world included her first encounters with the romantic ideas, her adoption of the 1848 ideals of freedom and emancipation, her deeply rooted humanism, and her sense of righteousness and humour. I still remember her amusing stories and funny poems she drew partly from folk literature and partly from her favourite poets, starting with Schiller[8] to Raimund and Nestroy,[9] most of whose works she knew by heart, but also popular sayings and proverbs that served to provide a comment or justify her every undertaking. It meant that whatever she then told me, and all of her actions, appeared indisputable and reasonable to me. She was interesting and funny, and thanks to her unique educational method, I started to understand and accept the world around me. If something escaped my understanding, she would cheer me up with the rhythm of her narration and a bright smile—which accompanied everything—and in that witty and energetic manner, she always managed to banish my discomfort. I was responsive to her every move, something no one else could ever obtain from me.

She was not a good-looking woman, and no one could ever call her a beauty, but her funny, good-humoured homeliness, which she herself made fun of, had an attractive appeal for me. Her face reflected kindness and understanding. At the age of sixty, she still used to comb her silvery-white hair in the same way she did when she was twenty. On both sides of a neat head parting, she rolled two firm braids over her ears, and at the nape she had an add-on chignon, which on occasional mornings I could see suspended on a hook above her charming little dresser while she was preparing herself for the new day.

She always wore the same dress—that is, all her dresses were made of the same material and had the same cut, with the exception of the heavy black silk dress that she wore on the Sabbath. Her skirts were always abundantly pleated, the waistlines fitted tightly, and she always wore a plissé insert covering her breasts. I never saw her inappropriately dressed. Fashion did not exist in her world. She wore her dresses until they appeared worn out and then gave them to the poor, but always making sure that they were still in a decent enough condition to be worn. She did the same with everything else she owned. In this same way, she donated groceries or clothing to people in need, careful not to hurt their feelings or humiliate them. After finishing her work in the kitchen and around the house, she would sit down and start knitting. She knitted hundreds of socks—white, black, and multi-coloured ones. Whenever she gave us a present, it was accompanied by a pair of cotton or wool socks with picot hemming. She liked talking to people about politics, a great passion of hers since her young days. She enjoyed even more to read a book and would get carried away by stories of heroic deeds, shed bitter tears over tragic situations and laugh heartily at comic scenes. Her favourite authors were Alexandre Dumas[10] and Eugène

Sue,[11] but also August von Kotzebue,[12] Heinrich Zschokke,[13] Jókai Mór,[14] and her dear Sándor Petöfi,[15] whose poems about liberty and freedom she was always ready to quote. Although the pathos with which she recited them sometimes sounded false, what she felt was authentic.

No person in the world is a mere result of coincidence. Also, no one can claim full credit for the person she or he has turned out to be in life, either in a good or bad sense. We are all inevitably just one small link in a chain of generations and only as such can we be genuinely understood and defined. I will have to apply myself hard to unravel the long thread of past events and reach deep into the past in order to both understand and define my grandmother's personality with all her spiritual and moral qualities, her remarkable vitality and passionate temperament—in short, all her explicit characteristics which made her so unlike an average woman of her time—and then be able to assess what she left to her descendants. The thread that connects our family with the past, with what constitutes our origins, can be traced back as far as the sixteenth century. It connects us with a particular past event, which is today regarded as part of history, but its traces nevertheless still inhabit us and have never fully faded away.

My grandchildren, for whom I am writing these lines so that something of the family history is preserved after my death, are largely ignorant about Jewishness and Judaism. They do not know that Jews, wherever they settled during the last two thousand years, were always perceived as foreigners, lived in constant exile with no legal protection, and were constantly at the mercy of unfriendly surroundings. The killing of Jews went mostly unpunished and those who participated in the persecution and massacre of Jews enjoyed practical impunity, guaranteed by the authorities. That a Jew was throughout the centuries considered a *Kammerknecht*, the servant of the imperial court, primarily meant that he paid customs duties and taxes directly to the imperial treasury. Jews were the emperor's personal property, which meant they could be leased out, pawned, or sold off, and were often used as a payment to settle incurred debts. Along with their subordination to the emperor, Jews were servants to bishops, local nobility, and town officials, who managed to drain most of what was still left.

Although they were prevented from earning any decent amount of money and were not allowed to run businesses, open shops, farm, or exercise any liberal profession, they were still subjected to additional heavy impositions. They had to pay the tax on Jewishness (for each family member separately) and on property, as well as municipal taxes, and the "third" and "gold sacrificial coin" used to finance incurred costs of coronation festivities, wars, Crusades, and church synods. With every extension of their privileges, they always had to pay new and higher taxes, under the threat of losing everything they owned, or to live in fear of being physically attacked or exiled from their homes. In urban areas, they were usually sequestered into separate Jewish quarters, where an officially appointed *Judenmeister* (Jewish Master) had full power over their bodies, their souls, and all their possessions. They were forced to wear a hideous Jewish uniform and a yellow badge so they would be easily recognizable and had to swear a shameful Jewish oath, which made them look ridiculous and contemptible in the eyes of their fellow citizens.

The first violent massacres, during which many thousands of people died, took place at the time of the Crusades. Attackers plundered Jewish ghettos, burning and killing everything that crossed their path. The fanatical masses of people accused the Jews of desecrating the sacramental bread and of killing children for ritual purposes. In Germany itself, hundreds of Jewish communities were destroyed, and their inhabitants burned alive in their synagogues. This happened in Munich in 1255, in Fulda in 1309, and in Frankfurt in 1349, all of it during the Black Death. During that catastrophic spread of the plague sweeping through Germany, Jews were accused of poisoning water wells. More bloody massacres took place in Switzerland, Alsace, south and central Germany, Salzburg, and the rest of Austria and Bohemia.[16] Hundreds of thousands of people were slaughtered, strangled, bludgeoned to death, and tortured on a breaking wheel. All Jews were ordered to leave the city of Württemberg in 1499, because of the Black Death, and so were the inhabitants of the old city of Ulm. The Jews from Ulm moved thereupon to Rhineland-Palatinate and central Francia, where they settled under the protection of the prince-bishop of Bamberg. My ancestors were among them. Since they came from Ulm, they came to be known as Ulmer or Ulmann. The family settled in Fürth, in the vicinity of Nuremberg, and were soon joined there by a considerable number of other Jewish families.

They lived peacefully until 1660, when the news spread across Europe about a man called Sabbatai Zevi from Smyrna,[17] a true wonder of wisdom, piety, and learning. His followers claimed that he was the true Messiah, whose coming was foreseen by the prophets and was confirmed by the appearance of a shooting star in 1648 and the apocalyptic prediction for the year 1666. It was said that the true Messiah gained the support of the Prophet Elijah, reincarnated in Nathan Ghazzati,[18] who sent his disciples wherever Jews lived to summon them to meet the "anointed one". My ancestor Mayer Ulmann and his family also joined the group of Jewish pilgrims who thus headed east, fully believing that the Messiah's arrival would fulfil God's promise, according to which the Jewish people would finally be redeemed and there would be eternal peace in the world.

The more misfortunes piled up, the more ardently the Jews believed in miracles and Kabbalistic teaching. They had been for far too long seriously troubled and the belief in the Messiah had consoled them and helped them persevere throughout centuries, filling their hearts with longing and giving them a certain purpose. The Kingdom of God would be realized here on earth, not in the other world. That faith and hope illuminated the dark world of their existence, as there was no doubt that the Son of David would appear and show mercy to his scattered flock. He would redeem them and reunite them. He would deliver them from grief and pain, exile and humiliation, and lead them back to the land of their fathers. Solomon's Temple would rise again in all its splendour and the light of life would spill over the people whose humble prayers would be heard.

This secret longing which they silently kept buried in their souls, this secret consolation in the midst of darkness, the certainty that the oppressed would triumph over their oppressors suddenly became real and close with the appearance of Sabbatai Zevi. The news from the east spread far west, from the south of France to Holland, from England to Poland, where at the time, Khmelnytsky's Cossacks led a major campaign of extermination of Jewish people, more violent and bloody than ever before. The news of the Messiah's appearance fell on fertile ground. It spread from one town to the other, from house to house, by word of mouth. People listened, their hearts lit up, they gained new courage. The word spread that the new Messiah from the east had performed great miracles and had proved his authenticity by loudly pronouncing the four forbidden letters of God's name. He had already gathered many followers, with thousands more rushing to the saviour from all parts of Europe.

What else could those unfortunate people possibly do? They left their homes, taking with them only what they could easily carry or hide away. Dangers of all kinds threatened them on their journey. Edicts were issued to deny them passage through certain lands. Some cruel provincial governors robbed the pilgrims of their meager belongings and threw them in dungeons. Highwaymen waited in ambush and attacked them. Many lost their lives due to hunger and disease. They travelled through foreign lands and were surrounded by people speaking foreign languages. The journey was long but illuminated by hope.

My ancestor also took part in that pilgrimage. He passed through Regensburg, Passau, and Vienna. Just like so many other pilgrims, he used the course of the Danube as guidance. His intention was to reach Smyrna, where the new Messiah could be seen. By the time he reached Vienna, the news spread that Joseph Escapa,[19] Sabbatai Zevi's teacher, proclaimed him a false prophet and banished him from Smyrna. Sabbatai left his hometown and took refuge in Salonica,[20] the centre of Kabbalistic teaching. My ancestor continued his journey along the Danube, through Pressburg,[21] and reached Buda,[22] which had been in Ottoman hands since the Battle of Mohács.[23] There he received the unfortunate news that his holy man had been, in the meantime, thrown into an Ottoman prison and, under the sultan's threats to take his life, had renounced his Jewish faith. He converted to Islam, was named Mehmed Effendi, and given the title of the "imperial doorkeeper". But even as such, he seemed dangerous to the sultan since he continued to attract and gather followers. He was therefore banished to Albania. His follower and promoter Nathan Ghazzati fled to Skopje, where he died a few years later. Sabbatai Zevi, the false messiah, died in 1676 in the Albanian town of Ulcinj,[24] abandoned by his followers.

That is how my grandmother's ancestors arrived in Hungary from Germany. They settled on the shore of the River Danube, halfway between Buda and Mohács, and lived there for more than a century without taking proper roots, just as it was with all other Jews who were not allowed to own land or earn regular income. They had to be always prepared, from one day to another, to pack their belongings and resettle with their families somewhere else. The name Mayer Ulmann continued to be used in the family. My grandmother's brother was given that name, as was her uncle. At the end of the eighteenth century, a descendant of these early Fürth emigrants, my great-grandfather Carl Ulmann, moved to the ecclesiastical city of Pécs, where he was allowed to build a house and open an oil refinery.

Many other Jewish pilgrims who responded to the call of Sabbatai Zevi found themselves compelled to discontinue their journey east, but for some of them the glimmer of hope of experiencing the appearance of the Messiah never left them. To many it brought restlessness and carried them astray. It turned into a longing for something unattainable and distant, exceeding the boundaries of reality. It gave them an inner urge, which became eventually a characteristic trait of Jewish temperament. Even if not inherited, it was kept alive through tradition and oral history. That distinctive trait differentiated the Jews from other people. Something of that original faith in the Messiah has persisted in every Jew.

My grandmother, Sophie Ulmann, was born in 1827 in Pécs, as her parents' eighth child. Her mother was Charlotte Weissmayer, from one of the first permanently settled Jewish families in that town. The Weissmayers were a family of physicians, cultured and educated, as was common at the time. My great-grandmother Charlotte appeared to be a delicate and poetic soul, judging from one of her letters that has been preserved. She wrote the letter in question to her fiancé shortly before their wedding. "The day is approaching when we shall be chained to each other. I will, however, always try to weave a few roses into those chains, to make them more pleasing and less heavy for you to bear." This reference to the chain was not a mere metaphor. It referred to an old Jewish custom, according to which the fiancé is supposed to give his fiancée a wedding belt of no prescribed value, from cheap to very expensive. The young spouses are bound together with that belt as part of the wedding ceremony that takes place under the *chuppah*. In the fifteen years of their marriage, my great-grandmother gave birth to five sons and three daughters. The birth of their last child, my grandmother, ended her life. The husband remarried and brought home a widow with three small children. Through the years, the new wife gave birth to five more children, so that there were eventually sixteen siblings in the family.

My grandmother could never stop talking about life in her parents' house, whereby she never differentiated between her real siblings and her half-brothers and half-sisters. The only thing that angered her was that her brothers had been given access to formal education while she had been denied it. In those times, girls had to content themselves with being taught how to read and write, and then receive some additional religious education. That was all. Her brothers, instead, were home schooled by private tutors from Budapest in a specially designed "school room".

My grandmother received no more schooling after she reached eight years of age. However, she was keen to keep learning. She was also smart and resourceful and figured out how to go about it. An iron door in the school room allowed a chimney sweeper to slip into the fireplace, if needed. Behind that door was a small space, barely big enough for a child to hide by squatting down. She used to hide in there for hours, listening to the tutors' lessons. This is how she acquired the first notions of history, geography, and natural sciences. To commit what she had thus learned even deeper into her memory, she would offer to her sisters parts of her lunch in exchange for their willingness to listen to her retelling of stories about the Trojan War or the discovery of America. This knowledge was in her esteem more valuable than gold, and since she had an excellent memory, she never forgot any of it. By subsequent extensive reading, she broadened the scope and breadth of that originally acquired knowledge. Her great interest in history and contemporary politics had its origins in those humble beginnings. She continually wanted to know what was happening in the world at large and would frequently refer to the significant times of the French Revolution, when, for the first time in history, Jewish people were granted full equality by law. When that law was repealed during the reactionary Restoration period, those who experienced the effects of that short-lived freedom could never forget it. The seed was planted, the potential was there. More and more people openly proclaimed and wrote about the idea of freedom and equality for the Jewish people. The call for full emancipation, both economic and personal, was greatly encouraged by the writings about freedom by people as varied as Friedrich Schiller, Victor Hugo, Mihály Vörösmarty,[25] and Sándor Petőfi. Jewish painters, poets, musicians, and philosophers who began emerging straight from the ghetto, and by skipping within the span of one generation many stages of cultural development, succeeded in making an important contribution to European culture with their distinctively Jewish sensibility and intellectualism. Those distinctive Jewish traits found their expression in the sharpness of observations, in the ardour in controversy, in a good sense of satire, sudden mood swings, scepticism, and melancholy. These traits were soon reflected in the extraordinary artistic style of, for instance, Heinrich Heine[26] or Ludwig Börne.[27]

At the age of ten, in 1838, my grandmother undertook her first big journey away from home, accompanying her gravely ill father on a carriage ride from Pécs to Budapest. In those days, such a journey took eight full days. In Budapest lived her father's oldest brother, Mayer Ulmann, who was not just tolerated but rather considered a respectable citizen and is still referred to today as one of the founders of the Hungarian economy. He was a family man, cared for the upbringing of his nephews, chose their tutors, and paid the tutors' wages himself. My grandmother could in a way be grateful to him for her indirectly acquired basic education.

My ten-year-old grandmother brought her ill father to this uncle to seek advice and ask help from the best doctors one could find in town. It turned out to be an illness without a cure, namely lung cancer. Thus, after a stay of several weeks in Budapest, they eventually returned home. The father was on his deathbed following that exhausting and long voyage home and he died shortly after. He left behind sixteen children, half of them still infants. Despite the good reputation the Ulmanns enjoyed in all social circles, the family was after his death in a critical financial situation and without income. The eldest sons were merely fifteen or sixteen years of age. Their uncle in Budapest found for them their first employment in a couple of companies with which he had dealings. In this way, he launched them into the world of business. They were industrious and gifted, but it was not until 1848 that they successfully secured their own place in business and society. The younger siblings were distributed among various relatives in Pécs. Thanks to these relatives, the boys finished school and the girls were married off. The stepmother also died, just two or three years after the father. My grandmother found a home in the house of her eldest married sister, Veronika Fuchs, who did not have children. She was known in town as a particularly noble-minded woman and a most generous benefactor. People called her the "dear mother of all suffering and wretched people".

"For twenty long years, poverty has been a lasting bond between her and the rest of humanity. Misery and destitution were the only required credentials for being welcomed into her home and her heart." I found these lines in a newspaper obituary that my grandmother preserved after her sister's death in 1870, along with a pile of family letters and various memorabilia, which are still in my possession today. The article compares the deceased with the sun because, just like the sun, she radiated serenity and bestowed life and warmth upon everyone who happened to be in her vicinity. One can positively say that this remarkable woman had a crucial influence on my grandmother who grew up by her side. For the rest of her life, my grandmother used her as a role model and tried to continue her good work. When I was born ten years after Veronika's death, they gave me, following my grandmother's wishes, the deceased Veronika's Jewish name Frumet (or Fruma), which in Yiddish stands for righteousness and piousness.

The most important event, however, and the one that left an everlasting and indelible effect on my grandmother, to the point of defining her life (not to mention that it greatly affected my spiritual development as well), was the Hungarian Revolution of 1848. My grandmother experienced it firsthand, and on a daily basis, through all its inspirational and depressing phases—the coming and going of victories and defeats, calls for the liberation of peasants and bourgeoisie from the shackles of feudalism, and the uplifting slogans about freedom and equality, for both the Hungarians and the Jews alike.

Revolutions usually erupt after a long period of preparation, during which arguments take their full form and the spirit of action ripens. New slogans ignite ever more passions and the tension reaches its maximum. The pre-revolutionary atmosphere lasted from the July 1830 Revolution to the first armed clashes in 1848. It was the era of crinolines for women and stiff high collars for men and was marked by the arrival of the first railways. It so happened, by the way, that the first railway in Hungary on the line Vienna-Budapest-Debrecen was built by my great-uncle Mayer Ulmann. During that period, arguments with romantic intonations kept highlighting intolerable aspects of the ongoing political situation. Fanatics were emerging everywhere, carried away by their ideas and prepared at any time to take immediate action. Young people were burning with desire to free themselves of old-fashioned conventions and restraints. They were the most persistent bearers of revolutionary ideas. The Jewish youth was also among them, mixing Hungarian nationalist ideas with a desire for equality and their own emancipation. The latter was promised to them in fiery speeches and writings by the leaders of the revolution, Lajos Kossuth[28] and Ferenc Deák.[29]

Although acts of violence and persecutions of the sinister medieval kind were no longer perpetrated, the Congress of Vienna in 1815 engendered a new wave of reactions in Central Europe. Jewish rights were again restricted—their freedom of movement was once again limited, the royal, military, and Jewish taxes were re-established, as well as "head", house, and property taxes. The mass persecutions stopped but access to secondary schools and schools of higher education was still barred. The Jews were still not allowed to take up a trade of their choice, and apart from some rare exceptions, were still denied the right to practise a liberal profession. Different procedures were designed to make marriage more difficult, and in many countries, such as Bohemia, only the oldest son in the family was allowed to get married. Therefore, it is no wonder that under such circumstances Jews participated in proportionally large numbers in all revolutionary movements of the nineteenth and twentieth centuries. It seemed as if some century-long suppressed energy was suddenly let out in the open with a powerful liberating effect in both subjective and social terms. This was especially evident in the case of Hungarian Jews, who, even before their legally established emancipation, had been *de facto* integrated into the Hungarian society, spoke Hungarian, and considered themselves equally Hungarian as native-born Magyars. They sensed the approach of a new era; they felt deep emotional connection with the mass uprising of 1848, because, in Hungary, all layers of society were involved in the struggle and not just the bourgeoisie, as was the case in other European countries. It was nationalist in character and turned into a struggle against Austrian dominance. Out of 180,000 fighters of the revolutionary army, 20,000 were of Jewish origin, and the Jewish National Guard in Pést[30] constituted one whole division.

Four of my grandmother's brothers took part in the revolution. The oldest brother, Adolph Ullman (in those years the family name Ulmann began to be spelled as Ullman), joined the revolutionary army as a preacher and was for that reason executed in 1849 by the Austrians in his own house in Senta.[31] The physician Mor Ullman was an army surgeon in a field hospital. Her brother, Benjamin, was barely sixteen when he left home to join the fight. Several days later, he was brought back severely wounded in both legs. He succumbed soon after to his wounds.

It is important, considering our recent experience of the two World Wars and accompanying social changes, that we imagine ourselves, for a moment, a hundred years back in time and make an effort to grasp how people in those days perceived as an inspiring novelty something that we today consider as self-evident and ordinary. We must keep reminding ourselves that, what today sounds as empty phrases, was once new and unexpected, that long and loud tirades were effectively uplifting and attractive, that different political theses revealed new truths, that it took a lot of courage to utter them for the first time, and a lot of naive elation to repeat them. For the people in those days, a hundred years ago, who believed in the possibility of a better world, no sacrifice was too excessive. They were convinced that the wheel of history, once moved, could never again return to the same place; that there was no going back to the old prejudice, superstitions, medieval darkness, and ghoulish persecutions and accusations. They were convinced that people had awakened for good and their eyes would stay opened. Poets wrote rousing poetry about it, politicians made promises in their numerous speeches, and newspapers reported on it in detail. It was a topic of conversations in the street, on the main square, and at dinner tables in people's homes. My grandmother and her friends collected medicine, dressings, and linen to be sent to the front.

They urged young men to enlist and despised everyone who did not take part in the revolution.

She retold me all that hundreds of times. Her stories were vivid and detailed, accompanied by gestures, tears, and laughter. She was not just telling me stories; she was actually reliving them each time. She gave them form, refined them, and always adding new details she would suddenly remember while talking. I can still hear the sound of her voice in my ear.

She used to tell me about the death of her brothers, about the Russians troops, the defeat at Világos,[32] the arrival of the Schwarzgelben (as the Austrian soldiers were then called), the subsequent terror perpetrated by the Austrian General von Haynau, and the execution of Hungarian "Thirteen Martyrs of Arad".[33] Notwithstanding the bitter tears that accompanied her memories about the tragic suppression of the revolution and the loss of all hopes linked to it, my grandmother's optimism never failed. It remained with her not only during the critical period leading to the historic Austro-Hungarian Compromise of 1867, but for the rest of her life. In her view and in her heart, the revolutionary ideal had won. She believed that no bloody repression by the reaction could extinguish the burning energy that the revolution had set free, nor could it destroy the ideals it had been founded upon and which people continued to nurture in their hearts—particularly the claim to the right of freedom and equality.

Instead of the ordinary Jewish jargon of Osijek, my grandmother preferred to use the guttural Yiddish (Jewish German) with characteristic Hebrew expressions and intonations typical of eastern Europe. Yiddish was intended for communication within the Jewish community itself. When dealing with Christian house maids and customers at the store, or shopping at the market, she would automatically turn to Swabian German, the language generally used in Osijek, and as natural to her as the Jewish vernacular. The use of Jewish vernacular in front of strangers would appear an intolerable act of indiscretion, entirely inappropriate, as if one were wearing a scanty negligée in public or were found lingering in bed well into the morning.

In her writing, on the other hand, she exclusively used literary German acquired through her extensive reading. In a typical style of the period, her German was adorned with beautiful phraseology and imagery. However, the literary language she applied in her letters had nothing personal in it. It served only as a means of communication, which suited the requirements of polite social manners without stimulating any personal contact.

She used those three types of expression partly due to social norms and partly because of her innate sensitivity concerning finesse, according to which everyone had to be approached appropriately. However, there was no place for such "tactics" when surrounded by family. Then she was direct, spontaneous, temperamental, and open. She was always good at finding a suitable remark, or even better, at telling a well-pointed Jewish joke, at which she would be the one who laughed the most. Just as she was able to laugh from the heart, she could also shed tears. For forty long years after the Hungarian army had been defeated at Világos, she never spoke of these events without tears running down her face. Whatever she endured during her life—an everyday existence in practical confinement, full of restraints and sacrifices, with lack of outside stimulation—was overshadowed by the great drama experienced in her youth. The enthusiasm had never disappeared and her whole life was afterwards spent in the light of these early impressions. Her perspectives on life had been irrevocably broadened and due to her temperament and great spirit, she managed to see her narrow environment in a different light.

Between 1848 and the end of the century, the economic life in Hungary was assuming a new direction. Railways were being built, new factories constructed, and finances reorganized. The Jewish business community largely participated in this process. My grandmother's three brothers—Carl, Joseph, and Mayer—also played an important role in that process, although it is hard to tell who contributed what because they participated in it together. The aim was not simply to enrich themselves, but also to be of service to the country as a whole, to which they owed their gratitude for granting them their right to assimilate. They were representative examples of emancipated Jews, whose principal desire at the time was to prove, through their endeavour and hard work, to what extent they were prepared to fulfil the expectations bestowed upon them and serve their country to the best of their abilities.

The Ullman brothers always acted in that spirit. There is no institution in Budapest which is not in some way connected with their name.

They founded the Pest Lloyd's Association, the Commercial and Credit Bank, the first Hungarian insurance company, and the Danube Steamboat Association. They were behind the setup of the first large steam-powered mills in the country, of Budapest's first printing company and its first daily newspaper, as well as countless social and charity institutions in which they participated as directors and which they supported financially by making generous donations. Benefaction was the main virtue of all Ullmans. I do not know of any family member who was not generous. Another of their characteristics was that none of them became truly rich; no one owned land, big palaces in the city, or large assets in the bank. Despite their extensive business activities, they lived modestly and demanded little in life. In recognition of their public service, they were promoted into nobility with the titles "of Baranyavary" and "of Erenyi", and the right to be addressed as "Your Honour".

My grandmother was married in 1852. Since she was neither good-looking nor rich, she did not have the right of choice and had to be content with what destiny bestowed upon her. Love existed only in novels, so even if there was something secretly alight in her heart, it had to burn out in silence; in the practical world of Jewish families in those days, love was not a consideration, or at best it was viewed as of secondary importance. People married with the purpose of providing an independent life for themselves and not be a burden to the other members of the family. It was a duty of every man and woman to start a family. Such a pact was negotiated through "match makers". Young people did not have many opportunities to meet. The postal services were slow and means of transportation still unreliable. Match makers, however, had a large circle of acquaintances, had good knowledge of human nature, and knew well how to find compatibilities in people. Match makers used to negotiate, persuade, and mediate between two sides concerning financial matters. They were witty, eloquent, and full of indisputable arguments. They knew what the two parties needed, or at least they believed they knew. The two parties would meet when everything was already arranged. An obligatory third person was present during their introductory conversations. Sexual preferences were irrelevant, since marriage was not for pleasure, but an act of duty.

My grandmother had therefore no choice but to accept the suitor her family found for her. She did so with a heavy heart, but she was almost twenty-five years old—in those days considered past prime youth—and was advised to be glad that someone was still willing to marry her. My grandfather was not young himself, being already in his mid-thirties. It took him more than twenty years to open his own shop, after labouring first as an apprentice and then as a shop assistant and making endless and painful sacrifices to save one kreuzer at a time.[34] Even my grandmother's dowry, altogether some 120 guldens in coins, was invested in the shop. She was told that the man in question was hard-working, honest, and pious, and that sympathy among decent people develops gradually on its own. Truth be told, in my grandmother's case, no such thing ever happened. She shared with this man work, hardships, and worries, she took care of him until he died, but there was no mention of any affection. She found it hard to fit into the new environment, where everything was alien to her, including her husband.

Her hometown Pécs was an ecclesiastical city situated amid a vast agricultural landscape, with a lovely Romanesque cathedral from the time of the Árpáds.[35] When she came to Osijek in February 1852, the Lower Town looked, by contrast, like a village sunk in mud. There was no pavement, no streetlights, not a single representative building, and no green spaces, forests, or cheerful vineyards where people could meet and socialize in good spirit, as in her hometown. There was no theatre, no heated political discussions, no friends, and no books to read—nothing but the shop and the work connected with it. Moreover, her husband came from an Orthodox family and the strict observance of religious rules and rituals offered him daily relief from shop-related preoccupations and provided an escape from everyday life. My grandmother was religious too, but in a different way. For her, religion was a personal matter, apart from being also a series of inherited colourful customs, which she gladly practised and made even more festive with her cheerfulness, generosity, and spontaneity. Moreover, she was a city child, while my grandfather came from a Slovakian village situated at the foot of the Carpathians. The only thing I know regarding his family is that they used to be called Jasinger in the past. The family was hugely disappointed when, at the end of the eighteenth century, one of my grandfather's young uncles, driven by the desire to acquire more knowledge, left his father's house and set off into the world in search of education. I cannot say with certainty how he came up with that idea, but he was no doubt sufficiently gifted and energetic. He studied chemistry, which was a new science at the time, converted to Christianity and made his way up to become a professor at the University of Vienna. His son was a dedicated musician and became one of the founders of the Vienna Men's Choral Society. The family at home mourned the son who lost his faith as if he were dead. Not even on the deathbed did his father grant him forgiveness. The family then cut off all ties with their respectable Viennese relatives. They went so far as to change their family name from Jasinger (deriving from "jasno" or bright) to Weiss (meaning white).

When visiting my grandparents' house, I used to watch my grandfather at his regular morning prayer. He had a small velvet cap on his head and wore a white prayer coat. Over it he had prayer belts, from which hung leather capsules with parchment rolls containing texts from the Talmud. He would wrap these belts around his forehead and his left arm and chant, rocking the upper part of his body to and fro, and bending backwards and forwards. Since I had never before been in a temple and had not been acquainted with the Jewish religious ceremony, it all seemed most alien and frightening to me. I would run to my grandmother, who would console me by saying, "Grandpapa is speaking to Our Lord!"

I sometimes used to speak to Our Lord as well in my evening prayers. This was not a confessional god but a neutral one, whom I envisaged looking like my Uncle Strauss. The uncle owned a glass and porcelain shop on the main square in the Upper Town. He was almost entirely grey-haired, wore thick glasses, and had a long white beard and a moustache that was uncomfortably prickly when he kissed me. But every time he saw me pass by the shop, he would invite me in and give me a present. Among other things, he gave me a pink porcelain mug with small white flowers that I then regularly used to drink milk from in the morning. I could not have asked for anything better from Our Dear Lord, which was why I imagined him in the image of my uncle. While praying in the evening, I spoke on my own behalf, or that of my parents and grandparents, but also on behalf of all human beings, big and small. I imagined him as a universal god, who did not differentiate between big and small, Jews and Christians, Roma or black people. As long as I could believe in such a god, I was ready to love him, but I have never experienced religious mysticism and the ecstasy some people derive from it.

My mother was born after four years of marriage and was my grand-mother's only child. She named her Charlotte after her prematurely deceased mother and raised her in accordance with her free-minded and intellectual standpoints. Since she considered education as the greatest asset in a person's life, she enabled her daughter to take advantage of all the educational opportunities their small town had to offer. After finishing the four compulsory grades of elementary schooling, during which she was also taught a bit of Croatian as an optional subject (that remained all she ever learned of Croatian for the rest of her life), she was tutored in all secondary school subjects by a professor from the Osijek Gymnasium. She was taught French by a certain woman of French origin, and German and English by Miss Schulze, who ran a private school in the Fortress for the girls of "elegant family backgrounds". On top of that, there were piano lessons with an excellent pedagogue, Mr. Joseph Schwartz, whose son was later employed at the Music Academy in Zagreb. She was taught how to dance and swim, she read classical authors in the original, and, in my grandmother's eyes, was an epitome of perfection, a fairy bestowed upon her by Providence to make up for all the privations she herself had been obliged to endure.

My mother was petite, delicate, and frail, with long ash blond hair falling in gentle curls over her shoulders, which, when pinned up, formed a gleaming crown above her forehead. She was dressed according to the fashion of the day consisting of wide skirts and small tight jackets with square-cut necklines, most often decorated with light-blue or silvery-grey ribbons and velvet bands on her dress and in her hair. Wide-brimmed hats and small coquettish parasols were sent for from Vienna. My grandmother wished her daughter to have all the things she would never have cared to ask for herself. Everything had to be the best. When my father, a handsome and well-educated man, fell in love with her and married her, their love story was, for my grandmother, a source of as much joy as if she herself were the main protagonist.

~~~~

The return of my parents from the sanatorium in mid-August would mark the end of my stay in the Lower Town. Saying goodbye was never easy, but I found consolation in knowing that I would soon be spending a whole hour riding on the omnibus. The carriage, much like an old huge chest, was pulled through dusty streets by a skinny horse. I would kneel next to my grandmother on the seat covered in shabby red velvet and look out of the window. Houses, trees, meadows and vegetable gardens were passing fast before my eyes. Then came the Fortress casemates with their dilapidated brick walls, appearing strange and eerie. I asked about them fearfully and was told that bad people were imprisoned there. I wanted to know who those bad people were. Soldiers, I was told, who instead of fighting ran away from battlefields. My next question was why they were running away. Because they were scared, she said. I found it difficult to understand. I feared the dark myself and was sometimes scared, even in broad daylight. Was I bad, because of that? To avoid answering, my grandmother told me instead that we would soon be entering the Fortress, where a military orchestra would most likely be playing music on the main square. I was, however, still preoccupied by the casemates and moats. I was convinced that those high walls, narrow gun chambers, and dark corridors were hiding places for mysterious and ghost-like creatures, perhaps even captured princesses and vicious dragons, just like the ones found in the fairy tales my nanny Rozi used to tell every day.

A piercing sound of the trumpet could suddenly be heard from one of the barrack courtyards and my thoughts returned to reality. There were soldiers everywhere doing their exercises, and loud commandments could be heard echoing in the narrow streets. On the right side was the Water Gate covered in ivy and opening in the direction of the River Drava. On the left was Novogradska (New Town Street), which ran across the glacis towards the Stone Cross monument and the large army exercise ground near the City Garden. The military were everywhere around. There were officers with their sabres rattling as they strolled in front of the club

Ressource. There were soldiers with their rifles in the ready position standing guard in front of their black and yellow guardhouses. As predicted by my grandmother, an orchestra was playing military music on the main square in front of the Holy Trinity Barracks and the main guard hall, both of which dated from the eighteenth century and the times of Empress Maria Theresa. The omnibus slowed down and stopped at the corner of the square. A potpourri of operetta tunes replaced the military marches. Brass instruments were blaring, flutes whistling, drums storming. I was so excited that it left me breathless. As the omnibus started bouncing again, the bells from the Franciscan church tower suddenly started ringing and the entire hubbub and uproar gradually swirled up into a sound vortex which made the air quiver and windows clink. I was still kneeling on the velvet-clad bench and was all eyes and ears. Images were sliding fast before my eyes, as if it was not us moving forwards but the outside world moving inexorably towards us. These impressions were usually accompanied by the evening skies, the colour of translucent light red. The dome above our heads was often deep blue with clouds of strange shapes sailing across the sky. It also sometimes happened that the sky was low and drops of rain would trickle down the windowpanes.

Such were my first impressions of those omnibus rides. A good walker would require a mere half an hour to make the distance on foot, but for me the omnibus ride was as impressive as a real journey. I would become restless only by the time we started approaching the first buildings in the Upper Town on Kapucinska (Capuchin Street). The first building to appear was the house where the photographer Graff had his studio. I knew it well because I would go there yearly to have my picture taken.

House after house would pass by, greeting me as if we were old friends. The omnibus would stop, and my mother and father would stand there waiting for me. I would run into their arms, burning with impatience. The rooms I knew so well, my good old bed, and darling Rozi were waiting for me. There were also heaps of toys which I seemed to have forgotten all about and now appeared even more precious in my eyes. I was also being observed and admired. They would put me up on a chair and conclude that I had grown a bit taller. They would say that I had grown smarter as well during that time, and since I was very much aware of my importance, I would boast about all the things I had learned at my grandmother's house. In a child's life, two months mean a lot. During that long period, a child inevitably begins to see things differently and discovers new aspects and details. What was once big becomes smaller and what was small becomes even smaller than it used to be. All of a sudden, everything is shifted and changed. New knowledge engenders a different way of reasoning. A child feels a change of atmosphere in her environment instinctively rather than consciously. She can feel that the mood of the grown-ups has changed, as well as their focus, and that change becomes even more evident in their relationship with her. Sometimes these changes are small, but often the foundations of old habits seem shattered. There are new expectations a child needs to fulfil. Time is organized differently.

My grandmother knew of no other pedagogical methods but her warmth and spontaneity. My mother, however, abided by certain principles that she considered indisputable and I strongly resisted them from my early days. It is hard to say whether that urge to resist came naturally or was the consequence of my upbringing, but one thing was certain: throughout my life, I abhorred authoritative norms. As I could not at the time differentiate between what was useful and what superfluous, I used to resist everything that could in any way repress my freedom and independence. Not even today can I understand the cause of that fierce spiritual and physical opposition to any coercion, to every categorical "you should" or "you must". I even used to resist doing things that I would have done on my own anyway, had I not been forced to. I equally abhorred the principle of the "golden middle", which I was firmly urged to follow, and which *a priori* anathematized any kind of exaggeration, in either a good or a bad sense. They used to tell me, even before I could truly understand its meaning, "Be moderate in everything you do!" This was precisely what I detested most—stop playing when I was having the most fun, finish a meal when it was the most delicious, be satisfied with less, refrain from setting out to do something the moment it came to mind, or be silent in other people's presence even if I wanted to talk. These were all demands I rebelled against, if not always openly then certainly in secret, in my inner self. This sense of protest, interpreted in my childhood as disobedience, rebelliousness, and defiance, was at the heart of all I did in my later life—defy restrictions, narrow-mindedness, pettiness, social conventions, and formalism, all of which, in the time of my childhood, stood for supreme law.

The house where we lived at the time and where I was born on 8 February 1880, was located on the secluded Šamačka[36] Street, surely one of the most inconspicuous and ugliest streets in the entire Upper Town. Popular taverns lined the street. Adjoined to our house, on the left side, was notably the Piller beer pub. It was often considerably tumultuous in there, especially on Saturday nights when Osijek burgers were joined by fishermen, coachmen, and wood depot workers, as well as by some people from all over Podravina.[37] They had little money to spend, and what they did have, had been earned by taking odd jobs along the river. They spoke with a genuine Esseker accent and behaved like true troublemakers. In those days, the Piller beer pub served a good fish stew (*Fischpaprikash*) and cheap house wine and the place resounded with loud yelling, singing, and screaming long after midnight. The yelling could be heard in my room and would sometimes wake me up and frighten me. I would claim that there were thieves in the house and refused to remain alone in my room any longer. I wanted to sleep in my mother's bed, and by using this excuse, I was usually successful.

A few paces to the left was the Scheper beer house. Their beer was so light that one had to drink litres to become at least tipsy. To get seriously drunk was practically impossible. The town's prominent and distinguished citizens such as civil servants and merchants were regulars at the beer house and had at their disposal separate private rooms. What went on in there was usually commented on in a subdued voice and with a knowing smile by those sitting in the public area. I could not comprehend any of that. On one occasion, I figured out that certain young ladies were involved. My father declared it shameful and suggested that the participants should be more careful as they might likely face some serious trouble. I grasped the meaning of those words only twenty years later when a real scandal did blow up and several older city dignitaries were severely compromised.

Close to our house was a fish market that I had to pass by whenever on my way somewhere. The sight of a large pike or a Danube carp splattering in stagnant water and gasping for air, and the stench which came with it, formed one of my first gruesome memories. I used to watch them with their mouths agape and their eyes motionless as they floated in that water half-dead. They were compressed against each other, thrashing around and slowly suffocating. The fish that wrenched too violently would get a blow on the head to calm down before a customer put it in her basket or a shopping net. In such moments, I hated not only the customer or the vendor who acted this way, but also Our Dear Lord, who let it happen! This is where my aversion towards animal abuse came from, and for that matter, towards any method people apply when dealing with caged animals. I particularly disliked visiting menageries, which in those days existed on every large market square. They would have on display wolves, lions, and tigers, all of them with maddened eyes, frantically circling their cramped cages, looking for a way out. I saw it once and nothing in this world could have made me go there again. Even seeing dogs on chains disturbed me profoundly. Whenever there was a bird in a cage, I would find an opportunity to open the door of its cage and let the bird fly off free. My disapproval of these practices did not cease with time. I'd rather say it grew stronger and I personally never owned an animal in captivity.

From our front yard, a set of descending narrow stairs led to the lumber storage which belonged to Furtinger's cooperage. It took another few steps to reach the river, where I would often go, despite my parents' firm interdiction. Whenever unsupervised, I would take the opportunity to rush down to the River Drava, sit on a grassy slope, and watch the grey-yellow water slowly flow by. Weeping willow trees grew on the opposite bank. In spring, they would be full of fluffy yellow catkins, and soon after, small silvery-green leaves would replace them and appear like a thin veil spread over the trees. Only in summer would the treetops intertwine and create a shady roof that concealed the view beyond them. It was most enjoyable to sit down there on the shore and watch steamships go by pulling a long line of heavily loaded barges behind them. The ship's bells would ring, the smoke would billow towards the sky, and large wheels would turn and splash into the water, with gleaming droplets of water tearing themselves off their paddles. Above the river stretched the summer sky, blurred by haze and entirely colourless. Only at dusk would the sun manage to penetrate through the milky fog, shoot its sharp rays of light through it, spill over the woodlands, and turn the sky, the earth, and the water into an enchanted world. I would sit on my slope, bathing in the glow, unable to comprehend the suddenly occurring change, but nonetheless taken aback by the thrill, which exceeded everything that I had ever felt until then. I used to watch the red colour of the sky turn deeper purple, the gold turn into lighter yellow, and everything eventually fade further and slowly lose its warmth. Only a few more silver rays would be left dancing on the surface of the water, then they would also sink in and everything would disappear. This is how the light created a world of beauty around me, which was in reality not there and yet remained indelibly carved into my memory, forever rescued from transiency.

I have before me on my desk a handful of yellowed pages of a diary my father began to write on his twentieth birthday, 20 April 1873. They mostly refer to his early childhood and to the first few years of his education in Mohács.[38] He complains, for example, that he never owned a toy in his life:

I never had even the smallest playing ball of my own. I used to be bitter with envy because some of my playmates owned a fine sabre, and sometimes even a shotgun and I had nothing. It was the same with my clothes. My suits and coats were always patched together from different leftovers. My father considered it a waste of money to buy useless toys or give me decent clothes to wear, and my mother was too meek and mild to do anything against his will. At the age of five, I was sent to school, which consisted of going with my two older sisters to the house of a Serbian woman, who taught us how to knit! I started real school when I turned six, and that was pure terror.

Our teacher had the habit of arriving in the classroom already partially drunk, and always had a bottle of brandy on him. From time to time, he would pull the bottle out of his pocket to take a sip. His eyes were bloodshot and his nose red, so we children called him Palinkas, meaning a guzzler. He used to punish us for the smallest of faults. We had to lie down on the dirty floor, and he would then knee down on the victim's back and whip the boy until he felt the need for another sip of his drink to regain his own strength.

My father noted down that between the ages of five and eleven, he was whipped in such a manner almost daily. After leaving the elementary school and successfully passing the required entrance exam, he pursued his high school education in Fünfkirchen.[39] He wrote about it in his diary: "The town of Pécs made an awe-inspiring impression on me. I had never seen so many tall buildings in my life! I could not have ever dared dream of such splendour! Seeing the majestic old cathedral made me feel transported into some other world!"

After the gymnasium, he went to Vienna, where for four years he attended the Commercial Academy, which at the time ranked as a university. It was in Vienna that he became truly acquainted with a big city life and all its spiritual stimuli. However, there was no mention of that experience in his diary. He did talk about it during my own stay at a boarding school in Vienna, as he often visited me and kept drawing my attention to various points of interest.

He did talk in his diary, however, about his visits to his grandparents in Beli Manastir (also known as Pél Monostor), where they owned a few fields and vineyards and a small shop in the same house where they lived. Each year he would spend his school holidays with his grandparents. The village was in the county of Baranya, on the main road that ran from Osijek to old Buda (part of Budapest). On one side of the village were the slopes of Batina Mountain, on the other, vast fields of corn and wheat. The undulating hills were covered in vineyards. At harvest time, my father would eat ripe grapes to his heart's content and spend time in the pleasant company of young people from the village.

He wrote the following in his diary: "My grandfather, Philipp Rosenbaum, or Veitl Monostor, as he is called today in the village, was born in Pressburg[40] to a respectable rabbinical family. According to his stories, which he likes to retell, the famous Chief Rabbi Loew seemed to have been our ancestor."

It is difficult, and often even impossible, to determine with accuracy the origins of a Jewish family for more than two or three generations. With so many synagogues having been burned and Jewish communities scattered in the course of their wanderings, all traces of everything that had once belonged to the history of these people were wiped out and disappeared in the darkness of the bygone centuries, with hardly any written documents and family records still preserved.

There were, of course, various legends that fathers bequeathed to their sons. Most often family names by themselves offered certain trustworthy explanations, especially if they referred to specific towns, for example Frankfurter, Krakauer, Dessauer, Wiener, Mannheimer,[41] etc. Other names, however, denoted various professions—Schuster, Schneider, Metzger, Rabbinovitsch.[42] The oldest names were Cohen, Kahane, Priester and Levy, and they indicated original connections with the Jewish priesthood. Furthermore, many Jewish family names corresponded to the decorative signs on their houses and over their shops in the Jewish ghettos, such as, for example, Nussbaum, Hirsch, Bär, Weinstock, and Stiefel.[43] The Rothschild family, for instance, used to be called Hahn. When the founder of the current dynasty Isaak Hahn and his wife Esther moved in 1567 to a new house called *Zum Rothen Schild*[44] on Judengasse (Jewish Street) in Frankfurt, they started being called Rothschild, first by their fellow believers, then by everybody else in Frankfurt.

Therefore, few Jewish families could claim to know their family tree. Even if recorded in some family prayer book that happened to be preserved, it was usually fairly sketchy and not entirely authentic. In the same way, the cherished legend about Chief Rabbi Loew being the forefather of our family, orally transmitted from generation to generation, was basically unsubstantiated. My father was intrigued by the story and wanted to find out the truth. During one of his frequent visits to Karlsbad,[45] he went to Prague and in the record office of the Jewish community kept at the Klausen Synagogue[46] he found documents regarding the rabbinical family Rosenbaum, including my grandfather, Philipp Rosenbaum. Having inspected the relevant records, he was able to determine with certainty that the Rosenbaum family effectively descended from Rabbi Loew. Rabbi Loew had many children, including a daughter, our ancestor, who was a learned Talmud student, something most uncommon for women in those days. She moved to Germany with her husband and lectured in his religious school.

The Jewish community office in Prague attested in writing that we were decisively direct descendants of Chief Rabbi Loew, one of the most influential people at the end of the Middle Ages. The full name of this Jewish Kabbalist and scholar was Judah Loew ben Bezalel, known in the Judaica sources as "The Maharal of Prague".[47] He was born in 1520, probably in Posen,[48] and was portrayed many times in German literature, notably in the novel *Der Golem* by Gustav Meyrink, in the historical novel *Tycho Brahes Weg zu Gott* (The Redemption of Tycho Brahe) by Max Brod, and in Hugo Salus' poems. His well-preserved tomb still stands erect in the old Jewish cemetery in Prague and my father visited it in 1886. It represents a house made of stone with a steep saddle roof, as is usually the case with most Jewish gravestones. The gables are luxuriously decorated, and the sides have the titles of fifteen of his works engraved in the stone, those published during his life and an additional four, published posthumously. In fact, all tombstones in that cemetery are of the same size and shape because, according to a Jewish belief, all people are equal in the afterlife.

Rabbi Loew's reputation as a great scholar, philosopher, magician, and Kabbalist has spread beyond the borders of the Jewish community in Prague and persists today in numerous legends. When, in 1592, Emperor Rudolf II received the respected rabbi in audience, their meeting lasted over two hours. The superstitious Emperor was evidently intrigued by the Rabbi's Kabbalistic extensive knowledge of foretelling the future.

Even common people believed he had the supernatural abilities of a real miracle worker. On one occasion, he succeeded in moulding a homunculus (a golem) and giving him life with Kabbalistic amulets. The golem was in his service until one day he sinned against the law of the Sabbath, and the Rabbi was compelled to destroy him. Another legend has it that the Rabbi once saved the inhabitants of Posen from the plague epidemic. In the midst of his prayer on the eve of a major holiday, the Rabbi saw the Angel of Death and he snatched from his hands the long list of those destined soon to die. A small piece of paper ripped off the list, however, and remained stuck between the Angel's fingers. The Rabbi's name was on it. After the holiday, the Rabbi suddenly fell ill and died. And so, the miracle worker managed to save the community, but not himself. Following the demolition of the Prague Jewish ghetto, the city council commissioned a statue of Chief Rabbi Loew to be placed against the wall of the New City Hall to honour his memory. The elongated figure of the Rabbi, wearing a tall rabbinical hat and a long robe with voluminous folds, has his eyes cast downwards upon a naked young person clinging to him and trying to stand up against him, a probable impersonation of diasporic Jews.

The teaching of Kabbalah had many followers, including, as mentioned earlier, this illustrious ancestor of mine. Its roots go all the way back to the very origins of Jewish religious tradition and probably even deeper in history. Some have tried to extend the existence of this "esoteric doctrine" all the way to the beginnings of humanity. Perhaps Kabbalah has its starting point in the old and forgotten cultures of the Chaldeans, the Manichaeans, the Babylonians, or ancient Egyptians, and their mathematical and astronomical knowledge, which, again, had its roots even deeper into prehistory. It was later influenced by Platonism, Pythagoreanism, and even Christian and Islamic teachings. It also contains concepts borrowed from apocalyptic literature and Gnosticism.

According to tradition, the teaching of the "esoteric doctrine" was, by the mid-eighth century, transferred from Babylon to Italy and cultivated exclusively in the Kalonymus family. One member of that family brought the teaching to Germany. The German school focused above all on the spiritualization of the religious living through mysticism. As the result of their exposure to the influence of Arabic thinkers, the schools in southern France and Spain, on the other hand, moved instead in the speculative direction.

It is significant that the Jewish Kabbalistic teaching flourished most intensely in the centuries of the fiercest persecutions of Jews. With their promises, prophecies, and announcements of miracles, which had either already occurred or were to happen, Kabbalah and Messianism sparked the hopes of those who lived in constant uncertainty, were terrorized by fear, and exposed to ridicule and abuse. These teachings provided comfort by announcing the imminent arrival of the Kingdom of God, thus giving people the strength to persevere.

They provided more than that. At the time when the rabbinical teaching, cut off from its sources, gradually began losing its power and vitality in favour of formalism, the Kabbalistic teaching and Messianism appealed to the inner energy of the sufferers to help them rise above their destiny. It was a call to revive their faith and open their souls to some fresh air which, they were told, would help them breathe more easily, and would provide a most beautiful *fata morgana* reflection of their dreams.

Kabbalah possessed precisely what people needed at the time. It embodied the ultimate wisdom concerning all aspects of life. By going back to the primordial man, to Adam Kadmion, Kabbalah established the principle of the primal male—the symbols of the Father and the King—as well as the primal female—the Mother and the Matron. It established the principles of an eternally positive and an eternally negative and validated the left and the right. It means it recognized the bipolarity of all things. It followed the postulates of Indian philosophy, such as the theories of reincarnation, transfer of souls, and overshadowing of one soul by another. This was, therefore, not about hope in an afterlife in the Christian sense, but about the purification of the soul that takes place already in this world, the expiation of sins from a past life, gradually, at each stage of one's reincarnation, until one reaches the highest form of perfection bordering on the divine. This provided a consolation over the death of the body. It meant accepting the principles of a higher justice, according to which those deeds which were not rewarded during one's lifetime can be recognized in the next life. Jews had been stimulated by these ideas for years, until they were pushed aside in the seventeenth century due to false Messianism of Isaac Luria, Chaim Vital Calabrese, and most of all Sabbatai Zevi. The ecstasy turned into an obsession, the enraptured enthusiasm into antics, fantasies of folly, and grotesque exaggeration, and the centuries-long grief transformed itself into exuberance. Suffering and fear were all too intense not to have caused violent reactions of the soul and, on many occasions, of the body as well. In such states of mind, people dismissed everything that was reasonable and were prone to finding sense in senselessness, following wrong callings and believing in falsehoods.

My grandfather, Philipp Rosenbaum, was since his early youth a serious student of the Talmud, something my father later highlighted in his diary. Studying the Talmud consisted of learning Biblical texts, principles of the laws that were preserved through oral traditions, including also numerous commentaries and dialectic interpretations of all that material put together. Such studies had often a purpose in themselves and in the case of pious Jews lasted for the extent of their lives. In the eyes of those who were busy earning their living, studying the Talmud was a God-pleasing profession. The well-off, and sometimes even not so well-off parents were proud to acquire a Talmud scholar for a son-in-law, even if it meant that he would not be contributing to the upkeep of the household in any practical way. Studying the Talmud was, after all, a religious duty.

The Talmud itself was a text written over the centuries by some 2500 people and contained the wisdom of all the Jewish people scattered in the world. In this way, it represented the spiritual core of Judaism. The Talmud comprised statements that could be interpreted in a multitude of ways and commentaries requiring additional interpretations. Often even the simplest of things would be rendered complicated, and someone's whole life would then be devoted to the study as to how to resolve it and make it right again. However, immersing oneself in those texts, designated as holy by tradition and customs and often elevated to the divine, was captivating. It had the power to distract from the reality of life and sharpen the mind, but it also often led to hair-splitting and unnecessary sophistry, pettifoggery, fallacies and nitpicking, the consequence of which was that the illusion became more important than reality and words more valued than deeds. For some fanatics, it was like a drug and so intoxicating that it drew them into isolation and made them completely unaffected by external influences.

That was exactly the case with my great-grandfather, Veitl Monostor. The only thing I have ever been able to find about him was that, thanks to his wisdom acquired from studying the Talmud, he was an exceptionally respected man and more knowledgeable than most of his contemporaries. At the beginning of the nineteenth century, he left his hometown of Pressburg and began wandering as a pious *Bocher*[49] from one community to the other, following the Danube in its downstream course. He stopped on his way wherever there were good Talmud teachers and learned book scribes. In this way, as he was gradually advancing further and further onto the Great Hungarian plain, he greatly extended his knowledge. One day, walking through the area called Baranya, he stopped in a small isolated village called Baan,[50] situated on the feudal estate of Archduke Karl of Aspern-Essling[51] and away from all major roads. There he met a pious man called Nathan Taussig (also known as Reb Nate Baan), who lived under the archduke's protection and goodwill and was thus allowed to settle permanently on the estate and open a shop, both otherwise prohibited to Jews.

Reb Nate Baan was born in Vienna. He arrived in Baranya as part of the archduke's entourage. His Viennese relatives, the entire Taussig family, enjoyed the protection of the Habsburg family, who were greatly indebted to them. The Taussigs not only had the right to live in Vienna permanently but were also able to own their house. Furthermore, they were exempt from wearing the "Jewish badge" and were allowed to employ numerous servants, which meant that whole families could become part of the household in the guise of servants and enjoy the same protection as their masters.

The "protected Jews" or "court factors" were in those times the only people entitled to handle money, since there were still no regulated monetary institutions in Europe and royal dynasties were up to their necks in debt due to constant warfare. They had the ability to raise huge sums of money to finance court prodigality, served as mediators in closing business deals, proved to be useful advisors, and thus gained a certain reputation as well, until their services were no longer required. For the smallest of offences, often based on a simple denunciation, they would then be thrown in the dungeon, executed in horrible ways, and their property confiscated.

The members of the Viennese Taussig family, including my great-grandfather Reb Nate Baan, were Habsburg court Jews. They kept that position well into the nineteenth century. The Austrian financier Theodor von Taussig, born in 1849, was the director of the Länderbank of Austria and acted as Emperor Franz Joseph's private banker. He greatly contributed to the advancement in the mining industry, the creation of the Danube Steamboat Shipping Company, and was personally involved in the process of nationalization of Austrian railways. The pretty and intelligent daughter of Reb Nate Baan, Theresa Taussig, was born and raised by the end of the eighteenth century as part of that Viennese family. In 1820, she married the Talmud scholar Philipp Rosenbaum, recently arrived from Pressburg. They were my great-grandparents. They moved to the nearby village of Beli Manastir (or Pél Monostor in Hungarian), also on the archduke's property and mostly inhabited by Swabian Germans and Šokci,[52] where her father made sure that they had the right to settle and open a small shop. My great-grandmother Theresa (known henceforth as Resele of Monostor) assumed from the start the full burden of running the shop. Her shop was the only one between Darda and Villány[53] and had loyal customers from all the outlying villages. She was selling printed fabric, linen, aprons and kerchiefs, household and farming tools, nails and mouse traps, petroleum, salt, and sugar. She was on familiar terms with her customers; she knew their circumstances and spoke their language. She would rebuke frivolous girls tempted to spend too much money on dressing up, telling them, "Didn't you buy a new kerchief and an apron just a few days ago? Get out of the shop or I will tell your mother!"

In the meantime, she had one baby after another, seven altogether, two sons and five daughters. Her eldest daughter, Josephine, was my grandmother. They all had typical Swabian names: Pepi, Hanni, Dinni, Mari, and Rozi. They socialized with local children and their mother raised them to be diligent and modest. They were dressed in the same clothes as the local Swabian girls in the village: wide skirts made of blue printed calico, one on top of another, bodices buttoned up to the neck, and colourful aprons. It was only after she was married that my grandmother put on her first city dress.

While my great-grandmother was thus running the store, standing behind the counter, weighing salt and measuring cloth, taking care of the cattle, fields and vineyards, raising the children, and making sure that servants did their work, my great-grandfather (still a relatively young man at the time) sat in the airy gazebo surrounded by a flowery garden. During the winter months, he would be in the warm back room, wearing his black corduroy cap on his head and studying his Talmud. He would often bend over his folios, frowning when he was tortured by certain indecipherable issues that could not be resolved regardless of his superb rabbinical knowledge. There were always the "pro" and the "contra" arguments, creating conflictual interpretations and, ultimately, made everything even more complex.

But it was a God-pleasing occupation. This is what his wife Theresa also believed and left him in peace. And so, while he was carefully reading aloud each word in a soft singsong tone all by himself, springs, summers, autumns and winters were passing by, without him paying any attention to his environment. He spent his days and years, in fact, his entire life, without even noticing that it was his wife who made everything around him run as it should. Even in her mature years, she was still beautiful. She had a gently rounded face, black hair, and large transparent-blue eyes, which she bequeathed to all her descendants. Her five daughters also had smooth black hair and the same blue eyes, in different tones and shades from azure blue to violet, occasionally dimmed with a bit of blurry grey, which made them look less shiny, or even with a tinge of green, which had something catlike about it. Since her first child was born, there was no descendant of hers who did not keep a glimmer of that blue alive. Her eyes continued glowing with that clear celestial blue well into her old age.

My grandmother Josephine was married in 1849 and moved to Mohács, a small town situated on the shores of the Danube, famous for being the place where the Hungarians were defeated by the Turks in 1526 and deprived of their national independence for a long period afterwards. I know little about the previous life of my grandfather Max Miskolczy. It is assumed that the family came from Upper Hungary, from a town called Miskolcz, hence their name. My grandfather was born in Bonyhád, in one of the largest South Hungarian Jewish communities. He moved with his brothers to Mohács but I know little about their families.

The story goes that in 1848 one of my grandfather's sisters followed the troops as army purveyor, so no wonder that she later did not enjoy a particularly good reputation. The other sister was our Aunt Strauss, whom I met when she was already old and an upright and unassuming woman. As a young woman, she was engaged to a young man from Bonyhád. The wedding canopy was put up in the garden, which, for Jews, symbolized a room for the newlyweds. The luxuriously dressed bride stood there sur-rounded by relatives and with a rabbi present, but the groom failed to show up, and was never found nor heard of ever after. The bride was so ashamed she hoped the ground would swallow her up. Everyone wanted to cancel the wedding when my Uncle Strauss took pity on the abandoned and embarrassed bride. He was at the time a glass repair journeyman and was travelling the countryside carrying his trunk full of tools on his back. He put down his trunk and exclaimed, "I like the girl and I will marry her." He took her by the arm and led her under the canopy, in the presence of many witnesses, which according to the Jewish law meant that they were wed. The abandoned girl thus saved her reputation and found another husband, to whom she was happily married for the following fifty years. The unexpected groom later opened a small porcelain and glass shop in Osijek. He was that good uncle who gave me the beautiful pink-coloured coffee cup when I was a child and, based on his appearance, I imagined how Dear Lord himself must have looked. He was a good and wise man. Some of his inspired remarks were often quoted in the family, even after his death. The rushed wedding was followed by a rushed pregnancy and the birth, way before the supposed due time, of a healthy baby girl. He accepted the situation without even discussing the delicacy of the matter. He did not go into any complicated calculations that might put suspicion on his fatherhood, and he loved his little Minna as much as his other children. It turned out that he spent his old age in her care and once he became blind, she devotedly looked after him until the end of his life.

In the meantime, my grandfather acquired considerable wealth. In 1870, he moved to Osijek and bought Hiller's House in Županijska Street.[54] The edifice remained in my family's possession until 1940. In terms of the existing building norms in Osijek, this was a solid and exceptionally well-built house, comfortable and as luxurious as could have been afforded at the time. It was in close proximity to the city's main square and opposite the parish church. The stairs leading to the first floor were made of expensive red marble, and the ceilings decorated with gilded stucco ornaments and paintings of idyllic landscapes. The rooms were large, with four-and-a-half-metre-high ceilings, and unusually tall windows. All rooms had attractive majolica stoves in pure Baroque style, just like those found in Count Pejačević's Manor in Retfala.[55] Underneath were the stores, one specializing in retail and the other in wholesale. They had high ceilings and modern display windows. The people in Osijek had not seen anything like it in their town before. The yard had stables and utility rooms. There was also a twenty-metre-long basement with concrete floors where goods were stocked from floor to ceiling. Hiller's shop had the reputation of a gold mine and no other shop in Slavonia could compare with it. My grandfather would never have dreamt of engaging in such a venture himself had he not been persuaded by his brother-in-law, already well settled in town, with promises to invest the same amount of money in the business and enter into partnership. In making the decision, my grandfather was also thinking of his large family: he had to provide modern education for his daughters and find them good husbands. This could hardly be achieved in Mohács, more or less a mere village. My grandfather agreed. He sold his by then already well-established shop in Mohács, along with his house and other properties which, all put together, allowed him to buy Hiller's House and move to Osijek in the mid-1870s. The family settled in the elegant seven-room apartment, occupying the entire second floor of the newly acquired house. He also purchased new furniture fit for a posh city apartment. The salon was twelve metres long and its main decoration was the representative marble fireplace with a brass griddle and a hearth made of the same material. The mirrors in wide golden frames reached to the ceiling, and the consoles were made of cherry wood and decorated with beautiful marquetry. The salon furniture set was in the late Empire style, consisting of tall chairs with their backs upholstered in brocade, and oval tables. Hanging from the ceiling was a gilded multi-arm chandelier with countless glass prisms, in conformity with the prevailing home decoration style of that period.

The three unmarried daughters played the piano, learned French, and overnight turned into elegant young ladies, dressed exclusively in Viennese gowns. All of a sudden, they had requirements and demands unheard of in their previous modest life in the countryside. They strolled with their friends on the glacis and displayed their latest fashion discoveries in the City Garden on Sundays. It took quite some time for the Paris fashion novelties to reach Osijek via Vienna. However, the fashionable ladies of Osijek did not take this delay too much to heart and believed that they dressed just like their distant sisters on the banks of the Seine and the Danube. Absolutely indispensable at the time were *cul de Paris* or *tournures*,[56] fashionable jackets trimmed with fringes, luxuriously pleated tunics, and

taffeta jupons garnished with ruching and lace. Included in the indispens-
ables was, placed on the top of the head, a heavily teased and pinned-up
high chignon made of a multitude of curls, with a small hat decorated with
flowers, ribbons, and feathers, precariously leaning over the foreheads.
Especially imaginative ladies would make their house dresses to look like
the gowns of their favourite characters in French sentimental novels. They
wore dressing gowns made of red and peacock blue plush with long trains,
all decorated with numerous ribbons, folds, and ruches. Scottish neckties
or lace insertions embellished the necklines. They would tighten their
waists, to the point of fainting. "Wasp waist" was one of the main requirements of female beauty. Hips and breasts were allowed to spill luxuriously
over the tight corset made of fishbone and steel, as long as the waist was
within the prescribed measures of not more than fifty centimetres in all.

The only opportunities a woman had to expose herself in her full fashionable glory were summer promenades in the City Garden,[57] where on
Sunday afternoons between four and seven, a military band played, and all
the elegant townspeople were to be seen. With its rich vegetation, the City
Garden was like a small version of Schönbrunn.[58] The strolling paths were
surrounded with tall hedges like stage backdrops, and there were beautiful shady avenues surrounded by ancient trees, the branches of which hid
the sun away. While the lovely Osijek ladies were strolling down the main
avenue, and the orchestra was playing one vigorous waltz after another, the
officers would be standing sidelong in a line and smiling with satisfaction
when a lady would cast a flirtatious glance from under her little parasol.
Usually those were just platonic looks because the officers, although
capable lads, were not well paid, and if they wanted to be married, they had
to secure a large cautionary deposit. And so, the young and elegant Osijek
ladies, my three aunts included, had to wait for their Prince Charming to
show up from somewhere else. The two eldest of my aunts were acclaimed
beauties, and since they also had a large dowry at their disposal, they could
be extremely finicky. No one in Osijek was considered a possible candidate.

However, it soon turned out that all the intoxication with luxury and the
rapidly awakened arrogance were ill founded. The brother-in-law who had
persuaded my grandfather into selling his successful business in Mohács
and had promised to invest a large sum in the business himself, turned out

to be unable to fulfil his promise, as he sank into the mire of his own debts and was left with no cash. This was a terrible blow for my grandfather. All his life he had been a respectable and competent merchant, almost of a proverbial strictness and thriftiness in the matters of business. He always used to earn more money than he was able to spend, and now, suddenly, he was faced with a task both physically and mentally beyond his power. His pride prevented him from burdening his family with his worries, so in the face of this grave situation he turned to his eldest son, my future father, who was twenty-three years old at the time and had been living in Vienna for eight years.

He was working in a large banking company and was intelligent, ambitious, and endowed with a versatile education. He was heading for a potentially successful career and was in general more suited for a life in a big city than a small provincial town with all its restrictions and middle-class customs. He studied economics in Vienna, read Proudhon,[59] Ricardo,[60] and Adam Smith,[61] had a few articles already published in current newspapers, attended the performances at the Burgtheater and the opera house, and socialized with intelligent people. Overnight he felt compelled to leave it all behind, respond to his father's appeal, rush home, and clear up the situation as best he could.

With the signing of the peace treaty with the Prussians in 1866, followed a year later by the Austro-Hungarian Compromise,[62] Vienna enjoyed a relatively calm period of peace and consolidation, propitious for economic growth and accelerated industrialization. It was a period full of promises never to be fulfilled. Everything around the dazzling imperial couple was done in grand style in Vienna. Thanks to the loosening of both foreign and internal tensions and the honeymoon atmosphere following the recently agreed upon arrangement of a Dual Monarchy regime, people hoped for an extended period of peace and economic prosperity. The luxurious buildings of the Ring were constructed in that period. Viennese universities and colleges, especially the medical school, became world-famous. Students from around the world attended its technical schools. The Baroque and Rococo styles of Old Vienna were overtaken by many changes and this flourishing new Vienna became one of the first European metropolises. The results of this new prosperity were to be demonstrated at the International Exposition of 1873 when, hardly eight days after its opening, the Vienna stock market collapsed and along with it, numerous companies and banks, resulting in a loss of hundreds of millions of florins. Many small enterprises had to shut down their operations, private banks had to close, and joint-stock companies had to stop their activities. This debacle was caused by unprecedented speculations in securities and commercial papers on the Vienna Stock Exchange. Even more to blame were the so-called politics of prestige, a practice of the ruling House of Habsburg to restore its shattered reputation after numerous defeats on the European battlefields. After the stock market crash, it became clear that all the splendour was built on sand and was untenable in the face of even a minor shakeup.

This crisis not only directly struck my father, due to the turmoil on the stock market and the depression that affected his bank, but also left a mark on his entire future life. His employment in a bank had naturally exposed him to the world of the stock market. He had witnessed the potential for making huge profits and so, as a twenty-year-old, he asked himself one day, why should he only work for the benefit of others. Why should only wealthy people take the profit from speculating with securities and investment bonds? He got carried away and began speculating himself. He invested all his savings into securities, expecting them quickly to increase in value. What happened was exactly the opposite. The value of his securities plummeted, and he suffered a great loss, causing him many sleepless nights. With great sacrifices and working overtime, he eventually managed to settle his finances. His lifelong aversion towards any form of financial speculation stemmed from that experience. He never again indulged in playing on the stock market, never touched a single deck of cards for the rest of his life, and repeatedly warned me about the danger of gambling, always arguing that only fools engage in games of chance.

He followed that principle when he responded to his father's call for help, abandoning his career as a bank employee and leaving behind everything that tied him to the big city—theatres, concerts, museums, libraries, and the company of like-minded and intelligent young people he had known since his school days. For a man of his abilities and ambitions, it was not easy to bury himself in the greyness of the province and he never truly got over that change. He profoundly disliked standing behind the counter and selling things to people. For that reason, he dispersed his activities into areas that had not much in common with his principal field of work—membership in different types of associations, honorary functions, and involvement in different public institutions and their new projects. It all, eventually, claimed most of his free time. His pleasant appearance, spontaneity, honesty, and kindness when dealing with people won him many friends, but naturally also attracted animosity and envy. In any case, he cut an above-average figure in the city.

How he managed to put his father's business back on track is only roughly known to me. He calmed the most aggressive creditors, took out new loans, and introduced various new products in the shop, including some items still unheard of in the region, for example, horse blankets and coarse cloth manufactured in Siebenbürgen.[63] He travelled each year to a small place called Heltau[64] near Hermannstadt,[65] where he could buy the particular white Loden fabric, the so-called halina-cloth,[66] which the Hutsuls,[67] the Csikérs,[68] and the Székelys[69] used in making their national costumes. The halina-cloth began to be in demand in our parts too, replacing the locally produced homespun cloth. He made business connections with textile factories in Moravia and Silesia, introduced a considerable number of novelties in customer relations, updated the accounts and management, reduced costs, and increased the income so that he not only managed to restore the old company back to normal, but he also made the business excel. He cut the oversized apartment in two and separated the two shop premises. He rented one of the shops to his brother-in-law Bauer and several former rooms in the apartment to the First Slavonian Savings Bank, and in this way considerably improved the family budget.

He was often seen visiting the Lower Town in these days, where my nearly twenty-year-old future mother lived. He fell in love with her at first sight. She was a petite, dainty blond, but regardless of her delicate appearance, also quite independent and headstrong. Alongside her distinctive, almost masculine intelligence, there was no lack of typically female flirtatiousness in her. The pair went through a series of lovers' quarrels of all possible varieties and in all phases, accompanied by numerous love letters, deliveries of flowers, and urgent visits, which altogether lasted almost three years until my mother finally decided to consent. Their relationship was from its beginnings founded on an aesthetic ground, greatly in accordance with the times but also their personal inclinations. They had both received an above-average education, which was obvious not only in their prolonged written correspondence, but also in the choice of books my father used to give her to read during their engagement. I still have today a luxurious edition of an anthology of best German lyric poetry, a collection of Lamartine's[70] poems in French, with my mother's name printed in gold on its cover, as well as a collection of letters written by Wilhelm von Humboldt[71] to a female friend.

When my grandfather passed away in 1878, my father felt obliged to postpone the wedding for a whole year. They eventually married on 3 March 1879, and a year later, I came into this world as their first child.

Several changes occurred in my life as I turned five years old, the most important being the birth of my sister Anny. That meant the end, once and for all, of my dominant position in the family. With a new wet nurse in the house, and as I was "a big girl" now, my old nanny (Kinderfrau) Rozika, was let go. That was the first great sorrow of my life. As long as I could remember, good old Rozi had been part of the household. The only exception was during my extended visits at my grandmother's house in the Lower Town, when Rozi stayed with her married daughter Berta, who once used to be our cook. And now she was about to leave us for good! I could simply not believe that was possible! Rozi had the patience of an angel and used to bathe me, feed me, tuck me into bed at night, and be there again in the morning, kind and ready to remove all obstacles from my path. My mother was often ill during the first years of my life. They used to say that she was too weak even to take me up in her arms, and so, I got used to good old Rozi. She and my grandmother were the only people who knew how to manage me without using any force. She used to tell me fairy tales. It was hard to tell which one was lovelier, and it is not clear to me even today where she picked them all up. Later, I came across some of them in the collections of folk tales by the Grimm brothers[72] or Ludwig Bechstein.[73] Some were folk tales assembled in various other anthologies, but many of them were of unknown origin. I was never afterwards able to figure out whether they were part of some oral tradition or she had made them up herself. It happened that from time to time she would be retelling them differently, introducing certain variations. That would disturb me and I would immediately protest, arguing that, for instance, the princess had blond and not black locks of hair, that she arrived on a white horse and not in a golden carriage, that the little goose shepherdess did not marry a common peasant boy but a prince, and that Hansel and Gretel did not really shove the old witch into the oven to burn, but only locked her in. Old Rozi would then explain that things in life did not always follow the same patterns and could sometimes get all mixed up, so why would fairy tales be any different? The most important thing was, nonetheless, that there was always the same moral point at the end of the story—the good wins and the evil gets punished. I could sit beside her for hours listening to her stories, my gaze fixed on her haggard-looking face under a white cap. Her cheeks were sunken and her lips thin, she had slightly red eyes and no eyelashes. In addition to all that, there was an aquiline nose and a long thin neck, which altogether gave her an unusual bird-like look.

I spent the first years of my life in an unfathomable but wonderful world of beautiful princesses, noble knights, evil wizards, and good fairies. It was a world where miracles happened at any time, where horses and birds could talk, where tiny elves lived in the calyx of flowers, where enemy forces threatened humans, and tender-hearted dwarves regularly saved them from trouble. I retained some of that fascination with miracles even as I was growing older, manifesting itself in the form of an intangible yearning for a world of unlimited possibilities, as revealed to me by my good old nanny Rozi through her fairy tales. I learned to enjoy the magic beauty found in the words by themselves. I believed in their deeper meaning, and the possibility of getting surprising results by arranging them in an endless number of varied combinations. I got used to personifications, transference, and symbolism. I learned to respect and love all that was small. But I simultaneously tried to imagine the essence of living as having some kind of a supernatural fourth dimension, and so have been hoping all my life for some unexpected, but nonetheless miraculous, solutions.

Never again did I hear someone tell stories in such a wonderful way as my old *nanny* used to. Her words fell like heavy drops upon my heart, all of them equally engaging and captivating. They were enchanting and their beauty lay in the way the stories were told. They were like a silken gown embroidered with pearls and bathed in sunshine. The storytelling was at the same time clear and well put together, and thus carved in my memory for good. Here is one of the most beautiful fairy tales she used to tell me:

"Once upon a time there was a poor old woman who used to go into the forest to gather firewood. She was frail and ailing and had no one in the world. One day she came upon a small creature, looking partly like a tiny child and partly like a lizard."

Of course, I knew right away that it was one of the spirits of the Earth, Air, or Water that Rozi often talked about. They were always around ready to reward or punish people, according to their merits. It was the same here!

"The small creature was lying helplessly before her feet shivering with cold. The old lady took off the scarf that covered her back, the only one she possessed, and wrapped the little creature in it. On the spot, the Earth spirit transformed itself into a beautiful fairy, dressed in silk and velvet. She raised her wand and everything around her started budding with life, turning green and blossoming. The forest was suddenly filled with sunlight and birds started chirping on the tree branches.

'You took pity on me,' said the fairy. 'So, make a wish and I will make it come true. Only be careful: you mustn't use more than five words!'

In all her life, nothing good had happened to the old woman except for the short time when she was young, so she uttered a sentence without a lot of thought: 'Let me be young again!'

The moment the fairy touched her with the magic wand, wrinkles disappeared from her face and her blue eyes glistened as clear as the sky. The old lady straightened up and threw away the walking stick she had been using until then. She easily lifted up the bundle of dry branches, which would have usually made her bend almost to the ground, and she hurried home."

Here Rozi suddenly went quiet but I waited, because each story good old Rozi told me ended with, "And if they didn't die, then they are still alive today!" This time it was different and Rozi continued:

"Fifty years went by since that day. It was again a cold day in March and the same woman, old, bent, and poor again, went into the woods to pick firewood. And once again, at the same spot as before, she came across the same fairy, young, dazzling, and clad in silk. The fairy raised her magic wand and spoke:

'I can see you haven't achieved much more than before in your life, have you? However, since you were once kind to me, I will grant you one more wish. Just be careful, it shouldn't be more than five words. Would you like to be young one more time?'

The old lady shook her head. 'Let me die in peace!'

'You have chosen well!' said the fairy, and she touched her with her wand and disappeared.

In that moment, everything around her started budding with life, turning green and blossoming. The forest was suddenly filled with sunlight and birds started chirping on the tree branches. A black starling with a yellow beak approached the old woman singing, 'All in good time! All in good time', and the words sounded like pearls falling from its beak. The old woman suddenly felt very tired and sleepiness overcame her. She dropped the bundle of wood from her back and said, 'I will lie down for a moment before I head back home.' She lay down on the soft, fragrant grass full of violets and anemones. On the branch above her head, the starling was chirping away, 'Good night, good night!' Small creepers and flyers were buzzing everywhere around her, and she instantly fell asleep, never to wake up.

Late in the afternoon, some women picking wild strawberries found her and carried her back to the village in their arms. Next day, as they laid her down in her grave, the black starling appeared again and chirped, 'When something is due to end, that's it. It's over.'"

And that was the end of the story.

"Why wouldn't she want to become young once again?" I asked my Rozi.

"Because, in the end, it all comes down to the same thing, even if you start it all over again ten times."

"And why does it all come down to the same thing?"

"Because you cannot be young without getting old. In old age, dying in peace is the best thing a person can wish for oneself!"

I did not quite understand her, but in that moment, her fairy tale world was also mine. It was a world of good and evil spirits which intervene in our lives and direct their course at their will. They have their own logic and moral message, and as they have existed since the childhood of humanity, they are close to and understood by children. They give life to nature and enrich it with content, meaning, and deep symbolic values.

In this respect, my grandmother had just as much decisive influence on me as old Rozi. She used to awaken and nourish in me the feeling of love for everything alive, a feeling I would later reinforce and expand with scientific knowledge. There was no room in that mystification of nature for any kind of superstition. It had nothing to do with transcendence of souls, resurrection, or sadomasochistic legends of martyrdoms. Because my first questions about life did not evolve around the realm of a mysterious divinity, whom I should fear more than love, or the question of whether or not it existed. My interests gravitated towards the mysteries of the natural world—the growth of plants, the life of animals, the universe of a starry vastness. My hunger for knowledge was so powerful that everything I learned in that field felt like the enrichment and expansion of my own life and filled me with excitement.

Most children gain their first spiritual experience in the church. The acts of devotion impress them, lives of saints fascinate them, customary ceremonies are loaded with symbolism of something incomprehensible to them and infinitely great. I knew nothing about those things and there was later nothing for me to deal with in order to overcome it. I presume that mature rational dealing with childhood religious experiences can lead later in life to deepening one's thinking. It may bring people to espouse opposite viewpoints, but also often mobilize them to the best of their abilities, increase sensitivity, and sometimes become the source of amazing artistic inspirations. On the other hand, those of us who have grown up without any religious experience have, in comparison to others, a certain advantage. We can neither gain nor lose anything in that respect. The direction of our development since our youth does not have to face setbacks or reactions. New understandings will build upon existing knowledge and avoid contradictions.

My little sister was a delicate child and kept my mother constantly busy. Once my *nanny* was let go, I was sent to a recently opened, modern kindergarten, established thanks to the initiative of a few progressive, public-minded citizens. It was set up in Schreiber's House in Kapucinska Street. It had a well-illuminated and spacious hall with a few low benches and a full set of pedagogical materials for early childhood education as prescribed by Friedrich Fröbel.[74] The educator's name was Eleonore Partl. She was a handsome, slim, and well-dressed young lady from Vienna, hardly twenty years of age, and was immediately welcomed with open arms by Osijek families. She began receiving invitations to daily afternoon coffee gatherings (the so-called Jausen), offering marvellous coffee with whipped cream, *Gugelhupf,* marble cake with raisins, small pastries and walnut, chocolate, or punch cakes. The entire city was suddenly interested in playing with sets of wooden blocks, and some dads chose to accompany their young ones to the kindergarten themselves, declaring with a lot of praise that Miss Partl was a perfect educator.

I hated the kindergarten from the bottom of my heart. I found the mechanical activities boring—neither useful nor attractive, with no positive effect on a child's sense of good taste or the development of its basic skills. They were useless tests of patience, which forced me to sit still for hours. I detested silly activities of paper folding, aligning small sticks and tiles, or putting disparate parts of a cube that had been cut criss-cross back into the shape of the original unit. When I think about it today, all I see is a senseless drill aimed at instilling the first rules of blind subservient mentality in the minds of little pre-school children. The only two pleasant hours I had at the kindergarten took place when I was once punished for disobedience and had to stay overtime. Old Nanči Mahm, who worked there as a cleaner, was given the task of keeping an eye on me while I was enduring my punishment. The moment the others left, the two of us set off to work. She was sweeping the room and I was collecting the paper cuttings off the floor. Then we dusted the desks together. I drew water out of the well and we sprinkled the floor with it. Then we cleaned up the scattered toys and put them back in the boxes. At the end, I was allowed to take the waste basket to the garbage heap at the bottom of the garden. In a few words, it was wonderful, and I was deeply aggrieved when my two penalty hours were over and Nanči Mahm took me home.

Most fortunate for me, the kindergarten experience was abruptly cut short, due to a considerable scandal. The pretty Miss Partl—who had, in the meantime, added quite a colour to her cheeks and roundness to her physique, thanks to many fine treats she had been consuming—was, according to the claims of a few jealous spouses, receiving male visitors in her room! She, however, defended herself by saying that those were only the officers from the local garrison, and, moreover, they were all her "cousins". This latter detail incensed not only the wives, who worried about their husbands' morals, but also the husbands themselves. If officers were allowed in Miss Partl's room, why not them as well? Anyhow, the immoral ways of this young lady's life resulted in the closing down of the kindergarten. She left the city and was not replaced by any other "perfect educator". What a lucky and unexpected turn for me it was! An interregnum of several months of regained freedom lasted until the following autumn, when it was time for me to start proper schooling.

The next important event in my life was our family's relocation to Franjina Street,[75] where we lived from when I was five up until thirteen years of age. We had at our disposal four rooms, an alcove, and a large entrance hall, which led to the front yard full of flowers, and was therefore used as a veranda. The style of most middle-class dwellings, both in their interior and their exterior, was in those times an expression of nothing but bad taste. Houses built between 1860 and the end of the century on Anina, Franjina, Njemačka,[76] and Duga Streets were perfect examples. They were built by some ignorant and non-imaginative masons, following the same cliché. This was the transitional period between the comfortable bourgeois style of the *Biedermeier era* and the extravaganzas of the Secession which, around 1900, dominated the *fin de siècle*. For half a century, however, both houses and furniture were entirely devoid of any personal touch. Beauty was measured by what the people of good financial standing could afford and how it would reflect the level of their standard of living and improve their reputation. Every "better-off" family had a dining room in old German style and a plush settee, with a wooden shelf above the head-rest displaying an array of kitsch made of glass, porcelain, and ceramics. These were collected by the family over the years and kept up there with the only tangible outcome—to make sitting under it a considerable risk, and to oblige someone in the household to dust it daily. The elaborately carved sideboard cabinet displayed valuable silver items—carafes, platters, and bowls.

All respectful families had a salon with a red velvet sofa set, decorations of palm leaves made of canvas, and huge bouquets of dried grass and flowers (the so-called *Makart-bouquets*[77]). The salon was considered the best room in the house and used only on rare occasions. It was not heated in winter while, in summer, the velvet upholstery was usually covered with a huge non-descriptive cloth and protected with camphor and naphthalene. All houses, ours included, were low-built, uncomfortable, and damp. The wide entrance gates occupied a good third of the street facade and were used in summer as outdoor dining rooms. Each house had at least one dark windowless room, which was unsuitable for living but people still used it. It usually served as a bedroom with the explanation that there was no need for light to fall asleep. Sometimes it was a room reserved for children, as they usually had the tendency to destroy things and a space like that would be good enough for them. This should not be judged as a lack of parental love but, rather, as being in accordance with the prevailing puritanical method of bringing up children in those days, namely that children should learn to be accustomed to modesty, simplicity, and even a certain amount of deprivation. Children had to understand that they could not have everything they might desire.

Our house on Franjina Street was a so-called throughway house. Next to our flower garden was a courtyard that looked like a long village street with storehouses, stables, workshops, and many damp nooks that served as homes for several proletarian families with numerous children. That courtyard was the longest in the entire city.[78] It led directly from Franjina Street into Županijska Street, and then connected with Wildermann[79] Street, and finally Vukovarska.

It was considered the shortest route to reach the Lower and New Towns. For years, inhabitants who lived in the vicinity used that appropriately called Long Courtyard as a convenient passageway. My parents wanted to stop that practice, and, as soon as we moved into the house, ordered that both the large street gate and the small latticed door, which separated our yard from the long public one, be immediately closed. There were no unsocial motives behind that decision. My parents were simply, and rightfully so, afraid that the Long Courtyard, with its countless hiding places and nooks, its unlimited possibilities for adventures and, above all, the presence of a pack of children roaming around all day long, would be an irresistible attraction for me. From the very day we moved into the house until the day we moved out, my parents and I were constantly fighting over it. Despite all pedagogical countermeasures, persuasion, threats, and punishment, the struggle ended in utter parental defeat. Nothing could ever prevent me from playing with the children from the Long Courtyard. In any case, my parents had to yield to the pressure of the street, unlock the house gate, and open the small garden gate. The passageway was thus free again, not only for the outside people, but for me as well!

The closest to our house, immediately on the other side of the latticed garden door, was the home of the Šufflays, consisting of a tiny kitchen and a narrow room with one small window and an uneven floor made of red bricks. Eight members of the Šufflay family lived and slept in that space—two parents and their six children, all girls under the age of ten. The father was a hatter and each Sunday would go to various village fairs to sell his goods. The trade seemed not very profitable because the family was obviously destitute and half starving. The eldest daughter, Anica, aged ten, looked as if she were merely one year old. Her legs were deformed with rickets, and she had not a single tooth in her mouth nor hair on her head. She could neither speak nor walk and spent her days lying in a trough behind the door. The second eldest, Helena, was my age and also my best friend. I would never have something nice to eat without putting aside at least one morsel for Helena. My parents too used to give her clothes and toys. She was as gentle as an angel, frail, and almost transparent, probably already suffering from a lung disease, since she died at the early age of twelve. I loved her dearly and in her natural gentleness, she would sometimes allow me to make her do things she would later have to account for. Thus, on one occasion, I persuaded her to cut a few leather thongs off the *kurbash*[80] that was always hanging on the wall ready for her father to whip her and the other children for the smallest of offences. I suggested that fewer twisted thongs would hurt less, and so she did cut them off, with my help. I assured her that her father would not notice a thing. Unfortunately, he did notice, and he beat her up, not with the thinned-out *kurbash*, but with a thick rope, which hurt even more.

Next to the Šufflays lived the laundrywoman known as Rezi. She had a sick child, little Franzl, who was said to be suffering from dropsy and was doomed to die soon. Since not even the old witch's remedy of throwing lime and coal into the water could help him, surely no doctor would be of any use either. That was the opinion of all women in the Long Courtyard and they did not hesitate to speak their minds about the matter in front of Franzl himself. The laundrywoman had three other sons, the elder boys already doing their apprenticeships. Her husband worked as coachman for my father, who was often obliged to travel out of town on business and therefore kept his own horse and carriage after we moved to Franjina Street. The coachman was a terribly rumbustious man and rarely sober. My father only kept him in service because he felt sorry for his wife and children.

Rezi was doing the laundry in the same kitchen where Franzl was, for months, lying ill. Suds would be boiling on the stove and the steam would be so dense that you could not see a thing in front of your nose. While coachman Ferdinand was spending his nights at the local pub, and then threatened and beat his wife upon his return, she was slaving by the trough from dusk to dawn in order to feed herself and the children. In the same cramped little kitchen where the laundry was soaking in soapy water waiting to be washed, also lay heaps of dirty laundry that Rezi would bring home on Mondays, and once washed, ironed, folded, and neatly pleated, return to "gentlefolk" on Saturdays.

Old women from the yard had the habit of coming to her house in the afternoons, always keen to gossip for a while and be able to complain, bemoan, and chat about whatever was happening around them. I would sit on top of that pile of dirty laundry and strain my ears to listen in. As usual, the woman who had most to tell was Wabi, whose job was delivering water to people's houses around the town. She lived in the courtyard and was housepainter Sokolay's tenant. Wabi was so thin that one could not help but wonder how she still kept her bones together. Although her job was to distribute water, it was obvious from just one look at her that she had never washed herself. There was no end to her gossiping, however. Her teeth would show up as she spoke, and it seemed as if she had more of them than any ordinary person would possibly have. Her tongue was also longer and thicker than other people's. Her words had therefore a guttural sound. As she was talking, spit would spray out of her mouth, all the more so since it did not cost her anything. When it came to water, things were different. Using water was quite a luxury for her. She used to sell one "*Pittel*"[81] of water drawn from the River Drava for two kreuzers, and goods at such a price should not be wasted flippantly or recklessly. As a result, the creases on her face were brown with traces of half a century of dirt deposits. Her hair was full of dust picked up on the countless streets of Osijek, through which she pulled her water barrel. No one could tell what the original colour of her hair had been. She had turned fifty. Her husband had passed away and so she had to earn her living. She had, poor woman, nothing to hope for! The children she used to have, eight or ten of them— she could not even remember exactly how many anymore—were all dead and buried. She lived by herself at Sokolay's and the Long Courtyard was her whole world.

The latest news she was thus distributing in her genuine Esseker German was that Keglević's son Tonči broke the shop windows at *Schnier und Urban* and ran away with a couple of revolvers. What a miserable "*šandkerl*"[82] to cause such embarrassment for his mother! Then, there is that guy, Mucki Fleitz. He broke into the cash register that belonged to his benefactor, who had been feeding him all these years, and he helped himself to a grand. He spent two years in Lepoglava Prison and then went to America. Only yesterday, Mrs. Fleitz blurted out that Mucki was a millionaire over there! And then there is the embarrassment in the Weifelds' house. The father is no good anyway and has eight children! The mother and the oldest girls, Fanny, Rozi, and Regi, are spending the whole day behind the sewing machine, sewing men's shirts and underwear. Now it is being said that pretty Rozi has eloped to Berlin with some guy. Oh, she'll be back in nine months with a child on her hands! Can you imagine—Sokolay's 120-kilo sow dropped dead at Christmas? And now his Mariči has fallen ill too, and it is said that the end will be a fast one! The Sokolay woman is really out of luck!

The Esseker German[83]—of which the locals were as proud as they were of their contaminated Drava water, city dust, and endless marshlands—was not even a real language, but a hard-to-describe mixture of languages, spoken and understood only by those who were born and raised between the two ends of the city. It was an idiom with suppressed final syllables, muffled vowels and consonants, without a clear intonation—in short, rather foggy altogether. There was not a sentence without something odd in it, and there was no trace of syntax, grammar, or orthography. This so-called language was actually a composite of the German dialect spoken by Viennese tradesmen imported in the times of Maria Theresa, the language of the local Swabian peasants, and elements of Württemberg Hessian dialects. One could also discern traces of Czech, popularized by military musicians of the 78th Regiment, numerous expressions found in the rich vernacular used by Jewish *Hauzierer*,[84] slang spoken by vagrants and journeymen on their way from Budapest, Prague, and Munich, and Serbian spoken by the original inhabitants of the Lower Town. One should not forget to add to all that the corrupted administrative German and Croatian languages used in the nearby Military Frontier, the bad style of the local German newspapers, and the fake theatrical pathos spoken by the visiting theatre troupes from Olmütz[85] and Pressburg.

I acquired the purest of Esseker pronunciation while playing in the Long Courtyard, and it remained stuck in my ear for the rest of my life. I found it hard to get rid of it, despite having a German governess and German language lessons with the Evangelical pastor Pindor, who spoke the purest form of German in the entire monarchy, Silesian German. I spent two years in a finishing school for girls in Vienna and I completed it with flying colours, and I could still not get rid of certain expressions that originated from Podravina and the Long Courtyard. The Esseker dialect found its way into my literary work as well, something I always considered a huge shortcoming. I fought it for years, trying to overcome the Esseker linguistic barbarisms of my childhood. I eventually succeeded, still only partially, after many years of absence from the region.

I must admit today that my parents were not wrong in attempting to make it difficult for me, if not impossible, to be in contact with the folk of the Long Courtyard. Besides the corrupted Esseker German that I was acquiring there, the place was known for a considerable number of other dubious aspects. Vice existed there along with self-sacrifice, good accompanied evil. There were drunks, thieves, and all sorts of ruffians. There was illness, hunger, and dirt. Tragic as it all was, it was also a genuine lesson of what life was all about, and I was given the chance to learn it at an early age. As I am writing this, I recall once bragging in front of Helena, who was always dressed in rags and was now admiring my new dress, "What I'm wearing today is nothing! I have ten more such dresses in my wardrobe at home!" I was making that claim in front of the poorest of all children, and, moreover, it was not even true because my mother was much too thrifty and sensible to buy me ten dresses! I honestly do not know what happened to me at that moment, why I felt like showing off in such a way. I had hardly even finished my sentence when I realized how disgraceful it was to flaunt in this manner in front of a child like Helena. I was terribly ashamed of myself and immediately began reducing the number of my "gowns" and felt compelled to add, "I might be wrong. Anny's dresses also hang in the same closet, and perhaps Mother put some of hers in there too!" Then I gave her my new pencil and after lunch brought her my dessert, as I often had the habit of doing anyway. However, that minor incident, which I have not been able to forget to this day, awoke something else in me. I asked myself, "Why do I have everything and Helena, who is a much better person than me, has nothing at all?" It was the first time that I asked that question, but it remained without a satisfactory answer for a long time afterwards. People around me, however, claimed that Our Dear Lord himself arranged it that way. "There have to be poor and rich people in this world," they would say, "because it is the only way in which we can exhibit our virtues. In the case of the poor, they resign themselves without grumbling about their fate and rely on the promise of a better afterlife. As to the rich, they give some of their excess wealth to the poor." This was the reason, I suppose, that I gave Helena a new pencil, knowing I would be getting another one soon. People also argued that there ought to be poor people around. Who would otherwise willingly accept to do dirty, difficult, or dangerous jobs? Only extreme poverty can force people to accept such jobs. All this did not sound plausible to me. My sense of compassion was awakened by that event and became, with time, a desire for justice.

A lot of playing took place in the Long Courtyard and I wholeheartedly took part in it, relying on my high sense of fantasy to escape reality. We used to play catch, hide-and-seek, hopscotch,[86] and cops and robbers. The most fun was when we staged whole fairy tales on the wooden *chardak*[87] that belonged to a leather tanner who lived and worked in the yard. He used the *chardak* to dry raw skins before he could process them. They lay there tied in large bundles, and since they were still raw, they stank, but it did not bother us kids. We would hide behind the rolls, ride, and do gymnastics on them. At one time, we played circus, at another, cowboys and Indians. There were times when we would imagine ourselves being in a knight's castle or an evil witch's cave in the forest. I usually played the part of an enchanted princess, while the others formed my court as brave knights, witches, dragons, or gnomes. I let them rescue me, kidnap or protect me, occasionally torture me as well, which I stoically endured. I would sit on my royal throne made of raw skin, with my hair tousled and my stockings pulled down, sobbing to break one's heart, or smiling in a dignified royal manner, depending on the role. I would act with such extravagance, so much pathos, genuine drama, and commitment to details that an actress playing tragic roles in our city theatre could have truly envied me.

The concrete base of the *chardak* was occupied by Romberg's vinegar factory. He had a large number of his barrels there, keeping their lids off to allow the draught of fresh air to accelerate the oxidation process. Thousands of bees swarmed around each barrel, so that this part of the yard seemed wrapped in a grey-green restlessly vibrating veil of mist. The buzzing was not necessarily loud, but the stream of that unusual music was unbroken. Swarms would be flying in and out like silver clouds and whoever carelessly approached the barrels too closely would hardly be able to escape a few stings. That was especially true for those who tried to defend themselves in panic, thrashing their arms around or revealing their fear in some other way. We children had a method of sneaking in without ever being attacked. We were actually grateful to these bees because they served as our "bodyguards", by surrounding our *chardak,* and, by creating a danger zone around it, protected us from unpleasant surprises.

Two important events took place in 1886. In August, my grandparents moved from the Lower Town to live with us, and, in October, I got a German governess, whom I liked even less than Miss Partl and her kindergarten. My grandfather suffered from progressive muscular atrophy, which made him move around with great difficulty. He had to give up his business and was from then on lying in a dark alcove made even darker by heavy curtains. My grandmother took over some of the household duties because my mother was constantly in bad health. She had been unwell since my birth and her general health worsened with the birth of my sister. She could only tolerate diet food, and even that in minimal portions. She weighed only forty-two kilograms, and there was constant fear concerning the condition of her lungs.

My grandmother also took over the upkeep of our small garden with its three mop-head acacia trees by the water pump and a gazebo covered in vines. In the middle of the garden was a large flower bed with dahlias and *Canna indica.* There were rose bushes under the windows and a spread of purslanes of all shades and colours growing between the red bricks of the pavement. Still, the most beautiful was the latticed fence, transformed by the climbing morning glory into a compact wall of flowers. Its buds would open in the morning in the shape of delicate and silky funnels of different colours, from the deepest purple red to peach pink, pastel blue, and golden yellow. There were countless transitional forms and variations and no flower looked the same. They opened up with the sunrise and withered away at sunset. They lived for only a day.

That was not all. The whole plot was full of flowers of all imaginable colours: mignonettes, petunias, phlox, and verbena. Although not having any real previous contact with nature, my grandmother loved it and this modest garden was for her not merely delightful to look at, but also a brand-new activity. She used to hoe, plant, weed, and look after her flowers with great love and extra energy.

My new governess was a Saxon woman from Transylvania with long blond hair, which was the only thing of beauty about her. She wore it arranged in two braids nested as a crown on top of her head. She had protruded, watery blue eyes and several nasty-looking scars on her neck. As a strict Protestant, she viewed everything as either black or white, good or evil, allowing for no mitigating circumstance, option, or psychological explanation. She insisted on blind obedience, with no concessions or pardons. Since her arrival, a thin rod had found a place on top of the wardrobe in the children's room. No matter how many times I tried to remove it and hide it away, it would be back at the same spot the following day. She used to say with her mouth full of saliva, "He who loves his child shall punish him most severely!" And she would refer to this maxim, however small the motive.

This person—and she stayed in our house for three years, between my seventh and tenth years of age—was a continuous nightmare for me. With her disposition, origin, and upbringing, she belonged to an entirely different world from mine. There was not a grain of either sensitivity or kindness in her and no capacity for lenience or patience. I would have found it much easier to bear sudden outbursts of violent anger than the cold calmness behind which she was hiding a pronounced sadism. It seemed even more tragic that my parents were impressed by her commitment to her principles and consented to submit me to her methods, all in their honourable belief that it was for my own good. I was not an obedient and easily manageable child—no question about it. However, with her despotism, moodiness, hysterical eccentricity, and complete absence of proper training, Miss Goldschmidt drove me into a deeply felt mental state of rebellion. I felt the same way about my other German governesses—Miss Kranich, Miss Kaiser, and Miss Seiffert—who stayed at our house, one after the other, until, at the age of thirteen, I left home to attend a boarding school in Vienna.

My protest was not merely directed against their insignificant personalities. It was levelled at everything that even remotely appeared to me as an imposition of authority, aimed at restricting my free will, reducing my freedom, and illicitly interfering in the exercise of my personal rights. That urge to resist authority remained with me, with some tragic outcomes later in my life until I learned how to manage it with logical reasoning.

The conflicts with Miss Goldschmidt occurred mostly because of my daily visits to the Long Courtyard, about which, it turned out, she was mostly powerless. The moment she turned her back, I would dash out there, out of the reach of her whip. It would be a short escape, of course, but who would ever think about some danger looming in the distant or even near future at such liberating moments? The vinegar factory with swarming bees flying in menacing circles proved to be an impenetrable mine field, which prevented Miss Goldschmidt from entering our realm. She could only call for me from a distance because she would rather have died than be exposed to the stings of those furious insects. Sneaking back home in the evening and trying not to be noticed, I would seek the protection of my grandmother who, I was well aware, had entirely different ideas about personal freedom from those of Miss Goldschmidt.

There was another educational method besides the Spanish rod that made my life miserable. It was the handicraft. Under the motto "Idleness is the mother of all vices", I was obliged to spend three hours per day crocheting. After I happily made the so-called *Musterstreifen*,[88] one in lace and one in Tunisian style crochet, each a metre and a half long, I had to make a lace tablecloth cover as a present for my mother. It was composed of small stars, twenty-five in width and thirty-five in length. I was convinced that it was simply impossible ever to complete such a work. The perspective of possibly still working on it deep into my old age seemed tragic. This pointless work, therefore, appeared to me as not just poisoning my present but also taking away any potential for a worthwhile future. Convinced that I would never finish the crocheting task anyway, I decided it was best not to begin at all. There seemed to be no escape from that flagrant act of cruelty, however, and I cried bitter tears, while the governess locked the door behind her and retired to the cozy vestibule, immersing herself in the enthralling reading of her favourite magazine *Gartenlaube (Garden Arbour)*.[89] Rivers of tears poured down my cheeks, neck, and dress. They streamed down my arms, the crocheting hook and thread. I had never cried more sincerely and more bitterly. I was hardly eight years old and the idea of crocheting my whole life out seemed pointless and useless. All this was too much to cope with. I would never, never be able to finish so many stars!

Twenty-five in width and thirty-five in length—that was what they were asking for! The thread turned so wet from my tears that it would not glide through the hook any longer. The hook itself soon became rusty as well. Everything before me seemed entangled, including my thoughts. I even forgot the pattern, although I had been doing it for weeks. Hours passed by, and I sat there with my hands in my lap and my eyes staring into space. Nothing was finished, nothing got done. The outcome was showers of customary punishments and interdictions principally concerning the one thing I yearned for most of all—to be allowed to play in the Long Courtyard.

They found yet another means to prevent me from playing—the requirement to go for a walk with the governess and Anny on the afternoons when I had no school classes to attend. Preparations for that activity were in themselves a special form of torture, since it was obligatory to be dressed following a prescribed elegance for those occasions. The fine dresses restricted all freedom of movement: they were uncomfortable, impractical, and required attentiveness when worn. I was lucky, insomuch as my mother was against any exaggeration when it came to fashion for children. But there were little girls whose hair would reach below their waist and had to be wound on to *papillottes*[90] once or even twice a day, followed by a good half an hour of combing and brushing. Quite a few girls as young as ten wore shoes with high heels, usually also too tight for comfort. As a result, they were unstable on their feet and could only take small steps. Many girls of my age already wore bras, even real corsets, because their narrow-minded and vain mothers claimed that it was never too early to begin the lacing-up, in the belief that it was the body, while still in the developing stage, which had to adapt to the form of a corset, and not the other way round. This was the only way to obtain the tiny "wasp waist", which in those days signified ideal beauty. Sensible mothers put off the wearing of the corset until the age of thirteen, but then it became inevitable.

Wearing a tightly laced corset was like wearing a stiff armour. Breasts were pressed upwards and the curve of the hips and the abdomen enhanced. At the early age of fifteen, girls already looked like bowling pins moulded out of a single piece of wood with a deep dent created by the forceful tightening of the waist, generating various difficulties and deformations later in life. Most affected were the liver and the stomach, and, in some cases, the damage led to premature death. Parisian painters complained of not being able to find a single good nude model on the streets of Paris. Corsets were deforming the female body to the same extent as did foot binding among Chinese women. Furthermore, newspapers published polemics concerning this delicate issue: artists, gynaecologists, and utopian eugenicists spoke up and wrote against wearing the corset. However, big Parisian fashion houses supported its use, and most women were on their side.

The extravagant outfits of elegant little girls included also various additional fashion follies, all according to the style of the day. Those were, for instance, shoes made of the so-called *"everlasting material"*, with twenty tiny buttons on each shoe that kept slipping through the fingers while being buttoned up. A huge sash made of satin and worn beneath the waist (and not easy to keep in place) supposedly provided a finishing touch to a girl's dress. It was tied in the back into a big bow which, with its exaggerated shape, corresponded to the bustle, a pad made of horsehair that adult women wore on their back under their heavily pleated skirts. A wide Florentine hat, swinging up and down, decorated with enormous ostrich feathers, covered the short haircut. A rubber band under the chin held the hat in place and its owner was thus transformed into a gigantic mushroom, looking utterly comical. Everything was distasteful, uncomfortable, and affected, nothing but a bad imitation of ladies' fashion whose trends between 1880 and 1890 adopted grotesque characteristics. Along with the "wasp waist", high stiff collars also became fashionable, as was the lavish use of dress fabrics by multiplying and extending skirt folds, as well as plastrons, ribbons, flowers, feathers, and lace. All this was eventually passed from the fashion for grown-ups to children's clothing and turned little girls under the age of ten into caricatures.

Our walk always followed the same route from Anina Street to Kapucinska Street, at the end of which stood the house of my photographer,

Mr. Graff. From there a wooden boardwalk led straight down to the avenue. Along the left side of the avenue were timber warehouses and two long black gunpowder storage buildings, while, on the right side, was a row of vegetable gardens, and an accumulation of stagnant water which often looked like a greenish and foul-smelling swamp. Once the road reached the moats and turned towards the *Tvrđa (the Fortress)*, a wide expanse of glacis reappeared, stretching, on one side, almost all the way to the New Town, and, on the other, all the way to the Lower Town.

Osijek was lacking in natural landscapes, with no forests or hills to speak of. Meadows of the military exercise ground provided therefore my first impressions of nature and the fortification moats and dungeon walls created an illusion of a rocky landscape. Some small things could be beautiful in themselves, while some individual segments could convey the beauty of the whole thing. For example, I had never seen a real forest until I was ten years old. A few spruces on the glacis, artificially planted on a surface area smaller than fifty square metres, appeared to us children as a little forest. In our thoughts it looked much larger and we convinced ourselves that it was a fully-fledged coniferous forest. In springtime, the glacis was even more attractive to me than the Long Courtyard. The first violets would spring out from the damp mossy ground of the glacis as early as the end of February, while the nearby moats were still under snow, which sometimes remained there, in some shaded spots until the beginning of April. The sun would work its magic and lure thousands of small blue heads to show up—and thus create a real miracle of gentle beauty, graciousness, and sweet fragrance, right there in the close vicinity of the flooded moats and the crumbling defence walls. Even more enchanting was their regular annual return. With each thawing of the snow, violets would be back. One could count on them spring after spring.

In summer, meadows would display their floral magic—mulleins, horned pondweed, dandelions, bellflowers, teasels, and clover. Little stars, small crowns, umbels, and goblets shielded by green leaves and protected by spikes and thorns. It was an immense and colourful carpet, with the grass so tall that one could easily hide in it. The damp and fertile ground that was for decades, if not even centuries, used for breaking in and training newly purchased cavalry horses, was rich in potent nutrients. Stalks of the plants were silky and long, and flowers clustered in a variety of combinations. The silver grey-green colour of the grass in spring would turn darker with the approaching summer and the grass became thicker. By the time of mowing, it would be totally dry and golden in colour. In some places, sticking out like spears above that wavy, slightly bent sea of grass, some firmer stems stood up. Others intertwined and formed a delicate lacework. There were those that displayed small clusters of grapes and beads, and those, powdered with golden pollen, that resembled the pussy willow catkins. The colourful carpet changed with every gust of wind, just as the kaleidoscope with its scattered pieces of coloured pebbles displays at each turn a new and wonderful combination of colours. And every new spring, it came back to life.

The final destination of our promenades was usually the Stone Cross, not far from the New Town. Another possibility was the obelisk at the end of the glacis, opposite the Drava and the *Kronenwerk* (Crown Fortress).[91] The obelisk was erected to commemorate the 1882 railway accident on the nearby bridge and pay tribute to the soldiers of the resident 15th Hussar Regiment, who had lost their lives in that accident.

The Stone Cross, hidden under the tall chestnut trees, was actually a Calvary with several stations of the Passion of Jesus Christ depicted in a series of panels painted by an anonymous artist—The Trial of Jesus by Pontius Pilate, the Flagellation, the Placing of the Crown of Thorns, the Crucifixion, and the Burial. The primitive paintings were in principle protected by glass, which was usually broken, and the paintings gradually became damaged due to rain, sun, and insects, to the point where the original shapes and colours were barely discernible. I often saw little old ladies moving from one station to the other on their knees, counting their rosaries and praying. I heard stories that the pilgrimage site had been built on the spot where, many years earlier, thieves and murderers used to be executed. The large stone cross and the Stations of the Cross were meant to help the souls of those sinners find peace after having endured their due punishments while on earth.

There was another story, of more recent origin, linked to the Stone Cross that created quite a stir in Osijek and was the talk of the town for years. One pious woman called Adela Dessaty made a solemn vow to go to the Stone Cross early each morning, when there was no one else on the glacis, to say her silent prayers in deep devotion. One day she did not return from her pilgrimage. The police were called in and they found her dead body in a nearby ditch, with none of her personal items missing. This was, therefore, not a predatory murder, and since she had no relatives at all, it could not have been greedy heirs either. She bequeathed her considerably large assets to the Osijek poor. The police were searching for the murderer for several days until, suddenly, the investigation was stopped, and the crime and its motives were never officially elucidated. However, everyone in Osijek soon found out what had actually happened.

A certain immensely rich old bachelor wanted to marry Mrs. Dessaty. Just as it happens in a trashy novel, the story inevitably involved a jealous woman. She ran the bachelor's household and was worried about losing her position and the advantages that went with it. The housekeeper in question had a no-good of a son, who left Osijek right after the murder and then soon emigrated to America. To avoid a scandal and not compromise the reputation of a respectable Osijek family, the crime went unpunished. The history of the town, as revealed by this story, obviously included some dark moments, although the people of Osijek always proudly claimed that their urban virtues and their homegrown, genuine set of morals, were exemplary and beyond reproach. The former Wildemann Street was renamed Desatičina (Dessaty Street),[92] and that was by and large all that could have been done.

The other destination of our long walks was, as mentioned before, the only other city landmark worth a visit. It was a small marble obelisk, placed close to the banks of the Drava, displaying an inscription in gold about the 1882 railway accident on the nearby bridge.

I often heard people say, including my father—who would speak about it in a voice trembling with indignation—how everybody always knew that the old railway bridge across the Drava had been crumbling and needed to be repaired, and how the relevant authorities were alerted to its condition on several occasions. However, those were the years immediately after the occupation of Bosnia. Trade with the newly acquired land was in full bloom, promising high profits. There were beautiful forests to be clear-cut, rich mines to exploit, and valuable raw materials to export. The only route between Budapest and Bosnia ran precisely across that old wooden bridge. It was out of the question to halt the traffic just then. Millions were at stake! Therefore, people in authoritative positions decided that the bridge would hold because it simply had to. The Budapest railway authority sent a committee to investigate and in a single day, it issued its expert opinion that the bridge was in the best possible shape. While the positive assessment was celebrated in the Casino with a festive banquet, the bridge suddenly collapsed under the weight of a passing train. It was full of soldiers from the local regiment who managed to survive the war campaign in Bosnia and were on their way home. They fell into the River Drava together with the whole train, and, locked as they were in their closed wagons, were all drowned like rats.

It was during my second year at school that I was, for the first time, made aware of the difference between me and my school friends. I was attending at the time a primary school on Anina Street, not far from where we lived. Most children from "better-off" Upper Town families attended the German school in the Fortress, originally founded for the children of Austrian officers and generally considered to be offering a higher standard of education than other schools in town. I am, however, to this day grateful to my parents for making me attend an ordinary primary school. There I learned to speak Croatian and immediately made many friends, but also became aware of the cultural separatism that later events in my life, in particular around the turn of the century, awoke in me an increasingly fierce opposition. My first-year teacher was Mrs. Dončević and I was her obvious favourite pupil. Since I could already read and write at the age of six, I only had to attend "repetition classes", held every morning between ten and twelve, following the regular lectures. Along with Croatian, I was also learning German, and by the time I was seven, could read and write in both languages.

My second-year teacher was an older lady called Miss Šestak, with a drawn-out face of a nun, full of pockmarks. Her brother served as a canon in Đakovo, which might explain her religious fervour, occasionally made apparent in her treatment of us children. Despite the ease with which I learned, I was viewed, right from the beginning of the second year, as an *enfant terrible*, since I had the habit of asking utterly impossible questions, which had nothing to do with the curriculum and were rarely properly answered. I managed, however, to interrupt the boring routine and make the whole classroom laugh, which was the main purpose of it all anyway. I usually knew everything in advance, having read the textbook from cover to cover the first day of school, and Miss Šestak had to acknowledge my accomplishments, even if she was not particularly fond of me as a person. But I was not just an excellent pupil. I also enjoyed the status of a "better-off" child. According to the educational system in force in those days, only the "less well-off" children could be subjected to corporal punishment. They were usually assigned to sit in the back rows in the classroom. The "better" ones would bring to school sausages, bacon, jars of stewed fruit or jam, apples and pears, or wine and brandy, and place them on Miss Šestak's desk or sometimes even take them directly to where she lived. The "better children" did errands for her, took her letters to the post office, and carried her messages to tailors, cobblers, and sundry others. They would do all sorts of needlework for her, although "worse children" could also take part in performing these more demanding tasks, and they did it with great enthusiasm because it meant less hand spanking and better grades. These efforts produced metres of lace of various widths and patterns, cross-stitched items, doilies, bedroom rugs, and wall tapestries, with all of it intended to decorate homes of various teachers. I also participated in that widely useful activity. Even though I had cried rivers of tears, a few years earlier, in protest against crocheting a star after star for my mother's tablecloth, I was happily prepared this time to produce two to three metres of lace, which most likely eventually found its place on some intimate garment of my teacher. It was quite an achievement for me as far as the effort was concerned. As to the quality of the product itself, there was hardly anything praiseworthy about it.

I was good at mathematics, excellent at writing and reading, but when it came to the recitation, I was simply brilliant. There was nothing I could be reproached for in this respect. At the exam time, I would stand up with pride and self-confidence and provide answers that usually surpassed what had been asked of me. I was thus one afternoon deeply concentrating on my calligraphy exam. The template read, "*Domovina kakva bila, rođenom je sinku mila!*" ("No matter what, the homeland is always dear to its native son!").[93] I had a good quill and I was successful in making all my letters lean at the same angle, with thick and thin lines neatly distinct. While I was so engrossed in writing, Melanka Matić, who shared the same desk with me in the classroom, suddenly gave me a push with her elbow. As the result, the entire examination sheet on which I was working got spattered with ink from my pen. The teacher had just stepped out of the classroom for a moment to have a brief chat with Miss Firly in the corridor, and Melanka was laughing at my state of despair. With a derisive expression on her face and in a superior tone of her voice, she declared, "Croatia is not your homeland, even if you write it out a hundred times! You may be a good pupil, but you will still not go to heaven, but to the place where only wailing and gnashing of teeth could be expected. The catechist told us that in class today!"

Growing up in the protected environment of my home, I had been unfamiliar with anti-Semitism. I made good friends at school and in the Long Courtyard and we went along perfectly well at all times. I was, of course, aware of my Jewishness because I had separate religion classes and did not participate in the religious practices intended for Catholic children. This was, in my eyes, only a minor difference in our ways of living but not a difference in the degree of our worthiness. That is why I did not suffer from any form of inferiority complex. I felt entirely at home among my friends and behaved the same as any other child. There was no doubt that Croatia was my homeland. That was what our textbooks were saying. My father also used to say, "Every person has to love the country in which he was born and in which he lives." I sang the anthem "*Lijepa naša domovina*" (Our Beautiful Homeland)[94] in unison with all the others and was annoyed if anyone maintained that Nikola Šubić Zrinski was Hungarian![95]

And now Melanka maintained that I was not Croatian and that I would never go to heaven but to some horrible place where wailing and gnashing of teeth were all one could hear! That same Melanka shamelessly and customarily used to copy from my mathematics exercise book! Now she intentionally made me smudge my exam paper, and that was bad enough for me. I had only a vague understanding of death, and heaven and hell were completely alien concepts to me. I knew nothing about angels and devils, or saints and martyrs, which play such an important part in the Catholic cult. What was I then supposed to be afraid of? But that event hurt my sense of pride. I felt humiliated and insulted by Melanka's words. She was a "better child" too, with her father being a lawyer. She used to organize snacks and dance parties for children at her home, to which I was never invited, although we sat at the same bench in class. That did not worry me much, but this assault on my patriotism and the story about wailing and gnashing of teeth were too much for me to tolerate.

"Why are you saying that Croatia is not my homeland, the same as yours?"

"Because you are a Jew and you Jews are nowhere at home. In that way, you don't have a homeland either."

"But I am at home here, just like you."

"Really, dearie? Well, that's not true. You can't compare yourself with me because you Jews crucified our Lord Jesus Christ. That is why you must now pay for it."

"I didn't crucify anyone!" I yelled, outraged. "I was not even born then."

"Doesn't matter!" declared Melanka spitefully. "So what if you weren't in this world at that time? Later generations must pay for the sins of their forefathers. That is what the catechist taught us today. It is in the Ten Commandments, he said!"

She persisted in her claims and called upon the other children to confirm: "Did he not say so, or what?" No one said a word, but they all looked at me with fright in their eyes. What a horrible destiny was ahead of me? The most horrible part of all was that I could try whatever I wanted and still not be able to escape my fate, because the catechist had said so!

The teacher returned to the classroom. Red in the face with excitement, I showed my spattered exam paper and explained what had happened. I also told her that Melanka insisted that I would end up in a place of wailing and gnashing of teeth.

She was silent for a moment, and, then, with her voice raised, she exclaimed that it was not for us to meddle in those things and we should leave it to Our Lord and the catechist instead to make a judgment. It appeared to me right there that she was on Melanka's side! Then she gave me a new sheet of paper to write on and rebuked me by saying that in future I should be more careful with the ink.

"But she pushed me! And she said I would go to a place of wailing and gnashing of teeth…" Suddenly I had a tight feeling in my throat. There was a coldness in the air around me and I was stunned. Did it mean that they were not my friends after all? They looked at me with pity but none of them offered help. And the teacher was unfair! She did not rebuke Melanka, who deserved it, but me. Why, I asked myself?

By the end of the 1880s, my father's social standing had greatly improved. He left the textile shop and took over the representation of the Franco-Hongroise Joint Stock Insurance Company. He also became interested in issues of political economy, published articles in local and Budapest newspapers, and was regarded as one of the best experts on the subject in the country. Several public institutions were launched in town, thanks to his initiative and active participation, including the horse-drawn tramway introduced in 1885 to replace the sluggish omnibus (but needed almost as much time to get from the Upper Town to the Lower Town). He founded a glass factory, the steam spa Diana, and the mill called Union. He sat on their boards of directors, was chairman of the Business Association and secretary of the Casino Society, as well as vice president, and later president of the Slavonian Chamber of Trades and Crafts. He was a good-looking man, tall in stature, with a likable and intelligent face. He was widely known as a good speaker and he dressed carefully and with taste, putting a lot of effort into creating a good impression of himself. He achieved it, above all, with his exceptional kindness, which was not merely a matter of civility, but stemmed from the goodness of his heart and a sincere interest in people and human destinies. He spoke in elegant and well-polished German that he had acquired during his studies in Vienna. In official speeches and when writing, he often resorted to rhetorical figures and ornate language. His sentences were complex, but always clear. Instead of expressing himself simply, he used stylish expressions that often lacked in candour and sounded affected. That was the typical way in which people functioning at the periphery of a linguistic community tended to express themselves. They learned the language primarily from books and never acquired the smoothness and the authentic tone of that language as if it were their mother tongue.

My father spoke only broken Hungarian. Mohács, the Hungarian town where he was born, had more Serbian and Swabian inhabitants than Hungarians. As a boy, he learned a bit of all these three languages, but none well enough. He learned to speak proper German when he moved to Vienna and adopted its literary phraseology, considering it preferable and more elegant than the usual German spoken in Viennese coffee houses. His speech style came from his readings, most of all the widely read daily *Neue Freie Presse (New Free Press)*, which helped generations of middle-class Austrians to form not only their political opinions and literary tastes but also a specific and bombastic style of expression.

At various public meetings of the Chamber of Trades and Crafts, the Business Association or the Casino Society, my father delivered his speeches in German. He regretted not being able to speak the language of the country he lived in and considered it one of his shortcomings. For a while, he even took private Croatian lessons with the attorney-in-training, Dr. Levinsky, but he never made it further than the basics. The hardest for him to learn was the correct declining of nouns in seven cases. I remember him, nevertheless, reading Ivan Mažuranić's epic poem *Smrt Smail-age Čengića* (The Death of Smail-aga Čengić),[96] which impressed him so deeply that several years later he encouraged me to translate it into German.

I was later told that I had inherited my father's fine style, which, of course, referred specifically to our use of the German language. Style, however, is not merely the manner in which thoughts are expressed, but rather how some impressions of outside phenomena are processed internally, in one's mind, and then formulated and expressed to recreate a similar impact on other people. In that particular respect, I believe I was ahead of my father.

In his time, people generally preferred to stay focused on the superficial aspects of an argument, under the assumption that going deeper would only generate new conflicts. They preferred simple solutions, opting for untroubled optimism, and nothing could please them more than an account which turned out balanced at the end of the calculation. In the case of my generation, we were young at the turn of the new century and more critical about things than our predecessors. That soon brought us into conflict with their views on life. The theory of evolution opened new doors for us. We lived in a new age of distinct individualism, so evident in the works of Henrik Ibsen[97] and August Strindberg.[98] By the turn of the century, we were already acquainted with scientific socialism, or at least with some of its largely utopian branches. We were sceptical, critical, and not even remotely as content as our parents with what a small provincial town such as Osijek had to offer. There was nothing intellectually stimulating in that town. The problem was that it lacked intellectually strong individuals of some high standing who would be capable of animating a true exchange of ideas.

While Zagreb and its neighbouring towns, such as Varaždin and Karlovac, were greatly affected by the Illyrian movement and all that it meant—awakening of the spirits, inspiring people to fulfil their higher ambitions, and making them conscious of their national identity and their native language—Osijek had none of that. Its lifestyle was defined by the Swabian presence in town. Moreover, in the course of two centuries, Esseker Swabians had lost touch with their original roots and degenerated into a well-established identity of their own. This was less the case with the inhabitants of the outlying villages, who kept to their old customs and folklore, cultivated the language of their forefathers and wore traditional costumes. City dwellers succumbed to an all-German influence, with various foreign additions. The Germans were, after all, considered a superior race and held most of the key positions in town, from the mayor himself to the simple policeman. Furthermore, the numerical strength of the German element in town was reinforced by the presence of the Austrian officer corps—Styrians, Tyroleans, Sudeten Germans, and the Viennese—who lived for years in the city, married, settled down, and considered themselves masters of the situation.

The nineteenth century Essekers were not exactly reactionary, but they were not progressive either. They were politically entirely indifferent. So, it happened that in 1848, Osijek was the only town that did not respond to Ban Jelačić's call.[99] It was not because the people of Osijek sided with the Hungarian Revolution, but rather that they preferred to preserve their peace and stay out of it all. They let the Hungarians enter the city without a fight as they sat comfortably at home by the fire. At the same time, people were dying for their all but justified ideals on both sides of the River Drava. In the 1870s, 1880s, and 1890s, political enthusiasm was unknown in the city. People abided by the old saying, "Near is my shirt, but nearer is my skin," and other people's concerns interested them only as far as suitable topics of conversation. Those who may have harboured some ideals in their youth and aspired to rise above the ordinary level of their surround-ings, soon found themselves submerged by the prevailing atmosphere of mediocrity, or kept being viewed as oddities, loners, and dreamers, because they appeared to be chasing shadows, and pretending to be heroes on toy horses. They adopted hobbies, such as collecting stamps or walking sticks, played chess and tarok, drank, exploited loopholes in law and litigation, and tortured both themselves and others with their fixed ideas. Or they simply found their peace in cultivating their small gardens and leaving it to their children to bash their heads against walls too thick to be either broken through or bypassed.

The curse of a small town lies in the fact that it is impossible to escape its grip. This was especially true of Osijek, where the poverty of ideas was compensated for by considerably well-stocked pantries. People are not predestined to be either heroes or martyrs. If life goes by without any problems, why pick a fight? Or so wondered the inhabitants of Osijek in those days. People earned their money without much effort and had plenty of food on the table each day—roasted or fried chicken, big fat carps, ducks and geese, sausages and ham, richly filled cabbage rolls, dumplings, strudel and Berlin doughnuts, and to top it all, fresh from the tap, a glass of Scheper beer. One could also have a game of cards in the Casino or even in a pub somewhere out there on the outskirts of the town, where men could secretly give in to their vices and still behave as exemplary husbands or small family tyrants on the home front.

Every good Esseker was proudly displaying his large potbelly and had the habit in summer to take a trip to Marienbad,[100] finances permitting, to get rid of the excess weight. The vast plain along the River Drava called Podravina was highly fertile, well watered by the surrounding rivers, and home to large flocks of wild ducks and geese in its marshes. The wine from the nearby Baranya and Fruška Gora Mountains was light and easy to drink. Quaint Swabian villages produced boundless amounts of thick cream, butter, cheese, and white bread. Apples, watermelons, grapes, peaches, and pears brought by peasants to the market in autumn were juicy and sweet. In such a world where there was little to worry about, there was also not much to think about.

In the last two decades of the nineteenth century, approximately eighty percent of the Osijek population belonged to the category of good Essekers, with the remaining twenty percent far below that standard. Among them were the three "beggars" of Osijek, well known by every child in town. One was an old, grey-haired Roma man with one leg and a wooden stilt that he used with remarkable skill, as if he were preparing for a race. The second was a young man who also had only one leg. While the first man could stand straight, the prosthesis of the second was a few centimetres too short and he hobbled heavily. The third beggar was "Baba Puchpuruch," a crazy and constantly drunk old woman. Children used to run yelling, "Yuck, yuck, old hag Puchpuruch!", after which she would fly into a rage and begin shouting obscenities and wielding her stick to chase them away until they ran off in all directions, laughing with joy.

Podravina, in general, was not lacking in thugs, boozers, and layabouts with no regular income. Among them were occasional thieves, burglars, and murderers. In other words, life in Osijek was not exactly an idyllic pastoral play. There were always those ready to disturb the peace, who went astray, put too much hot pepper in their soup, and were ready to launch a fight in the pub, which sometimes ended with heads being smashed. There were fierce inheritance feuds over an old hay barn, for instance, a piece of land or a cow. Axes would then be wielded, and roofs would catch fire. There used to be on the town's periphery a few genuine dives, places where thieves would arrange a rendezvous with their accomplices and stolen goods would change hands. One such place was the notorious Palilula pub, on the road from Retfala[101] to the small village of Kravice, or the inn called Csingi-lingi-csarda, a gathering place for all kinds of shady characters. In short, there was a real underworld, existing right there in the face of Osijek's smugness. Provocative columns were published in local newspapers referring to these matters with a lot of humour and local colour. Every year there would be a few good trials, and the public would dash to attend them as if they were opening nights at the opera. Besides small offenders, who, after their trial, could be cheaply hired for sawing wood and who peacefully roamed the streets followed by a bored single guard, there were also political detainees kept in the Fortress. Their shaved heads, pale grey faces, and grey-striped prison clothes evoked anxiety. But one could see those "big shots" talked about in the newspapers on only two occasions: the day they were convicted, and then, at the break of dawn, when they were transferred to the County Palace to be hanged in its courtyard.

The County Palace was situated right in the centre of the town, across the street from the Casino and the theatre. Its clean, paved courtyard looked like an idyllic spot. There were scattered patches of green grass all around, with elderberry shrubs and lilac trees along the walls. In spring, they would be in full bloom and smell most pleasant. A nightingale would sing on their branches, oblivious to what was occasionally taking place in that courtyard. We lived only three houses away and I walked by it every day. Sometimes I would peek through the gates and there would be the gallows erected the night before on the lawn, ready for someone to be hanged a few hours later. I was greatly troubled by that thought. I could not believe that people had the right to condemn other human beings to death in cold blood, invoking their own reputation of irreproachability and some law devised by humans against other humans. I have never found it justified and still do not today. I do not think such a procedure is defensible on the basis of an ethical motive. It is a vengeful act by those who have acquired the power to follow the principle of an eye for an eye, a tooth for a tooth. Something in me has rebelled fiercely against it ever since, especially nowadays as we witness mass killings being considered legal in different parts of the world.

Among all the people I knew and were also close to me, my mother succeeded most effectively to break away from the restrictive atmosphere of a small town like Osijek, where she was born and lived most of her life. She succeeded, despite her frequent migraines and other health problems. She made great efforts, without any help from others, to keep up with the times. By nature, she was of an independent mind and self-confident. And she tried not to miss any opportunity that would allow her to experience something stimulating and new. Such opportunities were, however, rare in Osijek.

There were no impressive natural beauties in the form of forests or ranges of mountains, no occasions for artistic experiences, no historical references. There were no architectural monuments from the previous centuries, except for the old Ottoman fortress, which was already in a general state of decay, and, through time, partially transformed into Habsburg military barracks and painted black and yellow as required by Austrian military tradition. There were no churches built in a specific old style, no monuments, art galleries, or museums, not even a single written document to testify to Osijek's artistic past. There was nothing to recall a memorable battle, an unexpected victory, or a tragic defeat. There was no connection with the surrounding countryside as was usually the case with villages and small towns elsewhere. The easily acquired prosperity did not stimulate the awakening of spiritual vitality in people, but rather, it could be said that it prevented it from happening. There appeared no need to fret about anything. All one had to do was use a few typical phrases and posture around. And hopefully not even that.

It was different in the case of our family. There was something exceptional about our family that made us that way. It stemmed from our past and was evident in a variety of ways. It came from the atmosphere at home and the special kind of energy it engendered. It made us function the way we did, physically and intellectually. It was dominated by a high sense of responsibility towards everything and everybody, and not least towards ourselves. We seemed to have signed a special contract with our destinies. We were expected to act in a certain way, be aware that certain things depended on our goodwill in order for them to happen, and that we had many duties to fulfil. We were required to stay constant in life, regardless of obstacles or sacrifices imposed on us. Haggling and bargaining were not part of the contract, which had to be fulfilled in all its aspects.

That was the prevailing spirit in our house, without it ever being expressly discussed as such. It was the moral foundation of all our actions, without precluding differences of opinion on a great variety of issues, or differences in taste and temperament. My father's approach was founded on economic considerations and he observed everything realistically. In his view, first came progress and material prosperity, and only then could the artistic and cultural superstructure follow suit. My grandmother was an unreconciled romantic. What was valid in 1848 still had to be valid today. My mother had her own convictions and would express them calmly and logically. I would listen in on their discussions, which usually took place during mealtimes. My grandmother was extremely passionate in defending her views, with added insistence if she lacked evidence, which was in fact often the case. It was usually an issue linked to daily politics, her favourite pastime. She was, besides my father, the only other person in the household who read newspapers. My father would try to prove to her that she had misinterpreted this or that paragraph, arguing that, for instance, the aim of Koloman Tisza's policies was not to achieve conciliation but rather to deepen the conflicts.[102] Grandmother would be all fired up. My mother would in her calm way feel obliged to intervene and mediate. On one specific subject, however, there were no polemics whatsoever. All three agreed that one was obligated to perform in life in the best personal manner possible. And that was naturally also expected from me. The days of rattan cane were soon over, replaced by a new phase of categorical imperatives, and appeals to one's sense of duty and reasoning.

Along with moral dictates came also demands in the intellectual domain. In this respect, it was not merely a matter of overcoming the cultural limitations of a small provincial town, but also a matter of our view of Judaism. Centuries-long tensions and fighting for survival had kept Judaism strong. The need for Jewish solidarity may have disappeared with time, but the convergence with the surrounding society had not been fully realized. The only possibility for a breakthrough was through literature. We had in our house an extensive library containing all the classics, including Heinrich Heine,[103] Ludwig Börne,[104] and William Shakespeare. There was also Alexander von Humboldt's *Cosmos,*[105] *Karl Julius* Weber's *Democritus,*[106] and *Arthur* Schopenhauer's *Parerga* and *Perelipomena.*[107] There were many books on the political economy, among them those written by Proudhon, Ricardo, and Adam Smith, that my father had kept in his possession since his student days in Vienna. Attached to the only bookshop in town was a lending library where one could borrow German-language literature, such as novels by Friedrich von Spielhagen, Friedrich Gerstäcker, Georg Moritz

Ebers, Gustav Freytag, and widely read romance writers Eugenie Marlitt and Wilhelmine Heimburg.[108] The family subscribed to *Neue Freie Presse* (New Free Press) and *Pester Lloyd* (Pest Lloyd), as well as the two local papers, *Die Drau* (Drava) and *Die Slavonische Presse* (Slavonian Press). The latter two were government-friendly and subsidized papers, and although blowing the same horn on the political front, were engaged in a vicious feud between themselves. Unable to quarrel over political issues, they engaged on the pages of their papers in social gossip about each other, and even had recourse to personal attacks, slander, and fights, resulting in trials for libel, financial reparation, and detention, with younger staff members naturally serving as scapegoats and paying the price.

Along with the kitschy *Wiener Mode* (Vienna Fashion), read in every other household as well, we were subscribing to a more serious *Deutsche Rundschau* (German Review), published in Berlin by Julius Rosenberg, known for having been among the first to open its columns to the new realistic literature. The reading material that we as children had access to was of little intellectual value. It was chauvinistically and ultra-patriotically inspired literature produced to fill the hearts of German youth with a growing national self-identification and confidence after the successful conclusion of the Franco-German War. German virtues, German loyalty, German bravery, the goose-step and the helmet with its spike on the top, not to mention the technical wonder of German cannons, were incessantly glorified in verse and prose. The German Middle Ages were given an aura of a unique and heroic historical period. We read all about it and identified with it. In the absence of any other literary source, we had no option but to consider as valid what was presented to us. Apart from the heroic figure of Nikola Šubić Zrinski, regularly evoked as a last argument to be thrown into the balance during nationalist disputes (was he a Hungarian or one of us?), we knew almost nothing about the past of our country, its sufferings, or the economically and politically restrictive impositions which had maintained Croatia in a state of poverty and ignorance. We knew nothing about August Šenoa and none of us had ever seen a copy of *Vienac (The Wreath).*[109] In Osijek with its 23,000 inhabitants, there were only forty-three subscriptions to *Vienac,* all held by either public servants or high school professors. Our school subscribed to the only Croatian language magazine for youth called *Smilje* (The Everlasting Flower), but we found it utterly boring.

We were instead raving about the German Ottonian Dynasty and Heinrich the Fowler,[110] about "Der Alte Fritz,"[111] and, most of all, the great Kaiser Wilhelm,[112] about whom we kept reading in our children's books. To begin with, there was the *Töchteralbum* (Daughters' Album) by Thekla von Gumpert, published annually as an octavo volume of a thousand pages with covers decorated in gold. It contained stories of virtuous young German women who made the sacrifice of their golden hair braids at the altar of the Fatherland during the war of liberation against the evil Napoleon.[113] We read the newspaper for young girls called *Mein Feierabend* (My Free Evenings) in which the glorification of German countryside and family life was a regular feature. My favourite storyteller was Hans Christian Andersen, and my favourite fairy tale the one about the little mermaid who sacrificed her life for love. Apart from Andersen, I liked best Cervantes' *Don Quixote,* which I read at the age of ten in an abridged version for young readers. It was about that time that my family started taking me to the theatre, but I only remember three performances: Grillparzer's *Die Ahnfrau* (The Ancestress),[114] the dramatization of the story of Lucia de Lammermoor,[115] and the well-known sentimental drama *Der Müller und sein Kind* (The Miller and His Child).

This latter play was performed every year on Hallowe'en, not only in Osijek but in every existing theatre in the monarchy.[116] The main character in this horror drama was a terribly mean miller who sent his daughter to the grave. Scary, greenish-lit skeletons with rattling bones walked at midnight around the graveyard, where she went in secret to meet the poor mill helper called Konrad, whom she loved against her father's permission. She died of consumption in a dramatic manner on the stage. I kept crying heavy tears from the very first act, and so did the rest of the audience. For years afterwards, I was convinced that the quality of dramatic art depended on the quantity of tears one shed and I never went to the theatre without making sure that I had a couple of big clean handkerchiefs with me. The best performances that I still remember, however, were not those given in German in the Upper Town theatre, but rather those to be seen in the Lower Town Casino, where a company from Novi Sad gave local folk shows with singing and dancing. It was all improvisation and both the audience and those on stage participated. Only the front rows had chairs where dignitaries sat. The rest of the audience sat on narrow benches. There were easily twice as many people as there were seats available. My favourite was *Seoska Lola* (The Village Bum) with Mihajlo Marković in the lead role and the excellent comic actor Dobrinić, irresistibly funny in his grotesque appearance wearing a mask that made people laugh the moment he entered the stage. He created characters far more than simple caricatures, instilling life in the most ridiculous personages he performed on stage. It was there that I realized for the first time that good theatre was not measured by the volume of tears shed, but by how entertaining it could be.

Among my fondest childhood memories were the trips into the countryside I took with my father every summer, in June or July, shortly before my parents would take off for a holiday at the spa. We would first travel by train to the nearby town of Beli Manastir, and then continue by horse and carriage through the hilly landscape of Baranya to a small village called Baan.[117] This was where our uncle, Dr. Elias Rosenbaum, lived, and my father paid him a visit each year. Those were my first train rides and they left a deep impression on me. The only thing I regretted was that they were short—not even an hour long. My father was the best travel companion in the world. He would chat with me as if I were an adult and that was most gratifying. He would also talk to other people in the compartment, demonstrating in its fullness his characteristic congeniality. Each small matter stirred his interest and he would draw my attention to it.

The Baranya countryside consisted of mild hills, beautiful forests, vineyards, and fields. Until I was ten years old, the only landscape I knew was created by the river that flowed past Osijek. The river stretched northward where it began to branch out in several directions, forming vast marshes covered in reeds and sedges. Since I had never seen a real hill before, I was impressed by every elevation higher than twenty-five metres and imagined it to be a precursor to a real mountain range. I was delighted at the sight of every farmhouse, of cattle grazing in the fields, of a rabbit jumping out of a thicket and then, startled, dashing back to hide. The ringing of Sunday church bells in villages sounded more beautiful to me than any music I had heard before.

By that time, I had already read quite a few books, mostly fairy tales and poems, with Andersen naturally topping the list. The reading made me aware of two things—that beautiful words could help form ideas, and that words were important in themselves. On many occasions, my impression of something was pushed into the background, and the word describing it would come to the fore! Words made things become what, in my mind, they supposedly were, or the way I wanted them to be. I had learned quite a few poems by heart, either at school or during my private lessons, notably those by Johann Ludwig Uhland, Emmanuel Geibel, and Ferdinand Freiligrath.[118] Due to the images I had gathered from those poems, I was seeing a world as if through tinted glasses, not in its immediacy but rather through these literary filters. I had to make a real effort later in life to find the lost simplicity, but no unaltered impression could compare in strength with those acquired through literature. They continued to serve as a connection between me and the real world, no matter how distorting, glorifying, and transfiguring—and fortunately, sometimes also critical—they may have been. I kept trying, later in my life, to get rid of all that, so that the nature I was observing would be what it truly was, rather than as seen through the prism of the romantic renditions found in the drawings of Wilhelm von Kaulbach and Adrian Ludwig Richter or the cajoling lines by Uhland and Freiligrath, in my *album of German art and poetry*.[119]

We would get off the train in Beli Manastir, where Uncle Rosenbaum's coach would be waiting in front of the station with old coachman Martin at its side. As the coach carried us through the town, my father would be sure to point out to me the old family house where his grandfather and grandmother had lived, and his mother was born. The coach would soon start bouncing on the bumpy country road that wound around the foot of Mount Batina through meadows, fields, and vineyards, towards the village where Uncle served as a doctor. As was his habit never to miss an opportunity to meet new people and learn something about their lives and prospects, my father kept talking with the coachman. On one such occasion, he asked about the living conditions in the village, the forthcoming harvest, last year's grape yield, and the coachman's family. He did this with such kindness and sincerity that the old Swabian with sunken, unshaven cheeks, and his chest hair sticking out of his collar, who had been in Uncle's service for almost forty years, completely opened up and talked extensively about his children and grandchildren. How his cow had just had a calf and he was also lucky with his pigs. Only recently, the sow had given birth to nine piglets, four of which would be fattened. His youngest daughter was helping the doctor's wife in the kitchen, where she was bound to learn a lot of useful things. And the doctor had helped his eldest son to go to Budapest to study agronomy. Such good people they were! The doctor travelled around the countryside in this same coach and the peasants from the nearby villages worshipped him as if he were God himself! Lately, however, he had seemed to be a bit rundown. He was coughing and his voice was hoarse, but he refused to stop. God only knew how much longer he could last that way.

Uncle greeted us with evident joy as we arrived, but he quickly started to apologize. "You must excuse me for leaving you for a while with my dear Rozi. I still have a few cases to look after!" He was over sixty and had been working as a village doctor for forty years. Those had been, exactly as coachman Martin had said, forty years of committed work in the village and nearby hamlets, over a total area of at least thirty square kilometres, always on the road, wind or foul weather, sunshine or rain, day or night. He had delivered babies, treated the most severe illnesses, dressed wounds, drained boils, fixed broken bones, relieved pain, fought against death, consoled, and given strength and hope where nothing else could be done. His old, frayed leather bag contained a complete pharmacy, and when people were really poor and unable to pay him, he would leave behind a gulden or two on the table, and allow only the people who could afford it, to pay for his services. His patients would force him to get out of bed well before sunrise. They would come to his house and wait, sitting on the two benches in his front yard or standing at the entrance to his surgery. And although a day was only twenty-four hours long, they would all have their turn, and even those who could not be helped went back home consoled.

He was unimposing and short in stature, with a finely shaped head and the piercing blue eyes he inherited from his mother, "Resele of Monostor". His gentle smile revealed a deep understanding of human needs, deepened and shaped by being constantly in touch with human suffering. Medicine was, in his opinion, more than an exact science. In practice, it assumed the most varied of forms and covered all areas of life. It required the understanding of psychology, sociology, economy, law, ethics, philosophy, and agronomy, not to mention the various branches of medical science itself. In this way, general medicine had a part to play in all specialized areas, and vice versa. A field physician was never allowed to disregard a patient's general condition by concentrating on individual symptoms, or to neglect the social factor that might have an impact on a specific clinical case.

The doctor's house had originally been the dwelling place of old Reb Nate Baan, his grandfather. It was a nice-looking, comfortable stone building, shaded by tall trees. While Uncle went to attend to his patients, some of whom had been waiting since early morning, my aunt showed us in, where we washed our hands and shook off the dust from the road. There were no decorations in the house, and the furniture and various other household items seemed slightly shabby due to years of use, but still pleasant in their simplicity. Most importantly, however, everything was spotlessly clean.

Aunt was proud of her flowers and in her caring hands, they truly thrived. She had big, lush fuchsias dotted with red-blue, cup-like flowers with calyxes full of silky stamen threads. Not normally highly valued as windowsill plants, her geraniums became under her care a magical display of colours. She would get her grafts and shoots from the women in the village and by early spring, her geraniums were blooming in all available colours, from ivory white through to deepest red.

She had the most beautiful oleanders in her garden. They were over a hundred years old, two to three metres tall and covered in red flowers that filled the garden with the intoxicating scent of cinnamon and vanilla. The white clustered flowers hanging from the tall acacia trees also exuded their own heady perfume. At the far end of a spacious yard were stables, storehouses, servants' quarters, a bread oven, and the summer kitchen— another source of alluring aromas coming from the various dishes being prepared for us. Aunt set the table in the shade of the acacia trees and served us mid-morning snacks—a wonderful homemade ham, eggs, radishes, and fresh home-baked white bread. She had decorated a little wicker basket with green leaves, filled it with gooseberries from the garden, and urged us to help ourselves.

One could hear Sunday church bells ringing in the near distance. Sunlight poured through the branches above our heads, creating restless arabesque forms on the ground below. Aunt joined us at the table. She was a petite woman, even smaller than her husband, with shiny black hair and always wearing the same black taffeta dress and a small white lace bonnet. Her manners were refined, she spoke well, her bearing was dignified, and her gestures harmonious. The villagers would come to her for advice on all matters of practical life, and many a peasant girl came to work for her and learn how to cook, do the laundry, iron, and keep a household clean and orderly. Uncle joined us after a while. The conversation switched to family matters and health problems. He was planning to travel to Bad Gleichenberg[120] the following month to undergo treatment for an uncomfortable hoarseness, that had bothered him since the previous winter. He would do it only, of course, if his practice permitted it. His voice truly did sound strained and husky, but he was in a good mood, showing us the pet pigeons he had been breeding in his free time. Some were small greyish-yellow turtledoves, constantly cooing, others entirely white with little coral-red legs and beaks. There were also some with funny-looking beaks, helmets, and tufts of feathers on their heads. But that was not all—there were several pouters strutting around and showing off, a few with peacock-like elegant tails, that they kept spreading open in the shape of big feathered fans as soon as anyone looked at them. Some pigeons looked as if they were wearing funny feathery trousers over their little feet or had their curly feathers ruffled up. All displayed luxurious, gem-like colours enhanced by a shiny metallic overlay that melded the colour tones beautifully. Many had wide rings under their necks, symmetrical stripes or striking zigzag lines of alluring colours. Altogether, they looked very impressive.

The birds had their nests sheltered under the roof. They kept fluttering around and cooing insistently. A whistle from the doctor sufficed to make them land on the table and peck at the crumbs. They were so tame that we could catch them and hold them in our hands. They kept landing on the doctor's arms, hands, and head, and even snatched seeds out of his mouth. They let me hold them, which made me very happy.

We had our lunch behind the house in an airy gazebo made from trailing grapevines. The table was covered with a beautiful white damask cloth and the porcelain plates and dishes had a faint mother-of-pearl shimmer. We were served a lovely chicken soup, roast chicken and a delicate green salad, stewed fruit, and cake with mountains of whipped cream. It was a long and leisurely lunch spent in conversation. It was not long enough for me, however, considering all the delicious treats piled on the table.

By the time black coffee was served, the village priest had appeared and joined in.[121] He was the doctor's close friend and a frequent visitor at his Jewish home. They had developed a habit of playing chess during the long winter evenings. On Sundays, after the Mass service, the priest would regularly drop in for a cup of coffee. The two had philosophized and politicized for the full forty years. In the process, the *plebanus* (as the priest was called in the village) had picked up some Talmudic wisdom and the doctor heard many dissertations on dogmas and the teaching of the Catholic Church. Both were none the worse for it. They had started from different viewpoints, but they met halfway and agreed that people who suffered spiritually or physically deserved to be helped by all available means. In their fight against human failings and suffering, the village doctor and the village priest were comrades, despite their different convictions and confessions, which seemed of no consequence in comparison to the enormity of their pure humanitarian task. They had stood at each other's side at countless deathbeds and accompanied hundreds of people to their graves. The doctor may have been an expert in his profession, and a wise man as well, but so was the old priest, a good philosopher in his own way. In this remote place where they had both ended up living and working, their worldviews had gradually changed and adapted to the circumstances, becoming less exclusive and dogmatic. Even when observed from the religious perspective, a person's genuine human qualities had to be recognized, and the priest was compelled to admit that there was nothing wrong in the way Dr. Elias Rosenbaum conducted himself in life. Nothing was lacking, either. Perhaps God's mercy, upon which, said the divine law, depended all that was good in this world. But, was that mercy not obvious in his deeds, words, and thoughts? Did it not radiate from him constantly? The priest could not overlook that fact and was thus forced slightly to adjust his *credo*.

My father was also of a philosophical temperament, and, as far as mutual tolerance was concerned, in favour of cooperation and concessions. He had been aware since boyhood of Lessing's allegory about three seemingly identical rings, and how nobody could tell which of them was the genuine and original one.[122] He believed that evidence of the value of a genuine ring could only be perceived through manifestations, whether small or sizable, of our humanity. Acts of humanity endowed the ring with its inherent "magical power", while the religious message was conveyed by the ring's external shape.

While I was occupied with exploring raspberry bushes in the garden, the three disputants sat around the table with a bottle of aged Villány wine, sipping, toasting, and discussing Hungarian politics, always with a dose of circumspection. The issue regarding universal suffrage soon came up in the conversation. The subject was under discussion at the time in the Hungarian Parliament, less in terms of its social implications and more in terms of Hungarian chauvinism and the question of ethnic minorities— Serbs, Slovaks, Croats, and Romanians. They were all given the common name of "tinkers" and were considered illiterates and at the bottom of the social and national hierarchy. How could such people be included in universal suffrage? Once given the political voice in this country, they would start blowing up buildings, because they were not just only illiterates but also rebels, terrorists, and anarchists by nature. This was the common belief in those times, when political and economic liberalism was a sort of state religion, concerned exclusively with the well-being of the top ten thousand privileged people.

On the issue of universal suffrage, the doctor was in favour and the *plebanus* naturally against. My father tried to view the problem from the broader perspective of political economy. He put forward the thesis that people usually acquire their political maturity through active participation in politics, and even the uneducated people should not be treated all their lives as mere objects of politics in the hands of those in power. As the conversation became more and more animated—not least due to the effects of the good old wine which, soon after a few small glasses, blushed their cheeks and made their eyes sparkle—Aunt showed up with afternoon refreshments consisting of iced coffee with whipped cream, Gugelhupf with raisins, a cake, and raspberries. I had unfortunately already eaten too many raspberries and was still full after my lunch. The sight of the table all set up again filled me with deep *Weltschmerz*. It was warm. The pigeons retreated to their nests. I was not interested in the conversations and the time seemed to drag. I was bored, moody, and disappointed, as it usually happens when the expectations are unrealistic.

Finally, we said goodbye to Uncle and Aunt, and I was glad to regain the coach and drive back to the station. Father would not let me stay grumpy for too long. When we sat down in our compartment, he summarized all the experiences of the day and everything was again within reach and lively, in the right place, presented in a suitable way and appropriately to the point. The experience was described in a plastic way, in the form of a well-written newspaper report. Thanks to that remarkable presentation and entertaining explanations, which included even the smallest details, I felt I had spent a wonderful day and that I would remember it forever, which I did. This was our last visit to the doctor's hospitable home because he died a year later of laryngeal cancer, which turned out to be inoperable. The whole area grieved deeply for him. People were intrigued by the fact that the Catholic priest came with many grateful patients to attend his funeral in Darda. The priest delivered, after the rabbi's service, a farewell speech over the open grave, expressing his own gratitude and that of everybody else for all that his friend had done as a person and as a doctor.

On the second day of our trip, we dropped by to see my other grandmother, Josephine Miskolczy, and gave her news about her brother and sister-in-law. She was, in contrast to my other grandmother on my mother's side, an imposing woman, above average in height and heavily built. She was dark-skinned with a high forehead and prominent cheekbones. She had fine facial features and those distinctive light-blue eyes inherited from her mother. Even in her old age, she retained her shiny black hair.

My grandmother was a woman of great tenderness, fine manners, and endless generosity. She had lost her hearing quite early in life and by the age of fifty was completely deaf, which made any communication with her particularly difficult. My dealings with her were limited to her constantly giving me sweets, our joint visits to the confectionery store, and me enjoying mountains of chocolate-covered doughnuts, *Schaumrollen*,[123] *Cremeschnitte*,[124] and cakes, all of which remained inseparably connected with her in my memory. There was never any need to appeal to her generosity. It was automatic with her, the moment she would see me. She always had in store something she could cheer me up with, some kind of a treat, a ticket for the circus or the theatre, or a nice book that I had wished to read for a long time. She used to bring piles of presents from her annual visits to the spa in Marienbad or Karlsbad.[125] Everyone would get a present—her children, sons and daughters-in-law, grandchildren, friends, and servants. And it was always precisely what we had hoped for, whether it turned out to be a charming purse, a small brooch, a Karlsbad porcelain cup painted with flowers, a decorative item made of glass, a hand-crocheted lace collar, an embroidered handkerchief, or silk stockings. She believed that gifts were a luxury and had to evoke joy, and she instinctively chose the right thing each time.

She was in general used to quite a high standard of living. She wore fine silk or *barège*[126] dresses made in Vienna, and, depending on the occasion, small black or white toques made of finest lace on her head. She owned expensive jewellery, bracelets, brooches, a pocket watch on a long chain decorated with diamonds, as well as beautifully fashioned diamond earrings. Her elegant reception salon had furniture made of light cherry wood decorated with incrustations, consoles, and a mirror in a gilded frame, which reached to the ceiling. There was also a crystal chandelier with twelve gilded arms, artfully moulded wax candles, and a multitude of Venetian glass prisms, through which light refracted in all the colours of the rainbow.

There were still four daughters living at home by the time my grandfather died. Aunt Lina had been married twice and both times widowed in her young age. While still living in Mohács, she first married a certain Mr. Fritsch, who owned a shop in Osijek. She was twenty years old at the time, petite, sweet-looking, with a beautifully shaped face, and a profile reminiscent of a Greek cameo. Her sense of duty was so overpowering that she did not dare go to Osijek with the groom right after the wedding. First, she had to restore order in the house—tidy everything up, wash and scrub, and put everything back in place as it had been before the wedding hubbub. Only then was her young spouse allowed to show up again and take her with him to Osijek. He was, however, by that time already suffering from a fatal disease and died only a few years later. Their daughter was my cousin Theresa and their grandchildren, Vera and Harry Drucker.

Her second marriage also ended abruptly after a few years. My thirty-three-year-old Aunt Lina was again a widow, forced to take care of the family business and run one of the most respectable shops in town all on her own. She looked after her children, raised them and cared for them, never asking for anything for herself. She acquired quite a bit of wealth and moved to Zagreb in her old age, where she built one of the first villas in town on Mošinskijeva Street,[127] which she eventually bequeathed to her son and daughter. At the time of the big debacle in 1941, her son Max Bauer perished in the infamous Jasenovac concentration camp. Her daughter somehow escaped deportation and survived.

Three more girls came into the world after the birth of my father and his only brother, Alexander Miskolczy. The two eldest were exceptionally good-looking. The sisters grew up convinced of their father's affluence and demonstrated exigencies and pretensions beyond the family's means. Following the death of their father, it fell upon my father to find husbands for his sisters. Aunt Laura had already refused several suitors when a certain wholesale merchant from Budapest turned up. He was a middle-aged man with good looks and big-city manners, who impressed even my twenty-five-year-old father. During a short conversation, he managed to convince my father not only of the solidity of his intentions, but also that his wholesale shop in Budapest, dealing in fabrics and hosiery, was prosperous. He even produced his account books, which looked fine. Information collected was positive and the pair fell deeper and deeper in love. The wedding soon took place, with all the accompanying pomp, as expected. The couple took off for Venice, the Eldorado for all newlyweds. While they were feeding pigeons on St. Mark's Square, trunks and suitcases containing the bride's trousseau, expensive wedding presents and huge amounts of linen, clothing, porcelain and silver, were expediently sent off to Budapest, where, before the wedding, the groom had rented an elegant and luxurious apartment on Váci Street. The dowry was paid in cash and invested in the business.

Everything was so lavish that it was no surprise to anyone when, a year later, this man's brother, who also had a share in the business, showed up and asked for the hand of the younger sister, Matilda, a ravishing beauty, not yet twenty, with whom he had fallen head-over-heels in love at his brother's wedding. This time, my father thought it unnecessary to ask around about him or check his business records when everything seemed to be proceeding so smoothly. He paid the dowry, the newlyweds rushed to Venice, and they too were feeding the pigeons on St. Mark's Square while trunks and suitcases were being packed and sent to their destination. A year later, however, the *wholesale* firm was facing bankruptcy. Both my aunts' dowries were barely enough to delay the catastrophe a little longer, to calm down the most assertive creditors and obtain new credits. Then began a direct attack on my father, with express delivery letters sent as registered mail, urgent telegrams, pleadings, explanations and implorations, containing excuses, sentimental allusions to destroyed family happiness, and compromised family honour. There were documented referrals to the latest fluctuations on the stock market regarding securities, which had caused the trouble in the first place, as well as references to our merciful Lord and attempts of covert blackmail and open threats.

Father then travelled to Budapest. This time they showed him entirely different business records. The company's liabilities had soared to 175,000 guldens, which was at the time an enormous amount. If they went bankrupt, everything would be lost—not only my aunts' dowries, but also their furniture, linen, and everything else they owned. Worse, a judicial procedure could be launched, and the two men called to account for their responsibilities and maybe even jailed. They would lose their good name and never be able to expect to own another company. What would happen to both families in that case? There were already children to consider and everything had to be done for their protection. That was, in my father's opinion, more important than guilt and atonement. He decided to help. But this could only have been done if he were to invest all his assets, and, moreover, his mother's property would also be at stake. He would have to guarantee any further creditors' claims with his signature, which in short meant that he would have to risk everything he possessed himself.

Father hesitated. The two brothers-in-law were threatening suicide, and he was afraid not only of a tragic incident in itself, but also of a potential scandal. Nothing like this had happened in our family before. Never had any member of the family, be it grandfather, father, brother-in-law or cousins, owed anyone a single penny! Everyone had been cautious in doing business, always operating on a small scale, without expecting high profits. No one close to him had ever lived beyond his means, including himself. He was suspicious of big profits, or wealth acquired overnight. I often heard him explain, "By working diligently and honestly, a man can earn perfectly well as much as is necessary for a reasonably comfortable life but cannot accumulate excess wealth. All ambition in that direction must rely on deception." He may have drawn that assertion from reading Proudhon, whose books held a prime spot on our bookshelves and my father kept reading them. It may also have stemmed from his innate social consciousness. I am at any rate grateful to him for thinking that way and creating on that basis a distinct ambience in our home. To my surprise, I often heard him say that people who became rich overnight should be prosecuted and without delay sentenced to twenty years in prison. After subsequently checking their debt accounts, it would surely turn out that the sentence had even been too lenient. It was, in his opinion, not only a crime to circumvent enforced laws but also a dubious act known in business circles as "usances", which meant skilful and moderate circumvention of business ethics that remained unsanctioned, provided it was accompanied by success.

That view hinged on his standpoint on assimilation and Jewishness. Up until the beginning of the 1890s, assimilation was, in the eyes of Western European educated Jews, the most acceptable—and, one could add, the only—solution to the problem. The Jews had by then acquired political equality, but the struggle did not end there. What they wanted was an assimilation satisfactory to both sides. Even though they had regained equality rights, after their being removed for a while at the beginning of the century, it had become important for the Jewish people that the recognition of those rights be equitable and inalienable. This was also my father's conviction—full evidence of equity would signify true victory for the Jews. Assimilation should not bring about the destruction of their cultural identity. Quite the contrary. Assimilation should not mean an automatic absorption into the social surroundings and an indiscriminate adoption of the national and traditional peculiarities of that society. At the same time, the surrounding society should be convinced that Jewish intentions were respectable and should discard the long-standing perception that Jews were outsiders and pariahs, presumptuously pushing their way into a foreign community. Jews should endeavour to provide proof of their high intellectual and moral qualities and their capacity for a top-notch performance. Through the demonstration of personal virtues, they could also prove not only that the Jews were gaining something by joining another community, but that the receiving community was also enriched by incorporating this way the best aspects of Jewishness. Every Jew had two reasons to provide evidence of high personal standards—first for himself, but also for the Jewish community as a whole. A Jew's moral integrity pertained to a mission. A committed crime could never be dealt with in isolation, based on the clauses of the civil law, as would have been the case if a Christian had been involved. Everybody had to assume the burden of the responsibility and be judged and condemned accordingly, as if it were not a mere act of stealing or cheating, but a betrayal of the community and one's own family. That was why the case of his two brothers-in-law deeply distressed him. The days he spent in Budapest on that occasion must have been the hardest of his life.

Before fully committing himself, my father decided to seek advice from a trustworthy person who would judge the situation impartially. He went to see Georg Mayer Ullman, the last surviving brother of my grandmother. Much like his two elder brothers, Karl and Joseph, he too had gained a respectable, one might even say a leading, position in society. He was president of the Louisen Steam Mills Joint-Stock Company, president of the newspaper committee of the Pest Lloyd Society, as well as the founder and manager of the Pest Printing Joint Stock Company. He was short in stature, surly in looks and abrupt in his manners, with my grandmother's piercing grey eyes. He could see through people and not be fooled by their exterior. He wore the so-called Kossuth beard, which framed his face, and the way he dressed revealed that he paid no special attention to elegance. Even his "presidential" office gave away his exemplary simplicity—a middle-sized desk made of softwood, a simple glass case, several shelves with bound documents and books, a brown leather canapé, and a few wooden chairs.

He let my father talk and explain the situation, and then asked in his usual straightforward manner, "What is the extent of the debt?"

"Around 175,000 guldens."

Uncle muttered something to himself and said, "A nice sum. And you intend to pay it off?"

"One part. The rest in warranty bills that I would have to sign."

"Do you have that sort of money at your disposal?"

My father said he did not. He was at the early stage of building his business, only recently married, had two children, and made a good living, but was by no means a rich man and disposed of no large sums of cash.

His uncle studied him with his penetrating eyes. "And you are still ready to sign? Don't you know that to sign means to pay? And since you don't have the required amount, in a few months you will find yourself in the same situation your brothers-in-law are now in, except that you will pull more people into this misfortune, for example your wife."

In his matter of fact and abrupt manner, he then said it again, "To sign means to pay!" This irrefutable fact required no further comments.

Then it dawned on my father. He said thank you and left. He explained to his brothers-in-law that much to his regret there would be no settling of their debts. He resisted all further insistence and requests. He suggested his sisters return home with him, where they would be most welcome, along with their children. When they refused to do so, partly out of their sense of pride and partly due to loyalty to their husbands, my father pledged to provide a monthly support until the time their husbands were back on their feet.

The company became insolvent and painful bankruptcy proceedings took place, the course and resolution of which was never discussed in our house. If I am not mistaken, my father never stopped paying the promised support, because neither of the brothers managed to make a comeback. They worked as travelling salesmen for another company and my aunts shared their woe with much dignity. They never complained nor admitted that they lacked anything.

My father's youngest sister, Adele, was married to Salamon Berger,[128] a distinguished merchant from Zagreb, who later became known as the founder and first director of the Ethnographic Museum in Zagreb. Their wedding was a pompous affair, which remained deeply ingrained in my memory. First, it was because of my beautiful pink satin dress with wide red ribbons. Second, for the first time in my life I was wearing low patent leather shoes, which were so tight that they hurt, but were in those days considered to represent ultimate luxury. Third, they used hot iron tongs to curl my unruly hair into a *frou-frou* hairstyle, adding a satin ribbon to keep it together, which made me look—in my eyes, at least—like a genuine fairy-tale princess. On top of all that was my role of a bridesmaid in charge of the bride's train, an honour I was sharing with my cousin Theresa. And all that in plain view of my curious classmates and friends gathered in front of the synagogue, watching me with admiring eyes, or so I imagined it.

The ceremony was followed by a splendid wedding reception at the Casino. A special table for the ten children was set in the side room, while a long and beautifully arranged table was provided in a big salon for the adult guests, who were all close or distant relatives. The menu had ten courses, alternating sweet and savoury dishes, fried and roast meat, fish, *poulardes*,[129] roasted chicken, stewed fruit and salads, strudels, Berlin doughnuts, cakes, ice cream, and fruit baskets. Roma music and speeches (serious and funny) followed in turns. There was good wine and even champagne as a final touch. Glasses were clinking and a few plates broken, all in the spirit of the old saying, "Broken glass brings luck". No one paid any attention to the children while this was going on. Once I was done with eating to the full, I became terribly bored with all the commotion, not least because my part in the wedding was over. I went to my mother. I could hardly recognize her. She looked wonderful in her silk atlas gown, with her hair piled high up and decorated with ostrich feathers. I told her I was terribly bored and wanted to go home. She whispered in my ear that my father would be giving a big speech in a moment and that I should keep quiet.

Father did get up with a champagne glass in his hand at that very moment and started talking. Mother made another quick dismissive gesture with her hand. I was not quite sure what her gesture meant, but I preferred to believe that she was telling me to go home because I was bored, and boredom was something I always found difficult to put up with. Once the wedding and the meal were over, everything afterwards seemed to me a waste of time. I had a whole life ahead of me, but I somehow considered instinctively every single hour too precious to be wasted. I had to keep in touch with the world, be continuously aware of my existence, constantly be involved in doing something, whether reading, learning or speaking, in order to avoid the threatening emptiness of an unproductive hour. From my earliest childhood, I hated doing things that were useless and of no worthwhile consequence. Hence my aversion to being forced to play with the educational toys of Dr. Fröbel,[130] do needlework with its only purpose to keep one's fingers busy, wear clothes that would not allow me to move freely, or put on tight shoes and gloves or those enormous hats with ostrich feathers. I did not like having anything to do with all those nice children from good families, who showed no resistance to behaving like young ladies and were constantly given to me as examples to follow. I did not want to be a "nice girl" and I insisted on being unruly and show my relentless resistance to all restrictions.

So, with my father standing there at the head of the table, holding a glass and toasting, with all the people present looking at him, eager not to miss out a single word of his speech, I grabbed the opportunity to make myself scarce. I sneaked down the stairs, a bit apprehensive because I was not entirely sure whether what I was doing was right. I was also afraid that I might be caught at the last minute. I ran across the street towards the cathedral and only stopped running once I felt sure to be finally out of sight. It was August and sweat was rolling down my face. The little curls on my forehead were gone, the satin dress was a mess, and the sash undone and loose. I stopped running when I reached Franjina Street and gave a sigh of relief—another five minutes and I would be home. I would quickly change and disappear into the Long Courtyard to play for a while with my friend Helena before the others returned home.

Things did not turn out that way. At the very beginning of Franjina Street, I came across the director of the savings bank, Mr. Andrić, who lived a few houses down the street from us. He was an amiable old man who often offered me sweets and invited me to visit his garden. This time he said that grapes and peaches had just ripened and that he had a lovely new swing, so if I felt like it, I could try it right away. The suggestion of the swing did it. There was no way I could resist such a temptation. I was unbeatable in mastering a perfect initial swing, and once launched, nothing could stop me. In the Long Courtyard, we used to make a swing out of my mother's clothesline. But this was something beyond comparison, because Mr. Andrić's swing was suspended on a crossbeam of a real swing frame. You could swing back and forth on its wide, solid seat whether standing up, sitting down or kneeling, and feel as if carried by the wind. I was in heaven and beside myself with joy, flying up and down and imagining myself to be one of those carefree swallows, way up in the blue sky, crossing oceans and living a free life—something I had always envied them for. I had by then lost my satin sash, and since my patent leather shoes kept hurting me terribly, I had taken them off too. I danced barefoot on the thick grass and good Mr. Andrić, whose lips were kindly smiling behind his curly white beard, led me around the garden, showing me everything. He had exotic plants I had never seen before, including an *alpinum*[131] with rare ferns, various succulents, and cacti. He explained to me that the Latin name of the royal fern was *Osmunda regalis, which* sounded like music to my ears. The most beautiful of the succulent plants had pale yellow and reddish flowers, resembling roses. The abundant vegetation of indeterminable colours and mysterious shapes brought to mind creatures from fairy tales. Among them were the green-winged orchids and the reddish-brown lady's slipper orchid *(Paphiopedilum)*—sometimes called the Venus slipper—which I had never seen before. It resembled a human face with pouting, honey-coated lips and gnats glued to them. Next to each plant was a wooden sign with its name in Latin, German, and Croatian. The names in Latin seemed especially melodious and elegant. I tried to pronounce them the way Mr. Andrić did because they sounded alluring and pleasant, like music. The names I liked the most were *Fritillaria imperialis* (Crown imperial) and *Osmunda regalis,* the royal fern with double compound leaves. I repeated these names several times so that I could not forget them. Since I was such a great lover of flowers, Mr. Andrić suggested I visit his garden more often, especially when one of the rare plants was in full bloom. Those things did not happen all at the same time, he said, but year-round.

I was astonished. "In winter too?"

He nodded. "Yes, in winter too. The Christmas rose (*Helleborus niger*) is an example. It blooms in December, under the snow. Many cacti also blossom in winter, of course, not outside in the garden, but on my closed-in, heated veranda. There is a small orange tree in there too, which also blooms in winter. You can come and see it one day!"

Then he invited me into the house and showed me his herbarium. The plants had been carefully pressed and organized by the species to which they belonged. Each had its name and history recorded. He told me where and when he had found them. One he had picked right here by the river, another high up in the mountains. Many came from sunbathed plains or the forest, and many others from the karst fields close to the sea. Each had its distinct characteristics and requirements. They could only grow where the correct combination of necessary factors was met. The living conditions of plants were at the time only partially understood and explored. Their functions were known but not the inexplicable stimuli to which they reacted. Plants seemed to sprout, bloom, and bear fruits following a certain inner law, all of which was taking place with an admirable punctuality. The enigma of that growth has remained unresolved.

The herbarium contained compressed images of what those plants used to look like. Seeing them in that way somehow made me feel sad, just as any death would. I perceived death as the negative of life in which I was fully immersed and which I loved in all its forms. I felt sorry for those dead plants that had once happily bloomed somewhere in a meadow, in the forest, or on a mountain. I have felt sorry in that very same way all my life—at first instinctively and later by conviction—for all those who were alienated, separated from an original environment, subjected to the will of other people, or forced to serve other people's causes and comply with their worldviews. I realized that sooner or later I would also be in the position of depriving a plant of its life. I became aware that plants suffer when mis-treated, that their inner purpose and the meaning of their existence could be destroyed, just as with all other living creatures on earth. Plants are part of a life cycle, the same as animals and people. But they differ in that they exist of their own free will and do not take part in fighting and destroying each other.

I was naturally not capable of formulating such reflections that after-noon in Mr. Andrić's house. I was capable nevertheless of being overtaken by an upsurge of great love. I was already at that age equally capable of instinctive aversion towards many things. The feeling was there, whether affection or repulsion, and in many cases fully deserving. It was usually so strong that it would manifest itself against my own will and carry me along. That was exactly what happened on that occasion. I was looking through Mr. Andrić's herbarium and carefully listening to his explanations. I was so taken by it all that it made me breathless. A whole new world opened up before me—the world of plants, about which I had known so little until then. Time was flying by. The stars came up in the sky and the light was switched on in the room. I had completely forgotten about going home. Only when the table was set up and Mr. Andrić was getting ready to have his dinner did I realize how late it was. As I was leaving, he suggested I return next day to see different things under a magnifying glass, or even a microscope, including the examples of animal and vegetable world float-ing in a drop of water. I keenly accepted the invitation.

What a surprise it was when I opened the front gate of our house, walked down the entrance hall, and calmly climbed the few stairs to the apartment, entirely oblivious to what was in store for me inside. Everyone in the house was in a total frenzy. It was eight o'clock in the evening and they had been searching for me for more than five hours. They were asking around, had checked with acquaintances, searched through the attic and the basement, and finally called the police. My mother was already practi-cally on the verge of passing out when the cook, Marija, concluded that I was probably snatched away by the "gypsies". Miss Goldschmidt was of the opinion that I must have wandered to the River Drava and drowned there. Aunt Adele went to the railway station on the way to her honeymoon crying her heart out, as she saw my disappearance as a bad omen for her marriage. By the time I finally arrived, the whole family, including a few aunts who had joined in the search, had gathered in one room and were sitting there in complete silence. It was hard to say which feeling predominated upon my sudden appearance—relief or anger for having needlessly frightened them to that point. My bridesmaid's dress was in a state beyond description, the patent leather shoes filthy, and my stockings torn. The ensuing punishment was one of the most severe I had been subjected to, as far as I could remember. I was forbidden ever again to go to the Long Courtyard or the street. From then on, I could only be in touch with my friends from the yard by talking through the garden fence. As for my new friend, Mr. Andrić, I was not allowed to see him at all. And so that unforgettable afternoon remained the only time I spent in the magical world of his garden.

Regularly, every year, Aunt Adele returned to Osijek to visit her mother. She held, unwittingly, the role of the kind and almighty fairy in the imaginary world of my childhood years. Every time she visited, she brought wonderful presents—be they treats, toys, jewellery, magically beautiful dolls with real hair (of the kind you would only be allowed to admire, with longing eyes, in a shop window), books with gilded edges and expensive bindings, and gold brooches and bracelets. She seemed to me altogether most unreachable and majestic. She was elegant rather than beautiful and all her attention was directed at appearing as distinguished as possible while observing, without fault, all social norms of refinement. Since her youth, she exhibited symptoms of morbid, neurasthenic sensitivity, which made her exaggeratedly circumspect and reserved in everything she did in life. She wore exclusively tailor-made, English-type suits, grey or beige in colour, lined with boning, which transformed the suit into an armour and restricted her movements to the minimum. She also wore stiff high collars, maintained in this way with the help of horsehair inserts. The times of Parisian *tournures*—those richly folded pleats with wide garnishing and tunics in the Rococo style—were over. It was now the era of long skirts and tight-fitting jackets, the front of which displayed a long series of little buttons. This English "old-maidish fashion" went well with the stiff Girardi hat,[132] usually worn low on the forehead with one's hair smoothly combed back and away from the forehead, giving the face a stern look. Simplicity was the order of the day, but it was a complicated, uncomfortable, and expensive simplicity, adding a masculine touch to the feminine chic. This style was imported from the leading Viennese fashion salons at the time when, in our parts of the world, there was still no mention of women's emancipation or of the suffragette movement.

Aunt Adele exaggerated in that respect. She never put any makeup on her colourless, sunken face with its pronounced cheekbones. On the contrary, her tightly pulled-back hair accentuated even further the hard lines of her face and her high forehead. She spoke a very correct version of German. She hardly moved her lips when speaking, making it look as if she were pressing her lips together after having tasted something extremely bitter. She rarely smiled and when she laughed, it was too loud and spasmodic. She was basically a good woman, but her overall mental disposition resulted in a tendency to exaggerate and to show a morbid obsession with prestige. She was not governed by real values but yearned for acknowledgement in certain social circles, whose sense of values she overrated.

Her precious gifts caused me more grief than joy because Mother would promptly put away the most beautiful things for "later". She rightly believed that expensive objects were not supposed to serve as children's toys. They only made children conceited, and the joy would not last long, because the objects would get damaged, even destroyed, through everyday use. I was only occasionally allowed to play with the doll with real hair, but always under the close surveillance of Miss Goldschmidt, which, by being by myself, was not great fun. I wanted to show it to Helena and, in general, to be able to take it with me to the Long Courtyard. By that time, the ban on playing in the yard had been for all practical purposes forgotten and I was again able to slip away. As for the doll and bracelets, there was no way Mother could prevent me from constantly thinking about them. I felt offended at being deprived of something that belonged to me by right. For that reason, on those occasions when I was allowed to play with them, I felt compelled to take them as quickly as possible to the Long Courtyard.

The three of us—Milena, Helena, and I—would find a spot in Helena's house or Georgijević's chardak and play with the wonderful doll. It had movable arms and legs, could say "mom" and "dad," open and shut its eyes, and had hair that we could arrange in complex styles. We took turns in combing it until we successfully removed the last of its strands. "Mom" and "dad" eventually became only sad-sounding groans and the eyes stopped opening, no matter how hard we jiggled and shook the doll. The bracelets and brooches I used to brag about would mysteriously disappear and my parading around made the children from the yard like me less than before. There was much envy going on—everybody wanted to have those things, touch them and try them. On one occasion, an especially malicious girl suddenly led me to the canal and fiddled there with my golden bracelet until she had unclasped its buckle and let the bracelet fall into the water, where it disappeared for good. Gloating in triumph, she claimed it had happened purely by accident.

There was only one coffee house in town in those days. It was not an elegant place. It resembled a common pub, and its premises were part of the Grand Hotel, located exactly across the street from the County Palace. The coffee house was mostly frequented by visiting sales representatives, local agents, and trade inspectors, who dealt intermittently with business transactions and noisy games of *Färbeln*.[133] In the evenings, fledgling folk singers and dancers would take to the tiny stage in the neighbouring salon, and entertain an exclusively male audience with racy, popular songs and provocative dancing. Respectable gentlemen preferred the Casino for their get-togethers after lunch, where they formed coteries depending on their profession and social status. Most numerous among them were businessmen and merchants, who, just like everywhere else in town, were setting the tone. A table reserved for the legal professionals occasionally included a judge or two. There was, furthermore, a table for dignitaries and another for wealthy farmers from the countryside, who would sometimes drop by. There was always a possibility to have a quick game of cards, take a turn on the billiard table, discuss a decision by the town council concerning the sewage system, waste disposal, or the Chimney Sweepers Act, or debate the foreign or domestic political situation in reference to reports published in the *Pester Lloyd* newspaper. There was also always a way to hear a spicy joke and exchange information on the stability of the market for a particular commodity, such as wood, wine, or grain.

Conforming to the norms of common decency, ladies never entered such public premises. They met instead in each other's houses for afternoon coffee, cake, and small talk. Conversations revolved around the latest fashions from Vienna, the progress of their sweet little children, and whatever amusing or racy story they could fish out concerning someone who happened not to be in attendance at that moment. Most of the discussions, however, dealt with matters of domestic service and gave rise to deep psychological analyses. It is important to keep in mind that ladies of the so-called good society were exempt from all potential work in a household. A dragon of a cook kept the kitchen in perfect order, a well-trained maid looked after the rooms, and an extra cleaning woman would come when required for heavier jobs. There was a laundry woman to do the washing and a seamstress to look after the clothes. If there were children in the family, they were first cared for by a wet nurse, then a nanny, and finally by a German *Fräulein* or governess, who often remained in the house to serve as a chaperone to still unmarried young daughters. The above-mentioned staff had full control of the area in the household they were in charge of, and terrorized anyone who wanted to intervene, including the mistress of the house, who had little to say anyway. That is why every change in the composition of the staff caused a major disturbance, bordering on a crisis. A new staff person would be discussed for days among the ladies, who took a wicked pleasure in guessing potential virtues or weaknesses. It usually happened that mistresses talked about their servants during the chat parties with an equal amount of misgiving as their domestics talked among themselves about their mistresses in their servants' quarters. Other people's children were an equally welcome object of frequent criticism. Ladies would typically dwell on the most unpleasant things about them, and those with no children were the most eager because they did not need to fear revenge. The ultimate maxim with which they tended to spice up their coffee and marble cake was straightforward: "Youngsters should be kept in check!" To start with, children should not be allowed to believe in their own personal value, as they tended to be presumptuous. They should be deliberately overlooked, their achievements underestimated, their claims ignored, and their opinions and efforts not taken seriously.

The supreme authority in all educational matters at the time was Mrs. Elizabeth Gersuny, née Schulze, born in Graz, who had arrived in Osijek some thirty years earlier, while employed as a governess in a colonel's household of some sort. In the 1860s, she founded a German-English private school for girls of "upper class" standing. It was that same school where my mother had acquired her extensive knowledge of foreign languages. In the 1860s and 1870s, girls had no educational options in Osijek after finishing four years of primary schooling, and Mrs. Gersuny (still Miss Schulze at the time) was highly commended for her initiative. She was considered a true female authority on all matters concerning higher education, culture, and upbringing. She had thorough knowledge of the vast German literature, from Robert Hamerling,[134] one of her fellow countrymen, to Schiller and Goethe. She was capable of throwing into a conversation a few French and sometimes even English quotations, and thus impress everyone around. Not only was she familiar with all issues of art and education, but she could also outsmart experts in the fields of medicine and law. It was not always her arguments, but her ironically superior smile, which made people surrender.

What she liked most, however, was, of course, to talk about pedagogy, from Johann Heinrich Pestalozzi to the fatal doctrines of the latest psychological methods conceived to find explanations for everything, and which were met with her total disapproval. Children were not individuals but small animals, and instead of using words to persuade them—a useless undertaking—one should apply the only systematic method possible, namely the drill.

I would shiver each time I spotted her during our daily walks on the glacis, rolling down the path like an unavoidable menace. She had become obese with age, was panting heavily, and was obliged every now and then to stop and take a rest from walking. There was no sign of any bone structure inside that clumsy and slowly approaching mass of folds of heavy black fabric reaching all the way down to the ground. One could not imagine anything human to be found under that mass of fabric, except additional folds of it. She had no waist whatsoever, and the heavy folds of fabric hid huge breasts. What was more, there was no visible transition to the neck, nor further up to her sagging cheeks. The only things visible were the drooping sides of her mouth, watery blue eyes protruding behind a wire-framed pince-nez, snow white, tightly pulled up hair with numerous cylindrical curls, and, like a crown on top of a pyramid, a wobbly small hat decorated with feathers.

To the great surprise of her former students, she even managed to find a husband at the age of forty-two. She married Mr. von Gersuny, an unprepossessing and shy little man, who, besides his two carefully tended strands of side whiskers, had nothing else worth mentioning. He belonged to a respectable family, had a substantial income, and had been running around the former Miss Schulze like a miserable pest. Occasionally she would teach him a lesson and send him to the corner, the way she would do with an impertinent brat. He would then be obliged to do his penance, beg her pardon, and wait until she deigned to forgive him.

She was known in town exclusively as Gersuny. It was at once a family name, an honorary title, a nobility title, and a seal of recognition for an established authority after thirty years of a successful service to the towns-folk. During that time, several generations had had the good fortune to be associated with her and acquire remarkable linguistic knowledge, without ever having the chance of applying it in a town like Osijek, and therefore slowly forgetting it all. In all those years, she had never lost her Styrian accent, changed her style, nor modified her way of thinking. She had never had even the slightest reason to doubt her own worth, and never noticed any changes in the ways of the world, or public opinions. It was as if time had stood still for those thirty years, just as she had.

During the promenades in the glacis, she used to speak to everyone she met, always in the same ironic way, high and mighty, so that the other person was disempowered before even uttering a word. The moment I saw her approaching from a distance, I would feel shivers through my whole body, in anticipation of an inevitable encounter. She would intercept me immediately with a barrage of questions, to which I did not know the answers. She would then supply my mother with a new pedagogical recipe and discover in me a failure that not even someone like Miss Goldschmidt had noticed before. With every minute that passed, I was decreasing in size because I could clearly feel that nothing could ever escape her perceptive eyes. This did not only apply to small sins, of which I had plenty on my conscience, but to my most hidden thoughts, which I knew would not go unnoticed by her. She seemed to me like a supernatural creature endowed with mysterious powers. To make matters worse, she managed to convince my mother of the validity of her viewpoint that strict discipline was the only effective method of education.

Mrs. Gersuny's method proved to be fatally wrong in the case of one person at least, and ironically, it was her own son. She had him late in her life and brought him up not on mother's milk but on lofty pedagogical theories. He was three years younger than me and surely the unhappiest child I had ever known in my life, even more so than the poorest child in the Long Courtyard. They used to be beaten and went hungry, but possessed something young Oskar Gersuny lacked, namely freedom of movement and the possibility to play with other children, to compete with them and potentially get ahead in that way. Oskar Gersuny received everything in homeopathic, rationed doses—food, sleep, play and work, permission to speak or stay silent. His punishments were not as brutal as those received by my friend Helena, whose father used to hit her with a horsewhip, but none the less cruel, cold-heartedly deliberate, and inescapable. They would be announced to him in the morning and applied in the evening before bedtime, so that the entire day was spent in anticipation of the forthcoming terror. According to his mother's theory, the delay of the punishment and its cold-blooded execution were supposed to increase its effectiveness. She had an ideal image in her mind of what little Oskar should become, but he was incapable of fitting the picture. He was an anaemic and perturbed child, suffering from nightmares, digestive troubles, and bronchial asthma. His condition was worsening due to the systematic procedures his mother subjected him to in order to strengthen him physically—ice cold showers, cold bandages, and half-body bathing. If he dared to resist, he would be locked up in a little room at the back of the house. He would find this utterly terrifying. None of this was done out of malice *per se*, but as part of a deliberate training to transform little Oskar into the ideal child his mother had in mind. With appropriate treatment, every child could, in her opinion, become an ideal child—most of all, and naturally, her very own.

It was no fault of little Oskar that the experiment he was subjected to did not work. Whatever he did or did not do was not an expression of ill will. It simply meant he did not know any better. Fear was the most destructive factor. His gaze was erratic and full of fear. As far as his mental and physical development was concerned, he lagged behind children his age. He had a hard time learning to spell or to execute basic calculations. His little legs were thin, his neck skinny and his spine curved. He had sparse, thin flaxen blond hair, and skin so pale and so transparent that his blue veins showed through. The corners of his mouth drooped sadly, and his eyes looked worried. He seemed like a sleepwalker or an automaton. He was afraid of everything, both people and animals, but most of all, his mother. He was startled whenever she addressed him, was unable to give an answer, kept biting his nails, stammering, and slouching forward. As a consequence, he would be subjected to new punishments under the premise that one should stand up straight, speak clearly, and not bite one's nails. He would occasionally walk down to the moats with me to pick a few flowers, which he would then hold tightly in his hand for the entire afternoon and observe with fondness. His mother would not let him bring such "weeds" home, and would order him to throw them away, which he would do promptly and carefully, but not without regret.

Then, unexpectedly, people started gossiping that little Oskar was ill, which it turned out to be indeed true. I was unable to obtain any specific answer to my initial inquiries about his illness. From conversations that I managed to overhear, I soon learned that something horrible was going on with that dejected, quiet, and dispirited little boy. Overnight he turned into a wild animal, baring his teeth, biting, kicking everything around him, refusing food, and not allowing anyone to come close to him—least of all his mother. All the city doctors were called to help but they seemed helpless when confronted with his case. Opinions were conflicting. Was this a psychological state caused by a mental stress, or were those manifestations symptoms of a serious and progressive mental illness? Medication, massages, counselling—nothing helped.

What happened to little Oskar Gersuny? What drove him to madness at the age of eight? Even the most loyal supporters of Mrs. Gersuny began to wonder. Her system of strict drills and character building had proved imperfect, not to mention that the victim of her system was her own child. Doctors advised a change of environment. Little Oskar was sent first to a hospital in Graz, and a year later transferred to the house of a country teacher, where his condition slowly improved. We never saw him again. These events made Mrs. Gersuny suddenly twenty years older. And not just that—she changed and became more thoughtful and humane. After considering her for years as the supreme authority in matters of education and intellectual refinement, some people began to express doubts, most of all because she had ruined the life of her own child. She must have recognized it herself. Even though she still appeared on the glacis, under the same cover as always (wide black skirts, white hair ringlets, wire-rimmed glasses), she was far less high-handed and judgmental. There were occasions, while we, the children, played around on the meadow or in the moats, that she would, albeit briefly and imperceptibly, observe us with wistful eyes.

Since our house in Franjina Street was close to the main promenade, where ladies regularly went for late afternoon walks, various friends and acquaintances got into the habit of coming to our apartment. There, the table would be set, and they could stay for an afternoon coffee or tea, and sometimes even stay over for dinner. My parents were hospitable and rejoiced at having visitors. People could count on my mother and grandmother to be home at that time of the day. Besides their welcoming faces, there would always be refreshments—coffee, stewed and fresh fruit, and delicious pastries. My grandmother found great pleasure in preparing these refreshments as she seldom went out and visitors were a most welcome diversion. While other people sometimes had to make serious efforts to be successful in entertaining their guests, she was naturally witty and entertaining, read all the newspapers that came to our house and was well informed about all current issues. Her remarks, skilfully thrown in during conversations and very much to the point, did not just entertain everyone present, but gave her personally a lot of pleasure. People in her company never stopped laughing.

My mother was also sociable. She was, however, far more intelligent than other people and fully aware of it. She did not know how to entertain and make people laugh the way my grandmother could, and she took everything in life seriously, something many of her so-called friends found annoying. In consideration of my father's standing in some important social circles, she forced herself to socialize with people with whom she had very little in common. For years, she was thus obliged to cope with futility and squabbling, and it was only later in her life that the full potential of her exceptional abilities was properly revealed. To this day, I am unable to comprehend why she wasted so much time interacting with so many shallow, superficial, and ill-intentioned people, who were mostly on bad terms among themselves anyway, and why she kept receiving them in her house and entertaining them. Presumably, the basis of those social ties rested in an almost mystical sense of belonging to a clan. Individuals might feel mutual aversion or affection in their relationships, but the worthiness of a clan in itself was beyond any doubt. Under its wing, people were ready to help one another in times of hardship, which was effectively the case on far too many occasions. They defended one another particularly when confronted by someone outside the clan. No matter how different they were individually, everything about them was founded on the same principles and standardized rules of the clan—clothes, homes, level of education, manner of speaking and behaviour. People were subjected to the laws of "people are saying" and "it is expected". Deviations were judged as tactless or lacking in good taste, and, in especially blatant cases, as an attack on the unity of the social circle. Everything that crossed imposed boundaries, whether it amounted to personal preference or natural talent, was quickly nipped in the bud under the pressure of public opinion, the most effective format being constant mockery. It was in fact considered in good taste to make fun of everything and everyone. But that persistent jocularity, in the form of playing with words, resorting to distortions and false attributions had nothing in common with scepticism. Not even my sensible mother considered her "friends" to be stupid, spiteful, or frivolous. They happened to be the constituent part of her world, which also included conflicts and contradictions. She was herself never aggressive by nature, but she knew how to react to aggression by others. It became evident when people made clumsy allusions about her married life. My father liked to extend his charming attention to pretty ladies and my mother's good friends never missed an opportunity to inform her about it. The stories were unfounded and driven by jealousy and my mother dealt with these hints of potential infidelity with razor-sharp rebuttals.

Some of our afternoon guests would visit us on a daily basis. Others would come weekly. Miss Kitty Lipschitz, my mother's old friend from the times they had attended Miss Schulze's classes together, came each day. Miss Kitty was, so to speak, part of the household inventory. She was tall, skinny, and showed no evidence of any typical feminine curves. She wore her hair short, which made her rather conspicuous in those days. A peculiar gait due to the flat-heeled shoes she wore provided an added touch of masculinity and made her recognizable from afar. She was known to have been Gersuny's best pupil, which meant a lot to her, and she never missed an occasion to mention it, even twenty years later. She even adopted Gersuny's attitude of intellectual superiority and was held in high esteem by that otherwise particularly critically inclined lady. They often strolled on the glacis together, and people would watch them pass by with curiosity. Every few steps they would stop. Miss Lipschitz would be standing upright like a grenadier while Gersuny would be panting and catching her breath. They were always immersed in some stimulating conversation and vigorously gesticulating. While Gersuny held firm convictions and never had any doubt about where she stood on any issue, Miss Lipschitz was, despite her energetic appearance, not so sure of herself. She was mistrustful, constantly claiming to be overlooked, especially in the company of pretty women for whom she had little respect. Men in her view fared even worse—with the exception of an occasional exemplary specimen—and were as a whole disposable.

All her friends had been married, had their own homes, and had given birth. In a small town such as Osijek, full of evil tongues, it was necessary to have a solid dose of egotism, even a definite strength of character, in order to avoid the usual classification of "old maid". What kept her going in that embarrassing situation was her closeness to her mother, which had evolved into a real cult. Her mother was once an acclaimed beauty, and Miss Lipschitz had lived under the spell of that long-gone glamour. The old lady, on the other hand, was endowed with unusual energy for her age. The seventy-year-old woman treated her children as if they were kids and, driven by her sheer egotism, was preventing them from getting married. She found fault with every suitor who approached her daughters. One suitor was too tall, the other too short. One seemed too fat, the other too skinny. One had flat feet, another sloping shoulders. If a man was withdrawn and shy, she considered him stupid. If he was assertive, she decided that he had to be a drunk, a spendthrift, a brute, or not serious enough. There were men who appeared, in her opinion, entirely unsuitable to be good husbands, and would squander the dowry and abuse the wife. The mere thought of handing over to such a monster a helpless creature, who happened to be her own daughter, simply terrified her. She would explain to the suitor that her daughter still had plenty of time and was in no hurry to get married.

Miss Kitty's younger sister, Berta, was a good-natured and amiable person in her mid-thirties of indifferent looks, who spent her days in a corner of their living room occupied with needlework—whether crocheting, knitting, embroidering, or threading—and always relying on well-tested patterns from Blatt der *Hausfrau* (Homemaker's Journal) and *Wiener Mode* (Vienna Fashion). She did not command much respect in the household because she was considered apathetic and dull-witted, especially when compared with the exceptionally intelligent Kitty. Besides the two daughters, the Lipschitzes also had two sons, Gustav and Hugo, who jointly handled the family wholesale business in agricultural commodities after their father's death. They also remained unmarried, to the great satisfaction of their mother, who claimed that her darling boys could not afford being away from their store and that there was not a single woman in the world worthy of them.

Miss Kitty also put her brothers on a high pedestal and would cite their opinions as irrefutable arguments whenever she thought, and it happened often, that her own supposedly inconsequential female opinion might not have enough weight. Hugo and Gustav were in fact good and diligent lads, not so young anymore, bald, and with rather large bellies. Due to their regular interaction with agents and inspectors involved in buying and selling transactions, generally in the coffee room of the Grand Hotel, they adopted the jargon of the place, spent their time playing cards and chatting, and felt more at home there than in the fancy Casino. They also dressed rather casually and had mistresses of a lower social standing than their own, something their mother was never supposed to find out.

The Lipschitzes lived in a house by the river in an area surrounded by a flood of mud in winter and fields of dust in summer. They had to wade through their spacious yard in the rainy season. On market days, the yard was full of heavy carts delivering sacks of wheat, corn, and oats for sale. At the bottom of the yard were warehouses built in concrete, where the merchandise was stacked up to the ceiling, waiting to be sold to local or foreign retail companies.

The yard was full of discarded building material, planks, beams, lime and mortar, garbage bins, full and empty barrels, heaps of sawdust, and ash, all of which had accumulated there for at least fifty years. In the long and vitrified corridor—a typical feature of every "better" house in Osijek—more piles of useless objects had been lying around for years, including broken chairs and other furniture removed from the rooms, jars of all sizes, broken mirrors, a rusty old stove, bundles of old business ledgers, and years of issues of popular *Gartenlaube* (Garden Arbour)[135] and *Vom Fels zum Meer* (From the Cliffs to the Sea)[136] magazines. There were also empty flowerpots and withered houseplants, mousetraps and rat traps, broken paraffin lamps and lanterns, a rusty sitting bathtub, broken window blinds, and a torn runner carpet. That overcrowded vestibule led directly into the apartment, where, the moment the door was open, one could immediately detect the characteristic odour of unaired rooms. Besides the dominant smell of mould from the walls, there was a mixture of scents from hair pomade, bed linen, stale food, human sweat, old shoes, camphor oils, menthol extracts, soot, naphthalene, lavender, and scented candles which kept burning all day long to eliminate all the other odours.

The rooms were packed with old furniture, carpets, and a myriad of objects. Each carpet was covered by another to protect the one below. Various covers protected every piece of furniture, with a washed-out cretonne dust cover on top of them all. Tens of thousands of useless items were piling up in those rooms, or at least that was how it appeared to me whenever my mother and I visited the Lipschitzes for major holidays, bringing along a bouquet of flowers for the occasion. Before each visit, my mother used to explain to me in detail how I should behave, because Mrs. Lipschitz paid much attention to social norms and would be offended if they were not observed, especially in her own home. For some inexplicable reason, nowhere else did I have as many mishaps as in her house. I tripped on the carpet, bumped into a small gilded rococo easy chair, pulled on the fringes of the tablecloth until silky threads got stuck to my fingers, and entirely unintentionally stepped on the tail of Mrs. Lipschitz's favourite cat and made him run away howling. I once even overturned a vase of flowers, causing the water to spill out on the silk tablecloth and creating a turmoil as if the house were on fire.

Wherever you looked, whether it was on the sideboard, chests of drawers, or shelves, there were plates, cups, and bowls stacked on top of each other, as well as all kinds of knick-knacks in ceramics, flowers and butterflies made of silk, along with gnomes, dragons, little dogs and cats made of various materials. Porcelain shepherdesses were in constant danger of falling off the shelves. On the table and sideboard were business card trays, displaying greeting cards, and condolences from people already deceased themselves. The windows were decorated with heavy corduroy curtains at each side of the frame and sheer curtains in the middle. Cushions of all colours and shapes lay on sofas and the floor. There were hand-painted plates and screens, family albums with covers in plush and embossed leather, encrusted with mother-of-pearl and ivory, and, on the walls, daguerreotypes and miniature paintings of great-grandparents. Among them, in a wide gilded frame, was a life-size portrait in oil of the very lady who had created that milieu and was firmly objecting to it ever be changed. Mrs. Lipschitz was by that time mere skin and bones. Her bald skull was hidden under a ginger-red wig. As she spoke, her badly made set of false teeth would shake and even be at risk of falling out of her mouth. Her tiny, watery eyes were buried in deep eye sockets. Thick layers of powder and makeup could not disguise the wrinkles on her face nor provide the illusion of the former freshness that was beaming in full splendour and beauty from the painting on the wall. In a vain effort to keep the image on the picture alive, she always wore the same peacock blue corduroy gown with a collar of white lace, elegant long diamond earrings, and a mass of rings and bracelets on her fingers and arms.

And so, for years, everything was taking its usual course at the Lipschitzes until clouds suddenly gathered, and an unexpected storm broke. Kitty's sister Berta—the one who had been crocheting, knitting and embroidering non-stop since she was fifteen years old, had mastered various lace and needlework techniques, and had produced hundreds of metres of lace, along with a few dozen tea towels, doilies, bedside rugs, tapestries, and cushion covers—stood up one day in front of her stupefied family and announced that she was engaged to be married.

The effect of this event could not have been more devastating if the house had been struck by lightning! The future husband in question owned a farm, had a fully furnished house, fields, and vineyards, and was a widower with two children who needed a mother. This last circumstance was crucial, and Berta said yes. Mrs. Lipschitz was wringing her hands in desperation. There were objections, discussions, beseeching, energetic bans, and threats. There were hysterical tantrums and fainting. When none of that had the desired effect, the offended mother declared that she would renounce and disinherit her degenerate daughter. However, Berta explained she had anticipated that and taken it into consideration. Her youth was gone, this was her last chance, and if she missed it, it would be all over for her.

This event had a most harmful effect on Miss Kitty. No one knew what had happened to her mental balance, but as soon as Berta left home, she had a nervous breakdown. She suffered from insomnia, was consumed with a dark melancholy, refused to eat, lost fifteen kilos, and eventually made a serious attempt to commit suicide by taking several doses of sleeping pills. She was taken to the "Maria Grün" sanatorium near Graz and she spent several months there. She was treated by the famous psychiatrist, Professor Richard von Krafft-Ebing and, with his help, made a miraculous recovery and mental regeneration. On one hand, she realized the advantages derived from her illness, as it enabled her to be once again the centre of attention. On the other, her daily association with a personality such as Krafft-Ebing gave her a new sense of importance. She found a new person to admire and keep in close contact with, and she submitted herself fully to his treatment, analysis, hypnosis, and massages. She abided by each of his directives and managed to identify with him entirely through complex mental transformations.

From then on, there was no longer any other meaningful logic than his, no binding truth except the one he acknowledged. The whole world could be explained in neuropathological terms. In the light of his scientific theories, all phenomena became comprehensible and admissible. Miss Kitty Lipschitz had discovered a new world, conceived by her doctor, in which everyone had their psychopathological characteristics and where a "normal" person was nowhere to be found. She strictly followed the daily programme developed especially for her by Krafft-Ebing. She ate everything he prescribed, and soon recovered the fifteen kilos she had lost. She regained her poise and self-assurance and took over her own care following his instructions. In the final analysis, her refuge from all problems, the excuse she used to gloss over her deficiencies and help her restore the lost balance, evolved around this heaven-sent illness. The Krafft-Ebing sanatorium was from then onwards her Mecca, the site of annual pilgrimages. It was a place where she would lay all her spiritual and physical shortcomings before a sacred altar, recuperate from any type of depression, come across new theses, and spread them around. The name of Krafft-Ebing was continuously on her lips and in her circle of friends and acquaintances, it secured for her a new level of authority.

Among our daily house guests, besides Miss Lipschitz, was also Aunt Tinka Vesely, a married cousin of my mother. The talk of the house was that Aunt Tinka had never forgiven my mother for the fact that her husband had been in love with my mother in his youth, and that she had refused him because of my father. Aunt Tinka would cast a meaningful glance at my mother and declare that her Heinrich was the most boring spouse on earth, a typical bookworm and a total drag. "A pity," she once said, looking at my mother, "that you didn't take him. He would be much more suitable for you! Or Miss Kitty! Apparently, he was courting her too at some point! Imagine the deep conversations they would have been engaged in during their moments of passion! I have no patience for such things, because, luckily enough, I am not an intellectual!"

Miss Lipschitz replied with a circumscribed smile, "Mr. Vesely has once and for all demonstrated the extent of his bad taste in women." Then she gave Aunt Tinka a crushing look from head to toe, which left the latter quite undisturbed. On the contrary, she seemed to enjoy herself and have a great time because the more other people were angry, the more satisfaction she drew from a situation. And so, day after day, they would sit at the same table and exchange caustic remarks. It is hard to say what was predominant, the contempt they felt for each other or the enjoyment derived from constant goading. No one could match them when it came to enliven their social conversation with innuendos, inferences, and a range of disguised attacks, always accompanied by an amiable smile.

Aunt Tinka, who had a high opinion of her physical appearance, was in fact a small, chubby person, tied up firmly in a high, steel-hard corset. The more her waist was tightened, the more her hips and breasts swelled over it. It looked as if her body consisted of two bowling pins glued together at their heads in its middle. On top of her short, fat neck rested a small round head with a wide double chin, beady black eyes, a tiny rounded nose lost between her cheeks, and a rounded, fish-like mouth with sparse, pointed teeth. Her sarcastic remarks were accompanied by gurgling laughter, in which neither the eyes nor the lips participated. It was the kind of laughter emerging from somewhere deep inside her that produced a sound resembling liquid running out of an overturned bottle and spilling all over the place. Occasionally it was interrupted by short, abrupt sentences, also uttered in the same irregular chuckling way even when there was nothing to laugh about. No matter how innocuous her remarks may have sounded, Aunt Tinka managed to use them to rip someone to pieces, whether present or not.

Aunt Tinka had no children, no interests, no concerns for people, events, or any earthly phenomena. Everything that existed was, in her opinion, a perfect object for mockery, unless it concerned her own person, her self-confidence, or needs and wishes, because she took those things very seriously. She was convinced that she deserved the best of everything—life with no worries, good health, distinction, luxury, the most beautiful apartment in town, the most expensive Persian lamb coat, the loveliest silk gowns, the most valuable jewellery, and finest food. And all of it was due to her without any effort whatsoever on her part, and with no mention of reciprocity or gratitude. She was Tinka Vesely, née Basch, who enjoyed special privileges under the contract she had signed at birth with the heavenly forces.

On top of everything else, she also had the best and most devoted husband of them all. She exercised a domineering control over him in that same mysterious way as so many other women manage, without it having anything to do with their beauty, brains, or some innate virtue. The man who was superior to her in every possible way and who had once apparently loved my mother, now saw in that huge body, in those beady eyes, and in that utter lack of intelligence and discernment, the embodiment of an ideal that he looked upon with devotion.

Heinrich Vesely had been my father's friend since their study days in Vienna. He became a well educated and an above-average, polished lawyer. That intelligent man, prone to quiet contemplation, succumbed during ten years of marriage to a gradual process of personal transformation. His limited, banal, gossiping, and derisive wife, who could barely be deemed attractive, acquired such an influence on him that he never missed an occasion to mention her name, and asked for her advice, even in connection with matters of which she had no knowledge whatsoever. With each success or failure, he claimed that she had foreseen it. Tinka's judgments were instinctive but still indisputable, especially when it concerned people and their character, whose trustworthiness she claimed to be able to assess at the first glance. Her antipathy to this or that person would eventually prove to be inevitably justified. He even consulted Tinka on questions related to high politics. Of course, he had to admit that she did not know much about politics. Nevertheless, she had an infallible flair, a sixth sense. There was something witchlike in her, enabling her to assess things she knew nothing about, and he would subscribe to her conclusions, even if they were contrary to his own best judgment.

I could not make much sense of those conversations around our table. While eavesdropping at the door, or during those short moments when I was allowed to show myself in front of the guests while getting my piece of cake, all I could hear were unintelligible murmuring voices, mixed with Aunt Tinka's gurgling cascades of laughter. In those moments, my full attention was focused on the cake stand, hoping that by the time I arrived, my share of the cake would still be there waiting for me—which was not always the case. There were fewer guests on fair-weather days, but when it was raining or snowing, there would be a constant flow of people through the front door. People we had not seen for a year would suddenly show up and we had to bring extra chairs from the bedrooms and children's room to accommodate them. All sorts of wet overcoats, jackets, capes, pelerines, and raincoats would hang in the lobby, water would trickle from umbrellas, and the cake would disappear before my indignant eyes, until there was nothing left but crumbs. Mother would wave to me to go away and, unhappy and disappointed, I would retire to the kitchen, to grumble with the servants about the unexpected invasion that caused me to lose my share of the cake, filled the rooms with the smell of damp clothes and burdened the staff with extra work. The person who grumbled most was the cook, Marija. She always kept strict track of who, among the guests, had left her a tip and who had turned a blind eye when she had "accidentally" intercepted them in the hallway for the tenth time. In her opinion, they were black sheep—people without good upbringing and with no manners. Take Miss Lipschitz for instance, who was there every day, always with a friendly greeting, but not a penny to give out. Niggardly Aunt Tinka would rather die than open her wallet, but, luckily, Mr. Vesely would hand out very generous tips behind her back. Marija's sharp assessment was straightforward—fine people were givers, while those who refrained from giving had no upbringing and no class. She could not stop wondering why my mother kept socializing with them at all.

Marija was talking this way while sitting on the wood crate by the oven, her bloated face full of broken capillaries caused by the heat from the stove. My arrival in the kitchen would not stop the torrent of her words. The only thing she insisted upon was that I never repeat anything said in the kitchen to my mother, and even less to the German Fräulein, whom she could stand even less than I did. It was no longer the Goldschmidt woman, but Miss Kaiser, a rather hysterical person, who luckily took little care of us and spent her days writing letters. Cook Marija claimed that those were all love letters and the chambermaid Eva confirmed it. She got into the habit of going through Miss Kaiser's drawers while cleaning and dusting her room. And there were things to be found! Photographs of young men with dedications of the kind "Forever yours" and love letters, but mostly curt goodbye notes. There were also Miss Kaiser's personal sentimental outpourings. Sometimes Eva would bring some of them to the kitchen and would laugh her heart out with Marija beside her as they read them, and each time I would have to promise anew that I would not blurt it out to anyone. I kept my promise, but with an unclear conscience because I had never before hidden anything from my mother.

It was about that time that one of my grandmother's nephews arrived in town to start his medical practice. Hs name was Doctor Karl Reinfeld. He came to our house regularly every day following his consultations and house calls. One could declare with certainty that he soon became the central focus of our social circle. As far as I can remember, all the physicians in Osijek until his arrival were elderly men—Dr. Zechmeister, Dr. Reiner, Dr. Knopp, and the county physician, Dr. Gottschalk. They must have, no doubt, cherished some ideals in their young days and shown due respect for medical science and an interest in their profession. But in their provincial surroundings, cut off from the vibrant resources of big-city clinics and without any supervision, their enthusiasm soon faded, and they found themselves pursuing the usual well-trodden path, devoid of ambition and curiosity. They kept prescribing sedatives, chamomile tea, quinine, bromine, and the so-called *"Bitterwasser"*, a natural bitter laxative. If patients recovered, the doctor would be credited for it, and if they died, it would simply be God's will.

Osijek was by no means a healthy city. It was situated on the Drava Delta, a well-known marshland, with its network of meandering beds of stagnating water, called "dead Dravas", which in autumn and spring would regularly spill over their banks and flood the entire area. There was not an inch of dry land anywhere around the town for miles. Lush reeds and swamp weeds looked like forests. And yet, regardless of the abundance of water, or rather because of the amount of water continuously seeping into basements like a subterranean river and covering the walls of houses with saltpetre and mould, there was not a drop of healthy drinking water to be found in town. The water from wells contained saltpetre and that from the river was contaminated with typhus. There was no end to epidemics, and it was even claimed that there had not been a single Esseker who had not fallen ill with typhus, usually unknowingly and in early childhood. Those who survived developed a sort of immunity, and the typhus from the river water could no longer harm them. Still, the fear of this disease was the reason the town scarcely grew in population. Nobody from the surrounding area, especially rich landowners, wanted to risk their lives by settling in Osijek, preferring instead to move to Zagreb, where the drinking water was clean and safe. Water from the River Drava was nevertheless consumed in private houses in town, but only after undergoing a complex purification procedure. This was indispensable, because the town sewerage system drained into the river upstream rather than downstream, so that the water picked up for everyday usage was the same as that already disposed of as sewage! Special water carriers would fill barrels with river water and transport them around town on small carts. Each water carrier had his or her own customers and would bring water into the house in special containers called *Pittels*. The water set aside for drinking was immediately poured into a special filtering machine in the kitchen. It consisted of a metre-high clay or tin pipe with a diameter of approximately twenty centimetres. The water was let drip through wide layers of river sand, which purified and cleansed it, of course, only of the crudest dirt, so that the filtration mainly resulted in improving only its appearance. At the bottom was a small drainpipe with a tap, sometimes only a goose feather, through which water would drain out. In especially conscientious households, such as ours, water was then boiled and taken to the basement to cool. It was an elaborate procedure that only partially fulfilled its objective. On its long journey from the Drava to the barrel, the filtering apparatus and, finally, the kitchen pot, the water lost all its taste. In addition, it had to be used sparingly, because each drop of clean water was precious.

Also troublesome in the area were mosquitoes. Of all the existing varieties of these insects, there were none as bloodthirsty and aggressive as those in Osijek. They hatched in the wetlands and in reed forests stretching for kilometres along the Drava. They would arrive in town in thick swarms, filling all the treetops in parks and avenues, dancing inside each ray of sunshine, flying and buzzing around lamps, invading yards and houses, sticking firmly to the skin on the arms, legs and face with their burning stings, and infecting their victims with malaria, known in Osijek as the "relapsing fever". The local sour wine was believed to be the best remedy against the fever. Another consisted of throwing hot coals in the water and invoking old women's abracadabra, especially performed by women from the town periphery who had mastered the magic passed to them by their great-grandmothers. Fortune-tellers were also helping as best they could. It was a well-known fact that no herb in the world could really save people from dying. As for doctors, they were only there to collect money, their bitter medications being of no use anyway!

Until the appearance of Dr. Reinfeld on the scene, the medical practice in town had been neither particularly strenuous nor lucrative. Bacteria had been left to spread at God's will. Knowledge of sterilization, antiseptic prevention, and disinfection was scarce and vague. Typhus, dysentery, and cholera were perceived as one and the same and dealt with identically—by applying laxatives, bloodletting cups, and sweat baths. Suddenly, a new doctor was showing no intention to resort to these common treatment practices. After completing his studies in Vienna, Dr. Reinfeld practised medicine at various clinics in Berlin, Vienna, and Paris. He was acquainted with all the branches and methods of modern medicine and seemed remarkably keen to exercise his profession the way he had learned it. In severe cases, he would make a house call two and sometimes even three times a day. He would accept emergency night calls without notice and did everything possible to save a patient's life even when others had given up. This was all the more unusual as family doctors had not been paid in those days according to the number of house calls. Instead, on 1 January each year, they would receive a lump sum in the form of an advance payment, established according to the patient's own estimates and discreetly slipped into the doctor's pocket in a sealed envelope. Depending on a family's financial circumstances, the sum varied between fifty and one hundred and fifty guldens. My parents were paying the highest rate out of gratitude. From the start of his first year of practice in town, Dr. Reinfeld had managed to cure my mother, who had been ill for a long time and become excessively frail. He had simply prescribed bed rest and a special diet to help her gain weight.

There was in those days a definite lack of young men of marriageable material. The officers of the 78th Regiment were rarely welcome pretenders due to the fact that the military authorities required a deposit of some 30,000 guldens to issue a permission to marry. Their presence therefore caused more panic than joy in families with several marriageable daughters. Besides officers, there were also occasional short-term-contract employees and legal trainees, a few government and private employees, and students back home for summer vacations. Under such circumstances, Dr. Reinfeld was perceived as an ideal Céladon[137] as well as a great catch! Not only young girls but also mature women had their eyes set on him, the latter either on account of their marriageable daughters, or because of their own need to break away from the monotony of a long marriage and to enjoy some liberty in their life. The doctor was a good-looking man, tall and blond, with a fair complexion and delicate hands. I am bringing this up here because it was an entirely unusual feature for such an impressive man. He completely occupied my thoughts at the time, and in fact, he was my first great, unrequited love, which lasted from when I was twelve until I was sixteen, adding a lot of bittersweet emotional content to the general state of crisis during my years of puberty. During that period, I was enjoying an exalted sentimental state of bliss, which was my deepest secret and from which I could find no relief beyond a few silly love poems, which I wrote down in iambs and trochees on pink paper and ripped into small pieces right away, feeling ashamed of myself.

Puppy love should never be taken lightly. By its intensity, it is just as powerful as that felt by adults. In fact, it is often deeper than adult love. It sprouts in virgin soil and its power potential is still unexploited. It harbours no frivolous or dishonest thoughts. And since it finds no understanding, it enhances the feeling of spiritual loneliness and easily becomes a source of apathy, which is difficult to cure.

Our afternoon refreshment offerings gained in popularity with the arrival of the doctor because meeting him at our house was practically assured. Several new ladies joined the get-togethers at that time, among them a certain Frenchwoman, Madame Gabrielle, an excitable lady of that hazardous age once called *entre deux ages*, who fell madly in love with our doctor. Since he failed to acknowledge her affection, she resorted one day to swallowing several morphine pills. The doctor was immediately summoned, and he managed to bring her back to life. From then on, he was considered not just her personal physician, but also a saviour in distress and the comforter of her wounded soul. She would come to our house every day to be at least for a while face to face with her "Mr. Wonderful" himself.

Miss Stella Hayek was, like Madame Gabrielle, a newcomer among our guests. Her reputation had been rather tarnished, due to two previously broken engagements. The rumour was it that she was about to become engaged for the third time, when she asked my mother's permission to pay us a visit. They had previously known each other. One day at lunchtime, while I was dispatched to the kitchen to fetch bread, my mother declared—admitting right away that it might sound judgmental on her part—that it was well known that Miss Stella was chasing after men. If she suddenly wanted to pay us a visit, it was merely for the sake of the doctor! Still standing by the door, I could overhear my father replying that it was all sheer small-town gossip, and that we should, as always, keep out of it. So, from then onwards, Miss Stella could be counted as a regular guest at our afternoon gatherings. She was charming and I liked her. She wore a tight-fitting green suit made of woollen fabric lined with fur, and on her head a tilted little hat, from under which spilled thick curls of reddish hair. She had large eyes full of childish wonder and a small, always slightly half-opened mouth revealing her shiny teeth. Since I knew that she was there because of the doctor, I watched her every step. I would be waiting for her at the front door and, while she sat at the table, would lean on her shoulder, inhale her fine perfume and fiddle with the watch chain wound around her waist.

It is amazing how I remember it all in such detail! I can still visualize the room and the people—their joys and sorrows, insecurities and aspirations, their petty barely concealed animosities and childish jealousy, obsessed with the desire for self-affirmation and assertion. I can clearly see the round dining table, mounted on a massive, finely carved foot featuring animal motifs in the Late Renaissance style. I can also see the beige checkered tablecloth with its red embroidery in an *à la grecque* style and long fringes. Or the even prettier one made of the finest silky damask, rose-coloured, and embroidered with huge birds, butterflies, and all kinds of fluttering creatures. Sixty years have gone by since then, and it gives me great joy to be able to write about it and, by putting it all down on paper, rescue from oblivion some of the things once so dear to me. I can still see the large teacups, white on the inside, and beautifully light blue with intertwining gold lines outside, adorned with little gold handles and gold edges. There were also silver baskets and platters on the table. The serving glass bowls bore my mother's monogram. Depending on the time of the year, different seasonal treats were served—small walnut-filled croissants for Christmas, Berlin-style doughnuts (*Krapfen*) for the carnival, and on the occasion of the Jewish Purim festivities, the gorgeous Purim kindle cake, the mere preparation of which provided us children with the fore-taste of the approaching celebration. All the almonds, raisins, arancini, lemon juice, cinnamon, and vanilla that went into its preparation created an impression of a divine abundance that seemed way beyond what I imagined *manna* from heaven itself could have been like. Only my grand-mother knew how to prepare it with such unsurpassed mastery and with her death, the recipe was lost forever.

In the corner of the living room stood a piano. It was the same one my mother used to practise on when she was a girl but had rarely played since. It was a long yellow trunk occupying half of the room. There were two engravings hanging on the wall above it: one showing Bach giving a morning concert surrounded by his numerous family members, and another of a dying Mozart listening to the performance of his own requiem for the first and last time. It was now Miss Stella who sat at the piano and played. She looked charming in her pink silk blouse, with her white round face and dimples in her cheeks when she laughed. The doctor would stand close to her, leaning on the piano. I forgot to mention earlier that he gave the impression of being a rather surly person, abrupt, austere, and unap-proachable, much like the typical heroes of numerous novels written in those days for adolescent girls. I was not allowed to read them at the time, but devoured them despite the prohibition, as they were able to transport me to a sphere of the highest emotions and made my heart beat faster whenever, after a long period of hesitation and apprehension, the "wonderful" hero would finally reveal his true feelings and choose the humble and adoring Cinderella for his bride.

Miss Stella and I were both experiencing all the well-known phases of trepidation of a heartfelt love. I could notice the way she looked at "Mr. Wonderful" and that it was for him alone that she played the piano and sang. Her repertoire, to tell the truth, consisted only of arias from popular operettas such as *The Beggar Student, La Belle Hélène,* or *The Gypsy Baron.* "Let me tell you who married us! A bullfinch[138] in the woods, with a blue dome like a cathedral above our heads, and a nightingale singing nearby," she sighed and sang with tremolos and flamboyance. At that point, poor Madame Gabrielle, who had meanwhile been conversing in broken German with my grandmother, suddenly became ill and had to be taken to the bedroom to lie down on a sofa, upon which the doctor was forced to stop the concert and check the afflicted woman's pulse. The following day, before the other guests arrived, Aunt Tinka told my mother, "That little schemer wants to ensnare the doctor, but there are a few things that should be outright and openly said about it. If nobody decides to speak, I surely won't keep quiet!" Upon which my mother dispatched me out of the room, as was usually the case whenever "such matters" were discussed. There was nothing else for me to do but disappear to the kitchen, because, much as Miss Goldschmidt had taken care of me, Miss Kaiser, in contrast, neglected me. She made her own life easier by declaring that I was irreparable, that I refused to follow her advice and ignored her punishments, and therefore the best thing for her was to leave me alone. I was entirely in agreement with that new educational method and she busied herself thereupon with some secretive occupations of her own. Marija, the cook, explained to me that Miss Kaiser was herself in love with the doctor and that she was busy writing him love letters.

One day, Aunt Tinka barged into the room earlier than usual, the ribbons of her hat untied, and her jacket buttoned up the wrong way. I first thought that there had been an accident. Then whispers and muttering began, from which I could only discern that it was about my beloved Stella and that something had happened to her. Miss Kitty arrived earlier than usual as well, all flushed in the face, due to haste and excitement.

She went straight to the dining room, threw herself into the nearest arm-chair, and took a few deep sighs before regaining her voice. I heard her talk about some great disgrace facing the doctor, and how only God would have been able to advise him how to entangle himself. But it served him right, because, as the saying went, "Don't look at the jug, but rather focus on what is inside it!"

Miss Stella did not show up for tea that afternoon, and the doctor excused himself as well, being detained, as he explained, by an emergency. When Stella did not come the day after, or the following day either, I became worried and insisted on being told what had happened to her. Mother refused to say anything. I was so concerned that I went to the kitchen and inquired with Marija, who at first did not want to talk either. I would not let it go and I kept asking, so she finally exclaimed, "Stella is expecting."

The explanation only partially satisfied me. Something unclear was hovering in my mind, something that girls at school whispered about in secret, about having children and certain inappropriate and incredible activities connected with that. I knew there was something mysterious behind it, which was bothering me and which I was unable to resolve. I had often heard women in the Long Courtyard talk about it, but never in a clear enough way for me. I knew, though, that women bring children into the world. Cats and dogs have their young ones, too. I saw it with my own eyes down in the yard. But everything else was vague and I could not understand what my beautiful, beloved Stella had to do with such stories. I was sure the cook was mistaken. She must have been confused, because what she was saying could not have been true! Only married women could have children! So how could then Stella, without a husband?

The cook laughed. "She does have a husband. That is the thing. She has even got two, and now she wants to catch the third!" She could not stand Stella because, to begin with, Stella was beautiful and young, and secondly, because she was one of the worst tippers among our guests. What was someone of that kind even doing in our house?

I was speechless. How could it be? My ideas about strict marital monogamy were forever shattered!

The cook continued. "She had her fun with the First Lieutenant Dobrzhinski. They were very much in love together. But Dobrzhinski can't marry her because officers are expensive, and Stella doesn't have the money for the required deposit to get married. That is why she had her mind set on our doctor. For him, however, it has turned into a huge embarrassment because he was entirely unaware of what was going on. Then Aunt Tinka intervened and enlightened him. She did it because her plan was to see him marry her sister Adela and there was no way she would let 'a girl of that kind' snatch a good match in front of her nose."

The cook told all that with obviously malicious pleasure, adding a few more moralistic comments that could all be summed up as follows: "Men are not to be trusted! At first, they are God knows how polite, promising a girl the stars and the moon from the sky, and then they leave her hanging, in disgrace and stuck with a bastard child." The cook also had a child, a little three-year-old boy, and that made me think. Maybe she had gone through the same thing herself? But even then, she must have been mistaken and the explanation must have been elsewhere, because making mere promises to someone, even if they were stars from the sky, could not bring little children to this world! Even more confusing was how to figure out why all this should be shameful!

My frequent visits to the kitchen gradually led me in the right direction and my sexual enlightenment finally developed so much that I could conclude certain things even from partial hints. But the moment my curiosity was satisfied, and I found out everything Marija had to say about the topic, I kept avoiding conversations of that kind, both in the kitchen and at school. Moreover, it was not that those ambiguous allusions had any appeal to me. On the contrary, I found them repulsive. Since early childhood, I had had a lot of understanding for all the natural occurrences, whether it concerned plants, animals, or people. I sensed the meaning of motherhood early. That is why I could not connect that phenomenon with any kind of indecent thought. I had already acquired notions of the cyclical aspect of life on earth, including that of human beings. The mystery of birth and death engaged my thoughts and awoke a deep sense of wonder and respect. I thought it was a miracle and I could never understand why people talked about the birth of a child in a secretive and obscure manner or made stupid jokes, as was common at the time.

The social coercion in such matters was in those days more rigorous than today. Remarrying after a divorce was out of the question, and a divorced woman, whether guilty or innocent, was forever socially stigmatized. It was even worse for so-called seduced girls. There was no way they could recover from their "fall". A man was allowed to break a marriage, but never a woman. In order to get married, a girl had to wait for someone to choose her, and, if she had no proper dowry, her marriage prospects were generally slim. Old unmarried relatives were superfluous appendages to their families and a typical laughingstock in popular literature. They could only find relief in silly chatter and idle gossip about things they had themselves been deprived of forever. People enjoyed speaking about these topics, sometimes ambiguously but also in straightforward terms. It tickled their lascivious imaginations, prompted laughter, spiced up conversation, and chased away boredom. When such subjects were raised at our afternoon gatherings, I no longer waited for my mother's signal, but left of my own accord and with a look of contempt on my face. It annoyed me that they were letting me know that these conversations were not for little girls, as if I cared about them anyway! In fact, I could not stop wondering how grown-ups could entertain themselves in such a childish way.

As far as Stella is concerned, I found out only several years later that she had left Osijek, had a baby, and later sang and danced in a big city music hall. She used to be so beautiful and sweet and I felt profoundly sorry for her! It might have been that, moved by the story of her misfortune implicating the object of my own first love interest, I experienced a transference of my feelings from one object to the other.

It could be said that by the end of the 1880s and the beginning of the 1890s, Western European Jews had not yet truly espoused Jewish nationalism. That came later, triggered by various events, but most of all the rise of Zionism. Being Jewish was founded on religious grounds and on the fact that persistent resistance and societal and religious pressure from the outside had reinforced and tightened the sense of community. There was no doubt that, notwithstanding the legally sanctioned equality, Jews had remained outsiders. The host community refused to accept them as equals. I paid no attention to such things. I felt much closer to my friends from the Long Courtyard than to the "nice" Jewish children my German governess wanted me to befriend. While I rejected refined snobbery, there was still something within me, in the way I spoke or in my temperament that distinguished me from the children in the Long Courtyard. At issue was not only my stronger power of imagination, my inquisitiveness, my quest for knowledge or my spiritedness, but my tendency to be critical and my definite scepticism.

In that vein, my attitude towards Judaism was also more negative than positive. Why did I have to be different from other children? Why could I not join in their attractive religious celebrations? Why could I, all dressed in white, not walk with others in the procession on the feast day of Corpus Christi? If all my friends at school could do that, why could not I? My mother explained, "They are Christians and you are Jewish." I then wanted to know why I was Jewish. "Because you were born that way!" I explained to her that all children are born equal. In the Long Courtyard, at the house of the Sokolić family, I saw a small, newborn baby girl. Why was she a Christian and I was not?

My mother explained, "You are of a particular descent. All your ancestors, grandfathers and grandmothers, as well as your parents, are Jewish, so you can't be anything else. We Jews have a different confession of faith." This did not enlighten me a great deal because I actually was a non-believer. More to the point, I was born here, just like all the other children from Franjina Street and the Long Courtyard. I knew every stone there and loved every blade of grass growing there. It never occurred to me that I should have some other homeland than this one. What was the origin of my Judaism? I had no knowledge of its rituals and had never practised them. I retained vague but pleasant memories of the Sabbath celebrated at my grandparents' house in the Lower Town, but in my parents' house, we never followed the rituals surrounding the Sabbath, the Passover Seder, or the autumn festivities. We never observed the regulations concerning ritually prepared food and looked at it as an anachronistic encumbrance.

My father was the vice president of the Jewish Community, but he based his active participation on ethical and charitable principles, which had no specific Jewish, but rather universal humanistic foundations. Here I must point out right away that the charitable work of my mother, and even more so, my grandmother, extended beyond the religious confines. My grandmother used to give a lot, and with pleasure, wherever it was most needed, regardless of religion, and since there were more poor Christians in town than poor Jews, she mostly helped the Christians. Each first day of the month, old women (her former laundrywomen, maids, servants, and other poor people) appeared at our house door and received a gulden each. She was giving away clothes and food, and I never again in my whole life met someone who knew how to give with so much tactfulness, cheerfulness, and kindness. At Christmas, she put together heaps of gift baskets, each containing the flour, eggs, butter, and walnuts necessary to prepare the obligatory Christmas croissants, with an additional apple and walnuts for children. No woman who happened to knock at my grandmother's door asking for charity was ever turned away. She was never left waiting outside, no matter how ragged she was. My grandmother would lead her to the kitchen, offer her a warm cup of coffee, and treat her the same way as any other guest. She asked about her miseries and circumstances in life and wanted to know how she could help. And she did help many of those who were still able to do some work by finding them jobs. In the case of the poorest and most helpless, she used to inform charitable institutions about them and made sure they received help. She did all that bursting with happiness for being offered a chance to help. She invested all her energies into it and was pleased to be of service to another human being.

That same bright tone and spiritedness characterized her religious devoutness. It mostly consisted of celebrating religious festivities. Even though I knew her quite well, I would not be able to say anything more on her personal relationship with God. I could not tell how deep her belief was, how she imagined Him, how much of her service to God came from long-established habit, and how much of it was related to her inner need. Besides, I think these things could hardly be kept separate. Old habits with time turn into irrefutable truths, just as people become attached to useless old objects and losing them is painful. Since she rarely went out of the house in her old age, attending the holiday service at the temple became her favourite pastime. After moving to the Upper Town, she had her permanent seat in the temple, in the first row of the women's balcony. There she sat leaning forward, as if in a theatre loggia, intensely watching either the balcony on the opposite side or the ground floor where men, covered in their white prayer shawls, performed the actual rituals. On those occasions, my grandmother wore a dress made of light black silk, a triangular shawl around her shoulders made of Venetian lace, and her golden watch on a chain around her neck. On holidays, she wore a dainty bonnet made of lace, which in her younger years, had been of a lighter colour—beige or cream with purple or violet ribbons—but became later in her life exclusively black, in perfect contrast to her grey hair. She used to order her bonnets from Mrs. Galimberti, one of the leading Viennese hat makers in those days.

When I turned ten years old, my grandmother suggested that I should be at least symbolically involved in the half-day fasting in the commemoration of Yom Kippur, the Day of Atonement, dedicated to the alleviation of all mental strains caused by oppositional forces that inflict our life. In the name of repentance for all committed sins in the previous year, the holiday was usually a period of fasting and prayer. My grandmother explained to me that it was a wonderful feeling to be able to bury one's hatred and pave a new road to love. However, my father got angry and told her that it might be so in her case but not for his children, who should grow up to be modern people. He did not want us to take part in such old-fashioned rituals, including fasting, be it half a day or daylong. His wish was for us to blend into our surroundings, to look for human values in all people, to love our neighbours, avoid injustice, and acquire a good education. Religion was not a question of the stomach, but rather an innermost need— or nothing!

My mother tried to intervene as she found it most inappropriate to expose young children to doubt. From time immemorial, religion had been the centre of Jewish life and it was impossible to disassociate the two. Maintaining public forms of practice was a matter of an innate sense of solidarity. My father was upset because my grandmother brought up a sensitive subject, about which he was rather inflexible. It was his opinion that, since Jews had been finally accepted, it was up to them to dispel any prejudices still existing against them. They should, under these new conditions, abandon the centuries-old ghetto mentality that continued to define their separatist attitude, and occasionally amounted to Jewish self-sufficiency. They should overcome that tendency towards separatism and accommodate themselves in the outside world. There should be nothing about them to make them different, whether in their dress, speech, or customs. They must be good Jews inside the temple and, with equal conviction, good citizens outside it. Solidarity should not refer to the mere solidarity among Jews with a potential aim of creating a state within a state, if necessary, but rather a solidarity with all good and decent people, wherever they were.

Discussions of that kind did not contribute in any way to the strengthening of my religious feelings. I preferred to think about that topic as little as possible. I considered the religion classes I was obliged to attend twice a week, as a necessary evil and their pointlessness drove me to despair. We children approached these religion classes with an attitude of passive resistance by not doing our homework and spending the time in the classroom staging mischief, shouting, and making all sorts of noises. We would eat our sandwiches in front of our teacher's nose, laughing in his face when he scolded us about it, tapping our feet against the floor and banging the lids of our desks. As for studying, we did not learn a thing. In the first four years of primary school, we never went beyond the rudiments of Hebrew, reading from our Hebrew textbook. Under the Bible studies, on the other hand, we covered the narrative from Adam and Eve to the Deluge in a very primitive manner, and that was more or less all. The classes were not held at school but in the derelict building of the Jewish Community in Njemačka ulica (German Street). The classrooms were stuffy and stank of mould. Everything exuded poverty, backwardness, dirt, and disorder, the blame for which lay partially with the teachers who were not up to their task, as much as with the pupils themselves. This confessional school was once attended only by the poorest of children. Many of them did not go home for lunch at noon, but ate "per day", which meant that every day they had lunch in a different, well-to-do family house in town. It was a long-standing custom among Jews but, although conceived as an act of generosity, it hardly evoked pleasant feelings in its recipients.

The religious education given to us in such a way contributed little to our edification and did nothing towards developing our sensitivity or stimulating our thinking. We knew almost nothing about the classical Judaism of Biblical times (except for a few legends from the Book of Genesis), and nothing about the fate of our brothers in faith from the early days of exile onwards. Nothing about cruel persecutions in the Middle Ages and Catholic superstitions and fanaticism directed against Jews, nothing about mass killings during the Crusades, the false blood libels, and the slaughter of innocent women and children. Nothing about harassment and restrictions or material penalties and charges imposed on them. Nothing about mass expulsions from Spain and Portugal, the Inquisition, and the fate of those Spanish Jews who converted to Christianity. Nothing about the malicious and perverse accusations of ritual killings, host desecration and well poisoning, and so many other imagined sins that Jews had to expiate with their lives and their possessions for centuries. We learned nothing about their tenacious resistance to all those abominable deeds against them. There was not just one, but thousands upon thousands of messiahs among them, who suffered on the cross because of their beliefs. We had no idea about the mental strength, which kept them going, or about the optimism in their perception of life, which had inspired them for centuries. We were not too young to be told about it, however. Children always have a lot of understanding for heroism, both admiring it and trying to imitate it. But we were taught none of that. We struggled to spell the letters in our Hebrew textbook, listened to the squawky voices that came out of our teachers' mouths, and sang in a choir, without ever realizing that it was the great common suffering of those people, our forefathers, which brought them together, strengthened their awareness and sense of collectivity, and became the foundation of the Jewish religion. We learned nothing about Jewish spiritual values or Jewish humanism, which recognized the presence of God in each living creature and inevitably led to the awareness of the unity of all life on earth. Furthermore, we were not taught to look at the Bible with the respect it deserved as one of the first written records of the power of human spirit, as a narrative of people's varied destinies, as an anthology of human wisdom, and a stream of beautiful poetry contained in "The Song of Songs" and the psalms.

In the last two decades of the nineteenth century, Jewish children were kept oblivious of all that. Our religion teachers did not recognize the necessity, felt no inner drive, nor possessed the skills to raise us as Jews. They were uneducated, inert, phlegmatic, with no understanding for young people and the times in which we lived. The old world was dying out and the new one emerging with its outlines blurred in the hazy distance. We experienced a period of disconnectedness during our youth, and as life went on, we got the impression that in fact a superfluous burden had been lifted from our shoulders. It was, nevertheless, during that time, that Arthur de Gobineau[139] developed his new and extremely dangerous racial theory; that Houston Stewart Chamberlain[140] wrote his book on the foundations of the nineteenth century, imbued with hatred towards the Jews; that the first anti-Semitic fiery speeches were delivered in the German and Austrian parliaments; and that, in Russia and Romania, pogroms were the order of the day. It was at that time that Karl Lueger[141] established the Austrian Christian Social Party and Jewish students were physically harassed at the University of Vienna. While all that was going on, our class was told to continue reciting out loud and in unison from our Hebrew textbooks, regardless of the fact that we could not tell the meaning of a single word we read. Our teacher, Mr. Essig—uncombed, unshaven, and wearing a dirty shirt and a crooked tie—would meanwhile sit in his chair in front of the class, absorbed with extracting raisins from a paper bag he was holding in one hand, throwing them into the air and into his mouth, while at the same time chasing annoying flies buzzing around his nose. From time to time, his head would drop to his chest, we would stop our monotonous singsong and without delay dash out of the classroom and into the yard, yelling and bawling. The noise would wake him up. He would then grab his stick and rush angrily after us, hardly ever managing to catch us and making us return to the classroom.

I stopped playing in the Long Courtyard by the time I began attending the secondary school for girls and its more comprehensive curriculum considerably broadened my interests. I had no difficulties with my studies and was always good in composition and mathematics. My weakness was discipline. I was bursting with crazy ideas that would make the whole class laugh and was therefore more popular among my classmates than my teachers. In addition to school, I was attending private lessons in drawing, German language, and piano.

My drawing teacher was a certain Mr. Waldinger,[142] an artist of great talent, especially in the field of graphic art. The people in Osijek did not appreciate his art and he was forced to work as an office janitor for the Business Association to provide for his family. Lacking in options, he was mostly working on his paintings along the shores of the River Drava, where he could find countless motifs to paint in different seasons and under different effects of light. He was an obsessive loner of his own making, drawing thousands of sketches that he kept for himself and showed to no one. His paintings were done in the Albrecht Dürer's style in an exceptionally wide range of delicate strokes. His pictures of the River Drava with weeping willows, grey skies, and the sluggish muddy water were the expression of his deep melancholy. Each detail of his paintings had a meaning of its own, the river, the horizon, and the willow trees were always different, and not only due to the changing natural lighting but according to the painter's mood—because it was only while painting that he became alive and delighted in unveiling things undetected by other people.

As a painter, Waldinger was undoubtedly an unrecognized genius. As a pedagogue, on the other hand, he was unfortunately hopeless. He was terribly pedantic. All he cared about was practising technique and that obsession of his turned out to be a torture for me. He never thought of teaching me how to observe, so that I could identify on my own the particularities of the things he forced me to draw. As a result, I never properly learned how to do it. In the course of two years practising drawing with him, I never drew what I saw or at least what I thought I saw. To my misfortune, Waldinger had a thick folder full of samples and he made me copy them again and again—eyes that were open wide or shut halfway, their pupils directed upwards or downwards; eyes showing surprise or fear; but most often eyes looking empty, with the face turned forward or in profile. I drew dozens of earlobes, with only minute features to distinguish one lobe from the other. Then came noses with dilated nostrils, mouths smiling or sulking, hair curled into wonderful locks, and then again eyes, with or without any expression.

I kept copying for a year, and then for one more. In all that time, I never drew a single human face in its entirety, nor a landscape, or a house, or a tree, or anything that had something to do with real nature or be the expression of my own creative ability. I must admit, though, that my hand became so skilled due to constant practice that I did not even have to look at his samples anymore. I could have easily copied them in my sleep. I remained, however, forever incapable of drawing a real person's face, or anything in its completeness. It could easily be said that my acquired virtuosity prevented me from doing so. Of course, it would be unfair to put the whole blame on the teacher, his collection of samples, or his methodology. Someone like the great painter Raphael would have probably managed to overcome it. But I was no Raphael and I finally gave up.

A similar thing happened with my musical education. It was not because I had no sense for music, but rather because of the teaching methods applied by my teachers. I changed teachers five times and each time I had to start with a different system of education and a different fingering technique. I would hardly get used to one teacher's whims, when there would be a change and the new "music master" would decide that everything I had learned so far was wrong and my playing technique ineffective. I was taught to play by using my fingers, my wrists, my elbows, and shoulders, with the result that I started experiencing the playing of music as nothing more than a physical exercise. My first teacher was Mr. Schwarz, who lived with the Mihajlović family in the building situated at the end of the Long Courtyard facing the street. He cared for two things in his life—music and his small silky pinscher with overgrown curly hair. His name was Popocatepetl, but mostly called Pompush. Mr. Schwarz was tall and gaunt in appearance, with a beard that reached to his waist, the longest I had ever seen in my life. As he played, the beard would slide over the keyboard along with his fingers, turning his playing into a highly compelling thing to watch. He was a typical Protestant, born in Klagenfurt—petty, stuck in his ways, and incredibly patient with his pupils. However, that patience was so unswerving and endless that it would occasionally bring me to despair. It made the piano lessons excessively boring and continually forced us as students to achieve something impossible.

He had his own method, based on a specific hand and finger posture. The wrist had to be raised high up, hands steady and stiff, making the fingers do all the work. He would place a coin on the sloping back of our hand, insisting that it should stay in place and under no circumstance be allowed to slide off while we were practising scales, chords, or finger movements. The coin inevitably kept falling off, which meant starting whatever we were practising all over again, for the tenth, twentieth, and even the hundredth time. The sound and keystrokes would become weaker because all the attention would focus on that small coin, ready to slide down as soon as the playing began. It would keep gliding up and down and, before you noticed it, land on the keys. In the end, there was no point in trying anymore—the attempt failed, the fingers stiffened and turned more and more wooden until the music stopped altogether! A brilliant musician like Wolfgang Amadeus Mozart might have overcome such obstacles, but I was no Mozart. That realization made me shed angry tears before and after each lesson, as it became more and more obvious each time that I would never be able to master what was required of me.

I also had private lessons in German with an evangelical pastor who lived nearby. I am grateful to him for helping me master my German orthography at the early age of twelve. This enabled me to pass with success the entrance exam to the finishing school in Vienna and skip the whole final year of the high school for girls in my hometown. During pastor Pindor's lessons, I began reading German classics. My first assignment was Goethe's *Hermann und Dorothea*, followed by Schiller's *Wilhelm Tell*.[143] Since classes at school lasted from eight until twelve in the morning and from three to five in the afternoon, and walking to school and back took up another hour and a half—not to mention numerous hours of private tutoring—I hardly had any free time left. At the same time, I was a passionate reader and read everything I could lay my hands on. Being by nature outgoing and excitable, I felt a great need to report to other people about things I had read or experienced after I had first thoroughly processed their impact in my mind. My joy doubled if others became involved as well. I must admit that I did not always report my experience in a fully truthful manner—I allowed myself considerable poetic freedom and often presented things as I wished them to be or to take place, and in that way made "reality and poetry"[144] inextricably intertwined.

It was at that time that I made a new friend, Ana. We had already met in primary school but became inseparable only in high school years. We lived next door to each other, and it seemed natural that we walk the long way to school, located in the Fortress, together. That provided me with a lot of time to tell my stories, and Ana was an appreciative listener. Often the stories I told were for mere amusement, but mostly they were my renditions of whole sections of the most recent books I had read. Sometimes I would fail to dissociate my daydreaming from reality. I probably was not even capable of making that distinction at the time. I would succumb to the appeal of the images provided by my imagination. They would carry me away, as they were so convincing, and the daydreams so perfect and so much happier than my actual experiences, whether at school or at home. I was overjoyed that Ana trusted me and without any doubt followed me on that path lined with roses. She was not of a critical mind and I have been grateful to her for that to this day!

We sat next to each other in class and helped one another with schoolwork. She was better at handicraft and drawing and I did better in other subjects. That friendship was so deep and heartfelt that I simply cannot remember being friends with anyone else in those days. However, a few other familiar faces occasionally spring up from the darkness of oblivion, and with them specific events and anecdotes from my school days. The event that left the deepest and unforgettable impression on me took place in the fifth year of high school and, at the time, made me immensely happy. Our headmistress in those days was Miss Klotilda Cvetišić. Due to her professional qualifications, powerful personality, and understanding of youth, she stood out among other teachers. She showed a lot of consideration for my restless temper, particularly evident on one occasion. I was absorbed in composing some poetry under the desk during her history class, when she suddenly startled me out of my poetic trance and asked me to repeat what she had just said. In that moment, I did not even know where I was or what was expected of me. I kept staring at her, frightened and silent. She took from me the notebook and with it my pathetic poetic composition in iambic hexameter, in which I was expressing in most loving terms my admiration for my best friend. The way they were written, my exalted phrases could have just as well been directed at a male person and be considered a serious offence for a pupil attending the school for girls. It was interpreted as a manifestation of a corrupt character punishable with a bad mark in behaviour. There were known cases of slightly more mature girls attending fifth-year classes accused of going out with boys and consequently receiving lower grades. For that reason, with my heart pounding, I went that same afternoon to see the headmistress in her office with the idea of explaining my situation and getting my notebook back. The sight of Miss Cvetišić's lovely, kind face looking at me filled me suddenly with so much loving emotion that I could not utter a word. Instead of scolding me, she surprised me with a question: "Do you often write such things? I heard that you were competing with Rety recently. You were both writing a poem on the same topic. That was very brave of you, considering that you are only in the fifth grade and Rety is in the eighth, and she has the best mark in German composition."

"That is exactly why! She is terribly conceited, and I wanted to tell her off."

"And how did that thing end?"

"Very well!" I exclaimed, with evident pride. "I won."

"And what was the topic?"

"We were both writing about motherly love."

Miss Cvetišić then expressed the wish that I bring her my poem the following day. But I was so pleased with her interest that I did not want to postpone the big moment until the next day. I told her that I knew the poem by heart and that I was ready, if she so wished, to recite it right there. She agreed. I was suddenly as excited and shaken up as a debutante on her very first audition that might determine the course of her entire future life. I took my position and began. I was whispering at first because I had a lump in my throat, but then I let go and declaimed my poem with the ultimate available pathos. Then a miracle occurred. As I finished, I could see gleaming tears in Miss Cvetišić's eyes. She was obviously touched and left speechless for a moment, but then she put her arms around me, pulled me close and kissed me.

I was in a state of total bliss! Miss Cvetišić had kissed me! I had touched her deepest emotions. She stood close to me, I felt her warmth and the light smell of her clothes and saw her kind, still beautiful face leaning towards me and I kissed it back with trembling lips. I put into that kiss all the affection I had in me—all veneration, and even idolization. I was astounded that something so miraculous could have happened to me. I felt immense gratitude along with an exalted admiration of her as a person, as well as satisfaction and vanity, that I was loved and that I had actually managed to touch someone's heart with my poem! All of that filled me with immense pleasure and joy. Except that the joy turned too soon into an unfathomable sadness, as it became immediately clear to me that the occasion was unique and would never happen again. It was a star shining for a while over my horizon as it was shooting across the sky and, before I was even aware of it, faded away into the darkness. Miss Cvetišić gave me my notebook back, with no mention of punishment or consequences. I closed the door of her office behind me and soon realized the following day that the usual relationship between pupil and teacher had been duly re-established. She behaved as if nothing had happened the day before and treated me in the same way as all the other girls in the classroom. In a romantic outburst, I dedicated a poem to her, inscribed it in ornate letters on a pink sheet of paper rimmed with roses and blue forget-me-nots, and carried it personally to her apartment. An older lady I had never seen before opened the door and explained that Miss Cvetišić was not at home. Miss Cvetišić made no mention afterwards of that poetic masterpiece of mine, but that short moment of happiness has never been forgotten nor surpassed in its importance during the rest of my life. Miss Cvetišić, however, left Osijek while I was in my sixth year and Miss Pinterović took over. She was a good and fair teacher, but she could never properly replace my beloved Miss Cvetišić.

I walked to school with Ana, but according to my parents' wishes, my German governess was supposed to accompany me on my way back home. She thus dutifully came every day to school to pick me up. I found, however, no pleasure in being taken home on a leash like a poodle and often managed to avoid that embarrassment by resorting to skilful manoeuvres. It was my luck that the school had two exits. When lessons were over for the day, I would send one of my girlfriends to find out at which exit the governess was waiting to take me home. Of course, I chose the other door where there was no danger of meeting her. I would waste no time and dash out, and then take a quick turn around the first corner, with a whole gang of my accomplices behind me. Ana was naturally one of them, serving as a rearguard. We would quickly reach the ivy-covered Water Gate, and from there descend straight to the ditches at the bottom of the fortress walls.

Nothing in the world would have made me give up the pleasure of sidetracking on my way home into this romantic world of moats and casemates. There I felt as if I were in an enchanted garden, that I was unbound and free, and occasionally also admired as a heroine by my girlfriends, who would cheer loudly at the daring things I would risk undertaking. Everything was exotic and unusual in those trenches, abandoned for decades to rot and decay, starting with the heavy musty smell of the old walls and the ancient legends about them, through to the abundance of plant life growing there. Plants of all sorts were rooted in the walls, branching out, their vines intertwining and trailing up the walls, some like thick cords, others as tiny delicate threads. They were so entwined that they provided a firm footing for potential climbers. I often climbed up to fetch a bunch of fronds of a particular fern that grew there and nowhere else in Osijek. In certain places, among yellow or greenish-grey coloured lichens and moss, one could discover tufts of beautiful bluebells that looked as if they were embroidered in silk. There was also a succulent plant carrying pink flowers, and heather with red flowers turning into violet, and blooming only in May. A variety of small shrubs conveniently served as footholds while climbing, because they were solidly rooted in the deep cracks in the walls where they could find traces of earth and moisture.

This was the general decor. The main attraction was down in the moats, amid stagnant waters, where white water lilies quietly floated. Their roots spread for several metres in all directions, while, on the surface, huge, round, dark green leaves provided a contrasting backdrop for the wonderfully beautiful flowers glowing shiny and white in that poisonous green swamp. We would have loved to be able to pick them, but they seemed out of reach, surrounded by all that water and mud. One awkward step forward would suffice for our feet to sink into mud and get entangled in the roots. I had tried several times. On one such occasion, I took off my socks and shoes, tucked my dress up to the waist, and waded in. I immediately started sinking into the ground and sliding into the web of all kinds of roots, although the water hardly reached above my knees. There was no firm ground, nothing to grab and hold on. I was sinking so fast it seemed as if some magic force was working against me. I was a good swimmer, but there was no way one would possibly wish to swim in that water. Images of vicious wingless dragons from my fairy tales, dangerous Medusas grabbing people with their tentacles, and even venomous snakes hidden in those waters came to mind and I became frightened out of my wits. The task of those creatures was undoubtedly to guard the White Princess from a bold snatcher like me. I suddenly could not make another step forward.

Swarming around above the surface of the water were greenish gnats, glimmering mayflies, dragonflies, and hornets. Duckweeds were floating on the surface of the water everywhere around me. I stood there for a moment until I realized that the hem of my rolled-up dress was wet. I had no choice but to go back, without even coming close to a water lily. However, there were other flowers on the banks—yellow buttercups, blue forget-me-nots, and marsh marigolds. Countless frogs could be heard in the grass. As we moved around, the frogs took flight into the water and the lizards hurriedly looked for shelter in the cracks of the walls. We picked as many flowers and greenery as we could carry along with our school bags, and as the sun began sinking behind the horizon, it was time to start slowly on our way home.

We climbed onto the riverbank that ran along the Drava and floundered on the narrow path by the Regiment Garden, all the way to the Upper Town. Then the most beautiful thing happened—the western sky was inflamed by the setting sun, rays of light refracted on the water, and a waterfall of light flowed over the clouds and the poplars by the river. I cannot recall encountering anything comparable to that spectacle in my life. I have seen Swiss Alpine lakes, the Rhine Falls, the banks of the River Seine upstream and downstream from Paris, the Rhône where it passes through Lake Geneva and then runs all the way to the Mediterranean Sea.

I have seen the Loire and its castles, the Garonne and its estuary on the Atlantic coast, the Danube all the way from its source near Donaueschingen, through the entire Swabia, Ulm, Regensburg, Passau, Linz, Vienna, and Budapest, down to Belgrade, and from there even further to Orşova and Turnu Severin. I have seen the two sources of the River Sava, one near Kranjska Gora, the other at the lake Bohinj. I have visited all these places during my long life, experienced them in the light of changing seasons as well as the historical and romantic aura attached to them all. Yet the River Drava, the river of my childhood, neither beautiful nor romantic, and of no historic and geographic importance, still evokes today an indescribable longing in my heart. It is the kind of longing only marginally connected with the actual landscape. It consists of delicate and inextricable threads of memories, immediate observations, associations, and childhood dreams, which, combined into one, appear vivid and colourful before my eyes. I see the sluggish waters being pierced by a sunray and turning gold. I see white foam glitter on its surface, the colour changing from soft rose to darkest purple at the spots where the river is at its deepest. I see the windblown waters dissolve into tiny hopping waves sprinkled with silver, or, under the cloak of heavy lead-coloured clouds, change colour from a dull grey into frightening tones of black and blue. I see waves swelling and racing each other, while the wind picks on the willows on the banks and bends their branches to the water. The old willows, knotted and hunched like old gnomes, resemble beasts ready to leap. The sandbanks are as smooth as melted glass and bare feet leave no trace on them. One suddenly becomes consumed with fear in the face of all that magic—the unstoppable flow, the eternal and steady rhythm, the balanced inhaling and exhaling of the surge and the calm of the water, the predestined route into the unknown distance, the streaming that never stops.

As we continued, it turned uncomfortably cool by the river and we decided to climb onto the embankment. The vista of the city spread before our eyes, with its well-known silhouette and its three distinguishable towers—the bell tower of the parish church, the shapeless water tower next to the fire station, and the funny turret on top of the City Hall. The streets were already enrobed in dusk, and houses shut tight and surrounded by silence. I finally arrived home. I was late and dishevelled, my dress was torn and dirty, my skirts wet and full of weeds, with bits of damp soil still clinging to their roots. A shower of reproaches, sanctions, and punitive measures followed. Life was again restricted, dictated by the inevitable habitual rules and overtaken by daily chores. What was left of forbidden detours, fortress moats and fairy and romantic meadows by the river turned into vague memories, although they still sometimes visit me in my dreams. I find myself stumbling around vast fields in the desperate search for something long gone. I am not just referring to the extravagant products of a schoolgirl's imagination but also to the Osijek moats, which no longer exist. It has been years since they were razed to the ground and the defence walls and ditches flattened. In their place now stretches a wide street with lovely apartment buildings, parks, and villas surrounded by gardens. What is left of their original magic is an image floating around like a restless apparition or a faded mirage from my distant childhood dreams. The person I was at the time is also long gone, as are the joys I experienced in those days. So are the sorrows. What has remained intact are fragments and details that I laboriously try to glue together into a whole.

I was in the seventh year of high school in 1893. While still the top-of-the-class student, I had never stopped being the *enfant terrible* in the classroom and never ceased making my classmates laugh. My usual tactics consisted of asking questions of our teachers that were way beyond the prescribed curriculum material. The teachers would be embarrassed and showed difficulty in answering them, sometimes even preferring not to answer them at all. The classroom would cheer which was most satisfying, primarily because I cared more about entertaining my friends than impressing my teachers with brilliant answers of my own. I always did my schoolwork in a hurried manner. I excelled in mathematics and composition but used to prepare for a lesson at the last minute and had to depend on my verbal skills to pull myself out of an occasional awkward situation.

At that time, I was mostly busy with setting up theatre presentations at our house, usually in our spacious gateway, purportedly for charity purposes. I used to write the scripts myself, direct and stage the plays, and rehearse the performances with a few girls from the neighbourhood or my school. Naturally, I always reserved the leading role for myself. Once I was a fisherman's wife, a poor widow with four starving children, all of them at least a head taller than me. One of my plays, entitled "The Rose Fairy", was written in verse. Playing the leading role, I wore my cousin Theresa's pink dancing gown and I felt like an actual creature from another world. Wardrobes of various family members were the source of most of our costumes. Otherwise, bed covers, curtains and tablecloths served equally well for makeshift costumes and stage backdrops. But that was not all. I used to write and make copies of playbills, one of which I would stick on our gate entrance door to inform our esteemed audience about the upcoming artistic event. I would also go from house to house along Franjina Street to sell tickets—three kreuzers for a balcony seat and two for a standing place on the ground floor, explaining that the proceeds were intended for charity purposes. We then bought pencils, notebooks, and sweets with the money we collected. In addition, I urged some shop owners I knew to donate as well and received from them gloves, handkerchiefs, and socks for that purpose. We would then distribute the items into ten packages and organize Christmas gift-giving for the ten poorest children at our school. I derived exceptional pleasure and happiness from those moments.

My girlfriends and I were at the time turning fourteen and some of my classmates who were more mature than others, began flirting with boys attending the boys' high school across the street from our school. I was not interested in their constant whispering and secret talks and preferred not to be involved in any of it even if my life had depended on it. I refused to grace any of those immature schoolboys with a single look the way other girls did while standing by the classroom windows and flirting while the teachers were not around. I refused to walk even a few paces with any of those boys and resisted any attempt on their behalf to approach me. I was at the time hardly a beauty. I had a chubby baby face, large, inquisitive, grey-blue eyes, and two thin braids. On top of that, I paid no attention as to how I was dressed or how my hair was done. As I did not consider myself especially good-looking, I made a point of openly showing how little I cared about my appearance and opted for a tomboyish style of my own. When my friend Ana, who was quite pretty, became an object of keen attention by the boys across the street, I urged her to behave as moralistically indignant, aloof and irritated like me. And when Ana received a beautiful rose from a shy sixth-grade schoolboy as a sign of his admiration, I coerced her into throwing it away with indignation. But I still did not find that enough. I persuaded her to come with me to the headmistress's office and report the boy's misdeed.

However, I too had my big secret, my hidden heartthrob! I would rather have died, however, than confided in anyone. In my mind, that love was, of course, something entirely different from Ana's superficial flirts. It was boundless, predestined, soul-wrenching, and nothing like the frivolous affairs my girlfriends were involved in! There was another important aspect too—my love was unrequited! When a fourteen-year-old girl is happy in love, her deep feelings do not get the chance to find their full expression. The tragedy of one-sided affection provides for the full depth of feelings to come to the fore. In addition, the awe-inspiring nature of the object of my desire was exceptionally satisfying.

"Mr. Wonderful" was, of course, Doctor Reinfeld, who had even married in the meantime. That made my martyrdom even more painful. My lovesickness increased at the mere thought of the happiness that another person must have been enjoying in his presence. It became evident soon enough, however, that the imagined happiness was highly improbable, as the marriage turned out to be a bad one from the start. That revelation further enhanced the intensity of my feelings. I was now able to feel sorry for him from the bottom of my heart, and I imagined all sorts of romantic situations in which I would be consoling him and uplifting his spirits. In reality, however, I never dared to look him straight in the eye. I knew well that in a face-to-face situation, I would have simply melted into nothingness or faded into a cloud of mist carried away by a breeze. In short, I would have gone through a state of disintegration, because, at the mere sight of him, even at some distance, my heart would stop beating, my face would turn bright red, my throat would become dry and hoarse, and I would be speechless. He never looked at me and did not even acknowledge my existence. There was nothing else left for me to do but transpose my love misery into verse, which I did, but always secretly, and quite often hiding in the attic staircase. My grandmother would occasionally find me there and, upset with my flustered appearance, would prepare linden tea and make me undergo steam inhalation treatments, worried that I might be running a fever.

Luckily, I actually did develop a chronic throat inflammation in that draughty staircase and consequently headed twice a week to pay a visit to my adored doctor's surgery and have him smear my throat with *lapis lunaris*. It burned like hell and brought tears to my eyes, partially caused by the caustic application, but equally due to my mental state. The happiness of being in his proximity surpassed the pain.

One of the most significant events during my school days was Ban Khuen Héderváry's[145] visit to town as part of his election campaign, devised to strengthen the support of the loyal city of Osijek for his government programmes. In his honour, the town organized a big welcome reception, with all the important personalities of both military and civilian establishments present. Villagers from the surrounding countryside also took part, and some of the younger ones wearing colourful national costumes came riding into town on white horses, adorned with ribbons and flowers. Also in the crowd were beautiful Croatian girls from Đakovo and the entire Podravina, some arriving all the way from Virovitica. They were all dressed in wide, white, richly embroidered skirts, wearing ducats around their necks and flowers in their hair, strolling arm in arm down the streets in groups of three or four. The guard of honour was composed of local dignitaries in their tailcoats and uniforms, joined by members of different associations of war veterans with their various banners floating over their heads, rifle shooting club members with their bugles, and the brass band of the fire station. Naturally, schoolchildren also had to line the route and we stood in dense double rows from the train station to Županijska Street. We were extremely conscious of our importance, although it meant waiting under the scorching sun and with empty stomachs for more than four hours to witness the big moment that eventually lasted a bare minute. Ban Khuen Héderváry, accompanied by the county prefect (veliki *župan*),[146] Count Pejačević, flew past us in his carriage driven by four horses in less than a blink of an eye, and we had hardly time to call out "Živio!"[147] before it was all over.

But in the city, which was generally apolitical, people talked about the grand event for a long time afterwards, be it in the Casino, the town council, or coffee houses. It was claimed that this important visit would create unimaginable perspectives for the city and would most likely, and in no time whatsoever, help Osijek overtake the arrogant city of Zagreb. The latter was, of course, run by the troublemaking followers of the Party of Rights[148] and *Obzor (Horizon)*,[149] whereas the well-disposed Osijek inhabitants—the Essekers—were always dependable. Did not His Excellency himself declare something of the kind at the banquet held at the Casino, promising a considerable subvention for the city that supported his politics so efficiently? This seemed quite possible in the eyes of Essekers. After all, looking at it from a purely objective view, one could ask oneself, why should Zagreb be ahead of Osijek? If I remember correctly, Osijek at the time had a population of 23,000, and Zagreb no more than 27,000. That was hardly a difference worth mentioning. And, if you asked Essekers what else could be thrown in as ballast to redress the balance, the answer was unanimous and accompanied with a self-assured smile: "Our German culture, of course! Our sense of order and progress. Our realism, our political loyalty, called '*magyarophilia*'[150] in hostile political circles, and last but not least, our business flair." People in Osijek perceived Zagreb as a typical bureaucrats' town, with all its advantages and disadvantages. A bureaucrat was a hair splitter and a stickler for the rules, and worse, his stomach was empty and the hems of his trousers in shreds. In such conditions, anyone could easily become a frondeur. From there stemmed their constant recriminations, their political dissatisfaction, their demands for more than they were entitled to, and their street demonstrations and incidents in the Sabor.[151] Essekers were well fed and, thank God, required nothing of the kind—they were happy with what destiny had in store for them! They respected the authority and all honourable and eminent people and paid no attention to things that were none of their business. As for politics, let the fine gentlemen rack their brains over it if they so pleased, but Essekers had no interest in the political opposition. Roasted lamb on the spit at the restaurant Pakao (Hell) in the Lower Town, the spicy fish stew at the inn by the bridge, or a couple of tender roasted chickens served with green salad at Zlatan Bunar (The Golden Well), appeared to them far more important than political demands by those nagging people from Zagreb, which had so far produced no tangible result other than, in the worst of cases, an increase in taxes.

It is interesting to note that Essekers did not excessively care, if at all, for their great son—in fact, the only one they could be proud of—namely Bishop Josip Juraj Strossmayer.[152] On the one hand, this was due to their sense of loyalty towards the political authorities, but on the other, it had a lot to do with petty small-town opportunism. They identified Strossmayer with the newspaper *Obzor* (Horizon) and its followers, perceived by Essekers as a mixture of notorious street mischief-makers and people prone to scandalous behaviour, never shy of disturbing peaceful deliberations in the Sabor with poisonous speeches in support of that extravagant idea of Yugoslavism,[153] of which no one in Osijek approved. Besides, Bishop Strossmayer did not care much for his hometown. He made enemies in the city when he asked the town council to give him a suitable piece of land where he could build a cathedral and move the seat of his diocese to Osijek. After long discussions, the council refused the request, partially for political reasons and partially out of sheer narrow-mindedness. Their excuses were unfounded, petty, and dictated by personal animosity. It was argued that there was no suitable location for the construction, and that Strossmayer's presence in the city might upset the peaceful, unified community and cause its break-up into two camps. The Swabian and pro-Hungarian members of the town council were afraid of the very idea of Yugoslavism, whose meaning they could not grasp, and saw in *Obzor* the prime propagator of that idea. From their point of view, *Obzor* was just another name for the opposition, considering that its columns publicly and regularly preached against the political directions the government in place was taking!

Added to all that were specific recommendations issued by the county headquarters, where the bishop of Đakovo was viewed most unfavourably. No question about it, the bishop was their fellow countryman, and they were mostly good Catholics, but in their eyes, he was nevertheless—with all due respect to His Excellency—reckless and foolhardy. Did he not dare to contradict his Imperial and Royal Highness? He opposed His Holiness the Pope, too. His spirit was dangerously rebellious and disobedient and his very presence, especially that of his entourage, could—with his unacceptable ideas and pronouncements—infect the entire city, especially the young and inexperienced. This would lead to quarrelsome arguments in one's own house, around the dinner table, between fathers and sons, among people who had until just recently been friends. In no time notorious loudmouths would begin agitating people and rebelling against literally everything that had been put in place. And as is usually the case, once the first stone is loosened, the second and third follow, until gradually the entire building collapses.

It was that kind of reasoning that good old Essekers were sharing over their mugs of Scheper's beer. They feared the wise bishop so much that they preferred to forsake the potential benefits which might derive from his presence in town. The county authorities put in place a secret surveillance service, under the direct control of the deputy prefect, Adolf von Čuvaj. He had his exponents in the bishop's closest circles. They not only watched his every step, but also kept track of his plans and ideas, and reported their findings back to Čuvaj, who then forwarded them to Ban Khuen himself.

Čuvaj kept local newspapers well informed of his findings, as well. They regularly wrote about the bishop in unflattering terms referring to him as "*vladika*"[154] and occasionally issued entire pamphlets against him. For years, he avoided coming to town, and when he eventually did for the consecration of a seminary, he was welcomed with no enthusiasm—one might even say that the reception was cold. Those same Essekers expressed their dismay years later when he bequeathed nothing to his hometown in his will. They did not get a single kreuzer from him for the city's cultural advancement. His precious collection of paintings ended up in Zagreb, where he also founded the Yugoslav Academy and the university. The people of Osijek were extremely annoyed, and I often heard, as a child, people saying, "What a shame that we denied him that land for the construction of the cathedral! That was bad business, in fact, more like a business running on a deficit. The city gained nothing from its loyalty to Hungary or the Magyarization politics of Ban Khuen Héderváry. His promises have turned out to be nothing more than words."

Time moved on, however. The wheel was turning. Whatever had seemed so far firmly established became shaky, including all the inherent assumptions and prejudices. Not even the most cautious burghers could prevent it. The soul, along with the body, eventually succumbs to corrosive elements, no matter what. Something new emerges. New ideas and outlooks. No matter how cautious old folks may try to keep doors and gates shut tight and retreat to their fortified positions—a behaviour proven rather profitable and advantageous otherwise—the collapse is inevitable and will originate from within. It was inevitable even in Osijek, the stronghold of devotion for everything Hungarian, including "*Khuenovština*".[155] It all happened simultaneously in both political and social domains. Young people from Osijek who were studying law, philosophy, or liberal arts at the University of Zagreb came into contact with supporters of Ante Starčević's Party of Rights and *Obzor* and brought these new ideas with them when they returned home from school. Furthermore, by the 1890s, the city slowly entered the era of industrialization. The working class became acquainted with socialist theories. Soon there were the first strikes and the first mass demonstrations in town. The First of May was celebrated with red flags and the singing of the *Marseillaise*. The peace was disrupted, the continuity broken. The Croatian national propaganda was out in the open for the first time. Croatian could be heard spoken more frequently than ever before in the past. The first Croatian newspaper was published, and for the first time, an opposition candidate defeated the long-time supporter of Magyarization to sit as the local representative in the national parliament (*Sabor*), despite threats of severe repressive measures.

In 1894, my father was elected president of the Slavonian Chamber of Trades and Crafts. He was, without any doubt, the most knowledgeable person on the subject of our local economy. What was even more important was the rectitude of his character and steadfastness with which he resisted every temptation. Despite his social position, he never gained great wealth, nor accepted money for services rendered. Not only like-minded people who shared his political ideas, but also those from the opposing party valued his integrity. On the occasion of the Sabor elections called by Karól Khuen Héderváry in 1897, the opposition candidate Josip Horvat, the parish priest in the Upper Town,[156] made it known to my father that he would be prepared to give up his candidacy if my father were to accept the nomination himself. My father refused this honourable offer with the explanation that his work in connection with the Chamber of Trades and Crafts would not leave him enough time to fulfil, conscientiously, and responsibly, whatever would be required of him as a member of the provincial parliament. In addition, the suggested mandate would involve several months spent out of town. But I know that Horvat's suggestion gave my father the greatest of pleasure. It was, undeniably, the confirmation that even the opposing political party acknowledged and valued, not only his integrity and intelligence, but also his efforts and initiatives at the head of the Chamber for the benefit of his adoptive fatherland.

In his numerous speeches, my father frequently emphasized the social aspect of an issue and placed social interests above all else. I suspect that he considered living conditions and the economic development of people as individuals to be above the national interest. In his capacity as a member of management committees of numerous institutions, he had many opportunities to put that into practice. He never refused anyone who approached him asking for advice or help. On the contrary, he served the society as a whole by catering for each person individually. He favoured a utilitarian rather than an ideological approach, and the latter only if practicable. In his view, the defence of freedom of conscience, tolerance, liberalism, and social well-being depended on the prevailing economic conditions in the country, not on utopias. Petty chauvinism was not in his nature, but he did identify with the interests of the country in which he lived and for whose benefits he worked.

At the turn of the century, many influential thinkers were convinced that people would reach their desired goals through a gradual evolutionary process. This conviction was based on a lot of goodwill, short-sightedness, and optimism, and the belief in an unimpeded, progressive build-up, allowing one generation to bequeath still unresolved issues to the next generation, with no upheavals and external disasters jeopardizing what had already been achieved, or destroying what had been realized through the hard labour of preceding generations.

Such optimistic assumptions did not just refer to economic and social development, but also to the problem of Jewish assimilation. That was my father's firm belief. On no occasion did he conceal his Judaism. He would not stoop down and seek recognition and gain favour on the basis of false assumptions either. But he was convinced that it was a duty of every conscientious and honest Jew to serve his community and to do his best. Each mistake a Jew makes harms not only himself, but the whole of Judaism. In the same way, a Jew's earned reputation does not remain his private matter alone but concerns the whole community. That is how prejudice is overcome and pure human spirit prevails. He believed in this unwaveringly, but gradually and due to certain indisputable facts, he was eventually forced to recognize how very wrong he had been.

It was roughly at that time that he was elected secretary of the Alliance israélite for Slavonia, an institution with its headquarters in Paris. It was concerned with the status of Jews in the eastern world and, where necessary, provided material help. The Alliance also organized and financed the emigration of refugees from countries in which they were the object of violent persecution. They helped victims of pogroms and secured new life opportunities for them. Under the motto "All Israel bears responsibility for one another", they founded hospitals, old people's homes, schools, and work colonies across Eastern Europe, Asia Minor, and Palestine, as well as the southern coast of Africa.

Frequent contacts with refugees from Russia and Romania provided my father with a better insight into the destinies of Jewish people. Images of the past were coming back, that same past he was so sure had been overcome—once and for all. I too was deeply impressed with the melancholy appearance of those unusual, gaunt and black-bearded people who came to our door asking for help more and more often. While talking to them, we found out about outrageous things—masses of people breaking into their quiet neighbourhoods, pillaging and burning houses, slaughtering women and children, and how they had been forced to leave their homes naked and barefoot. The tragedy befell not those reviled Jewish capitalists portraited as objects of mockery in various humorous papers or as protagonists of shallow burlesques on stage. No, those were dedicated workers of all sorts—tradesmen, cobblers, locksmiths, tailors, and factory workers, who all lived from hand to mouth, in closed communities, strictly abiding by their traditions and speaking a common language. Their national and religious attachments went hand in hand. It was impossible not to realize it. It was impossible to overlook it. Judaism was suddenly presented to us in an entirely different light. The destinies of those people did not depend on their own will. No matter how hard they tried, they were pushed back against a high wall. There was no way they could avoid bumping into it, and no way to surmount it.

Father did everything to help them. He was an excellent organizer. He took the necessary steps quickly and energetically. He found temporary shelters for those without a roof above their heads, opened a soup kitchen where they could eat, acquired travel documents and ship tickets for those who wanted to cross the ocean and go to the United States, Brazil, Argentina, or Central America. He acquired licences for those who preferred to stay put and work as trades people—cobblers, tailors, weavers, furriers—something he did not find difficult to do in his capacity as president of the Chamber of Trades and Crafts. He found for them suitable workshops, supplies, machines and tools, household items and beds, and where necessary also linen, clothes, medical help, and medicines. Since my father preferred getting to know people on a personal level, he had long conversations with people whose life experiences were mostly unfamiliar to us, questioning them about their home countries and their personal destinies. He became acquainted with their living conditions, their religious and social convictions, and the way they had reacted to the pressures they had been exposed to. He inquired about persisting physical and spiritual consequences of the violence they had endured. He was amazed that those people still lived with the hope of salvation, harboured for centuries among the Jews, namely that the promised Messiah would one day appear after all. That faith and hope had helped them pursue their lives full of misfortunes, persecutions and abuse.

The arrival of those people was like a sudden gust of wind creating waves on the sluggishly flowing river, affecting our lives and demolishing the impression of serenity. We had, until then, either consciously or unconsciously, excluded from our lives any disturbing element, and kept believing in an ever more powerful unity of people of goodwill on earth, in eternal peace, unstoppable progress, and an equitable distribution of wealth. I might have been young at the time, but these events had an effect on me too. Hardly anything else was talked about at mealtimes and some-thing inside us and around us had changed. The prism through which I had been looking at the world from that point of time onwards reflected a different kind of light. This was not literature, but real life! It made me mature faster and in barely a few weeks, I turned more thoughtful and serious. I asked myself, "Can such things really exist? Can all that injustice and abuse of power against the weak take place, with no hand being raised to stop such outrages? Was there no voice of condemnation uttered loudly enough to be heard? Should we not therefore learn all about the existing injustice in this world, form our own opinion, and identify with those who have encountered and suffered from it? Should we not arm ourselves and be prepared for whatever fate befalls us today, and someone else tomor-row? A fate from which one cannot run away, from which salvation cannot be found, whether by virtue or noble thoughts, cunning or wisdom, grit or passiveness!" The black figures who knocked on our door asking for help provided a living proof that there was no escape from the fatal sidetrack on which they had found themselves. This was no game. One had to be ready, take one's own destiny in one's hands and be responsible for it.

My father and his friends still refused to give up on their optimism. They claimed that circumstances of that kind had long been eradicated in our part of the world. Those were testimonies from barbarian coun-tries such as Russia and Romania, where European civilization had hardly penetrated. Those were outbursts of barbarism, religious fanaticism, and political despotism. In Western Europe, such things, thank God, could never happen again!

Then, in 1894, newspapers brought the first information concerning the Dreyfus Affair. In France, the Affair had turned into a conflict between right- and left-wing parties, and in other European countries divided people into two camps on different lines. Artillery captain in the French Army, Alfred Dreyfus, of Jewish origin, had the inexcusable ambition of being part of the French General Staff and when a spy was detected among them, the general opinion was that the traitor could be none other but the Jew in question! Who else would sell his own country's defence plans to a neighbouring country? How could one ever suspect a French person of such an act? Dreyfus was charged, demoted, convicted, and deported to

Devil's Island off the coast of French Guyana. He was eventually exonerated and reinstated in the army, but not until 1906. It is hard to imagine today how shattering that affair was for Jews and Christians alike. In comparison to the storms of two World Wars, the event seems insignificant. But it represents a prelude. Since then, hecatombs and revolutions have shaken the foundations of the world and changed the face of the earth. Six million Jews were incinerated in crematoriums, drowned in rivers, suffocated in gas chambers. The atomic bomb fell over Hiroshima and hundreds of thousands of men, women, and children perished. Still, the Dreyfus Affair, which concerned a single man, ripped the spirit of an entire generation out of its phlegmatic state of existing, destroyed its optimism, and opened its eyes. It was the first crack in an established system, the uncovering of a cynical crime committed without concealment or shame, and of the heartless mechanism of the state against one human being. It was Machiavellianism stretched to the extreme, the reversal of all hitherto held principles in favour of absolute evil. The Affair offered to the world the first premonition of what people were truly capable of. This was the atomic bomb Europeans hid in their midst and suddenly became aware of. For European Jews, though, this was an exceptionally heavy blow by the mere fact that it originated in the civilized West. The Dreyfus Affair gave anti-Semitism an occasion to flourish and ended all hope of a possible Jewish assimilation.

There was at the time not a single Jew who was not affected by the event. It was not merely a matter of a French officer of the General Staff having his epaulettes publicly torn off his shoulders under the pretext that he was unworthy of wearing them and was now slowly dying on Devil's Island. It meant that all Jews were thus demoted and dishonoured. In an instant, they became aware of how much their situation was once again insecure and under threat, how their fitting place in society was once again denied them, and, what exactly, a full century after the French Revolution, people still thought about them. The issue was no longer religion, but race. Imaginary tales of well poisoning and host desecration were replaced with numerous tales about superior and inferior races, containing biological and psychological evidence to give the arguments a pseudo-scientific foundation. It was once again all about atavistic instincts, jealousy, competition, bigotry, superstition, in the same vein as the acts of Jew-baiting, burning, and cudgelling were in the Middle Ages.

The Dreyfus Affair was not an easy subject to handle in the circle of our family friends. The afternoon gatherings continued, but the atmosphere had changed, and the conversations were marred by insoluble problems. Miss Lipschitz had to admit that her omniscient Dr. Kraff-Ebing, no matter how excellent a neuro-specialist he might have been, was, nevertheless, most likely influenced by his surroundings in Graz and had turned out to be a full-hearted "anti-Dreyfus" supporter. As of recently, we also had the occasional pleasure of receiving Mrs. Gersuny at our afternoon gatherings. As was her usual habit, she opted for a golden middle position in her assessment of the situation. She considered Dreyfus guilty. Numerous indices made it impossible to doubt. The *Grazer Tagespost* (Graz Daily Mail) demonstrated it clearly. Why then call it a Jewish question when it was an issue that exclusively concerned the French General Staff? Mrs. Gersuny's apodictic opinion was that the Jews committed a cardinal mistake by showing their solidarity with a criminal and thus inevitably provoking the rise of anti-Semitism.

For Aunt Tinka, the Dreyfus Affair was merely a question of prestige and she knew something about it herself. She was a social leader and kept in close touch with the wives of the county prefect (*župan*) and the town mayor, but they stopped attending her afternoon parties, saying that the conversations were of no interest to them. Was it not rather because they had suddenly discovered that her elegant, seven-room apartment with a hall, salon, and man's den, had just been completely refurbished by a specially commissioned interior architect from Vienna, or that Tinka Vesely, née Basch, of that objectionable race, could afford to serve excellent liver pâté from Strasbourg, ice bombes and canapés with caviar at her tea parties?

Notwithstanding her advanced age, my grandmother did not lose touch with the mood of the time we lived in and could not talk about anything else but the Affair. She would get upset when someone contradicted her and would not keep silent like everybody else when the person indulging in contradictions was Mrs. Gersuny herself. Her indignation was so strong that she would forget all about having lived and breathed German culture for sixty years of her life, and would turn to the fully fledged jargon of her childhood, with its highly colourful imagery, to be able to express herself as forcefully as possible. The juiciness of that unique language could only be appreciated and understood within the narrow family circles. Her moods oscillated between hope, outrage, enthusiasm, and despondency. How was it that people of another faith could not see clearly why there was so much talk about the Dreyfus Affair in the newspapers and elsewhere? The Jewish people had turned mistrustful, were mentally exhausted, and saw scorn and blame everywhere around them. A friend had overnight become an enemy. As a result, Jews had no choice but to revert to freemasonry and community as a source of their self-identification, where people could tacitly recognize themselves in each other, and make all those "others" feel excluded and cut off.

From the start, my father tried to preserve his calm and keep away from the general hysteria. He viewed this event as purely a matter of French domestic politics, as an act of revenge taken by the royalists and *revanchistes*, namely the French aristocracy and military circles, for having been politically sidelined. He did not believe in the possibility of a new hunt on Jews flaring up, and, as proof that times had changed, kept pointing at personalities such as Lord Beaconsfield,[157] Baron Moses Montefiore,[158] Adolphe Crémieux,[159] or Gerson von Bleichröder, Bismarck's financial and political advisor.[160] Among other noteworthy figures at the end of the nineteenth century was Baron Hirsch,[161] who devoted his entire wealth to philanthropic ends, established numerous humanitarian institutions in the Balkans, and advocated and financed the mass settlement of Jews in Argentina. My father was one of his most passionate adherents. He supported, with both words and deeds, his idea of a Jewish agricultural colony in the scarcely populated Central and South Americas, where soil properties were excellent and climatic conditions corresponded with our own. This was also the time when Herzl wrote the book *The Jewish State*, advancing the idea of a massive settlement in Palestine.[162] The two concepts, by Herzl and Hirsch, were juxtaposed, and both weighed serious arguments into the balance. In those days, the Arab question was already a critical issue. The Zionist idea was not initially well received by Western Jews either, as it implied a complete change in an established mindset and lifestyle, based on Western cultural foundations, finally espoused by the Jews after many sacrifices, struggles, and difficulties.

Another frequent guest at home in those days was Dr. Levinsky. Father told me that, due to his erudition and intelligence, Levinsky had been a real wunderkind at the age of twelve. Since he was poor, the Jewish community took charge of him and enabled him to go to school. He was asked to finish the gymnasium in Osijek and then attend a seminary in Budapest, in order to replace our old rabbi one day. The Jewish Reform congregation in Osijek wanted a modern rabbi, locally born and fluent in Croatian, who would not, as far as religious practices were concerned, require more from the good old Essekers than they were themselves prepared to follow. And they worked out a plan. In accordance with an established custom, poor Jewish children, so-called dailies, ate each day in another house at another table, and the young boy, Levinsky, was nicely fed at the tables of well-off families in Osijek. To what extent such charity, no doubt driven by the best intentions, was beneficial or damaging to the character of the recipient is today difficult to assess. The practice had existed well before psychologist Alfred Adler defined his theory of inferiority complex. But the feeling of envy towards those who are better off needs no special theoretical definition in order to exist and awareness of one's humiliating condition has surely always been present in humans. One could assume that the children fed "per day" transferred a certain amount of bitterness onto their future life and that their gratitude for the benevolent acts towards them, while young, was most likely problematic.

It happened that young Levinsky had an unpleasant surprise in store for his community in Osijek. He continued being an excellent student, but his progress did not head in the directions his patrons were hoping for. He fiercely disagreed with their unpreparedness to assimilate, and with their loyalty and friendliness towards Ban Khuen Héderváry and his government in Zagreb. To the astonishment of his sponsors, he joined certain Croatian nationalist circles and, along with a group of young oppositionists, participated in forming a political faction of their own. He read *Vienac* and *Obzor* and energetically demonstrated against Ban Khuen

Héderváry's politics. This was around 1884, when it became evident that Khuen's politics were vastly anti-Croatian in nature. At that time, opposing them meant playing with fire, especially in a town such as Osijek, where the opposition's demands were unanimously refuted. There was absolutely no sympathy for either their purpose or their justification. Among the voters, all of whom voted for the government, there were in the first place "virilists",[163] meaning local landowners, then government employees, who felt obligated to vote for the government, and finally the so-called minorities—Serbs, Swabians, and unsettled Jews—who expected the government's protection in return. The country was governed almost like a colony and its resources were exploited by foreign capitalists. As foreigners, and even more so as businessmen and traders, they were pushing the government to grant them low tax rates, provide suitable import-export regulations, and most of all, guarantee freedom of enterprise, invoking the mottos, "Where some people make money, others can't be found lacking," or "Rich people allow the poor to live too. One person's luxury provides a loaf of bread to another". No one had any appreciation for anything else beyond one's own profit, which was always considered to have been rightly and justifiably acquired. Politics meant prosperity, and prosperity meant profit. All respectable citizens of Osijek shared that view and considered it to their credit that they did so. In fact, everything that diverged from such thinking was unrealistic, a pure fantasy, and a total waste of time for any mature and serious person.

The moment Levinsky passed his final high school examination, his frightened patrons warned him not to meddle in things that were none of his business. Especially as he was a poverty-stricken Jew, who should be more than happy to have a secured existence ahead of himself!

"This is a matter of my convictions!" he replied.

"A poor young Jewish man fed 'per day' cannot have different convictions from those of his benefactors, especially when that person is a future rabbi!"

"I don't want to become a rabbi at all. It's out of the question! I don't want to go to Budapest and your seminary. I want to go to university in Zagreb and study law."

"And how do you intend to live in that Zagreb of yours? You are a nobody and have nothing!"

"Fine, I will have nothing to live on, but that will be better than whatever you might be proposing."

He really had nothing to live on for four whole years. He was occasionally tutoring, did a copying job in a lawyer's office, ate in soup kitchens, and slept at friends' houses, depending on where he happened to be. My father helped him by sending regular monthly support money, because he liked the fact that the young man was guided by his beliefs and wanted to become a lawyer instead of a rabbi.

His studies finished, Levinsky returned to Osijek with the intention of joining the local judiciary. But that did not materialize. His political reputation was not good, and, more to the point, he was a Jew! And so, his four years of starvation brought him a thin harvest. He had to be thankful to find employment as an articling clerk in the office of one of the town's lawyers, which allowed him to work in the legal environment and acquire experience. In that skilfully run lawyer's office, he soon came across all forms of corruption, bribery, and justice trafficking that was kept successfully concealed through astute legal manoeuvres. His boss was a long-time member of the Sabor and a devoted supporter of the regime. He also held a seat on the town council, where he pushed for everything that would bring him personal gains and opposed measures of no use to him, no matter how much they would benefit the city. In court, he would conspire with the opposing party in cases where it provided greater financial advantage than what he could obtain from his own client. He drank and fraternized with judges and made deals with them in critical cases. He was regarded in town as an excellent lawyer, who could negotiate a favourable outcome of a case, even when it stood no chance, mostly thanks to a generous advance the client would discreetly slip into his pocket. The legal merit of a case was irrelevant. After all, in the final analysis, a clause could be interpreted in this way or that. What mattered was to find the right approach, which is what he wanted Levinsky to do. When the latter stubbornly refused, he was dismissed.

His second job was entirely different. His new boss was a downright ignorant, elderly gentleman. He dragged his trials on for years, and his main effort, if one could even call it an effort, was to keep adding more folders full of documents to an already huge pile, and leave things unresolved, which, in his opinion, made more sense than finding a hasty solution. He was not acting that way in bad faith. He was simply a cautious man, who wanted to preserve his peace and avoid excitement. He drank cold beer with his friends at the pub and let Levinsky run the business. He became apprehensive when Levinsky found on top of a bookcase a pile of dusty case folders dated 1880, became engrossed in the cases, and started solving them. It was Levinsky's best moment. He possessed solid judicial knowledge and was astute, expeditious, and agile. In no time, he began resolving the most complex matters and successfully closed one case after another. His cautious boss was shaking his head with concern. What possessed this super-smart Jew to come and disturb his quiet life in this manner? Instead of going to the pub, he was now obliged to listen to legal deliberations. It went so far that his own clerk, still wet behind the ears, tried to prove to him that a case that he had been dragging on for years could be resolved in a single move, and that there was no need to waste more time and harm the client by preventing him from obtaining what he was legally entitled to. It was then that Levinsky was fired, under the pretext that the office was not making enough profit to keep an additional articling clerk.

His third boss was an avid card player, constantly in debt, highly strung and peevish, always making a mountain out of a molehill and, without hesitation, insulting his employees in front of the clients or slighting the latter in front of the employees. This time Levinsky himself gave his resignation and left. The next job turned out to be quite good. His boss was a good lawyer, highly respected both among the citizens and the legal profession, so that his candidature for the government party in the upcoming parliamentary elections seemed a sure deal. Already planning his future political career, he entrusted the running of his entire office to Levinsky.

Levinsky had been married a few years earlier, and according to the so-called society, committed a terrible mistake. His young wife was a hat maker, just as poor as he was, so that even before he started a family, he was already indebted up to his neck. He never did get rid of those debts, which simply grew as the years went by. Then there were interest rates, which he could not pay. There were medical bills and children, and always unexpected expenses. Those external difficulties were now accompanied by Levinsky's spiritual apathy. He had struggled for years, eaten at other people's tables and starved, fought for his ideals and suffered for it. And now, at this crucial moment, he had no more strength to fight. He was supposed to pass the bar exam and become independent, which my father kept persuading him to do, but he just nodded and let everything take its usual course.

He was embittered, disappointed, overwrought, and in that condition, wasted his energy on trifles, while his vital problems remained unresolved. We were the only people he still visited. Father respected him because of his logical mind and his uncompromising attitude. Levinsky did not know how to assert himself. His broad general knowledge and the huge enthusiasm he had shown in his youth did not, however, just disappear into nothingness after his student days, as was the case with so many other people. He was a keen student of history, in search of solutions to current problems. He enjoyed discussions with my father, who, apart from newspapers and economic publications, no longer read much else. But those newspapers and publications catered for a specific social class and were, therefore, tools of a specific propaganda, while Levinsky already knew a few things about scientific socialism and tried to prompt my father in that direction. He was the first person I heard speak about the difference between working people and the propertied class, and the fact that the real issue was not the extent of charitable work we were willingly and generously prepared to do, but the need to fight for one's rights. Father also viewed these matters critically, but his criticism dealt with the method, rather than the facts themselves. He had read and studied Proudhon enough to admit, at least theoretically, that property ownership represented theft. And so, one such subject led to another, and I had the privilege of sitting at the same table with them and listening. Levinsky was of the strong opinion that the world's balance had been disrupted. Evidence of anarchist tendencies were discernible everywhere, as was an atmosphere of agitation in politics and art. Things became derailed and seemed on a collision course.

Occasionally, they would tackle domestic politics and Levinsky would speak emphatically against the government and its stand on Magyarization. My father had this to say:

"You will forgive me for saying this. Not being a nationalist myself, I cannot regard the subject from this single standpoint alone. I do admit that the nation is being treated unjustly, but I look at the problem from the political economy point of view—as a need to improve the living conditions of every individual. Peasants could be advised to intensify their agricultural activity, and craftsmen to broaden their production capabilities, by taking advantage of the current greater availability of cheap materials and good market relationships. The workers they employed would, as a result, have secure, paid jobs. Private initiative can do a lot in this matter."

"It cannot do a thing!" cried out Levinsky, suddenly becoming excited. "Without national liberation, the initiative will always come from above."

"You are probably right," my father replied. "As Jews, we cannot, however, but look at that question from where we stand today and recognize that the Ban has been politically loyal towards us."

Levinsky laughed. "Loyal? Maybe. But he reminds us all too well of an autocrat from the Middle Ages, who let Jews become rich and thus made them double victims. To begin with, everybody around them hated them because of their wealth, and then he robbed them of their money for his own benefit. He waited for them to refill their coffers and then let the cheering people massacre them. I guess you know the story of the *Judenschwamm* (The Jewish Sponge)?[164] Shouldn't it also apply to the Ban's regime?"

It did not take long before something happened, which deeply upset my father. In view of the upcoming nationwide elections for the Sabor, Dr. Levinsky began campaigning to run as the opposition candidate. At one of the meetings, he gave a speech in which he criticized Khuen's methods, his budget, and especially his electoral system. On the one hand, Khuen kept tightening the income-based prerequisites for census suffrage,[165] while at the same time using the police force to keep the peasants in check. In that way, the right to vote was a privilege enjoyed only by the wealthiest, who had already been his supporters anyway and helped him govern by successfully stymieing the voice of the opposition. Dr. Levinsky spoke about people's complaints on that subject, told his listeners the truth right to their faces, the way no one else had done before. He unleashed an immediate and stormy reaction. Upon instructions from "above", newspapers could not find enough damaging words to describe him, calling him an eccentric, a crackpot, or a grouch, who had decided to meddle in things that were none of his business. The gentlemen at the Casino were of the same opinion. His former friends suddenly remembered that he was a Jew and started avoiding him. The Jews were upset with him, because he had put them in an awkward position. With his public behaviour, he set townspeople against them as well, when all they wanted, both individually and as a community, was to keep the peace. His boss was also angry—the man whom he had kept on his payroll, thus allowing him to put food on the family table, dared to challenge him publicly, reducing, if not destroying, his chances for re-election! He also received a sign from "above" and fired his refractory employee shortly before the election.

This happened at a time when Levinsky's children were ill and when the last object in the house they could spare was taken to the pawnshop. His wife was causing scenes and kept nagging. Another employment would have been impossible to find at short notice, considering the circumstances, and Levinsky had had enough. Deeply depressed, he went to the bridge over the River Drava, took off his coat and his watch, and jumped into the waters. In the pocket of his coat was a short letter saying it was not worth living anymore in such times, in such a world and under such conditions. His body was washed away by the waves, all the way to the Danube. It was never recovered.

Meanwhile, I completed my seventh year of high school and my parents decided to take me out of school without finishing the eighth grade. They sent me to a Viennese boarding school where, besides the necessary refinements, and the discipline I so badly needed, I would be able to acquire a good education. The new environment did not, at the start, inspire my confidence. It was obvious I could no longer behave like a princess, the way I used to in the Long Courtyard. I had to give up my role of *enfant terrible*, with which I had charmed my girlfriends and made them laugh. I could not behave towards the children at the new school in the same authoritarian way as I had treated my friends in Osijek or make them believe in my tall stories. We were twenty-four girls at the Viennese institute, some younger, some older than me, and many had already attended the same school for a considerable time. They had become used to being there, developed their own style, and a special manner of speaking. There was a firmly established hierarchy between them, with several acclaimed leaders and star students. I was forced to change my game by letting go on many fronts and winning on others. From the very first moment, I felt I was on shaky ground in this new environment and my former self-assuredness failed me. But I soon discovered that the new environment could compensate for many things that I had been forced to leave behind. For the first time, I was attending a school where every subject taught interested me and I eagerly wanted to learn. Each lecture my professors gave was a revelation. I had the first glimpse of an endlessly attractive and challenging world, as yet unknown to me.

But that is a whole new chapter. There was at first an abundance of tears and sadness at parting with my father, who had been protecting and consoling me for years. This time he advised me to take full advantage of the two upcoming years and to do my best. When his loving figure disappeared from my sight as the door closed behind him and I was left alone, I was seized by a feeling of utter abandonment.

PART II

DEFYING CONVENTIONS

The seventy-year-long reign of Emperor Franz Joseph, considered by some as the last "legitimate European monarch", is referred to as the Francisco-Josephine era of the Austro-Hungarian monarchy, which corresponded in many ways to the British Victorian era. Its main feature was a government exclusively in the hands of an aristocracy, which, in contrast to the Prussian Junkers, was known for its bigotry, philistinism and a Catholic-clerical orientation sustained by the Vatican. That aristocracy formed a tight, anti-Slavic coterie, which successfully hindered any possible resolution of the tense political relationships dominating the domestic front. Despite their lack of talent, along with their spiritual and physical degeneration, this group was the Austro-Hungarian ruling class, which held all leading government, military, and diplomatic positions in the empire.

Nonetheless, the Francisco-Josephine era was also marked by the awakening of nationalism and a visible effort towards democratization, particularly strong in the last years of the emperor's reign. A good illustration of the ethnic makeup of the state, maintained together by purely artificial means, was the diversity of people in its capital, Vienna, the majority of whom were not of Germanic descent, but newcomers from around the country. It was precisely that heterogeneous mix of languages, behaviours, lifestyles, and cultural manifestations that gave the city that typically Viennese atmosphere—a happy-go-lucky, even can't-care-less attitude, boisterousness and gallows humour, shallow sentimentality, affinity for art and beer culture, paucity of ideas, combined with intellectual arrogance, and an instinct for form for its own sake in the service of aesthetics, all of it with no earth-shattering consequences. If there was anything valuable in the city, it was most likely a thing of the past. The glorious tradition extended all the way back to the medieval German Empire and ended with the operettas of Johann Strauss. The Baroque of Herrengasse Street and its surrounding area gave the city its prime architectural look. Everything that came later was an imitation.

It was within the confines of the Museum of Natural History and the Art History Museum that one could find things worth seeing. On the performing arts front, those would be found in the great theatre classics performed at the old Burgtheater, in the tearful charm of some Biedermeier[166] plays and the humour of Raimund and Nestroy.[167] In music, it would be in the works produced from the great era of Mozart, Beethoven, and Schubert to Gustav Mahler's epigones. In the last decade of the nineteenth century, all of that had already reached a dead end and we, the latecomers, were living on the interests generated by the former treasures, wrapped in vague contemplations, impeding prepossessions and tragic misconceptions of the present as much as of the future ahead of us. This was all part of a fragile superstructure, built upon a solid, but already bygone, foundation. The superstructure itself consisted of idle chatter, fantasizing, and an exaggerated emphasis on details. It was all a game of words, colours, images, and forms. It was easy to topple that whole fragile structure down. It required an equilibrist to keep the things in balance, be it in politics, intellectual life, or artistic innovation. In an attempt to escape serious aspects of life, people in Vienna opted for gaiety. There were masquerades and masked balls, flower shows, carriage rides to the *Prater,*[168] and Imperial Court balls during the carnival season. The majestic "Ruler of the People" grew into a legendary figure in that baroque atmosphere. When the emperor rode along the streets of Vienna in his golden carriage pulled by the traditional set of white Lipizzaner horses, his subjects bowed down to the ground with joy (out of reverence, they bowed even when the carriage was empty!). When, on the occasion of the Corpus Christi procession, His Majesty—revered by the crowd as "the last legitimate monarch in Europe"—walked under the ceremonial baldachin, surrounded by court dignitaries, ministers, and diplomats, the delighted common folk lined the route all the way from the Hofburg to Saint Stephen's Square. Wealthy people instead paid big sums of money to watch the spectacle from one of the overlooking windows and the sight, it was claimed, was, for all those people, a lifetime experience.

I arrived in Vienna with my father on the first day of September 1893, with the purpose of spending the following two years in one of the

Viennese boarding schools for young girls. Well-off parents found placing their young daughters in boarding schools a convenient way to extend their schooling beyond the age of fourteen. Moreover, while essentially beneficial for the general education of an adolescent girl, the placement effectively put her social life on hold, before she could be declared "marriageable" at the age of sixteen or seventeen and be introduced to society.

The choice of a boarding school and the level of comfort it could provide depended on the parents' taste and financial means. There were convent schools run by nuns, the Ursulines, for example, where young girls were exposed to some diluted general knowledge and a considerable religious education, with a subsequent lifelong impact. The most prestigious of those convent schools was Sacré Coeur. It was there that some lucky girl could find herself sharing the same school desk with a genuine countess! Besides these confessional institutions, there were also girls' boarding schools operating on a purely commercial basis, where more attention was paid to the father's financial status, than the daughter's religious beliefs. Such schools offered boarders a fitting education for someone of their social standing. They learned foreign languages, piano, and singing. They were given some finishing polish in terms of their looks and demeanour and acquired a definite affinity for Viennese operettas. They also acquired some ability to chat with ease about their appreciation of art, something that would serve them later in life as valid proof of their extended education.

The institute where my father brought me was not one of those designed to instill in me an elevated sense of my own social importance. Rather, my parents chose it exclusively because of its legitimate reputation as an excellent school. The headmistress, Mrs. Szanto, came from an old scholarly Prague family, whose male members were all either high school teachers or university professors, and whose wives and daughters had also taken active part in the family's humanistic pursuits since the early years of the nineteenth century. Mrs. Szanto was approaching her seventieth birthday at the time. Her snow-white locks of hair with a neat middle parting resembled a small bonnet encircling her small but elegant face. I liked her from the start. Her relaxed attitude inspired confidence. She asked me a series of questions regarding the extent of my knowledge and affinities, even my personality traits, and I gladly, and without reservation, answered them all. We quickly established a relationship. This was important to me, since I had now been in a big city all by myself, in a foreign environment, among strangers, without my parents' immediate support, and away from the safety of my family home.

I must add, that out of desire to make progress as soon as possible and to learn as much as I could, I had decided at the end of my seventh year in high school that, once in Vienna, I would not automatically enrol in the eighth grade. Instead I would skip it and take an entrance exam to enrol in the so-called extended education level. I passed the exam with good results and was overjoyed to become one of the "older girls", although, at the age of thirteen, I was the youngest in my class.

The institute was located in the city's second district, on the corner where the narrow and unsightly Negerle Street met Schöllerhof Street, and then headed along the left bank of the Donaukanal, between Stephanie and Ferdinand bridges, towards the district's commercial neighbourhood. With its barricaded doors and shuttered windows of the storage rooms and offices on the ground floor, the entire outside appearance of the building resembled more a prison ward than a legitimate boarding school. At first sight, I was disappointed, even frightened. The school itself, situated on the second floor, along with the dormitories which were annexed to it, appeared dark, stuffy, and far too confined, considering the large number of its pupils. Besides twenty-five full boarders, there were also half-boarders, as well as external students, which easily brought the total number to one hundred pupils. The school had already been in operation for forty years and had never been renovated during that time. The furniture was shabby, the paint on the walls faded, and the desks uncomfortable. Even the spirit of the school had hardly changed. The educators and teachers were, with few exceptions, older people. They were idealists *par excellence,* who perceived the educational task as their mission in life. Boarders were crammed in a few small bedrooms, usually four in each room. A spacious dining room served as a communal space where we did our homework. There were no bathrooms, only a small washroom with five washbasins and no running water, so that a girl who happened to be the last to arrive would sometimes find barely enough water to rinse her hands and face.

We had to dress quickly, which was no easy task. We were already wearing fishbone corsets. They had to be buttoned and tied up, which amounted to a lot of work. We wore low shoes in summer and high boots with a huge number of buckles in wintertime. The fixing of our long hair was a time-consuming procedure—we had to give it an oil treatment, comb and brush it thoroughly, make two braids, and, with the help of a set of hairpins, coil them up in the form of a nest or chignon at the back of our head. Miss Johanna supervised our morning toilette and helped us with fixing our hair. It all had to be done by half past seven, when we were expected at the breakfast table. The lessons began at eight and lasted until one o'clock, when we had an hour of lunch break, followed by a stroll in line and in pairs, usually down Prater Street to the Praterstern intersection and back. From then until seven o'clock, more lessons, handicraft, and piano practice. We did our numerous written and oral assignments after dinner, and precisely at ten o'clock returned to our beds. Ten hours of mental work was a strenuous programme for adolescent girls. I was nonetheless satisfied with this schedule and would have gladly added ten more hours to a day to have even more time to learn. The lessons were interesting and of good quality. There was a conceptual uniformity in the way they were taught, with an organic interconnectedness in everything we learned, which made it easier to understand.

Apart from being genuinely interested in learning, I was also ambitious. I was the youngest in my class and, furthermore, "new", but I absolutely wanted to be equal to the other girls, many of whom had been at the institute for some years, with a clearly established hierarchy among them. I quickly figured out who were hierarchically at the top and who were at the bottom. I refused to be pushed around and wanted to be among the best and to belong there either due to my audaciousness and ruthlessness, or through my exceptional and impressive success in the classroom. The hierarchy, with Miss Johanna, our teacher, at the top, stretched from favourite students to black sheep. The favourites formed Miss Johanna's entourage and could do things others were not allowed to. The *raison d'être* of the black sheep, however, was to be the laughingstock for the privileged girls. No matter what they said or did, they were ridiculed and exposed to mockery.

Miss Johanna taught French and spoke to us exclusively in that language, including outside the classroom. She spoke fluently and correctly, but her French sounded affected and elaborate, obviously acquired from books. She shared the life with us—she sat at our table during meals, slept in our dormitory, supervised our homework, and had the role of the final arbiter in all disputes. She was in her forties with a snub nose, protruding eyes, and shapeless lips. She wore her corset tightened to the maximum, and her overall figure resembled more an artificial mannequin than a living body. She wore high, stiff collars, and kept her mirror-shiny hair (with its visible streaks of early grey), parted in the middle and pressed tightly across her ears. She abhorred curls and with firm combing and brushing, managed to tame even the most capricious strands on her wards' heads so that at the end of the daily, early-morning procedure everything looked sleek, tight, and shiny with oil. Not a single stubborn curl was allowed to show on our young foreheads! She simply detested all forms of coquetry and condemned all attempts at expressing femininity as signs of shallowness and frivolousness. That had been her life for some twenty-five years, always surrounded by new groups of young girls. Often among newly arrived girls were daughters of former pupils she had taught some years earlier. Generations of girls came and went, but she always remained true to herself, as alienated from the world as ever, because she knew no better. She was raising us in the same spirit as she had raised all the other generations before us, guided by the belief that avoiding the realities of life was the ultimate virtue.

I shared my small, modest bedroom with three other girls. Olga Gussman's family belonged to Viennese theatre circles and from her we got an inkling of the mysterious world behind the stage. As a grown-up, she became an actress herself. She had a job at the Raimund Theatre[169] and married a well-known author, Arthur Schnitzler, creator of such plays as *Anatol*, *Reigen* (Round Dance) and *Liebelei* (Flirtation).[170] My other room-mate was a small, chubby Hungarian girl, Ilonka Dénes. She spoke broken German and whenever at a loss for a word, resorted to whole sentences in Hungarian and countless *"kérem szépen"* (if you please) and *"jaj istenem"*

(oh, dear me!) The third roommate, Sofie Hartwig, was, in my opinion, the most interesting. She was the indisputable star of our institute. Her considerable talents and confident demeanour were impressive not only to us, her colleagues, but also to the professors, and especially Miss Johanna.

I, too, found Sofie impressive. In fact, I adored her and my love for her was unrequited for a long time. I admired all her good, and bad, qualities. She was from Vienna, two years my senior, almost a grown-up. She had by then spent six years at the institute, although her parents lived only a few blocks away from the school. She rarely spoke about her own family. Once she mentioned in passing that she preferred staying at the institute, rather than with her parents and her three older sisters of marriageable age, none of whom she could tolerate. She was well provided for. Her allowance was three times larger than ours and the drawer of her night table was always full of sweets, milk chocolate, and bonbons, which she generously shared with us. She also possessed a distinct kind of elegance that the rest of us lacked. It had less to do with better clothes and more with the way she wore them. Although she was not exceptionally beautiful, her olive complexion, slightly slanted and half-closed, greenish-brown eyes, as well as her nicely lined lips, made her look unusual and attractive. She had far-reaching plans for the future but had not yet decided whether she would dedicate herself to music—as she was a talented musician—or make a career on stage. At the time, she was fully engaged in exercising her superiority on those weaker than herself, which, unfortunately, also included me during my first weeks at the institute. She did not like me, although we shared the same room and sat at the same desk in class. Here is an example. We had no textbooks. Instead, the professor would write down our lessons and homework in one notebook, which Sofie looked after and let the rest of us copy, one by one, into our own notebooks. Lessons in mathematics took place on Wednesdays. Most of my colleagues copied everything from the notebook in the following few days, but my turn was always at the last moment. No one helped me because Sofie's authority was indisputable and I was, for weeks, forced to do mathematical assignments in the greatest of haste and at the last minute.

Still, I did not even consider complaining. I was a new student, with no support from other girls or teachers, and complaining might not have been looked upon favourably. I kept my silence and accepted Sofie's challenge, determined to be her equal with regard to excellence in studying, and even better than her, if possible. As far as that competition went, the situation gradually turned in my favour. It took some time for my isolation to be broken and for me to find myself on an equal footing with her.

I was most successful on that front in our literature class and in essay writing, taught by our director, Professor Max. I had always been good at essay writing and Professor Max would ask me outside the classroom additional questions about various literary topics that seemed to interest me and he was always pleased with my answers. His lessons were particularly stimulating, because he extended his teaching considerably beyond the prescribed curriculum. He did not present literature as an exclusive phenomenon, but as inherent to a specific historical period, offering us striking cultural panoramas of entire epochs in history. He was a great admirer of Schiller and preferred him to Goethe. He had memorized entire sections of his favourite poet's works, both in verse and prose, mostly monologues from his plays, which he recited in class with a lot of pathos and a voice trembling with fervour. We would then learn those monologues by heart and surprise him at the next lesson by reciting them back to him with equal pathos and fervour.

In the course of the first year, we read in class all Schiller's plays, from *The Robbers* to *Wilhelm Tell*, with each of us assuming the role of a particular character in the play. We only left out *Intrigue and Love* because it was not considered "classical" enough and therefore not in the proper spirit of the school. Sofie enjoyed the privilege of being regularly assigned the role of a leading character in the plays we read. Since she was truly talented— one could even say a born actress—she was not satisfied with just reading the parts, and she actually played them out. She would recite the text in a thundering voice, exclaim and sigh in a deep suffering tone, as if already standing on the stage of the Burgtheater itself. Unlike her, Jeanette Azriel from Belgrade read her parts, Thekla[171] or Amalia,[172] in a dull, deep voice, with no evident empathy for the characters. I usually got to play the villains and schemers, such as the old and treacherous Octavio Piccolomini[173] or the insidious Franz Moor.[174] I used to be brilliant at home with my recitations, delivered with maximum pathos, but the texts I had recited on such occasions were of the modest calibre of an Uhland,[175] Geibel,[176] or the melancholy Chamisso.[177] That is why my personification of a cowardly murderer of Octavio's sort was an inevitable failure!

Then something unexpected happened. We were preparing to read Schiller's *Don Carlos*, and the professor, to my great surprise, assigned me the part of Marquis of Posa, and asked Sofie to read that of King Philip! Of course, I was thrilled because Marquis of Posa was my favourite of all Schiller's characters from his entire opus of work. I already imagined myself falling on my knees and beseeching Philip, "Sire, grant us the freedom of thought!"

Sofie seemed stunned. Such casting was a personal insult to her. Her lips tightened and her green eyes flashed a fluorescent glow. She then said with her characteristic mocking smile, "After all, Philip is a king. To kneel in front of you as Posa? Never!" Then she became silent, as if nothing had happened.

The next day, my beautiful copy of Schiller's collected plays with gilded inscriptions on its cover, which I had only recently received as a birthday present, disappeared. It was nowhere to be found, even after I had thoroughly searched my own and all the other girls' drawers. The only thing I found hidden in a corner was the opening page of *Don Carlos* ripped into tiny pieces. At our next literature class, I told Professor Max that I was not up to playing such an important role as Marquis of Posa and I politely asked him to assign it to Sofie.

Upon hearing what I had just said, Sofie turned crimson red and stared at me speechless. I said it spontaneously without even knowing myself where that idea had come from. But Sofie refused to accept my apparent gift. I remained firm and repeated my request. The professor kept looking at us in turns. Did he realize what was actually going on? Finally, he said, "Very well. Sofie shall read Posa." And then he turned to me. "I have a special assignment for you. You will write a paper about *Don Carlos*, taking into account not only individual characters but also historical circumstances. Do you feel up to that task?"

Yes! I was up to it and I was overjoyed! Full of gratitude, I looked at my teacher, who knew how to solve a conflict with necessary tact. I looked at

Sofie too. She was perplexed and looked the other way. The ice was still not broken.

It took me several days to complete the assignment and it came out well. Professor Max read it in front of the class and added that I showed a good grasp of the meaning of the fight for freedom and human rights, and that I correctly described Philip's character. I recognized the fact that his tragic loneliness was the inevitable cause of his profound insensitivity and hatred of people. I emphasized that only when in touch with other people can one realize one's full potential. Using red ink and in calligraphic style, the professor wrote "Excellent" next to his signature at the bottom of my paper. This was my first success at school, which I reported back home glowing with happiness.

This time Sofie was not expressing envy. Turning to others rather than me, she remarked that the essay was really good and beyond her expectations. She took the whole incident with apparent indifference, but she harassed me much less afterwards. She even made discreet moves to get closer to me, which I accepted with enthusiasm. What a joy it was when she asked me for information or wanted to borrow my pencil. And one day, as a replacement for my lost copy of Schiller's works, I received from her an even more elaborate edition.

We became friends. We were seen more and more often together, whispering to each other in confidence. We now formed a pair during our daily afternoon walks, and she would confide in me about things that interested her in particular. I was immensely proud of that friendship and admired her so much, that I compliantly succumbed to her influence. She was not just ahead of me by being a few years older, but also due to her experience in life, self-confidence, and vitality. She had been through quite a lot in her life and must have witnessed a few unpleasant things too, most likely within her own family—something she refused to talk about. How otherwise could one explain her precocious scepticism? I had been exposed to nothing but good things at home. My parents were well-intentioned people and demanded of their children that they perform their duties and be tactful and good-mannered, as they themselves had always been. Many of their good deeds in life were based on those principles. Was I not then supposed to believe that the whole world fostered the same or similar virtues? But Sofie claimed that such views were obsolete and that no one would get far in life by abiding by them. She said people should not be respectful and good in life, but rather inconsiderate and tough. They should not let others see through them, nor should they say what they really meant, especially if they intended to be in control of their own lives, as opposed to letting others control them.

I was aghast at her precocious outlook and asked, "Does it apply to women too?"

"Even more so to women!" she exclaimed. She then explained that all that nonsense about a woman's special role as a submissive servant to her husband and master was outdated. It was something one could still find in reading Chamisso. Equally outdated were the precepts of a particular female morality. One should read modern books, such as Ibsen's *Nora*, or *Hedda Gabler*,[178] Wedekind's Frühling Erwachen (*Spring Awakening*),[179] and Strindberg's *Miss Julie*.[180] There was no point to discuss the matter with me until I had properly read those books. They showed what a real woman looked like, what she wished for and aspired to, without that false decorum, which people like Miss Johanna, who had never experienced anything in life, tried to instill in us. Miss Johanna's prudery engendered erroneous notions and warranted inevitable disappointments in the future. This was particularly so in the domain of love, something everybody was making so much fuss about. Sofie did not care much about it personally and was a hundred times more disgusted by hypocrisy than by the naked truth itself.

We would usually have these conversations during our breaks between classes. Sofie would casually sit on top of the table and look at me from above. When she became passionate about something, her greenish eyes would sparkle, her forehead would frown, and her nostrils would quiver. I would, meanwhile, look at her admiringly. While the rest of us were still not fully developed—either too tall or too plump, awkwardly put together, badly dressed, and, with our sleek, stern hairdos, seemingly lacking in feminine charm—Sofie, seated the way she was, with her body bent forward and her legs swinging, possessed something supple and gracious, like a young animal. Furthermore, she was shrouded in mystery, which even I, who was so close to her, was unable to uncover. She had a private life of her own outside the institute. She could come and go when she wanted and without supervision, unlike the rest of us. They seemed to trust her when she announced that she would be visiting her parents who lived nearby. In any case, she had opportunities and time for small adventures, something entirely out of our reach.

While walking in pairs down Prater Street one afternoon, she made a gesture with her head in the direction across the street and said, "Can you see that grey house over there? That is where my parents live. We have all kinds of people come by, including artists and actors, and it is sometimes great fun. I could invite you one day, but I'd rather not. You are still so terribly naive, and I prefer to spare you any embarrassment. I have hardened up by now and it doesn't affect me anymore." She said all that with an indifferent expression on her face, as if she really was hardened up and immune to anything. As she spoke, her voice took on a deeper overtone and sounded different from usual. That same evening, before going to bed, she said to me, "You are certainly intelligent, and I like you a lot. I wouldn't have made friends with you otherwise. On the other hand, you are still such a terribly silly kid. For heaven's sake, you trust every bit of stupid nonsense people try to convince you about, and that is very dangerous. I don't trust anybody. But I am trying to get to know myself, namely, to find out what I am really like and not how I appear to others. That is more important than dates in history or math, which we have to learn here, and more important than that entire mess about love and marriage. It is all too shallow, banal, and boring! For instance, I already know now that monogamy isn't meant for me and I am unsuitable for marriage. I don't want children either, heaven forbid! I am for alternative experiences and more subtle relationships. But you don't understand it yet. By the way, more and more people share such views today. Why are you staring at me like that?"

I was truly taken aback, not so much with Sofie's openness, but more by the fact that she knew so much about those things. She explained to me that it was no surprise, considering she had three older sisters, who were emancipated and outspoken. In addition, there were in the library at home all sorts of books to choose from, including those written by Prévost,[181] for example, which were very educational, but also ordinary. She had more respect for modern authors who touched upon sensitive topics without being too direct, and who used certain allusions and detours in presentation, but were clear enough. In fine arts, too, she preferred modern art, which was closer to our sensitivity, because we had become keener, more sensitive and in need of more powerful stimulation—in short, New Art. Hadn't I noticed it myself?

Through Sofie I came across the names of many modern writers and artists, which I had not even heard of before. Thanks to the things she told me, I discovered a forbidden and magical world, a secluded garden where flowers blossomed in fantastic abundance and luxuriance. Once she brought me a small collection of poems in French: *Les Fleurs du mal* (Flowers of Evil) by Charles Baudelaire.[182] I read them with increasing excitement and delight, as never experienced before. What would Miss Johanna have said if she were to find out, considering that, for her, French literature began with Pierre Corneille[183] and ended with Jean Racine?[184] She considered Eugène Scribe[185] still potentially useful reading for a beginner, followed at best by *Corinne* by Madame de Staël[186] and *La Petite Fadette* (Little Fadette) by George Sand.[187] She had no great respect for Molière,[188] however. In her eyes, it was all lighthearted and frivolous buffoonery and she let us read it only because it was in French.

Besides her exotic exterior, nature also bestowed Sofie with extremely volatile moods, which I could not always comprehend in their many manifestations. One moment she was cold, the next, friendly; one minute she was offending people, the next, appear all sweet and caring. She was confusing with her shifting personality and dramatic ways of displaying her superiority, but I still loved her and put up with many things I would not have accepted from anyone else. Instead of evoking jealousy in me for being so superior, she triggered my admiration, which, more to the point, I saw only as a victory over my own weakness and the realization of that fact made me feel proud.

Our friendship continued after the years at the institute and we kept in touch by correspondence and saw each other occasionally. The last time we met was in 1909, when we were both already married. I already had three children. Sofie had just achieved her goal of becoming a stage actress, something she had dreamt of as a girl. She was given the chance to impersonate the problematic female characters that used to inspire her in Ibsen's, Strindberg's, and Hauptmann's[189] plays. Some years later, by sheer chance,

I learned about her tragic death and how that promising career had been cut short.

Oddly enough, it was in those surroundings, away from home, that my latent patriotism was awakened through my confrontations with impertinent Viennese and Hungarian girls—and it became increasingly pronounced. I was longing for the country I came from, the air of my homeland that had nurtured me as a child, for the Long Courtyard where I used to play and, in general, my carefree and safe childhood years. My patriotism stemmed from that longing. It was a love for my native land, without a trace of actual nationalistic feelings, which were totally alien to me. For me, homeland was the city in which I was born, with its drab streets devoid of any architectural charm, familiar to me backwards and forwards. I kept in my memory the image of the shores of the River Drava under the colourful evening lighting. Was there anything as beautiful as that? Seen from a distance, everything looked intensified, transformed into a fairy-tale setting, and appearing ever so enchanting. The moats and the glacis seemed veiled in a romantic light. I enjoyed remembering my bold climbing expeditions on the crumbling walls of the casemates and the first violets I picked in the ditches around the Fortress. That was all part of my memories, magnified and embellished, of something long gone and irretrievably lost, including my childhood.

Out of these vague feelings emerged something new to be idolized—a loving homeland. It was a purely platonic feeling based on mere illusions. I had no argument to explain that feeling, nor proof to justify it. The only thing I could rely on, besides my feelings, were phrases and tirades found in my textbooks. I knew by heart a few patriotic poems, and inspiring songs like *Lijepa naša (Our Beautiful Homeland)*.[190] I had, however, never paid attention to, and therefore knew nothing about, the political background to all that.

There were no newspapers to be seen at our institute. At least, I cannot remember anyone reading them or referring to something seen in a newspaper. I can only assume that, for pedagogical reasons, our teachers wanted to keep us away from the turbulent political atmosphere of the day.

Our discussions were always about questions concerning literature, our impressions after a visit to the theatre or a book we had read, sometimes even our personal likes and dislikes, but never anything beyond that particular framework.

In such a context, I approached my new patriotic interests from a literary perspective. I wrote to Osijek and asked my parents to send me a few Croatian books, which they did immediately. I wanted to find something there to be translated and make my colleagues appreciate the valuable aspects of our art and literature. The moment the books arrived, I translated a few poems by Petar Preradović,[191] trying hard to render, as best I could, their rhythm, rhyme, and content. Then I read them to the others. I could not tell how successful my attempts were and whether I achieved my goal. It happened that others were also proclaiming their patriotic love, especially a few Hungarian girls, who were particularly ostentatious about it. Sofie, however, claimed it was all nonsense and could not understand why anyone would want to waste one's time on such matters. Ilonka Dénes persisted, and as soon as we returned to our bedroom that evening, she began talking about politics, mostly, of course, to provoke me, because, just like me, she knew nothing much about it. Carried away by our patriotic enthusiasm and paying no attention to the fact that, according to the rules, we should have been asleep for a while already, we sat on our beds in our long white nightgowns, nibbling on chocolate and bonbons, and taking turns in delivering fiery propaganda speeches. These were, in our minds, of equal pungency to those given in the Viennese parliament. Our knowledge of the subject was minimal, and we instinctively followed our inner sentiments, which inevitably led to fantastic exaggerations. I began by saying that the Hungarians were our enemies and that was why I hated them. Ilonka Dénes felt the need to defend the Hungarian Crown of Saint Stephen and its prerogatives. She began yelling and put us all on edge because she had forgotten to be careful and not be too loud. Hungary could not care less about my hatred, she yelled. And she snapped her short fingers in front of my very nose. She was a small person, plump, with a tiny snub nose surrounded by two red chubby cheeks and lots of black frizzy hair, her unique beauty. She was hissing straight into my face like an angry cat. She argued that, as far as she could tell, there was no such thing as Croatia, be it a country or a people, that there was no constitution or law which provided for it, and that Croatia was illegal. There was only Hungary and nothing else.

I wanted to interrupt her. "What about those eight counties across the River Drava?"

Those eight counties across the Drava were nothing else but Hungary in her opinion. She triumphantly continued, "Kossuth Lajos[192]—how about him? Then there are Vörösmarty,[193] Petöfi,[194] Jókai Mór![195] How about them?"

I thrust forward the name of my Preradović again, unfortunately without success, because Ilona was louder than I was. "Who is that Preradović anyway? I've never heard of him!" She was laughing mockingly. But I did not want to be overrun just like that. "What about Nikola Šubić Zrinski?[196] You must have heard of him, I guess? He saved you Magyars when you were in trouble. At Szigetvár, you surely remember that!"

"Zrínyi Miklós? Are you calling him a Croat? Ha ha ha!" She burst into laughter. "He was a Magyar!"

The squabble turned more and more heated. We went all the way back into history to Koloman and Bela IV,[197] bickered over the unfortunate King Lajos[198] who drowned at Mohács, brought up Maria Theresa and the Pragmatic Sanction,[199] invoked the names of Baron von Trenck and his *pandurs*,[200] Napoleon, Deák Ferenc[201] and Strossmayer,[202] and whatever else we could think of at that moment. We would have probably gone all the way back to Adam and Eve, had we not finally managed to wake Miss Johanna, who appeared on the doorstep, looking like a ghost in her white robe with a candlestick in her hand. Angry at us for disturbing the peace, she gave us a good scolding and sent us off to bed.

The most interesting lectures given at our school were those by Dr. Pick, our headmistress's brother-in-law, regarded in the world of science as a notable biologist. He used to live in Jena, where he was Ernst Haeckel's[203] student and associate, and had published an independent paper on the development of monocytes. He used to explain to us the structural developments of organisms in an easily understandable and distinctive way, all the way from amoebas up to humans. Most importantly, he knew how to make us passionately interested in those processes. We were breathless while listening to his presentations. It was during his lectures that I became aware of my special interest in natural sciences, which, eighteen years later, prompted me to study biochemistry. I had not believed in either the creation of the world in seven days, or God Almighty himself, since my school days. That left a certain emptiness instead, which I did not know how to fill or reconcile. Countless questions tormented me, above all, the origin and destiny of humanity. Not even Dr. Pick could answer those questions fully, but he led me to the right path that I then followed, carefully probing my way. The concept of the law of eternal becoming and passing away was enlightening. The professor's explanations introduced some order to my chaotic way of thinking, caused by sheer ignorance. Our world of solipsistic loneliness was suddenly shaken up by the liberating idea of the interdependency of all things natural. He also taught us that there are no big leaps in nature—rather, that nature is determined by certain stable evolutionary processes. He pointed to the fact that there were not just transitions from one species to another, but also transitions from plants to animals, most probably from the inorganic to organic matter as well, including the wonderful and entirely specific characteristics of crystals. He was telling us about the uniqueness of natural forces in the universe, of spectral analysis, astrophysics, and the fundamental cosmic laws based on the sustainability of matter and energy. On this axiom, and in conjunction with Darwin's theory of evolution, he tried to explain all biological and cosmic occurrences. He was aware of the most recent scientific advancements made until 1895, which meant before Einstein's theory of general relativity or atomic theory and before Madame Curie discovered radium. At the time, only some seventy chemical elements were generally known, and their immutable nature considered established once and for all.

In those two years of his teaching, he gave us a solid foundation upon which to expand our knowledge, if ever so inclined later in life. He enabled us to understand all life phenomena and, with his interpretations, dispel for us the implied mystery. We were able to get rid of whatever religious prejudice was still left in us and be ready to espouse more sound, more flexible, and progressive ideas. I found out from Miss Johanna that it was entirely by chance that Dr. Pick happened to be teaching at our school. Despite his high academic rank as a scientist, he had earlier been expelled from the University of Jena, as a result of an anti-Semitic campaign. As a Jew who declined to be Christianized, more out of principle than religious convictions, he was not allowed to hold a full-time professorship at any university in Austria or Germany.

There was not a single Jew among the professors teaching at the University of Vienna in the 1890s. Each attempt to appoint one was nipped in the bud, either in the academic senate or by clamorous demonstrations organized by the German nationalistic or Christian-Socialist-oriented student bodies. Dr. Pick felt it on his own skin in Graz, where he was for a short time employed as a university lecturer. A crowd of politically organized students approached him from behind while he was lecturing and beat him up with clubs. He was carried out of the lecture hall covered in blood. Once recovered, he resigned and moved to Vienna, where he contented himself with the modest position of a high school professor at our institute.

The "case" of our beloved Dr. Pick was the subject of long discussions among us. Some of the girls had in general tried to forget they were Jewish, including me, and had, to a great extent, succeeded in this effort. But the insult suffered by such a remarkable man affected us deeply. Could it be true that the place of a Jewish person was outside the realm of law? How could one be denied the possibility to engage one's skills in the profession of one's choice? Must one really put up with bullying and insults by callous people, without the whole world becoming outraged? I was troubled by these questions and, for a while, found it difficult to come to terms with it all. Had it happened to someone else, I would have perhaps looked for certain logical explanations according to which the victim would carry part of the blame. But Dr. Pick was above any possible suspicion. He was a renowned scholar and a man commanding respect for his overall appearance and noble intentions. He was not striving towards material gain in life—he concentrated purely on his science. The fact that one such man could be beaten up and expelled from work, meant that raw violence could also prevail over everything else. I was increasingly aware of it. Various events taking place outside the secure atmosphere of our institute, news of which occasionally did reach us after all, reinforced my suspicions. There were brawls in the Parliament, hate mongering against Jews at the Vienna Town Council, and the renewed expletives, "Hep, hep!",[204] on the streets at the appearance of a recognizable Jewish person from the East.

A whole set of problems suddenly besieged me. I realized, for the first time in my life, that a person did not belong to oneself alone, not even to the close circle of one's family or to a selected number of intimates, but that we were all part of a hostile world which was not governed by noble and generous instincts, but rather obtuseness, pettiness, and even malice. The weak were the victims of the powerful, and none of that was mere coincidence, because it was never a single person's doing. On the contrary, it was a manifestation of a well-designed and solidly built system.

There was only one thing that helped me escape my troubling thoughts and restore my peace of mind. I am referring here to our frequent visits to theatres, concerts, and museums, which always made a deep impression on me. The effect of those cultural experiences was by far the most valuable of all the things I had availed myself of in those two years in Vienna. What I saw and experienced in those days provided me for the rest of my mostly provincial life with a lasting model and standard to help me distinguish the difference between good and bad art. Once a week, Miss Johanna would take us to a museum, either the Art History Museum, the Museum of Natural History, the Lichtenstein Museum, with its immense collection of paintings by Rubens, or The Belvedere, with its incomparably beautiful Gobelin tapestries. Twice a month we went to the theatre, and sometimes a concert. I could not, by any means, claim that my understanding of art had already been truly awakened by that time, but the sheer sense of marvel and awe at the sight of great artistic achievements was there to serve as the first criteria. That initial and genuine admiration gradually yielded understanding.

Those visits made me simply spellbound, fascinated, and exhilarated. There was, apart from the appreciation of beauty in itself, an additional sense of delight that those eternally beautiful things were there in front of me—works by Rembrandt, Rubens, "Hell Brueghel,[205] or Raphael and Titian, that I was able to absorb them, and that they were not mere concepts, but something I was personally experiencing. There was the house on Schwarzspanierstrasse, where Beethoven had died, as well as Saint Stephen's Cathedral with its towering pillars and incomparable, stained-glass windows, through which the light penetrated in silvery tones. There were Schönbrunn and the grey Hofburg palaces, the exuberant Karlskirche and the fountain on Neuer Markt built by Georg Raphael Donner[206] in his attractive Baroque style. I learned to differentiate between the Renaissance, Baroque, and Rococo, to find associations in shapes, colours, and sounds and then transfer all those impressions from emotion to thought. I was filled with gratitude towards life for all that was there, that existed, and even more so that it existed so that I could experience its enchantment.

The most beautiful, however, were our evenings at the Burgtheater, which was, at the time, one of the world's leading stages, and the best one in German language. Each of those evenings at the theatre was a big event in the monotony of our school life, with each of them seriously prepared for days in advance with reading and analysis of the plays we were about to see. In those two years, I saw the famous actress Charlotte Wolter[207] in her most important roles as Iphigenia, Mary Stuart,[208] Lady Macbeth, and Adelheid (in Goethe's *Götz*),[209] as well as actors like Adolf von Sonnenthal[210] as Nathan[211] and King Lear, Friedrich Mitterwurzer[212] as Othello and Wallenstein,[213] Bernhard Baumeister[214] as Götz, and Josef Lewinsky[215] as King Richard III. Most beloved by all the schoolgirls at the institute was Fritz Krastel[216] as the knightly Jean de Dunois[217] and the irresistible count von Strahl.[218]

The four of us roommates, headed by Olga Gussman and Sofie, were infatuated with Krastel. In the room next to ours, the girls were thrilled with Georg Reimers[219] playing the Templar[220] or Lionel,[221] or any of his usual roles impersonating a young lover with good looks and a curly blond wig. Typical, adolescent romanticizing set aside, there was also a much deeper foundation to our admiration. What captivated us was the magnificent collective performance of all those great artists, whether in leading or supporting roles. There were in fact no supporting roles—everything was in balance and on the same level. There were no tricks or special theatre effects, no gratuitous changes in the prescribed style, no star playing, no witty improvisations and antics. Everything rigorously followed the good old theatre tradition of the Burgtheater, including the strict use of the purest classical German (the so-called Burgtheater-Deutsch). Nowhere else was it spoken with equal beauty and clarity.

Although the ensemble had to follow strictly prescribed norms, the actors still had enough room to display their full personality and talent. Therefore, it is no coincidence that the Burgtheater ensemble yielded the greatest number of exceptional and distinguished actors. Oh, what harmony of gestures that was! What a euphony of voices! How much beauty there was in the suffering, in the fury of emotions, yes, even in the heroes' downfalls! What an extraordinary display of high emotions in the face of fateful events that inevitably and logically ended in tragedy—which we, as young girls, were privileged to witness unfolding before our eyes! Those were unforgettable nights. I can still see the noble character of Iphigenia; I can hear King Lear's laments; I can see Lady Macbeth with her demonic skill of seduction; I can listen in my mind to Sonnenthal as Nathan, reciting the parable of the three rings; and I can weep over the destiny of the unfortunate Mary Stuart, which sixty years earlier brought floods of tears to my eyes.

No wonder that we, as fifteen-year-old girls, were populating our world with heroic characters, and striving to measure our everyday reality accordingly. Everything happening under the limelight was convincing and resembling life. How monotonous and banal was reality without the reflection of that transforming light, makeup, heroic outbursts, tragic sequences of events conditioned by the forces of destiny, and their final resolution resulting in spiritual exaltation and beauty!

It was definitely no coincidence that four of our colleagues later worked on stage. People around us claimed we were out of bounds, unable to differentiate between illusion and reality, and were transposing our artistic and literary experiences into everyday life, where there was no place for such things. I admit we were hot-headed young people acting unreasonably in the given circumstances. It was not possible for us to think and feel differently, considering the education we were receiving—disassociated as it was from all reality beyond the walls of the school. They indoctrinated us with idealism and opened before us romantic perspectives. We were expecting far too much from the world into which we were slowly being introduced. We had too many demands and were fed on illusions that had to end in disappointment sooner or later. We lived in unnatural conditions, and we filled the emptiness of such life with delusions that we created ourselves and made into the foundations of our existence. We filled the horizons we gravitated towards with colours and light. We gave them shapes and sounds that were products of our imagination. We created our own fetishes that fascinated us, and deities that we worshipped. We were equally immoderate in assessing our own possibilities. They exposed us at school to the highest standards in art and literature as part of our overall education, without, however, considering how all that would serve us in our own future lives in a very different environment. How could they expect young people to be capable of separating one from the other? How could young people understand how temporary it all was, like a short flicker of light that quickly waned, with the subsequent darkness even deeper and harder to navigate through? Was it sensible or in any way useful to show us things which were not meant for us, and to give us tools to appreciate beauty that we would never again be able to encounter, only to be left, fifty years later, with the awareness of those things existing in another world from ours?

I admit we were a bit exalted, disoriented, and at a loss. I became most painfully aware of that state of mind as the time of my return home was approaching. I no longer felt the platonic nostalgia for the banks of the Drava and the Long Courtyard, but rather a certain unmotivated, undefined, but nonetheless agonizing, fear. I was afraid of going back to the life of my childhood, which I had left behind, and to which I was returning as half a grown-up. It was the fear of a life with no prospects ahead, and of the unknown that awaited me.

I can still remember the rainy autumn morning when my father came to fetch me. I was deeply distressed as I said goodbye to my teachers and friends and descended the dark winding staircase into the foggy school-yard. It seemed particularly grey and desolate at that moment.

"Aren't you looking forward to going home?" my father asked me, putting his arm around my shoulders and attempting to console me. I nodded. Oh yes, I was looking forward to it. "Why are you crying then?" I shrugged. I could not give him an answer, because I did not know myself. The tears had come spontaneously.

At the bottom of the dark yard, which seemed like a wide-open gorge, a trace of light appeared in the sky. The bustling city was out there. The streetcars were running along. People were mindlessly rushing about their business. It suddenly felt good to join the flow and stop thinking of the painful parting, not merely from the people I had learned to love, but also from a whole period of my life.

That same evening, we set off homewards.

While I was away, my parents changed residence. The familiar Franjina Street, where I had known every child who lived there, ceased to be part of my life. Gone was the old house and the Long Courtyard with its poor proletarian dwellings. Gone were the modest gardens in the neighbourhood with their raspberry bushes, mulberry trees, oleanders, and purslane among the red bricks of the pavement. Gone was the well, covered in vines, and the shady gazebo where meals had been served in summertime. The family had moved to a recently built and posh neighbourhood, where they settled in a comfortable apartment with seven rooms in a building on Jaeger Street.

The new apartment did have one big advantage. I had my own room where I could spend a few hours a day on my own, while reading and trying to find order in my unruly thoughts. After two years in Vienna, I was ripped out of all continuity. The old life was gone, and I was not prepared for the new, which seemed to have nothing particularly appealing to offer. Old acquaintances, schools, girlfriends with whom I had roamed around and played together—all that belonged to the past, overshadowed by more intense experiences in Vienna. I simply grew up and there was no way I could start over again. I was wandering the streets of Osijek like a foreigner. The streets had become narrower, the houses seemed to have shrunk, and people looked drab. The strict school discipline was over, and I could not reconcile myself to the fact that a sustained learning opportunity was no longer at my disposal.

The institutions of higher education were still not available to young women in those days. There was, since 1893, to be exact, a lyceum for women in Zagreb, the first of its kind in the whole monarchy. But in

Osijek, it was not considered proper to let one's daughter take part in such a revolutionary novelty. If they had the means, Essekers preferred to hire a German governess to act as a chaperone. As an alerted Cerberus,[222] the keeper of their morals, her task was to supervise the adolescent daughter and accompany her at every step. In any event, graduating from a lyceum did not open any doors to subsequent practical opportunities, because universities—with the exception of those in Switzerland—would remain closed to women for a long time to come. After finishing the lyceum, the best a woman could obtain as employment was to teach, be a governess, or a lady companion. Smart girls were not particularly appreciated in everyday life. The dislike did not come just from men—members of their own fair sex considered them as affected literati and bluestockings, and sometimes even more maliciously as amazons, to be mocked and avoided. It was difficult for them to find a marriage partner and they were often obliged to continue living with their parents as eccentric spinsters, which was not just burdensome to all concerned, but also considered a disgrace.

Men were against granting women access to university education or opportunities in the area of liberal professions, their explanation being that women were incapable of any independent cultural activity, that their way of thinking was insufficiently analytical, and that they were deficient in the area of original creativity or aptitude for abstraction. This is an assumption that is today[223] still maintained in the case of black people. Many profound psychological treatises were written about the difference between the sexes, in which it was claimed that "a woman in her deep commitment to her own being refuses everything connected to public life". There was talk about "the sex factor" in the definition of femininity, about the "organic unity" of the female nature, about the "accentuated instincts and vegetative life impulses in females", about their "oversensitive and unstable nervous systems", and their "by-nature-conditioned menstrual cycles and a smaller brain". There was talk of anatomy and physiology, as well as references to medicine, political economy, and aesthetic norms, and, as the ultimate argument, the claim that it would be dangerous to open the job market to women and create havoc on the wage front. Women would introduce unfair competition, which would make it difficult for men to start a family, and would, in many cases, end up by excluding men from certain categories of jobs. Entire books were written on that topic, which caused a flood of indignant replies from the feminine side. The indisputably worst pronouncement on that subject was put forward by a sociologist from Vienna, Professor Gruber,[224] who concluded in his treatise on social hygiene that women should under no circumstances be allowed to enter universities. Rather, they should, like cows, be left to graze in pastures, not be engaged in any activity other than to prepare themselves for their only proper vocation—breeding and motherhood. The men thus fighting to preserve their privileges conveniently kept forgetting that it was the women, prevented from studying medicine due to their alleged physical weakness, who were effectively engaged in the most physically strenuous professions of caregiving, nursing, and midwifery. They forgot that women stood behind machines in manufacturing facilities and factories, did the hardest agricultural work, and applied themselves as hard as they could in all other jobs they were forced to do during their lives. We should add to all of that such things as housework, giving birth, raising children, and being victims to endless abuse by their husbands, who were protected by law and tradition. Millions of women around the globe were forced to assume all forms of inhuman labour and not be appreciated for their sacrifice. In the male-dominated world, this was an accepted fact and met with no objection on behalf of men.

It was difficult—sometimes to the point of being impossible—to stand up as an individual against such an unreservedly sustained state of affairs by the society at large. It was impossible, with the simple use of one's own energy, to break the constraints of an entrenched tradition and prejudice, especially if that person was young and inexperienced, and lived in the oppressive atmosphere of a remote provincial town. There, everything was closely connected and every deviation from the norm was immediately confronted as if it posed a threat to the established order of things. I was aware—let us say, I suspected—that the position of a so-called upper-class woman was unfair, untenable and abusive. I was also aware that at issue was the welfare of only those women, since the welfare or misfortune of working-class and peasant women was an entirely different problem. In the time of enlightenment, liberalism, technical advancement, and unlimited possibilities provided by overall social progress, the position held by a woman in society represented a horrifying anachronism. In her role as a luxury object, she was denied the possibility of keeping up with the social changes of the day. Instead of her strength, she was required to rely on her apparent feminine weaknesses to attract the eye of a man. Women who dared to develop their own personalities were regarded as anomalies, and, in especially drastic cases, even monstrous phenomena, comparable to a calf with two heads or a similar circus attraction. If a woman happened to excel in a cultural domain, it was considered an exception to the rule. The time between the age of fifteen and twenty was considered nothing more than the waiting period for that great moment when "the most wonderful of them all" would step on the scene to reveal to his chosen one the heavens of love and the harbour of marital bliss. A woman's life could then finally begin. That is, of course, if one was lucky. It was a commonly held belief that the suitable time for marriage was over after one's twentieth birthday, when the bloom of youth began to wither. There was no more time to wait for a Prince Charming and one had to accept whatever became available, namely a marriage of convenience, for which material security was a decisive component of acceptance.

Time spent waiting for the big event was usually filled with all kinds of useless dalliances—foreign language practice, plunking away on the piano, silk painting, or painstaking handicraft, all under the maxim, "Decorate your home!" There were plenty of girls' afternoon coffee parties, with lots of giggling, whispering, sweet pastry, and whipped cream. There was also a bit of housework to be done, and I was put to that task as well. It did not amount to much, however. I was required to tidy my room every day, although we had an excellent maid. For the same pedagogical reasons, I was required to dust the salon and peel potatoes in the kitchen, to the great distress of our cook, who mostly found me to be in her way. It was still that same Marija, whom I had to thank for my sexual education some years earlier.

The educational programme to become a good housewife included setting the table for family lunches at noontime. Every afternoon I went for a walk with my mother, always in the same direction and with the same goal. We would start down the avenue, then walk across the glacis to the intersection of the roads leading to the Fortress and the New Town, and back again. At the turn of the first corner, we would meet someone we knew and stop. There would be expressions of great pleasure in meeting each other, although we would meet this way almost every day and talk about the same things—troubles with the servants, dinner menus, and matters of fashion and clothing. After a few more paces, we would run into more acquaintances, whom we would greet with the same dose of cordiality, as if we had not seen one another in ages, and discuss the same matters all over again. All those good friends of my mother paid no attention to me, as if I were invisible. The things they chatted about left me indifferent and I was bored to death. I would pull on my mother's sleeves to get going, but she was uncompromising when it came to tact and courtesy, and I had to stand there as mute as a fish while the ladies kept chatting. My annoyed grimaces regularly remained unnoticed.

Even more horrid were the occasional visits to our old aunts. I had the impression no one had as many of them as I did. They all lived in modest, mouldy, cramped apartments, which reeked of bodily odours and rancid fat. They were of melancholy predisposition, and nothing in their lives was joyful enough to change that state of mind.

Aunt Nina was harassed by her hysterical daughter, who had never married and blamed her aging mother for the failure. Aunt Roza was also unlucky with her children. Her only son had passed away when still a child, and her daughter, with three small children, was abandoned by her husband. Aunt Bettina was amiable and kind, and in a certain way cultured—she used to cite Heine and would sometimes refer to some lofty philosophical points of view. This was the only way in which she was able to bear her life next to her primitive and grumpy husband, who also had a heart condition. Aunt Fanny was not actually a real relative, but she had known my mother since birth and that was why we went to see her twice a year. Her husband had a grocery shop in one of the Lower Town's narrow streets. The store was certainly no goldmine. Its customers were the poorest of people and shopped there mostly on credit. Aunt Fanny, however, was known to be a big spender. Even on weekdays, she walked around in a rustling black taffeta dress with white lace cuffs and a gold brooch on her collar. She liked lounging on the chaise longue and reading sentimental novels, in which women of her type could still hope for something good to happen in their lives. In the meantime, her husband was toiling away from dawn to dusk.

"Why do we even go to see these people?" I asked my mother. "This can't possibly be amusing for you."

"It is our duty to visit our aging relatives whether it amuses us or not."

"But we have a duty to ourselves!"

I had read that phrase somewhere and I was pleased with myself to be able to use it at that moment. I tried to explain to my mother that we were a new generation and that we looked at things from a different point of view. It was no one's duty to be bored to death to please another person, as was the case with me that afternoon, but rather, by all possible means, to foster one's own self.

Mother retorted, "The best way to foster one's own self is to do one's duty towards others."

She truly believed in the necessity of fulfilling one's duty and never in her long life did she neglect whatever she considered that duty to be. I admit that "duty" belongs to the category of absolute necessities in social relations. But that term, used so frequently by my educators, had an irritating connotation when used in reference to me. Even when it referred to others, it seemed more like an obligation imposed by those more powerful on the weaker, for their own comfort, by making their lives at least bearable, if not happy. I knew women who used to perform their duties in sheer deference to their indisputably more stupid and ethically less worthy husbands. I knew men who stifled their striving for improvement in life, because of some official imposition of duty. Many girls were forced to sacrifice their personal inclinations, because duty required them to submit to their parents' wishes. How many unhappy marriages out there were maintained only out of a sense of duty, although the partners hated each other? All around us was a lot of denial of personal satisfaction, founded on the argument of duty. The sense of duty made people submit to quite ridiculous conventions, conform to outdated habits, act in a way that no longer had anything to do with tact and good manners, beyond being an automatic gesture, following years of coercion into a societally sanctioned social interaction.

Like so many others, I was also obliged to submit to these social norms. I had to fall in line with "people say" or "one should" and respect the laws of "the golden middle". I was not allowed to develop any personal affinities or have wishes or demands that would not fit within the prescribed standards imposed on me by my social standing. Having a talent was dangerous, and its public display was considered compromising for any woman, be it in fine arts, on the stage, or by pursuing higher education.

All this stood in the way of my continuing intellectual development in, probably, the most delicate phase of my growth as a person, and I was deeply aware of how unaccomplished I still was. My struggle for change required a great amount of strength and energy, because I kept facing constant pressures from people around me while having only one wish—to break loose and pave the way for my further edification. I considered it my duty.

By noting down these details of my growing-up days, I do not wish to advance the idea that this was some sort of tragedy. That would be wrong and pretentious of me. There were girls of my age who already knew what the struggle for sheer existence meant, labouring in factories up to twelve hours a day and living in unhealthy basements in an atmosphere of alcoholism, vice, and ignorance. Most girls from the countryside never went to school and could not read or write. There were poor seamstresses and couturiers, who were, in the eyes of good bourgeois men, not much more than easy prey for playboys, young and old, to seduce, ruin, and then ditch them. There was no possible comparison between my position and that of a young service maid, hired to take care of other people's children while still a child herself, and asked to perform tasks which were, besides a miserable pay and measly meals, far too hard and demanding for someone her age. I was not a daughter of a lowly clerk obliged to stand humbly on the side while the family's earnings were spent for the education of sons, who then failed to get married and therefore remained destined for the ungrateful "role of a daughter" and "the poor demurring one" until the end of her days.

I had no right to compare myself with those unfortunate girls. I was born into a respectable and prosperous family and was not obliged to take on any real work. My parents were loving and sensible, keen to prepare me for a comfortable and rather leisurely future life, which, if all went as planned, would last until my blissful end. But that was just it! I dreaded the idea of an indolent life in the Cockaigne land of plenty. I had too much of the innate élan to go along that path—too much initiative to become a mere object, whose fate would be decided by others. In all probability, however, I was heading towards leading the same life of empty existence as most of the ladies around me—a life of leisure and superficiality, with a total lack of interest in anything beyond oneself and daily gossip parties within the narrow family circles. The mere thought was already too much. I wanted to escape at all costs a fate that reminded me of a captured animal. I did not want to become one. Anything but that!

Since it was easier to determine what one really did not want, than to have a clear image of what would be worth living for, I directed my aspirations towards seemingly realistic goals that I hoped my parents would approve. First, I definitely wanted to continue my studies, and second, not to get married unless for love. It may sound simple today, but in those days, it was an entirely revolutionary idea.

Soon after my return from Vienna, I was allowed, upon my eager insistence, to resume my German lessons with Pastor Pindor. Since my grasp of grammar and spelling was by then quite solid, and I had either read or seen at the Burgtheater a great many German classics, the pastor chose to teach me a discipline which could suit my higher level of education. It was called "aesthetics"—the study of beauty or the science of good taste. We read Schiller's discussion *Über die ästhetische Erziehung des Menschen in einer Reihe von Briefen* (On the Aesthetic Education of Man, in a Series of Letters),[225] Lessing's *Laokoon, oder Über die Grenzen der Malerei und Poesie* (Laocoön, An Essay on the Limits of Painting and Poetry),[226] and Ch. Oeser's *Briefe an eine Jungfrau über die Hauptgegenstände der Aesthetik* (Letters to a Young Woman About the Importance of Aesthetics—also known as Aesthetics Letters).[227] Such scholarly reading made me feel important, but I was just as intensely bored as when visiting my old aunts.

The pastor approached the topic in an entirely academic manner and analyzed the concept of beauty by means of stretched-out, theoretical discussions, which added precious little to my understanding of the subject, and were so boring that they eventually suffocated in me all sense of beauty and aesthetic values. His office was painted white and the only decoration was a wooden cross. Its dark colour was in striking contrast to the whiteness of the walls. Under it was a lithography, featuring a portrait of Luther with his strangely medieval peasant face, and calligraphed quotations from the Holy Bible at each side. I still remember the monotonous buzz of flies, which made me feel even drowsier. The pastor kept pacing up and down the room, quoting and lecturing. He was a man close to forty, of sanguine disposition, tall, with wide shoulders, and fat, chubby cheeks drowning into fat layers of his neck without any transition. Worthy of mention was his smooth preacher's voice, with which he made even the most banal things sound special, pathetic, and eventually blown out of proportion. He used to explain to me, in the line of Schiller's precepts, that beauty was the apparition of freedom. It was important for a work of art not to stimulate any kind of "personalized interest" and instead be enjoyed dispassionately. Or put another way—beauty was meant to awaken affection devoid of possessive urges. I had difficulties in grasping it all. One single verse by Goethe contributed more to my understanding of art than ten pages of Oeser's letters to a young woman or Schiller's aesthetic theorems. I had yawning fits and kept looking at the clock, eagerly hoping that the lesson would soon end.

Somewhere around that time, I went through an emotional experience that increased my sensitivity and made me more intensely aware of my own immaturity and insecurity. That was my first encounter with death, an event which probably has the same unsettling effect on all young people. My grandmother on my father's side died that autumn after a long illness. It was not so much the loss of my grandmother which affected me, but rather the fact that it was my first direct encounter with the mysterious transition from life into non-existence, the annihilation of someone's vital living energy and the sudden disappearance from the sphere of the living. One day she was among us, sharing with us her happy and sad moments, the next, she was nothing but a shadow in our memories. I was suddenly aware of how incomprehensible it was to differentiate between being and non-being, how inescapable was our fate, how insubstantial was our existence. My standards changed. What was deemed infinite before, crumbled into nothingness today. I shed bitter tears, but I cried less for her than for myself. Why even live when the end was so terrifying, distressing and inescapable?

That mood increased my interest in mysticism, and I succumbed to the influence of certain irrational interpretations, which led me to an even deeper conflict within myself. I then did something I had never done before—I became interested in religious questions in the vague hope that I would find consolation and peace. I found a copy of the Bible in our book cabinet and began to read it. But instead of immersing myself in the Old Testament with its partially familiar legends, as would have been typical of me, I began to read the New Testament and encountered for the first time the figure of Christ. I found the figure highly impressive, but my admiration was soon accompanied by doubts. Why turn him into a godlike figure instead of venerating him for the man he really was, namely a human being like us all, who, by also being the son of God, conceived by the power of the Holy Spirit, dutifully performed his mission on earth? And his mission was love. Is that not the mission of us all? Is not love for humanity the only thing that can save us and help us overcome our personal loneliness? He died on a cross, and there were many others who came after him and died in defence of their beliefs. I have pondered over that thought with humbling emotions throughout my life. I have been inclined to worship all those who had remained faithful to their convictions and died for them, and I have always believed in the validity of their sacrifice.

There was, however, a factor that soon disturbed my burgeoning faith and quickly destroyed everything I had been painstakingly working on. It was the Gospel accounts of the subsequent miracles, such as Christ's ascension or his physical presence in the sacrament, and, above all, the horrible dogma of forgiveness of sins, and descriptions of the horrors of hell awaiting us upon our death. Is it possible to imagine God as an avenger of all sins, since he was the very same who planted their seeds within us? Just the thought seemed horrifying and absurd. Only a perverse brain could have invented such a thing! Already deprived of one's free will by the power of the unfathomable will of God, why should a human being be subjected to the torments of hell, even after death?

One day I revealed to the pastor some of my doubts and my religious confusion. I had no idea how it happened. But when you live with an obsession for a long time, when you are consumed with it, as I was, words start coming out by themselves. Giving shape to something one cannot comprehend and the act of stylizing it into words offers relief. Perhaps I was expecting him to say something special, some sort of enlightenment, which I was unable to find in Biblical representations, something more human and spiritual, something more than mere sentences. But I was wrong, because what happened was exactly the opposite of what I had expected. This man of God managed to kill at the start—and forever—that flicker of faith, which had illuminated my heart for a few days and was barely smouldering there for a few weeks, yearning for encouragement and validation. That period of a strained spiritual sinking into the irrational was the first and the last of that kind in my entire life.

The pastor was evidently pleased by this good pastoral opportunity and he used it to enlighten me. So instead of aesthetics, our lessons were from then on filled with religious thoughts. He was explaining the New Testament and the roots of Protestantism in the Germanic and Anglo-Saxon cultural realm. Then he crossed over to eschatology, namely the study of the Four Last Things.[228] He especially emphasized the fact that humans could not be saved by good deeds, but only by their faith. It was the only way to get redemption. Human actions could be valued only when inspired by the grace of God. Only if guided by that grace, could one find the way to salvation. Without it, all was in vain. I protested, "But in this way a person loses every personal initiative, all personal credit, any kind of motivation to be active or drive to create something valuable, every propensity for affirmation through one's own efforts. Instead of fighting, one is directed towards a passive surrender. In that case, why live at all?"

The pastor was up in arms upon hearing these remarks. He was trying to persuade me—by then entirely pursuing his pastoral mission—that a doubting person was condemned in advance. Such a person rejected God's revealed teachings and was therefore excluded from God's grace.

My next question came in a muffled voice, because of an uncomfortable pressure in my throat. "And what if a person can't believe?"

He replied sanctimoniously, "One should pray and wait."

I shook my head. Pray and wait? No way. My doubts became a certainty. I would never be able to find bliss! Luckily, my *Weltschmerz* did not last much longer. Young people have, for their own sake, an innate source of vital energy, strong enough to burst through, wash away layers of mental, mostly artificially constructed build-up, and prepare the ground for new stimulations and aspirations in life.

July was the month when we spent summer holidays in Velika, a small resort in the Mount Papuk region, near the town of Slavonska Požega. The main purpose of it was to escape Osijek swelters, clouds of dust, swarms of mosquitoes, and the bad drinking water. We stayed in an old Franciscan monastery, from where legendary Friar Luka Ibrišimović and his band of *haiduks* had launched many armed raids against the Ottomans.[229] The monastery and its vast estate became a seigniorial property in the eighteenth century, and in 1896 entered a new phase—it was converted into a summer holiday resort.

Velika had a thermal spring already well known in Roman times. It had numerous murmuring streams, and a fish pond teeming with trout and full of algae, which gave it its dark green colour. On top of the hill was a picturesque ruin. According to a legend, it used to be a church surrounded by tall defence walls and built by the Knights Templar. Other people claimed it had been a fortress owned by a cruel aga,[230] who had used it as the launching point for his pillaging campaigns around Slavonia. All that was highly satisfying for my need of romance. My happy disposition was restored in those surroundings. I went out for walks and long excursions. I enjoyed cool swims and the mysterious darkness of the forest full of cyclamens. I listened to bird songs and the incessant murmur of the streams. It was there that I also unexpectedly acquired a friend and a mentor. For a couple of weeks, and for the first time since my school days, someone paid a particular attention to me. It was the mayor of Požega, Franjo Ciraki, one of the co-founders and first collaborators of *Vienac (The Wreath)*, and already noted in literary circles for his poems and his *Florentinske elegije* (Florentine Elegies).[231]

He was at the time in his fifties, but to me, due to his age and wisdom, he seemed like Methuselah! He moved with a certain difficulty, since he had lost a leg and used in its place a simple wooden prosthesis. But he overcame his hardships with the strength of his will, and we took long walks together on the estate, studying and collecting plants, a particular hobby of his. I don't believe that anyone in the Požega surroundings knew as much about flora as he did. After one trip, during which we collected an abundance of plants, he prompted me to start putting together an herbarium. We bought paper and glue, improvised the plant press and collected more plants, among them quite a few species I had not known before. We pressed them, categorized them according to Linné's binominal nomenclature, and glued them into the herbarium. The result was not just a collection of plants. It reinforced my interest in the world of flora, which led me many years later to choose botany as my main subject of study when I enrolled at the University of Munich.

We spent hours engaged in eager conversations, while sitting next to each other, either in the cool portico of the old monastery, in the large square courtyard in the shade of giant chestnut trees, or in the small park by the swimming baths. Ciraki was the first Croatian intellectual I had ever met and a typical one, too. Deep down in his soul he was a passionate patriot, while being loyal to the ruling regime in his role as mayor. His public service restricted his freedom as a writer and created domestic difficulties as a man in his private sphere. He lived in a small town with no intellectual stimulations. At the same time, his prosthetic leg imposed considerable limitations on his movements. He showed more will than knowledge in all areas of life. He was misunderstood and bitter, and still haunted by the dreams and unfulfilled ideals of his youth. His energy stemmed from those constant contradictions, manifested in his eloquent outbursts full of noble clichés and slogans about freedom, equality, and patriotism being repressed under the Khuen's system. Like so many others in those days, he obeyed the regime out of necessity, exasperated that destiny forced him to make such a defeatist compromise, something he preferred not to talk about.

I should add here that almost all Croatian intellectuals in those days worked for their living as civil servants, because becoming independent professionals such as doctors, engineers, and lawyers was the privilege of the wealthy. Those professions required expensive studies abroad and significant initial investments. Lawyers, for instance, had to wait for a long time to obtain the *stalum agenda*,[232] and the financing required to achieve that goal was not always available. For people of more modest financial backgrounds, joining the municipal or government services appeared to be the only acceptable avenue. The ensuing rise through the hierarchy of rank was thorny, inevitably resulting in the last remnants of personal initiative and spiritual ambitions eventually being extinguished. Any kind of opposition was excluded, and all vitality drained by the dull routine of everyday life under a tyrannical boss, petty office troubles, worries in one's own household, pathetic tours of the pubs, and an accumulation of debt.

The result was a great number of our best talented people being wasted for good. With some negligible variations, the course of their lives was always the same. Many became used to such a life and gradually identified with it, found an anchor to hold on to and became undeterred representatives of a flawlessly functioning bureaucracy.

Ciraki was the first person to draw my attention to the difficult conditions under which our intellectuals were obliged to live and be creative. All I had heard before was, "A Croat is made this way! It is in his blood to accept a subordinate position and to have *Sitzfleisch*.[233] He is at ease when he is part of a hierarchy and reassured when there is someone supervising him. He is a born civil servant." I suddenly realized how much tragedy there was behind those facts, how many human lives were shattered, how much talent was wasted, how many works of art remained unwritten! Some promising attempts were abandoned in fragments, when their authors were suddenly frozen by fear that those from "above" would object and jeopardize their subsistence, because there was no way one could make a living from literature. In some of the best cases, books were printed in runs of three hundred up to four hundred copies, but rarely sold more than a hundred. This precarious situation could also be attributed to the fact that our literature in those days had hit rock-bottom. Everything published after the Illyrian movement had reached its zenith seemed mere anaemic imitations. There was evidence of goodwill but not much of a decisive quality. There were only cautious attempts to deal with reality, more likely by circumventing it, and hardly a sign to get the gist of it. It was difficult in those days to gather enough courage to disclose the truth and to give artistic shape to what people really thought. Authors were attached to classical formulas. Narratives were transposed into some romantic past and to other countries, and if possible, even to a distant continent. People searched for models in Pushkin's[234] and Mickiewicz's[235] epic poems, the Russian mysticism, and recently discovered French naturalism. Any echo of reality was a true rarity, and even then, merely hidden behind allusions. People were terrorized and the situation seemed hopeless.

Even Ciraki talked of those things with caution, worried that he might blurt out more than his official position would permit. He blamed the public for preferring to spend their money on foreign books, if at all. At home people read *Blatt der Hausfrau* (Homemaker's Journal) and *Gartenlaube* (Garden Arbour) and, at the most, lighthearted French novels. At the same time, *Vienac* had barely fifteen hundred subscribers. He told me it was the task of the young people to stop that unacceptable trend. He appealed to my patriotic feelings and the fact that I had been born in Croatia and was interested in all forms of life. I should not waste my attention on things remote to us, but on what was here and needed help—the homeland that was in urgent need of uplifting. I have forgotten most of the details of our discussions. Certain specific things, however, as is usually the case, have stuck in my memory. People store in their memory what appears valuable to them, what in some particular way was decisive as to the direction they have taken in life. Ciraki opened my eyes to a world unknown to me until then and which would become my own several years later. Since he was the first to do that, he left an indelible mark on my memory, and I have been grateful to him to this day.

Our discussions prompted me to write a newspaper article (my first!), which was published in *Die Drau* (Drava).[236] It was an enthusiastic tribute to Velika, which turned out to be quite a "sensation" among the guests at the resort. Ciraki liked it as well and, following that easily acquired success, he urged me to do more of the same. A few days later, he presented me with a scheme for a future novel and asked me to develop its ending, merely in the guise of practice. The novel was already entitled *Marica and Ružica* (Mary and Rosie), which did not really sound sensational. He explained that Marica and Ružica could be two young girls with different personalities—one would have modern views, be emancipated, clever, but eccentric, while the other would be unassuming and plain, but kind-hearted, and gentle. He let me put the two heroines in contrast the way I pleased, give preferential treatment to whichever of the two I chose, and present their life stories through as many different plots as possible. He wrote a plan for this "literary work" in a graphic format, organized in individual sections and divided into squares, each containing a few written notes, presumably to make it all easier for me to handle.

What a lot of naive optimism it revealed and how much he overestimated my modest abilities by assuming I could write such a novel at the young age of sixteen, and furthermore, on the basis of his scheme with all those compartments and squares! How much he actually underestimated the seriousness of a literary creation and degraded it to the level of primitive craftsmanship! I was occasionally able to put together a little poem, but to expect me to write an entire novel, on the basis of a ready-made, unfamiliar, Ciraki's cliché—exposition, story development, conflict resolution, catharsis, and the moralistic ending according to his carefully calligraphed notes on a few sheets of paper! No, that was impossible!

I could not execute anything of the kind. First, because I had already read far too many good books and had developed a true respect for literature and its meaning. Second, I lacked the experience to be the judge of the realities of life. There was more. I was in those days highly poetically inclined, and rather concentrated on myself, as is usually the case with young people during their formative years. In the course of our "intellectual" conversations, Ciraki must have seen in me more than I happened to be in reality. And he assigned me a flattering task to execute something that was way beyond my ability to fulfil.

In the last days of August, our Slavonian 78th Regiment held its summer manoeuvres in the area of Požega. The soldiers set up their quarters in the village and various officers of the regiment began visiting us at the resort. That provided the occasion for some dancing in the refectory to the sounds of an old piano. One afternoon, a young lieutenant appeared in the dining room, all prim and spruced up. A latticed barrier covered in vines separated our table from the one at which he was sitting, and through the leafy wall, I could see his silhouette and his lit cigarette. The sun was shining through the lattice, casting dancing shadows of the leaves fluttering in the wind on our bright white tablecloth. We had roast chicken with green salad for lunch, with a piece of strudel for dessert. I usually competed with my sister to see which of us could eat faster, but this time I could not swallow a thing.

He offered the first demonstration of interest that same evening. With a smile, half roguish, half friendly, our waiter, Sami, a pint-size of a fellow dressed in a smeared waiter's shirt far too big for him, brought and placed before me on the table a plate with two pieces of poached trout in brown butter sauce. He said, "The lieutenant shot them in the pond this afternoon and is taking the liberty of offering them to the young lady!"

It was an awkward gift! Flowers from an admirer can be pinned on one's bosom, a book given as a present can be read, a box of chocolates can be taken with gratitude and enjoyed in the solitude of one's room, but the trout had to be eaten while still warm! I had to eat it under his observing eye! I knew that he carefully watched through the latticed wall every move I made and every bite I took. The trout in its butter sauce was delicious, but seized as I was by awkward feelings, l found it hard to keep swallowing and was overjoyed when there were only fish bones left lying on the plate.

Naturally, I had to thank the lieutenant and that was the beginning of our short relationship, as fleeting as the last days of summer. It could hardly be called a flirtation (a word, by the way, that did not exist in our vocabulary at the time). The lieutenant was blond, good-looking, of fine manners, and well dressed. He was rather dim-witted, although in the state I was at the time, I would have fallen for a stupid ass just as much. Our conversations, accompanied by meaningful looks, limited themselves to a few phrases. He would ask, "Does the young lady dance?" I would say, "Yes." He would go on, "Waltz or polka?" I would whisper back, "Both!" A short pause would then follow, during which he would be thoughtfully pulling on his perfect moustache. Then there would be a new question.

"Does the lady ride?" I would say, "No." He would then reply, "What a shame. Otherwise I would have taken you to the riding ring to teach you some *haute école* movements." I admitted it to be a shame, although I had never even thought of riding before. "Do you at least play tennis?" "Not even that!" It was obvious that I was losing my reputation in his eyes. I was upset and saddened by that. I firmly decided I would at least learn to play tennis, maybe even to ride, since those were obviously proofs of social refinements. My father was laughing at me, something he did quite often in those days, but I was preoccupied. The image of the young lieutenant was haunting me day and night. What was happening to me? Love? But I barely knew him! I forgot all about my herbarium. I forgot about my unwritten novel *Marica and Ružica*. I even forgot about my friend Ciraki, who was hurt and disappointed and eventually withdrew completely.

I was no longer the person I had imagined being for the past several years. Gone were images of me as Sappho,[237] George Sand,[238] or Sofya Kovalevskaya.[239] My future worldwide fame toppled down in one stroke, like a house of cards. There were no more pretentious, philosophical thoughts about being or not-being, no more extravagant expressions of my intentions in life. I was nothing but a silly, excited, and gullible girl, like thousands of those to be found in every city and village, eager to be liked and to flirt, confused and disoriented by my foggy and misleading knowledge of people, exclusively based on literature, and fraught with misconceptions.

What I felt was not love as such. That my emotions were in turmoil was undeniable. It was more likely triggered by the overall situation in which I found myself at that moment (sunny days, fresh air, freedom of movement), which provided a perfect background for a new set of feelings. In addition, he was the first man in my life who was paying attention to me as a woman. His glances made me realize that I had become a woman and men would be able to see that in me from then onwards. I was over-taken by an upsurge of emotions. That realization suddenly became more important than anything else. Instinctively, but more clearly than before, I felt that whatever I might expect from life in future—happiness, love, successes, failures, struggles, and victories—it would be due to the fact that I was a woman! That realization did not emerge in the form of a simple thought, but as a powerful and suffocating fervour (with no defined objective yet), which spread warmth through my veins and made me feverish with an excess of joy and a strong feeling of anticipation. This transformation was triggered by the appearance on the scene of the first young man who had paid me a compliment. What he was actually like seemed of no consequence. He appeared by sheer coincidence at that particular moment of my great emotional awakening and that was all.

One day we went in the company of several other people on an excursion to the so-called Second Valley, in the direction of the waterfalls and the location of the former glassworks called Dubrava. We were too embarrassed to walk next to each other, so on the way to the falls, he led the group and I kept the rearguard. We reversed the roles on the way back. I was marching first with a carbine that he had jokingly hung on my shoulder at the waterfall, and in turn, I let him carry a posy of flowers I had picked along the way. The hard carbine belt cut deeply into my shoulder, but I heroically said nothing about it, plodding on while he was lagging more and more behind. Upon our return, he asked me whether the shotgun was too heavy for me. I said, "Oh, no!" Then he asked me if he could keep the flowers. I said, "Oh, yes!" That evening we saw each other for the last time. My shoulder was hurting, and I had to put cold compresses on it. My father was laughing at me, pointing out that it was the price of being in love. Clearly, he said, the thing was not worth it!

That autumn I began taking regular private lessons, this time with Professor Matić, a well-trained teacher with a lot of experience. He had been working for years as a private tutor for wealthy families, usually with lazy and untalented pupils, whom he would help prepare for a makeup exam and save them from failing to pass the grades. His method consisted in reducing the prescribed material to a bare minimum with the emphasis on fundamentals, such as dates, years, formulas, and rules, which even the thickest heads would have been able to memorize.

His methodology was certainly valid when applied to the black sheep he managed to get through the process of high school graduation in the least painful way. But once it was applied to me, it positively had its disadvantages. I also wanted to prepare for graduation, but I wanted more than that. I wanted to know everything! Lessons with Professor Matić, however, were the best I could hope for under the given circumstances, and I contented myself to profit from what he could offer as much as I could.

Matić came to our house three times a week. He was a cheerful and kind man and he could never stop marvelling at my eagerness. We did not stick strictly to the lesson itself and occasionally chatted along at the end. Matić knew everyone and everything that was taking place in town. He was retelling me all kinds of gossip, sometimes even serious things, especially the things which took place at school, where pupils in higher grades gathered to talk about nationalistic ideas and find ways to express them as best as they could. They were not publicly allowed to do anything of the kind, but they knew how to seize an opportunity for a spontaneous nationalistic demonstration of whatever kind, and whenever it presented itself. The Croatian professors, under all sorts of pressures themselves, would turn a blind eye. There were some younger ones among them who would even manage to instill patriotic feelings in their pupils during their lectures, naturally, always disguised behind the screen of pure scholarship. After all, scholarly approach was flexible and interpretations could vary, and there could always be a truth or two to smuggle in, especially in history or literature—discussions that would not have been tolerated elsewhere.

I liked that. It was precisely due to those informal moments of chatting that made me truly enjoy those lessons with Professor Matić. He was not just teaching me physics and mathematics. I also found out that behind the usual everyday superficiality and restrictiveness of Osijek, there were actually signs of a new and spirited life gradually emerging. That there were young people with the typical élan of youth as everywhere else, who were inspired by, reflected about, and aspired towards something new. Was there any chance for them to achieve it? That was the question which belonged to the future and which I was not even asking myself at the time. I saw the beginnings of a considerable strength in the mere fact that they harboured aspirations of some sort. Action might follow one day, maybe in a few years, or a few decades. I was deeply convinced that the attempt was not futile, that it would not vanish into thin air, leaving no trace behind. If

nothing else, it created at least an atmosphere from which future generations could draw new strength. That was considerable in itself.

One day, I showed Professor Matić a few of my translations of Croatian
poetry penned while in Vienna. He found them good and encouraged me to
do some more. He brought me an anthology of both older and more recent
poetry and I applied myself right away. The verses just kept streaming out
of my pen, as if I had composed them and was writing them down myself.
I did not find it hard to empathize with the poet's feelings and moods, to
follow his ardour and his suffering or find a suitable form and recreate the
rhythm of his text. What I was doing was not a word-by-word translation, but a poetic adaptation of the sentiments expressed in the poem. I
was translating Mirko Bogović, Hugo Badalić, Tugomir Alaupović, August
Šenoa, Đuro Arnold, Ante Tresić-Pavičić, Silvije Strahomir Kranjčević,
and Milan Begović.[240] Lyrical folk poetry with its melodic rhythm suited
me best of all, as well as the first section of *Smrt Smail-age Čengića* (The
Death of Smail-aga Čengić).[241]

The translated poems were published almost every week in the Sunday
issue of the Osijek newspaper *Die Drau* (Drava), occasionally in *Agramer
Tagblatt* (Zagreb Daily), *Agramer Zeitung* (Zagreb Journal), and in
Budapest and Viennese newspapers. That same year they were also published in the Stuttgart-based magazine *Aus fremden Zungen* (In Foreign
Tongues), in the issue in which they also published Maxim Gorky's short
story *Two Drifters* from his collection of *Essays and Stories,* introducing
him to the European readership.[242] What a joy it was when my first hono-
rarium arrived from Stuttgart—my own full five marks! Soon after came
also letters of gratitude and recognition from Croatian poets who were
very pleased with my translations. They sent me books of their poems, with
beautiful dedications. Milan Begović informed me that he had submitted
my translations to the well-known Austrian writer and leader of Viennese
literary modernism, Hermann Bahr, who considered them among the best
he had encountered. Vladimir Jelovšek sent me his book with the dedication: "To the only living *literata* in Osijek."[243] A correspondence on aesthetic themes developed between me and Ante Tresić-Pavičić and he even
asked for my photograph and some biographical details.

By now, my father must have noticed that I was increasingly determined about going in a direction that did not at all correspond to his expectations. Despite his generally liberal beliefs, he maintained patriarchal prejudices when it came to family life. Women who busied themselves with culture and art horrified him. He mocked them and was energetically against the emancipation of women—a sheer nonsense, in his opinion. This conviction was partially his own and partially keeping in line with the prevailing public opinion in Osijek that no woman should be anything other than what a man expected her to be. In that line of thought, my father demanded that I took this into account and not ruin my own chances of a good marriage. He was convinced that the whole intellectual business in which I was so deeply involved was not only alienating me from real life, but also from the circle of our closest acquaintances, and was dragging me in a direction which had nothing to do with my future mission of being a good housewife.

In order to avert me from that dangerous route, my parents introduced me into society when I was seventeen, altogether a customary practice in those days. I was given a gown which arrived straight from Vienna—my first long dress, made of *roshar* with a rustling silk lining. The skirt, with hip gores, was six metres wide and was, for the most part, trailing on the floor around me so that I had to hold it up at all times by my right hand. This was a complex procedure which required a lot of skill, but which, according to the norms of the day, gave the female figure the right touch of graciousness. Huge puffed sleeves and a high stiff collar garnished with all kinds of folds, laces, and ribbons completed the look.

Dressed in this outfit, in which even I could not recognize myself, I started accompanying my parents on their social outings. Afternoon parties were quite casual, and one could pay a visit without an official invitation and leave when one felt like it. The table was set and there was always something tasty on offer, since Esseker women were impeccable hostesses and their pantries well supplied with delicacies of all sorts. More food could be brought to the table at any time in case of additional and unexpected guests. Besides blushed pink apples (which could keep all winter), tall neatly labelled glass jars containing the most delicious compotes, thick quince paste, walnuts, and biscuits, as well as ham and liver pâté, there would be always something else available to bring up. For official occasions and events such as birthday parties, name days, wedding anniversaries, jubilees, engagement parties, and christenings, a special invitation would be required, and the celebrations would be observed according to a long-established procedure.

Such festive meals, real banquets in fact, were organized in our household as well. Foreign visitors who came to Osijek for talks with the board of the Chamber of Trades and Crafts or to attend a conference or a congress, were always invited to our house for dinner. An assistant cook, Mrs. Althofer, would then come to the house to help. She had apparently learned her craft at the famous Hotel Sacher in Vienna and she really was a great cook. The table was covered with a beautiful damask tablecloth, set with glistening silver cutlery, the finest china and beautiful flower arrangements. The dishes and the wines were exceptional, but the numerous speeches held at the table were boring, at least to me. The guests did tend to express their good intentions in those speeches, but considering the state of affairs in the country, it was empty talk.

The liveliest parties took place during winter seasons when the first soirée was automatically followed by a whole sequence of others, because all the invited guests had to return the favour presented to them on that first occasion. Naturally, the culinary pleasures constituted the most important part of the programme for these receptions. I still cannot understand how people managed to consume such quantities of food, especially the ladies, every one of them in tight corsets, which, like a steel armour, usually required a long procedure of lacing up with the help of one or even two people, until the right shape was achieved and everything was in its place!

I should mention some of the compulsory courses at such gatherings. As a starter, there would invariably be a cup of bouillon which was a small feast in itself. The appetizer usually consisted of a cold pikeperch in sauce tartare, garnished with hard-boiled eggs, lemon wedges, and caviar. This was followed by warm fish served with mashed potatoes, roast pork tenderloin in a colourful garland of baby vegetables, venison in cranberry sauce with sour cream (as a reminder that Osijek was situated in an area of Europe abundant in game!), then poultry, salads, compote, ice cream with whipped cream, cakes, biscuits, and a *jardinetto* (a display of apples, oranges, tropical fruit, candied fruit and almonds in their shells). To top it all were the best wines, plum brandy, liqueurs, and black coffee.

It took a full three hours before everything was eaten, and during that laborious exercise, and even later, everyone's gaze was fixed on serving bowls and plates, so as not to miss anything especially attractive that might have been brought to the table. Despite all that, there was always a guest, even with his stomach full, who would not lose his sense of humour, and as a special addition to the dinner kept providing funny stories, anecdotes, and casual remarks—in short, there was always someone with something to say. Such a person was considered the perfect "life of the party" and would always be gladly invited by every household. It is a common tendency with most Jews, and not just intellectuals, to try to abate a problem by finding a funny angle to approach it. This is, in fact, an old Jewish practice people have resorted to in order to overcome awkward and unbearable situations. Jewish jokes range from melancholic to self-mocking and have deep philosophical and psychological roots. They take the form of a wordplay, a pun, a clever aphorism, or an equivocation, and reflect the Jewish positive attitude towards life and the superior spiritual strength able to handle any absurd or tragic situation. I have been exposed to that sharp wit since I was a child. It is a characteristic trait of almost every Jew. A humourless Jew is his own worst enemy and far more likely to get into trouble. Words possess an inner strength of their own. They not only succumb to the simple dictation of logic but impose their own logic as well. They are not empty shells inhabited haphazardly by thoughts but have a reverse effect on thoughts by determining both their form and content. An uplifting word gives wings to thoughts and makes them lighter. A good punch line counterpoises seemingly irreconcilable opposites and creates a liberating effect by generating laughter.

Being in such an environment since I was small helped me gain an insight into human weaknesses and develop a sense of humour. I got used to accepting my fellow citizens, not only as they were, or as they presented themselves to be, but I tried to analyze their behaviour and guess their real motivations. That innate interest in people was overwhelming and observing them offered a treasure trove of discoveries. I realized early in my life that there were not simply good and bad people out there, but rather numerous gradations and contradictions, which made studying people so interesting. I was, however, mostly fascinated with the cases that deviated from the typical and appeared especially original in their particular ways. I could see in each of those "odd persons"—whether they had gone astray, were loners, or failed geniuses—something worthy of my compassion and sympathy, even more so because they were the objects of cheap mockery by Osijek society. They were despised for failing to achieve something in life. They were made into caricatures and were the laughingstock of the town, without taking into consideration their actual virtues, which had become stunted and degenerated, due to too many adversities.

Just as in any other small town, there were people in Osijek who, after a turbulent youth full of intentions, ambitions, and talent, suddenly got stuck on their way. Among them were former politicians, now only dabbling in politics, and, once fired up by a few drinks, would give inflammatory speeches in small pubs on Rokova Street or at Crveni kokot (The Red Cockerel) and then, between ten and midnight, stagger home on wobbly legs, believing they were still capable of inspiring the world. A few musicians who used to dream about worldwide fame, were now blowing into a brass horn in the theatre orchestra or making untalented pupils practise "salon pieces" such as "A Maiden's Prayer" or "The Bells of Corneville"—the two pieces most in vogue in those days. Furthermore, there were prophets of all sorts of theories, who "preached to stones"[244] in the absence of an appreciative audience. I will take time to describe just one familiar example, my former drawing teacher, Adolph Waldinger. He was indisputably talented and in his numerous paintings and sketches was able to create rewarding artistic effects from something as monotonous as the countryside surrounding Osijek, with its previously artistically unexplored, oak-covered woodlands. The townspeople considered him an eccentric and paid absolutely no attention to his paintings. To feed his family, he worked as an office janitor at the premises of the Business Association, a job my father had found to help him out. He was sweeping the floors and kept the rooms well heated. Nobody was interested in his paintings, let alone buying them.

From its abrupt rise in the 1860s, the Comitatsgasse, better known as Županijska Street, quickly became the central artery of the town. At its very beginning, on the right-hand side, was the Upper Town parish church, a discreet Baroque building of no distinguishable architectural style, but in harmony with the surrounding area of single-storeyed houses and large gardens. It was later replaced by a cathedral made of red brick in pseudo-Gothic style, austere and artificial as if built with the use of an Anker Stone Building Set for children.[245] Further down the street was the single-storeyed County Palace, which, in addition to its main purpose, also housed both the courtroom and the prison. Every year a number of people were hanged in its courtyard, usually at the break of dawn, with half the town out of their beds and on the street, eager to watch the hanging through the garden gates.

The left side of the street was reserved for wealthy tradesmen, who had come here in the 1860s and built handsome houses, with shops on the ground floors. The corner of the street was occupied by the home of the match factory owner, Adam Reisner, one of the richest people in town.

Right next to it was the so-called Hiller's House, which as I mentioned earlier, was purchased by my grandfather in early 1870. In that same row of houses was also the most beautiful building in the Upper Town, the Casino, the construction of which swallowed up the handsome sum of a hundred thousand golden guldens. Incorporated in the building was the Grand Hotel, considered to be the town's best hotel.

A spacious coffee room occupied its ground floor, where realtors and traders of all sorts discussed business and collected useful information. The first floor was taken by the Casino where well-to-do gentlemen gathered after lunch. Membership depended on certain criteria and was subject to the election, which signified the confirmation of the admitted person's good deportment, integrity, solvency, and political reliability. Count Teodor Pejačević[246] was the president and my father the founder and long-term secretary (later vice president). The exterior of the Casino was generally perceived as the most beautiful in town, and so were its halls with huge windows, parquet floors, and well-appointed furnishings. In short, it was the best thing Osijek had ever done in respect to culture.

There were billiard tables, a restaurant, meeting halls, and above all, reading rooms supplied with all possible newspapers available at the time. The most popular was the daily newspaper *Pester Lloyd*, the indispensable reading material for all those in need of business information, followed by the Viennese *Neue Freie Presse* (New Free Press), whose statements and opinions—although full of preconceived views and bombastic phraseology—were considered in the middle-class circles to be the ultimate in literary and cultural quality. They were blindly adopted and repeated by the entire German-speaking middle class in the empire as their own. Both government-oriented local papers, *Slavonische Presse* (Slavonian Press) and *Die Drau* (Drava) provided what was considered a sufficient amount of local gossip. *Obzor* (Horizon), mostly deemed highly objectionable, was read in that exclusively pro-Hungarian Casino only out of curiosity and so that it could be even more severely attacked for its "lack of ideas", indecisiveness, political charlatanism, conservatism, clericalism, and whatever other evils could be threatening the country. Finally, there were also *Narodne novine* (People's Gazette) with its government-issued announcements and *Hrvatska* (Croatia), the daily newspaper of the Party of Rights,[247] the latter read only rarely, and allegedly only to prove one's willingness to be objective.

Much more entertaining were the magazines *Leipziger Illustrierte Zeitung* (Leipzig Illustrated), whose function in those days corresponded to what documentary films provide today, the Viennese *Fliegende Blätter* (Loose Leaves), stereotypical and boring, as well as the offensively wicked *Wespen* (Bees), bordering on pornography, which all the gentlemen eagerly read and laughed over.

Croats, Serbs, Swabians, and Jews all sat together, day after day, in harmony and unity. There was no racial prejudice or nationalistic intolerance. They were all Essekers and incurable local patriots, for whom nothing outside their town could be of interest. Real moral values could apparently only be found in Osijek. If something was truthful, beautiful, or good, it was only so because Osijek estimated it as such. Naturally, even Osijek had its small worries. In no way could one stop time taking its course, not even when one had nothing better to do for years but make a good living and ignore all changes. Apart from communal matters, sewage problems, the tax rate, and the unfortunately never-implemented clean water supply project, the only other thing that irritated people was the disturbing news that kept coming from the rebellious Zagreb. What were they constantly nagging about up there? God forbid if anything ever upset Essekers to that point! Their calm temperament and inborn sense of loyalty could vouch for it. They were no rebels, but rather reliable businessmen and family men. Things were less clear when it came to the matter of the youth. Their sons studied in Zagreb and one kept hearing dangerous and hair-raising things that students were stirring up over there. For example, the dastardly act of burning the Hungarian flag on the solemn occasion of His Majesty's royal visit! In the eyes of Essekers, that act was shameful and had compromised the reputation of the country in the eyes of the outside world.

That was how the event was commented upon for a long time afterwards during discussions in the Osijek Casino. Essekers were not only pro-Hungarian but also consistently pro-Habsburg-oriented, which was not surprising in a garrison town like Osijek, with its Fortress and military parades being a daily feature. Since childhood, the citizens of Osijek were used to seeing the Austrian armed forces marching down the streets, the commanding officer wearing his shako,[248] proudly sitting up straight on his horse at the head of the troops. As times were becoming increasingly more restless, the spectacle served as a guarantee of the town's safety! And that was all the Casino gentlemen cared about!

Emperor Franz Joseph was fortunate that, after a period of wars and revolutions at the beginning of his reign, which cost him a share of his ancestral land and the title of Holy Roman German Emperor, the following forty years were marked by a continuous peace. He learned early that wars lead to nowhere good. That realization was his most important contribution to the improvement of his people's welfare. His people knew how to be grateful to him. Settled in his Hofburg palace, the old monarch became a symbol. For as long as he was alive, there was nothing to be afraid of—neither upheavals nor wars. He was keeping order and peace in his lands, made sure that nothing threatened that peace, and he kept handy, in case of need, a good fire extinguisher to deal with the fire, right from the start. Therefore, all the "constructive elements" in the country stood by him—that is to say, all those who would not gain anything by changing the status quo but instead lose everything—and so would he!

Every winter my father would rent a theatre box and twice a week we would go to a small theatre set up in the spacious complex of the Casino building. It was, by that time, already in desperate need of thorough refurbishment. The colours of the walls looked faded, the gilded ornaments had lost their shine, the red drapery was covered in years of old dust, the chairs had broken springs and the velvet on the ledges of the boxes was already worn out.

There was always a different German theatre company performing each season. With some occasional exceptions, actors were mostly second- and third-rate. The stage was equipped with a minimum of technical support and props, and the costumes were worn out and badly assorted. The orchestra consisted of musicians trained in military music, excelling in the use of wind instruments and in playing parade marches. There was no electricity, just small gas lamps, which would disturbingly flicker even in the smallest draught, and made people's faces appear chalk white.

A company would usually arrive at the beginning of September and leave after Easter, if it did not go insolvent sooner, which often happened as they were always on the brink of ruin. Actors were paid irregularly, which forced some of the valiant stage lovers to flirt with their landladies in exchange for belated rent payment. The ladies of those colourful companies relied on generous lovers, a few grey-haired Osijek playboys, who delightedly gave into sin for several months a year. They had a choice—the prima donna or the latest little chorus girl, whichever they could afford to support.

The director of such a travelling company had to be extremely skilful, well prepared for every contingency, a businessman, a charlatan, and a good psychologist, all in one. He had to know how to use promotional tricks and promise his audience the impossible. His repertoire had to include all genres—burlesque, grotesque, farce, salon pieces, Gothic drama, and comedy. He had to be able to offer Grillparzer's *Die Ahnfrau* (The Ancestress)[249] today and *Die lustige Witwe* (The Merry Widow)[250] tomorrow, not to forget operas, ballet evenings, matinees, gala shows, guest performances, benefit events, jubilees, new productions, and everything else that could possibly fill the theatre's constantly empty cashbox. It was because of a miscellaneous repertoire and numerous premiers that the Osijek theatre somehow remained afloat. No one cared to watch the same show twice. The audience consisted of a few hundred regulars from the Upper Town and the Fortress. The Lower Town citizens were mostly Serbs, who preferred to see their visiting theatre group from Novi Sad[251] or were simply hopeless plebeians, who did not feel like being dragged away from their warm stoves in wintertime to watch something like *Trilby or Die schöne Galathée* (The Beautiful Galatea) on stage.[252]

Sudermann's *Heimat* (Homeland), Hauptmann's *Hanneles Himmelfahrt* (Hannele's Assumption) and Hirschfeld's *Die Mütter* (The Mothers) were performed in Osijek already in 1897, soon after their creation in Vienna and Berlin, but none of them, I still remember, was on the programme for longer than a few days.[253] To keep up with such a tempo, the actors had to have a good control of their craft, be able to memorize quickly, and be alert and experienced, particularly so when you consider that the performances usually took place without sufficient prior rehearsing. Those were, of course, no exemplary performances—the limited number of lead actors and heterogeneous and randomly put together ensembles made it inevitable. Still, those were worthwhile efforts with interesting literary ambitions and, in the opinion of the citizens of Osijek, with their limited artistic demands, were fully satisfactory.

Our theatre did not differ much from other provincial theatres in those days. They all served as experimental stepping stones for the young actors to learn by heart a vast repertoire, from Sardou's *Fedora*[254] and Ohnet's *Le Maître de Forges* (The Ironmaster)[255] to Blumenthal and Kadelburg's crowd-pleasers *Im Weissen Rössl* (White Horse Inn), *Grossstadtluft* (Big City Air) and *Die Orientreise (The Orient Express).*[256] A young leading lover had to learn how to achieve credibility as a gentleman in his impeccable tailcoat, and a young actress a similar credibility as a genuine French marchioness with her lorgnette and a fake ermine cape. Besides acting, they had to know how to dance and sing. They had to play comic roles, speak Swabian, Yiddish, and the Viennese hackney coachman jargon. They had to be resourceful and know how to entertain their audience by inserting in their texts occasional and improvised allusions to local circumstances and personalities. The diva had to flirt with the theatre critic and the drama hero had to charm, with his irresistible performance, all those little schoolgirls eagerly waiting for him at the stage door of the theatre after each rehearsal. But that was the bright side of the stage life and concerned the young, who still had to overcome the occasional stage fright and use the Osijek experience to launch a career. It was worse for those whose career was ending with that final engagement on the Osijek stage—all those worn out, disappointed and failed actors, who via Olmütz,[257] Saaz,[258] Pressburg (Bratislava) and Eisenstadt[259] came back to our provincial town to find a final refuge for a short period of time. Their voices were worn out, sometimes hardly audible, sometimes rather squeaky and hoarse. Their faces were frozen into a grimace that made them look more like masks than their real selves. They suffered from rheumatism and joint stiffness. Their pathos lacked that necessary swing and their comedy acts the proper humorous effect, so that even a well-intentioned theatre critic could not help but offer friendly advice to Mr. X or Mrs. Y to retire from the stage and use poor health as an excuse. Once the season was over, Mr. X and Mrs. Y would then be unable to land a new engagement, be it in Olmütz, Saaz, or Wallachisch-Meseritch.[260] After more than forty years of life on the stage, they would find themselves tossed out into the street and slowly starve to death.

Winters were devoted to charitable activities, which, in the minds of Essekers, were inseparable from the pursuit of entertainment. There were three women's charity organizations in town—Catholic, Serbian, and Jewish. All three magnanimously cared for their local poor by organizing seasonal "charity balls". They were also involved in organizing occasional ladies' circles, masquerade balls, tea parties, amateur theatre shows with *"tableaux vivants"*, bazaars, raffles, "Venetian nights" with red and green lanterns and fireworks, the staging of tales from *The Thousand and One Nights,* and as the highlight of the season, a genuine Japanese cherry blossom celebration, including the obligatory kimono, to be worn regardless of one's sex, or how fat or skinny you were. Even when the needs of the local poor were met, there was luckily always a firemen's, a war veterans', or a riflemen's club whose benefit dances one could attend. There were also the *"Schlaraffia"*[261] and *Geschnasfest*,[262] which wholeheartedly welcomed all sorts of escapades. The entertainment at the officers' casino, the Ressource, was a bit more reserved, as was the most exclusive of all balls held at the Casino, during which Lady Patronesses of the ball were able to exhibit, on a specially erected *estrade*, their newest gowns from Vienna. In fact, there was always a motive to organize a dance or a party, whether it was a burned-down village, an earthquake, a famine, or a flood in a remote part of the country. As a last resort, one could always decide to collect clothes for the poorest black children in the darkest parts of Africa, for whom compassionate Esseker ladies developed a fondness. In those cases, there would be a committee under the leadership of such impressive ladies as Countess Lilla Pejačević or Baroness Marie Ottilie von Althann. There would be meetings and the ladies would then let their imaginations flow in setting up a plan of action. Several ladies would sacrifice their time to go from house to house selling tickets, while others would apply their creative talents to decorating the hall for the planned event. A few dedicated gentlemen of good social standing would take responsibility for the overall arrangement. Costumes of all kinds would be conceived and sewn in households where there was a grown-up daughter, or a mother still full of energy. Different dances would be practised, new hairstyles tried out. All those directly involved had no rest for weeks with all those responsibilities. They were rushing to their rehearsals and sang and declaimed as if their professional careers as performers were at stake.

I also took part in those performances, mostly in leading roles—once in a rococo costume and another time as a Russian noble woman (dressed in velvet and silk, covered in fake gold and frippery). Once I starred in a German comedy in the role of a "misunderstood woman". My parents were not pleased. They thought it was a bad sign and feared that people might make insinuating remarks on my account. Therefore, to forestall a disaster, they made me wear a white silk dress with a sky-blue scarf romantically hung over the shoulders and, on my head, a quaint little hat made of lace—in short, nothing that would resemble the usually prescribed casual clothes that would supposedly suit the image of a neurotic, silly, and laughable "misunderstood woman". There was a commotion when I arrived in my apparel, because the director was displeased with its inappropriate styling, but it was too late to make any changes, so I played the part wearing white and celestial blue and looked like an angel of innocence straight out of a novel for adolescents.

Despite the zealous promotion of these events, the net profit was usually negligible. The earnings were spent on decorations, hall rental, music, lanterns, confetti, paper garlands, and the overall cost of staging. And when everything was accounted for, there was just enough left for a symbolic gesture of giving consolation money to those fire victims, whom the whole enterprise was intended to help, and a few handkerchiefs to cheer up naked black children in Africa.

But for the young people that we were, the fuzzy accounting accompanying those efforts were of no concern at all. We were looking forward to those unique opportunities when we could socialize with the members of the opposite sex, meet different people, and establish some intimate contacts, which could potentially lead some day to the lucky tying of knots. Naturally, these occasions were, from the start, not propitious for getting to know someone. They were taking place under false assumptions, in the ambience of a dazzling ballroom, with music and flowers, silk, exotic scents, looks of admiration and compliments, in a mood artificially stimulated and entirely removed from everyday life.

I can still remember the powerful beating of my heart and the sensation of apprehension I felt the first time I entered a ballroom. I had to gather all my strength as if I were about to jump into ice-cold water. When the door opened, it felt like entering fairyland. Was that really my reflection in the tall Venetian mirror on the opposite wall? It probably was, because my parents were walking behind me. I saw them in the mirror, smiling with pleasure at the sight of me. I finally recognized myself in this elegantly clad young lady wearing a richly folded, sky-blue silk dress, her shoulders bare, with flowers in the décolletage and in her hair, neatly aligned along the two braids skilfully arranged on top of her head. Strapped into a tight corset and walking unsteadily in my high-heeled patent leather shoes, I was pale one moment and flushed the next, caused by the indescribable excitement and joyful anticipation.

In the ballroom, mothers sat in red velvet armchairs along the wall, dutifully playing their part as chaperones, watching the hustle and bustle and keeping an eagle eye on their brood. Fathers, on the other hand, usually found a way to withdraw as soon as they could. They would disappear to the gambling salon to take part in a game of cards or simply have a glass of wine to console themselves for the imposed role they were obliged to play. The daughters sat next to their mothers, peering at potential dancing partners on the scene from behind their open fans. Oh, what a joy when one of them did approach, introduce himself, and ask the young lady to dance! With pounding and grateful heart, you welcomed the young gentleman for rescuing you from the troubling state of waiting, in spite of the fact that you had not known him at all a mere few minutes earlier. You hesitantly touched the rough fabric of his sleeve, felt the firm grasp of his hand, and became aware of his breath and the movement of his muscles. Suddenly, all the conventions faded away and all that mattered was the dancing. You let the rhythm of the waltz carry you on and you let yourself enjoy the thrilling relaxation of the body, the freedom of movement, the coordination of your steps with those of your partner in the three-four time of the waltz. There was nothing more beautiful in this world than the breathless dance spin, the sliding in rhythm from one arm to another, forgetting everything that existed out there. It all made you feel transferred from everyday reality into a sublimated mode of existence. Those few hours of the night, between ten and six in the morning, gave rise to dreams, illusions, fantasies and a unique pleasure in playing a role of some kind and dressing up. There was no rest, no stopping. Feet were moving by themselves and the dance was the only driving force. You felt fully involved, intrinsically and organically, with every drop of your blood, and all senses on alert. We would be dancing until the break of dawn and would have danced longer, had the lights not been turned off at six in the morning and the exhausted mothers standing with our coats ready, urging us to go home. Only then would you once again be aware of the outside reality, and, with a wistful sigh, set off homewards through the cold, damp streets, which seemed even more dreary than usual.

Our dance partners were mostly officers. In principle, most parents in bourgeois circles were in a state of panic at the sight of a young man carrying the black and yellow insignia[263] because he was not considered an acceptable husband for their daughter. But on the dance floor, officers cut a fine figure and were most welcome as dancers. In fact, parents were proud if officers asked us to dance, so during the course of an evening we were able to encounter all military ranks, from ordinary infantrymen and sappers to quite conceited artillery officers, who considered themselves superior to all the others. We were occasionally asked to dance a quadrille by an officer of the general staff, or perhaps a heavily decorated major, while a junior officer fitted well for a polka or a gallop. Apart from a few exceptions, officers were not local people. They came from all parts of the monarchy and every few years would be transferred from Przemyśl[264] to Sankt Pölten,[265] from Pilsen[266] to Graz,[267] from Sarajevo to Osijek. They did not have a real sense of what a homeland could signify and their understanding of *Österreichertum* (Austrianism)[268] was also rather abstract. They had no deep attachment to a particular place or any other deep human connections, except for being loyal to their flag and to their own clique. Already at cadet academies, they were depoliticized and alienated from any reality that did not concern their military interests.

Members of the Royal Croatian Home Guard were an exception.[269] They were, in terms of the military prestige, at the bottom of the ladder, but held, for the most part, strong patriotic feelings, mainly because they were native-born Croats. In most cases, it was exactly for those patriotic reasons that they had joined the Home Guard, either after leaving the cadet academy, or directly as civilians after high school graduation and the completion of one year of volunteer military service. Among the older officers, there were also those originally from the Military Frontier,[270] who served there prior to coming to Osijek and made it up in ranks, from sergeant to captain, and, in certain cases, even to major. They had rough manners and had retained the warrior spirit of their Military Frontier ancestors. There was no trace of that snappy smoothness which characterized the "regular" ranks of officers, no trace of that exclusive *esprit de corps*, the narrow-minded self-overestimation and arrogance, which were partially a personality issue and partially due to the mentality of that entire class of people.

The military gentlemen had, in general, established an exclusive status of their own in town. The wearers of those colourful uniforms easily regarded an unfriendly look by a civilian as an insult. Consequently, some entirely harmless individuals found themselves unwittingly in the most awkward situations, which occasionally turned into duels with bloody outcomes, or vicious lashings in the middle of a street. I remember one such occasion during a promenade concert in the City Garden, when a journalist was heavily beaten up by a group of officers out of control, because he had apparently insulted them by publishing some disguised innuendos in his newspaper.

Roda Roda, who later made his name as a writer, was at the time serving in the artillery regiment in Osijek with the rank of lieutenant and was known to be responsible for some of those attacks.[271] Before he acquired his literary laurels, he used to be known as a dashing officer, a wild daredevil who paid no heed to anyone and who backed away from no obstacle. An accomplished and renowned horseman, he burst one evening on horseback into the house in which he lived at the time, forced his horse to climb the steps to the second floor, and broke into Professor Šičić's dining room just as the family sat down to have dinner. In another such supposedly "harmless" prank, Roda Roda attacked the young articling lawyer, Dr. K., by whipping him with his riding rod in broad daylight and on the promenade full of people. Dr. K. had apparently become too close to Adele Sandrock, an actress from the Burgtheater who was at the time performing as a guest at the Osijek theatre.[272] For Roda Roda, this was just another of many episodes that enhanced his popularity among like-minded comrades. But for Dr. K., humiliated and beaten in this way, the event had a fateful impact on his life with a tragic outcome. He was unable to overcome the shame he had suffered and left town and Croatia. He first settled in Vienna with the intention of disappearing in the large city crowds. He could not make a living there and he took off for the south of Africa, where all traces of him were eventually lost.

There was, besides officers, another distinct group of young people in town—the so-called *arrivistes*—who considered themselves part of the elite. They had university degrees and good jobs as articling lawyers, engineers, or economists. They were much more broad-minded and less dashing than the military men, but not of the courting kind either. They were extremely cautious in forming relationships, afraid that they might fall into a trap, fall in love and make a bad deal in marriage. They preferred to evade that danger by rigorously separating the concept of love from that of marriage. While waiting for their big opportunity regarding the latter, meaning finding a good dowry, they practised "love" with young house-maids, governesses, and milliners, who were easy prey, inexpensive, and could easily be got rid of. All that was needed was a small settlement to pay and the matter could be resolved. Unexpected and unpleasant conse-quences were quickly dealt with. The woman in question would undergo a horrifying and risky procedure carried out by one of those backstreet abortionists. If she got out of it alive, she would be careful not to reveal her shameful secret. If she did not make it, the lover would claim clean hands, because it was not his fault.

Relationships with married women caused even fewer complica-tions and "young gentlemen" perceived them as ideal for satisfying their sexual needs in Osijek. There was never a shortage of good young wives married to dull men engrossed in their work. They tried to compensate for the boredom of their marriage by a casual relationship outside wedlock. Seducing them was easy and in the newly established conjugal triangle, each party enjoyed certain advantages, even the cheated husband, who received his wife's special attention without having a clue about the real state of affairs. The lover for his part enjoyed all the privileges of someone else's nest and all the seductive extras the woman in love showered him with, in order to bind him closer to her. Furthermore, he enjoyed elegance and comfort financed not by him, but by the deceived husband.

There was another type of men—the lower-middle-class, badly paid civil servants, salaried employees, and small tradesmen—who primarily wanted to find someone who was thrifty, well mannered, and full of domes-tic virtues. Even before any engagement, their conversations centred on matters of family budget, favourite dishes and the number of children they hoped to have. They wore rubber overshoes, celluloid collars, home-sewn ties, refitted suits, and scruffy whiskers. In their eyes, beauty was a mere trap, and modesty the virtue that outweighed all external, possibly attractive traits. They also liked to go out with the lady of their choice for a year or two, to get to know her "innermost", before making the final decision. The resulting marriage was not happier, though, despite all those careful preparations, because sooner or later the husband was usually henpecked and under his wife's thumb. The lady of the house would stop cooking his favourite dishes or abiding by the pre-designed programme. There was no end to reproaches and real scenes when, regaining his old habits, the husband sought consolation from world troubles, with a pint of beer in the company of his mates at the pub. Celluloid collars and rubber overshoes disappeared as the victims of fashion, and the imposing whiskers were eventually sacrificed, too. In short, whatever they had carefully planned did not come through, and luckily for them, they usually only realized it too late or not at all.

The fourth group of young men in town were students enrolled in foreign universities, most often in Vienna, because Franz Joseph University in Zagreb had only three faculties, offering degrees in law, philosophy, and theology. Medicine and engineering had to be studied abroad, and the first option, of course, was the imperial capital, with its world-renowned schools and clinics. Students would return home on holiday armed with new slogans and ideas they had picked up in various social circles while abroad. Pan-Slavism,[273] social democracy, and "European horizons" were some of the buzzwords of those young people who would sometimes turn to the East, sometimes to the West for inspiration—from Turgenev's *Fathers and Sons*[274] and Artsybashev's *Sanin*[275] to Strindberg's[276] social nihilism and Ibsen's[277] high ethical demands. In the process, some of them managed to create a mental chaos and obscure any chance of thinking clearly.

A few of my childhood friends were studying in Vienna and as each returned home for holidays, they used to inform me about the hot novelties they had come across in the meantime. Rudi, my friend Lida's cousin, was a medical student—inconspicuous, middle-sized, baby-faced, with blond hair and pink chubby cheeks, and in certain aspects, a rather crafty fellow. His chief interest in life was his profession and he was made for it. The only other thing that counted for him was good food.

Fritz was Rudi's colleague who lived as a tenant in Lida's house. I learned from Lida that the two had agreed to marry once Fritz finished his studies. They had to wait as Lida had no dowry and Fritz lived for the time being on his scholarship. What would be their future was hard to predict at the time.

We met almost every day in the spacious garden behind Lida's house. Most old houses in Osijek had such gardens, with a few jasmine and lilac bushes in the corners, two or three colourful flower beds, and somewhere in the middle, a draw well covered in vines and a big mulberry tree. In the shade of that tree was a bench big enough for all of us to sit. Fritz would usually sit on the backrest letting his long legs dangle. He was well built, with a nice face and thick dark hair, which he kept adjusting with his fingers. He had grey penetrating eyes and there was something intent about his nature, as if he were always on the lookout for something new, surprising, and sensational, that would add validity to his convictions. He had joined the social democrats in Vienna, which had not made a significant effect on his sensitivity. Marxist ideas reached him only indirectly, through citations by speakers at workers' meetings and via the social-democratic press, and he adopted them in accordance with his romantic predispositions.

However, the person who dominated our conversations was my childhood friend, Vlado, who was perhaps not always making logical assertions, but was emphatic about everything he had to affirm. He was a sort of a firebrand, able to develop a passion for whatever issue crossed his path—feminism, individualism, anarchism, you name it, provided that in a given moment it offered a provocative topic for an ensuing conversation. He was older than the other two and had already twice changed universities. He first switched from philosophy to medicine and after a year of medicine, took up technical studies. He was thin and gangly. His suit was the worse for wear and so tight that it made him look even thinner than he really was. His head, mounted on top of a slender neck, with a sharply protruding Adam's apple, looked too heavy for his skinny physique. He was one of those students who supported themselves financially by mentoring and giving private lessons from the very start of their studies. He also worked as a draftsman in a technical institute of some sort, earning just enough not to starve. He was uncompromising in discussions because, as he claimed, life constantly forced him to make concessions everywhere else.

Vlado was four years older than me. We used to live next door to each other on Franjina Street and as children often played together. Later we used to come across each other on our way back from school, passing by in haughty and mutual disdain. I must have appeared to him too young for any real conversation and I found him boring with his exaggerated ideas. Now, however, back home on holiday, surrounded by an aura of importance due to his Viennese experiences, wearing big round glasses with a thin frame and his shirt collar worn open in the Byronic style, Vlado seemed intriguing. Straight on, at our first meeting under the mulberry tree, he told me that he was, as a matter of principle, as well as for biological, social, but mostly individual reasons, against female emancipation. The female belonged to an inferior category of beings, there was little differentiation between her physical and psychological existence, she was not capable of logical thinking and, instead of relying on reflection, she let herself be guided by emotions.

It turned out that Vlado was theoretically well prepared, as he cited Strindberg and Nietzsche,[278] and moved quickly from his specific hatred of womankind to the related topics, namely the hatred that encompassed society as a whole. He had thoroughly studied Bakunin,[279] whose ideas destroyed in one blow, like an exploded grenade, the solid petit-bourgeois conformism he had been exposed to at home. His father was an ordinary post office clerk and his Swabian grandfather an old-fashioned vine-grower. Vlado was now ripping to pieces all those inherited and, through early education, instilled principles of good and evil. All that was left were blue streaks of smoke whirling in spirals out of his newly acquired, short-stemmed pipe.

Fritz refuted him. Women's rights fell within the framework of all other social issues and their final solution could be achieved only through the evolutionary change of our entire social system in the spirit of socialism. Rudi shrugged and stated that he was much more interested in an ailing kidney or a fine specimen of a stomach ulcer than all those artificial theories people kept throwing up in the air in different phases of their intellectual development. A diseased kidney could be treated, and a stomach ulcer surgically removed, whereas resolving social problems was not within the powers of an individual. Those problems had been part of the human history. Therefore, it was wiser to concentrate, exclusively and intensely, on tangible matters alone. One could then achieve concrete results and each such result would then signify a step on the road to progress. While they talked this way, Lida would bring out a huge watermelon and the five of us would set out to eat it. We ate slowly, spitting the seeds around us as we meditated.

Vlado inevitably wanted to continue the conversation and he one day broached a subject we had never before agreed upon, but were all extremely interested in. It was the question of "free love", on which Fritz agreed with Vlado as far it concerned a woman's natural predisposition, or the issues of social hygiene, which made the whole matter more pressing and of a broader significance.[280] But while Fritz pleaded that it was a woman's natural right to do as she pleased with her own body, Vlado's opinion was that the problem should also be considered and resolved from the male perspective. According to him, a man was not by instinct monogamous. He was, however, in every way hindered in expressing his urges and was led towards solutions that were inadequately satisfactory, notably prostitution. While talking this way he revealed things that made our hair stand on end, and we girls begged him to stop. He argued in return that those were simply everyday phenomena that only silly geese could find disgusting, and he concluded that our understanding of "the problem of sexuality" was nothing but romantic platitudes.

After the women's issue came the question of personal freedom, followed by nationalist orientations—Greater Croatia,[281] South-Slavism,[282] and Pan-Slavism—followed by art and fashion, Russian realism, and the French decadent movement. Each of us said what we knew, and more often, what we assumed or thought we knew. We rarely reached any valid conclusion. Our conversations were magniloquent and packed with polemic sharpness. Still, that sober intellectualism was just a mask, behind which stood our desire for self-affirmation and assertion. We would bicker over trifles when, in fact, it was all about our own selves. Because the issue of what our own lives were all about was still unresolved, we were anxiously and impatiently turned towards that which lay ahead of us. At the same time, however, we could not free ourselves from our innermost fears.

In such an atmosphere, our discussions were more and more intense and there was no end to them—not that we wanted them to end. In those formative years, there was no final assessment for us on any matter, only stages, and an open road taking us from one experience to another towards an undefined objective. In addition, there was the purely egotistical desire to present ourselves to one another in the best light possible, to impress each other, and be judged in our responses to the other person's argument, not merely on the basis of the value of our exposition of truth, but also on the basis of our own personal worth. We indulged in discussions for our own sakes. That eagerness was all about us, even when we apparently advocated an abstract truth or an existential issue. Our personal self, with its dark cravings, its secretive turmoil, with that irresistible urge for something we as young people could not yet give a name—all that was the actual problem, the solution to which, life demanded us to find.

By the first day of September, Fritz and Rudi were ready to depart for Vienna to continue their studies. We met one more time to say goodbye, this time not in Lida's garden but on the glacis, where at dusk we took a walk together. The lads wanted us to kiss them goodbye. Lida granted them their wish and kissed them wholeheartedly. I categorically refused. Our relationship was based on friendship and kisses were out of the question. The phlegmatic Rudi retorted, "Fine, no big deal!" Fritz mockingly added that I should not have been afraid, as he was not planning to bite me. "One either gives kisses or not!" Vlado, however, claimed that it did not make any sense in attributing too much significance to one kiss, and besides, he was sure he would get that kiss upon his own departure. I repeated my decisive no, upon which he replied, "We'll see about that! I am not leaving until the fifteenth so you will have enough time to think it over. If you don't mind, I'd like to come over to your place tonight."

Since we had known each other from childhood, Vlado's visits were nothing unusual, and they occasionally took place in the evening. The two of us would then sit on our terrace overlooking the garden and chat about the same things as when all three or five of us were together. My parents were away on holiday at the time and my grandmother used to go to bed early.

That particular evening, we sat as usual on the terrace, listening to the chirping of crickets and watching shooting stars move across the horizon in beautiful golden curves and vanish into nothing. We were usually bickering over things but that evening Vlado started making strange advances. He moved his chair next to mine and said, "You will definitely kiss me. I am quite sure. Everything else is just talk, sentimental nonsense, and mawkishness. It is wrong to perceive natural things of this kind in such a way. You know well that I am not good at serenading around and am incapable of tender wooing. You are after all a modern woman, in whose company one can call a spade a spade."

I was proud that he considered me a modern woman, able to give up on chivalry and call a spade a spade. Nevertheless, I had been imagining a relationship between a man and a woman in an entirely different way based on descriptions in the novels I had previously read. It included ecstatic situations and lovers' blood in turmoil. And I did not feel any of that with Vlado.

He went on, "Love is today a mere matter of refinement and in its most exalted form is in general only possible among sophisticated and civilized people." That I found acceptable as an argument. I often thought of myself as a highly civilized person. Nevertheless, I moved my chair a bit further away from him because his hair started to tickle my face and his elbows were touching mine, and I did not want that.

Then he suddenly started talking about some shocking things that gave me goose bumps and had nothing in common with the "refinement" he had mentioned earlier. He talked about obliging Viennese girls who did not need begging and how he had met back in Vienna one such girl, who had always been ready to throw her arms around his neck and shower him with kisses. He talked of streetwalkers who were not disgusting, as some would claim, of ladies from cheap dance clubs, experienced in all arts of love, and of attractive waitresses in beer houses ready to serve more than just pints of cold beer from the keg. He claimed he knew them all, although I did not believe him, and as I kept turning my head and blushing, he argued that my education was incomplete, which was after all to be expected in the case of a provincial ingénue like me. In the big city, prudishness had become ancient history. Besides, there could be no talk of love between us, because I was far from being his type. His type was the real sweet little woman who was not acting coy and required no coaxing. That sort of woman admittedly lacked in substance, but when it came to love such things did not matter. Then he added, "As I said, there are all sorts of floozies out there, but not many girls you can exchange a few sensible words with, as one can with you. But you keep aloof. One gets the impression in your company of not dealing with a woman who is alive but, how shall I put it, an antique vase too fragile to be held tight in one's hands."

I liked the vase thing except that, despite the poetic comparison, he still kept getting closer to me and now he was not just touching me with his elbows, but putting one of his arms around me in an attempt to draw me nearer to him, regardless of the fragility of the vase he had referred to earlier. I was defending myself as best I could. It became a real chest-to-chest struggle. At the same time, neither of us made a single sound, because we did not want to attract the attention of other members of the household. He grabbed my shoulders and tried to come closer to my face. I was pushing him away with my fists against his chest, and my head leaning backwards. This mute wrestling went on for I do not know how long. I was covered in sweat and one could see heavy drops of sweat on his fore-head, too.

"You must kiss me!"

"I won't!"

"Please, do this for me before I leave!"

"No way!"

What had begun as a game turned into a real passion on his part. He was beseeching me, begging me, threatening. In the end, he declared his love for me, now in an entirely different tone from before. He announced that he would not go without that kiss and would have to miss his whole semester. Nonetheless, I stuck with what I had kept saying from the beginning. "No, no and never!" I was saying that with a triumphal tone of voice, because I was aware of my momentary superiority. I instinctively knew, however, that power would last only as long as I resisted his advances and, in that manner, add additional value to the kiss.

The game went on and on every night for a whole week. Vlado was no longer in control of himself and I believe that during that week he did fall in love with me and that he was in the end begging me for that kiss without any cynicism involved. His behaviour was altogether much clearer than mine and I wonder even today about what made me act the way I did. Was it girlish shyness? Still, why did I let him enter the house when he kept coming night after night? What was I thinking? I could have told him to leave once and for all, instead of sitting with him on the terrace, listening to the crickets, and watching the shooting stars—and then letting the skirmish begin once again, with us fighting chest to chest and I kept saying, "No!"

My parents returned and Vlado left town without getting his kiss. My mood was such that I did not know whether I was richer for the experience or poorer because I had missed out on an opportunity. My confusion, therefore, did not cease and my boredom after my friends' departure increased. I was reading a lot—whatever I could get my hands on. I did some laborious handicraft and took up my piano lessons again, practising with insistence Cramer and Czerny, all in order to reduce the waiting time. Because that was the basic problem. I was considering my life to be in an interim phase and its emptiness had to be filled with something before the big moment arrived that I was intensely anticipating in my dreams and spent time imagining.

It was not my mind, but my body energy, which pushed me in that direction. Nothing before and nothing later had I experienced with such intensity. Without being fully aware myself, everything within me was ready for that great experience of my life—falling in love.

My father used to say, "A person must concentrate on tangible things. A certain dose of opportunism is always recommended. We should be doing what is of use to us, provided it doesn't hurt the people around us. People should avoid all ambiguities and uncertainties and have a clear vision of all phenomena in life. One should practise logical thinking to avoid unpleasant surprises. That way, complicated problems can be resolved with nothing left in the balance."

I would shake my head. I loved mysterious uncertainties, I expected magical surprises. I was also against any kind of opportunism or far-reaching logic. I was against the obvious and against any simple, arithmetic approach that ensures a clean balance sheet as a result. With an understanding smile, my father would respond that I was indulging in youthful exaggerations which would disappear as the years went by. He could not and would not want to believe that his daughter would remain a bad accountant for the rest of her life.

We had this type of conversation during our evening walks. I was often, in those days, accompanying my father on his way home from the office. We would then stroll around for a while on what was known as the *corso*. There, on the corner of Kapucinska Street, on the ground floor of Reisner House,[283] was the newly opened Café Corso, mostly visited by the town's elite, higher-ranking employees, officers, and, in line with new big city habits, also a few ladies. We would promenade there every evening, passing by the brightly lit windows.

One day my father pointed at a corner window of the café and said in a good-natured but teasing tone, "Can you see the little lieutenant in the corner loggia over there? You have a weakness for original fellows, don't you? The lieutenant is just one such type for you. He must be a rare bird in the army, one should say. He knows his Schopenhauer[284] by heart, he has studied all eight volumes of Rolfes' *Metaphysics*,[285] and speaks about Kant[286] as if he had shared a bench with him at school—in short, a philosopher in uniform!"

All of that was, of course, meant as a joke, because my father had no interest in either Schopenhauer, Kant, or Rolfes' *Metaphysics*. Had he known at the time what an impression those words would leave on me, he would have bitten his tongue, rather than utter them.

It has been over fifty years since we had that conversation, but it has remained in my memory as if it happened yesterday. I can see the crowded promenade, the lit-up café, and behind the glass window, a thin face leaning over an open book. As I looked in his direction, he looked up. Our glances made instant contact. That single moment encompassed it all—my future life ahead of me and all the prior things which I had anticipated in my dreams.

I found out later from my father that the philosopher in uniform was Milivoj Vukelić. I felt sorry that such a man had to become an officer and I wanted to find out more about him. My father was either unable to or did not want to tell me anything more. But I soon discovered a new source of information, as is usually the case when one is really interested in something or somebody. Nothing is then left to chance. One uses all available means, with astuteness and resolve, consciously or subconsciously, in order to achieve that specific goal. We seek the company of those who know the person we are interested in and without others noticing we lead the conversation in that direction. We rejoice at each new hint and detail we can learn this way. We manage to find out a few things about the person's lifestyle, preferences, and abilities. We discover which books the person likes to read, and we accompany him in our thoughts on his daily walks. The image of that person begins to emerge from the mist of the unknown and is still not reality, because it is, for a while, mainly a construction of our imagination. It seems like reading an exciting novel that appears to be a mixture of reality and fiction, far superior to any already existing, with each new chapter bringing forward more intensity.

At that stage, there was nothing personal between us, apart from those secretive looks we gave each other. Those looks kept conveying our joy, our sadness, our yearning, and our eagerness to say how glad we were that the other person existed. The glances gradually became clearer, more eloquent, less concealed. They expressed everything—our courage and hesitance, our belief in life, which was supposed to bring us together one day, and the fear that we might miss out on the real moment, be torn away from one another without making our dreams come true. Day after day, we became increasingly aware from looking at each other that we were no more able to contain our feelings, that destiny was at work there and neither he nor I could escape it any longer.

He was twenty-four and I was seventeen. We should, at that time, have found our way to each other and been united, young as we were then, full of confidence, and in love. We should have experienced our happiness in that very early stage, before life had found ways to test our endurance with all sorts of tragic impositions. We should have been allowed to enjoy the magic of the unexpected and the instantaneous, instead of being forced to wait for years. It should have been an enormous and incredibly joyous gift from heaven. With the passing of time, however, the original feeling had changed and with it our attitudes and our belief in happiness. Shadows, like ashes, fell on our path and on our feelings. But destiny wanted it that way and it eventually took years from the moment we saw each other for the first time to the moment when we were finally united.

My best source of information was, as usual, Professor Matić, who knew everybody in town and also knew their secrets, both private and public. Between algebra and historical facts and dates, he was telling me about communal disputes at the municipal council, about possible upcoming betrothals and impending marital disputes. He knew my philosopher in uniform and supplied me with valuable information about him. Those details fuelled my dreams, but most of all provided concrete help to get closer to him.

Matić brought me a collection of poems by Lavoslav Vukelić,[287] my idol's father, entitled *Književno cvijeće* (Literary Flowers), edited and accompanied by an introduction written by his friend Bude Budisavljević.[288] I found in it numerous details that helped me form not only a portrait of the father, but also of his son. How precious was for me every single word that illuminated the poet's intimate life! I read with passionate interest about his progress in life, unaware that I was instinctively identifying the father's life with that of the son. I got to know the world of Milivoj's origins and his childhood. It all seemed distant in time and space, with an added touch of something tragic and a mix of unreality and romance. I did not actually want to get to know him in the greyness of everyday life, which would have rendered my feelings banal. I wanted to preserve the myth with which I could bestow an aura of glory on both the father and the son. I was not looking for realism, but a legend, nothing tangible, but rather abstract. I wanted to idealize and admire him in the way his father was admired after his death. I was not entirely mistaken in doing this close comparison, because, as it was later revealed, he truly resembled his father in his overall makeup, except that he lived in different times and was inclined to scepticism. No one was as strong-willed or tougher than him. His mother was from the Starčević family and he surely had inherited something from that family branch, too. Aside from vitality, he also had a dose of sobriety, persistence, and stoicism, all characteristics of the politician, Ante Starčević, his close relative.[289]

From what I learned in the writings of his friend Bude Budisavljević, my idol's father was a very engaging person in his youth and had left a strong impression on his entourage. His enthusiasm and tempestuous eloquence had a captivating effect on everybody around him, in particular his schoolmates at the Senj[290] gymnasium, who all perceived him as their indisputable leader. He was imagining wide-ranging plans for the welfare of his compatriots, and that ambition, when combined with his great talents, provided an assurance in the eyes of his friends that he would have an important role to play in the future. In any other country, this would have been the case. He would probably have become one of those who left their mark on their times. He possessed a comprehensive knowledge of history and literature, studied languages, and in his twenties had already read Dante, Torquato Tasso, Shakespeare, Goethe, and Mickiewicz in their original languages.[291] Furthermore, he was familiar with great Croatian Renaissance poets, as well as Andrija Kačić-Miošić,[292] whose many verses he could recite by heart, as he could the entire *Death of Smail-aga Čengić*.[293]

However, young men born on the Military Frontier[294] wishing to pursue their higher education had only one option available after they graduated from high school—to continue their studies in Austrian military or semi-military academies. There they would receive a rigorous military training as future servicemen or administrative officials deployed on the Military Frontier, where keeping your mouth shut was the ultimate rule of law. They were indoctrinated in the imperial spirit and stripped of their national awareness to the point of forgetting their mother tongue, as was, for example, the case with Petar Preradović.[295] They were forbidden to read those "shameful nationalistic newspapers" such as *Obzor*, and once they were well integrated in the military environment, with its well-structured hierarchical ranking system, they received their uniforms and ranks and were sent back home to Lika or Slavonia. There they had nothing else to do but obey the orders of their superiors and behave like puppets.

Lavoslav Vukelić was also educated in one such school for administrative officials on the Military Frontier. He was then sent back to his native Lika, and after a few years on the assignment, there was practically nothing left of his youthful élan. He was still considered one of the political rebels, but as was the case with so many other young men of his generation, his urge for revolt became seriously inhibited by the mindset that had been instilled in him from above. His revolt was extremely restrained, both by his military training and his patriotism, centred on his native region of Lika. Despite Dante and Torquato Tasso, Shakespeare and Schopenhauer, the drill to which he was subjected succeeded in infiltrating his whole being. His oppositional stand was a strange combination of *Weltschmerz* and political and legal concerns, altruism and personal discouragement, bad mood due to the hopelessness of his position, and the pain caused by the oppression of the Croatian people. Like so many of his compatriots, he also felt an urgent need to overcome the passiveness through occasional temperamental actions, and to find relief in words by giving passionate speeches and writing poetry. But there was no organized or concrete, goal-oriented rebellion in all of them—they were not attempting to shatter the foundations of the existing regime or rejecting the methods of the system. They focused instead on details and symptoms, on that which was visible and within one's easy grasp, on the calamities of an onerous service and the fact that "the ones with golden collars," meaning their superiors, held too much power. The real rebellion was, given the circumstances they found themselves in, something unthinkable. It would be equal to suicide, fighting the windmills, bashing one's head against the wall. There was no way, even from the inside, to resist the power in place. They were all just small cogs in the large wheel, bound by rules and ordinances to contribute to its faultless functioning. A life full of promises and plans was reduced to silence, and, apart from some forays in the literary domain, there seemed nothing else to do but keep quiet, because a single reckless word could have cost both the career and the unique source of an indispensable income.

This was the life experience of several generations of young men between 1840 and 1880. Lavoslav Vukelić broke free of those restrictions only on his deathbed. He got rid of clichés, returned to his promising literary origins, and wrote three really beautiful and moving poems that still stand among the best in Croatian poetry—the sonnet *Istina* (The Truth) expressing his yearning for the absolute, *Posljednja pjesma* (The Last Song) in which he was mourning for the life he had never been able to experience, and the poem *Kod Solferina* (At Solferino), which, with its humanistic message, represented the pinnacle of his literary expression.

I translated that last poem into German, and it was published in the Christmas holiday issue of the local newspaper *Die Drau*.[296] I was hoping it would attract the son's attention and bring us together, and so it did. Milivoj Vukelić read the poem, found out the translator's name at the editor's office, and soon after, in the spirit of the social etiquette of the time, asked my parents' permission to visit me and express his gratitude.

What happened next has so far remained undocumented, and not relayed in any narrative or literary form. It has been part of my deepest self, passed over through my blood to my children and grandchildren as the integral part of their own being. It contains both happy and painful elements. By writing about it, I wish to bring to light forgotten moments and give a new gloss to things that were obscured by the life that followed.

Milko's[297] visit was arranged for a Sunday afternoon. Nothing I had ever felt before could compare with the excitement I experienced in anticipation of that visit. I was insanely happy, but my joy was matched by just as much fear. How would it go? How would I feel standing in front of him for the first time? What would he say, and would I dare say a word out loud? Have I done the right thing by plotting this encounter, by trying to turn a dream into reality, bridge the distance that had been separating us until then, and allow an ideal image I had arbitrarily created in my fantasies to take the shape of a human being made of flesh and blood?

What was there to gain in the first place? I had not the slightest idea. Yes, I was about to meet him, but would I not at the same time expose our secret, which had for weeks been the backbone of all our thoughts and which had pulled us even closer to each other than any open form of an encounter could have ever succeeded? No one knew anything about it except the two of us. Everyone would now find out, become involved, burden me with indiscreet remarks, and pester with advice and bothersome directives. Worse, they would, in the future, be dealing with him, too—judging him, criticizing him, laughing at him, and mocking him—as was always the case in our circles if someone came across as being in some way different. Moreover, he might disappoint me as well, once I made his acquaintance. The mere thought was frightening.

He came at the proposed time and he did not disappoint me. Every thought I had in me was swept away by a torrent of emotions generated by his immediate presence. I could hardly hear what he was saying. The only thing reaching my ears was the warmth of his voice. We were sitting in my parents' red plush drawing room, facing each other for the first time. The whole family was there, but I only saw him. Of course, we talked about all sorts of things and touched upon various subjects. Everything seemed significant and wonderful to me but an hour later, I could not recall a single thing. He talked about himself. I do remember that. He garnished his talk with anecdotes and embellished his sentences with poetic images and lyrical observations. Even my usually level-headed mother got carried away by the torrent of his words. My grandmother later said that she liked the lieutenant because he spoke like one of those heroes from the romantic novels she used to read in her youth, when words had been important and people had allowed themselves to be carried away by their sounds.

To me, that afternoon remained equally inexplicable and as magical as that previous evening when we had first seen each other through the window of the Café Corso. I cannot remember the spoken words, because they were entirely insignificant. Whatever we might have both wished to say to each other was actually not uttered aloud, and we both knew it. As for my parents, in their opinion, once the courteous visit was over, the matter was all but concluded. The young man expressed his gratitude, as ordinary duty and form required, and any further interaction with the young man (considered entirely out of the question as a suitor) would have been pointless, even harmful. The two of us, however, were of a different opinion. After experiencing the joy of our first encounter, we were determined to continue our acquaintance, no matter what, and make it possibly even more intimate in fact, so no one could ever separate us. We managed to arrange short and inconspicuous meetings while on our outings. He was not on duty in the afternoons and I arranged my various errands accordingly. I would go out with my mother on a supposedly indispensable errand and as we walked down the street, he would appear from around the next corner and join us. He would lend me books and magazines, because he was not just interested in philosophy, but also modern literature, and that gave us an excuse for further meetings. He was the only person in Osijek to subscribe to Ludwig Jacobowski's magazine *Die Gesellschaft* (The Society) from Berlin,[298] dedicated to modern German literature by publishing works by Richard Dehmel, Detlev von Liliencron, Arno Holz, and other avant-gardes poets and writers.[299] He was also receiving the magazine *Aus fremden Zungen* (In Foreign Tongues) published in Stuttgart, which contained translations from a variety of languages, including texts from Emile Zola, Oscar Ivar Levertin, Arne Garborg, Henryk Sienkiewicz, and Maxim Gorky.[300]

Such reading gave me new insights into a diversity of cultures I had been unaware of. This was all the more important because people in Osijek were not really into buying books, with the occasional exception of something purely entertaining or to be read while travelling. Usually people read books they happened to come across by chance, or they borrowed them from Victor Frische's only lending library in town, where all they could find were books by Georg Moritz Ebers, Friedrich von Spielhagen, Friedrich Gerstöcker, and Gustav Freytag,[301] whose yellowing and tatty copies were still part of the collection ever since the library had opened some thirty years earlier. For birthdays, people received beautifully bound anthologies of entirely harmless poetry by Emmanuel Geibel, Ludwig Holty, and Anastasius Grün.[302] Families usually subscribed to *Gartenlaube* (Garden Arbour) and *Blatt der Hausfrau* (Homemaker's Journal) and, at best, *Vom Fels zum Meer* (From the Cliffs to the Sea) or *Wiener Mode* (Vienna Fashion). Magazines such as *Die Gesellschaft (The Society)* and *Aus fremden Zungen* (In Foreign Tongues) were considered a pure novelty in our town. Thanks to Milko, not only a whole new view of the world was thus revealed to me, but I also realized that my personal problems were by no means an isolated case, and that many other people struggled with the same issues as I did, shared the same thoughts, were haunted by similar conflictual feelings and adopted similar viewpoints. When Milko realized what an eager reader I was and that whatever we read always provided new topics for stimulating discussions, he started buying everything he assumed might interest me.

While we thus walked, I learned a few details about his personal life. He sometimes talked about his childhood. He seemed to have been a delicate child, sensitive, shy, and eager for knowledge. He grew up in the oppressive living conditions of a modest civil servant's family and he and his three siblings often went to bed with nothing to eat for dinner. The father was ill, distraught, and unhappy about his unfulfilled hopes and ambitions, a feeling he legated over to his children, along with the seeds of his illness. Milko was also infected by his father's disconcerted feelings, but he wanted to achieve more than his father. He looked way beyond the narrow scope of the military life and was interested in the broad world of contemporary ideas. He viewed his personal inner conflicts in the light of much broader human dimensions. Even so, he acted like his father—he never allowed himself to go all the way and assume the consequences.

Driven by his patriotic feelings, he chose, upon his discharge from the cadet academy, to join the Royal Croatian Home Guard, instead of the general army ranks. Interestingly enough, his patriotism was entirely apolitical, something he had in common with most officers. He managed quite well to keep in harmony his spiritual rebellion and the imposed military discipline, just as his disputing of the authorities was actually only theoretical. The love he felt for his homeland stemmed from a strong feeling of tribal identification and had a distinct aristocratic intonation. He descended from a long line of Vukelić generations, all the way back to the thirteenth century and the founder of the tribe, Vukelj, who had murdered his own father. Generations of warriors, heroes, and rebels ensued. One of Milko's ancestors was legendary "Crni Došen" (Black Došen), about whom folk songs were sung. On his mother's side, there was a pint-size Starčević who, notwithstanding his small size, pierced through a mighty-looking Turkish *aga* with his small sabre and made the surrounding Turkish troops flee in panic. Milko's grandfather was Colonel Petar Došen, who fought with Napoleon in Russia and was the first Croat to be granted the French Legion of Honour. There was also the old stoic and Eastern Orthodox

Church hater, Ante Starčević, who was so stubborn and tough that even the most convincing fact could not make him change his mind. Finally, there was Lavoslav Vukelić, the Croatian Hamlet, consumed by his own torments, who aspired for so much that he was in the end unable to achieve even what he could otherwise have been capable of.

That was the tribe Milko was devoted to—those thousands of tall, bearded men who inhabited Lika[303] and were credited for engendering enough sons to populate entire villages with the Vukelić breed. His sense of tradition, his pride, and his attachment to the land were entirely the result of that devotion.

He left Lika when he was just three years old and had since lived first in a small town called Sveti Križ Začretje in the Zagorje region, where his father died, then in Varaždin, where he attended the gymnasium, then in Karlovac, where he finished the cadet academy, and finally in Zemun and Osijek, his first garrison assignments. But the legend of his homeland accompanied him wherever he went. He was connected to it through unbreakable bonds, attached to its mountains, its boorish people, its tragedy, and its past. It was poor, neglected, and backward. He loved it all the more dearly. In those times, there was no railway in that wild mountain region, only a stagecoach, as in medieval times, which, in winter, would stop operating for weeks, due to huge snowstorms. Lika would then be totally isolated and entirely cut off from the rest of the world, with no mail and no newspapers.

Milko's bond with Lika was, just as much as it was for his father, predominantly poetic in nature. The connection was not organic, however, as was the case with his father, but rather stemmed from a commitment his father had transmitted to him. His own world was imbued instead by Western enlightenment and the historical and contemporary aspects of European culture. He learned French and English (the Vukelić tribe has always demonstrated an innate talent for learning languages!) Besides historiography and philosophy, he regularly read foreign magazines. His assessment of the regime's abuse of power in Croatia, or of the domestic political situation in general, was reduced to one categorical "No comment!", without going into details or giving any arguments to explain his views.

He was interested in everything to do with literature far more than in things political, which he considered as altogether immoral and repulsive. He was an enthusiastic supporter of the modernist trend in literature and was particularly fond of Scandinavian writers, such as Arne Garborg, Gustaf Geyerstam, and Jonas Lie.[304] They were advocates of a person's unlimited right to individuality and viewed politics entirely as affairs of corruption and criminal machinations. Such a stance neatly fitted his personal worldview and carefully maintained solipsism. He would reiterate with conviction that he wanted to stay away from the hustle and bustle of public affairs and not give it even a thought.

I believed at that time that this elevated and civilized worldview gave our protest a distinct European orientation. I had no idea then how easily that "European worldview" could, from one day to another, tip over and reverse itself in the opposite direction. I am aware today that the concept of a "modern civilized world" is fluid and overrated. It encompasses good and bad in human behaviour and could apply to whatever one chooses. Young people, however, must make choices to help them in their early endeavours in life and they must stand by their decisions.

In those days, I trusted Milko's superior mind, but he failed to give me a definite direction. I had to fight hard in later years to establish one of my own, by my own means. He failed because he himself had no direction of his own. It is no wonder that I was unable to find my proper perspective, with all that German education and youthful overestimation of German culture. Women in those days hardly read any newspapers and, if they got hold of one, they would exclusively turn to cultural pages to read reports on new books and theatre performances. Not only was there an evident lack of interest in politics and newspapers among women, there was also the fact that newspapers had very small circulation and readership in general. They were rarely read at home. Men read their papers in public places or at the Casino. Even intelligent women, like my mother, for instance, saw no interest in polemics found in newspapers. They viewed them of minor importance in their own lives, if at all, and only as far as they were relevant to their aesthetic interests and, even then, only as long as they had an effect on their narrow social circles.

I, however, wanted to break out of that circle. I was searching for higher values, most of all, knowledge. I knew instinctively that even in that area, my access was limited—mere ersatz and, in many cases, sheer bricolage. I was learning algebra, physics, and natural sciences from books for high school education, and Professor Matić believed I could soon be ready for the high school graduation exam. Important and vital questions had still not been answered, and Milko, from whom I expected to learn so much, was unable to help me find those answers. I read books he was passing on to me. They provided abundant material for reflection and revealed new areas of interest, but also created new conflicts in my life. The emphasis on individualism they were theorizing about had an impact on me, in both beneficial and disturbing ways. This put me further at odds with my surroundings and shook my trust in everything I had learned so far. The conflict was less to do with my relatives and more about my broader social environment. I lived in a small town and felt I was being constantly observed. People commented on the way I dressed, behaved, laughed, and expressed myself. They criticized my idiosyncrasies, my preferences, and my tastes. They knew what I was doing with my time, what I read and with whom I was socializing. The eyes of the whole town followed me around and nothing could be concealed or hidden from their merciless gaze. All mistakes were brought out in the open and registered, not to mention little acts of negligence or omission. It was even worse with certain choices made outside prescribed norms, since public opinion in a small town accepted no straying from the mapped path. Everything that stood out was interpreted as an insolent act of arrogance. Life had been once and for all times built on solid patterns, barely changed for decades, devised for the accumulation of possessions, the growth of businesses, and the reinforcement of business connections. People felt secure, content with the place destined for them inside a solidly built system they believed would last forever. They could not allow pushy, trend-infected people to disturb a world where everything had its name, its place, and its price. Only fools would be willing to pay more for things than they were worth and only those with criminal inclinations believed they could have whatever they wanted for gratis.

While in the eighteen eighties, everything was still moving at a slow and peaceful pace forward, the mid-nineties experienced a change. The clash between the old and the young generations—most uncommon in the past—had become in Europe more and more evident as a recurrent topic in literature and art. The reference to "youth" had become part of a new slogan and stood for the rejection of outdated prejudices and the intense clash of generations, as older generations showed no readiness to give in and grant young people the right to self-assertion and self-determination.

The impact of that struggle was so considerable that it even reached Osijek! Not just Milko, but several other Croatian young people declared themselves in favour of modernism. Interestingly enough, it was actually a few students from Osijek who began actively fostering the idea of a necessity for change, more in terms of literature than politics, it must be admitted. They recognized the role literature could play on the international stage by demonstrating the unique cultural features of individual nations, and furthering exchanges and contacts among them in order to enhance a mutual understanding and trust. This group of young people studying at the University of Vienna took upon themselves the forward-looking mission as a reaction, it seemed, to years of pressure they had themselves suffered in their small town. Among them were people like Guido Jeny, Dušan Plavšić, Vlado Schmidt-Jugović, Otto Kraus, and several others who, inspired by the ongoing cultural atmosphere in Vienna, embraced art and literature as their chosen field of action.[305]

Plavšić gave me my first copy of the Munich magazine *Jugend* (Youth). This innovative magazine, with its illustrations by Thomas Theodor Heine, Hans Thoma, and Ephraim Moses Lilien, and well-crafted and witty satirical sketches—along with highly popular chansons by Otto Julius Bierbaum and Gustav Falke, and cabaret songs by Frank Wedekind and Ernst von Wohlzogen—had a fascinating effect on the young, due to their brash lack of all respect.[306] *Jugend* was soon joined by the no less entertaining magazine *Simplicissimus*,[307] a change from the boring *Fliegende Blätter* (Loose Leaves) and equally dreary *Kladderadatsch* (Bust-Up) from Berlin. *Simplicissimus* created the character Serenissimus, an incarnation of a bigoted and medieval figure of authority, which served as an ideal object for merciless mockery of whoever held political power at the time.

"Older" folks were hit hard by the barrage of these attacks. But the struggle had just begun and, in the years to come, would only become more intense. It spread from the public sphere into family circles and manifested itself through the increased refractory behaviour of young people against the tyranny of their parents, without their ever having been particularly familiar with the theories of Freud and Adler and their implications. The "old" folk, on the other hand, were unable to understand that particular urge for freedom and the independence of their offspring. They considered it a highly objectionable sign of degeneration and an obvious digression. They perceived it as an attack on their life commitments and their political conservatism, as well as their safe deposit boxes, all of which was suddenly called into question. Irreverent hands dared to stir it all up. Their own progeny underestimated how much they had invested for decades in their life's work. The young people looked at it all with no objectivity and no sense of reality. It was tragic if a child in question was a son and heir, but even more tragic if a daughter was involved. The son's horns could become blunt with time and he might rediscover the right path, but, in the case of a daughter, disgrace was all one could expect as a result! She would be guilty of two *faux pas* at the same time—rebellion against not only the traditions and customs of her immediate environment, but also against the natural law, which had once and for all defined a woman's place in her family as fully obedient to her parents and her husband. She was not supposed to have any say in public affairs, whether political or social. She was required to refrain from expressing her personal opinions, as this would be considered "unfeminine" and susceptible to turning her into an object of ridicule and disdain. In the opinion of everybody around her, be they aunts, cousins, friends, or acquaintances, she could expect nothing but trouble in her future—and would never be able to find herself a husband.

On the occasion of my eighteenth birthday, on 8 February 1898, I pleaded with my parents to allow me to organize a dance at our home and invite guests of my own choosing. I did so, hoping I would get Milko to come to my house once again so I could spend some undisturbed moments chatting with him—something which had lately become more and more difficult. My parents agreed, and I immediately began the preparations. The large dining room was emptied and made into a suitable dance hall. The piano was brought in and I asked Milko to invite his friend Đuko Jakobac, a skilled pianist, who agreed to provide the music. Two buffets were set up, one in the salon for the grown-ups and the other in my room for younger people. I arranged the tables myself as best as I could. I set fresh flowers on the buffet table in my room and green plants in the background. I placed caviar and ham sandwiches on silver platters to make them look like colourful mosaics. I surrounded the cold cuts of poultry roast with a wreath of radishes and added pickled cucumbers and fresh parsley leaves as an additional decoration. I arranged cakes, petits fours, and fruit on tall stands behind the table, together with bottles of dessert wine, liqueurs, and flowers, all with the idea of making the entire arrangement as pleasing to the eye as to the palate.

My room had pink wallpaper and the sofa was upholstered in light green cretonne with pink flower motives. The dressing table was covered with a white lace drapery and on it were various shiny objects, as if on an altar. There was a small writing desk under the window, a bookshelf next to the sofa, and on the wall, two fine lithographic prints in their golden frames—portraits of Schiller and Goethe, which my father had given me as a present while I was in Vienna.

I also paid considerable attention that evening as to how I was dressed. I received as a birthday present an ivory white silk dress with embroidered floral patterns, ordered specially from Vienna. I liked it a lot and that night I wore it for the first time. I was glowing with happiness, aware that one's eighteenth birthday was not a minor thing to celebrate! I received many congratulations and presents. My grandmother gave me a gold ducat, just as she had done at every birthday for as long as I could remember. I had eighteen of them by that time—not a small sum—and I stored them all carefully in a safe place. God knows how many different things I had been planning to buy with them as a child! On that occasion, my plan was to save the ducats for my honeymoon, which was indeed what they were used for some years later.

Everything seemed nicely set up. The most beautiful part, however, was yet to happen. It was to be that one hour in his presence, that hour I had been anticipating for days, and the reason I had staged that whole complicated affair. It was the only reason why I had invited all those guests, most of whom were totally indifferent to me, why music was playing in the living room, why there were arrangements of fragrant flowers all around, why there were tempting fine wines and a choice of delicacies on the buffet tables. That was the reason why I also made such an effort with my outfit—all for the sake of that highly expected one hour. I kept standing in the entrance hall with my eyes constantly turned in the direction of the door, and at each ring of the doorbell, my heart pounded wildly with anticipation.

Of course, out of respect to my parents' social obligations, I had to invite a few young men of high social standing, who were still young in terms of their age, but represented exactly the opposite of everything I understood as being really "young". They had good positions, and what particularly infuriated me, were considered a good catch. They were fully aware of that reputation and believed it gave them permission to be arrogant in respect to young girls. Their prestige relied on well-tailored suits, a confident demeanour, and fine table manners. Their tastes were problematic, as was clearly evident in their conversations. In matters of theatrical performances, they preferred to talk about light operettas and prima donnas' fine legs, rather than actual artistic qualities of a show. They liked to read racy stories and preferred representations of nudes when it came to visual arts. If they started flirting with a girl, they always left a door ajar to provide for the possibility of a cautious escape. What disturbed me most was that they elevated coquetry above all other female qualities. According to their understanding, that was the only way a man and a woman could interact. They never looked for anything more than superficial entertainment, lighthearted chatting, meaningless laughter, and ambiguous looks from the corner of one's eye, always careful that it never led to anything serious and that they remained free of all responsibility.

Young girls played along. In fact, they did not expect anything more. On the surface, they were the perfect product of the education they had received from their governesses, conceived to turn them into so-called blank slates, to be formatted later at a man's will. While men preferred entirely different sorts of women for their own personal satisfaction, they did appreciate the pristine and inexperienced nature of those girls, when considered as potential wives. The lack of personality was just as valued as the sight of a pale face carefully protected by a parasol or a veil from the effects of too much light and sunshine. Neatly disguised behind fine manners, everything seemed intact and polished. It was the husband's task to bring to life the soulless doll he had married, to mould and shape her according to his wishes. It happened that not many men were up to the task. Most were no princes, who could wake their sleeping beauties and they rarely managed to fashion them according to their own expectations. A woman's hidden qualities sometimes came to the fore, but in most cases, it was a lost cause.

Milko arrived among the last guests. He saw me and smiled. I also smiled, and we shook hands with obvious pleasure. Jakobac was already at the piano and couples were swirling to the music. Milko explained to me that he did not dance. Out of principle! It seemed to me more out of uneasiness than principle. He wanted to avoid public exposure. I told him, "But I have to dance with my guests!" He just nodded. "I will be watching you." And he did. I kept catching glimpses of him while I was dancing. I noticed the expression on his face gradually turning sombre. He looked unhappy. He later admitted he had been jealous.

While the young people were enjoying themselves in the dining room, adults were sitting in the drawing room. It was the close circle of my parents' guests, who had been coming daily to our house, including Aunts Tinka and Sophie, Dr. and Mrs. Reinfeld, and Miss Lipschitz. The centre of considerable attention this time, however, was a newcomer—the young and elegant Mrs. Gerö from Budapest, whose husband had recently been appointed director of an industrial undertaking in Osijek. She was a freckled redhead with a tendency to mock and disparage those around her. The Osijek provincial setting in which she found herself, against her will, was way below the Budapest social standards to which she aspired. She kept making biting remarks, sometimes even strong insinuations, about people in Budapest she used to encounter while promenading up and down Váci Street. They drove past her in their elegant horse-driven coaches, never treating her as their equal, let alone inviting her to tea. Nevertheless, she knew what people in those circles considered chic, what they were thinking and saying, how they dressed and behaved. While Esseker ladies created their own style of fashion by imitating one another, Mrs. Gerö wore gowns produced by leading fashion houses, which appeared both posh and extravagant in colours and cuts, so far seen in Osijek only on the pages of Parisian fashion magazines. Outfits which they had previously declared among themselves to be the ultimate in fashion for that season were suddenly disputed.

In Osijek, women still used high steel-boned corsets and rubber belts to accentuate the waist curve as much as possible. Women wore puffed sleeves filled with bombast stuffing and skirts that spread right from the waist. Mrs. Gerö instead wore gowns with pleated skirts and a silk belt in a contrasting colour, slightly extended over the belly area, thus providing, seen from the front, a gently curved line, while the bust remained propped high up. Her sleeves were not puffed above the elbow, as had been the fashion so far, but rather below it in the form of an even larger puff, retained at the wrist by a narrow, tight cuff. The skirt she wore widened below the knees instead from the waist, which provided a totally new look. Mrs. Gerö also wore the most daring and clashing colours—black and white striped taffeta with cherry red garnishing, colour-changing foulard fabric in Nile green and silver-grey variations with incrustations of black lace, or peacock-blue velvet with gold brocade incrustations instead. Her hats were either trimmed with huge ostrich feathers, with tufts hanging over the eyes, or were small bibi hats, decorated with flowers and silk that looked like birds' nests in her puffed-up hair. "Phooey!" the former queens of fashion kept saying, because they could not match such extravagances and saw each of her outfits as an assault on good taste. At the same time, the sight filled them with awe, envy, and enmity.

Mrs. Gerö had an annoying and destructive effect on people's spirits, resembling an earthquake. To many ladies, she became an obsession that haunted them even in their dreams. "Parties" at the Gerős also initiated numerous controversies. She got rid of the existing custom of afternoon

Jausen, consisting of coffee with whipped cream and Gugelhupf cake with raisins. She received guests only on Thursdays, offering exclusively tea and sandwiches handed around by a maid wearing a cute white apron and a little lace headpiece. Both of her boys, aged three and five, wore little sailor suits with long trousers, which she claimed was the ultimate fashion in Budapest worn by the young Archduke Joseph Francis, son of Her Royal Highness Archduchess Augusta, Palatine Joseph's wife.

Between dances, I could hear the murmur of voices from the drawing room. I could also hear the clatter of plates, the clinking of glasses, and Aunt Tinka's chuckling laughter. The atmosphere was at its peak and I thought nobody would notice if I disappeared for a while. The couples were sliding on the dance floor. Soon the quadrille would begin, and I had not promised that dance to anyone, explaining that I already had my partner. I approached Milko, who was at the time sitting in a corner by himself, took him by the hand and said, "This dance belongs to you. Let us have a chat." I led him to my room, where the food buffet was, put food on his plate and filled his glass. We then sat down next to each other on the sofa.

It was the moment I had been waiting for the entire evening and all those days of preparations leading to it. He sipped his wine but had set aside the plate without touching it. I did not urge him to eat, as it was clear he did not feel like doing it at that moment. We barely exchanged ten words in that short period we spent together in my room sitting next to each other on the small sofa. The silence nevertheless brought us closer together than any words could have done. We looked at each other and felt utterly happy. We could have sat that way next to each other forever. All we wanted to do was to be together and our gazes to melt into one. Our hands were resting on the edge of the sofa ten centimetres from each other, but we did not think of joining them, not even to touch each other with the tips of our fingers.

Couples in love are convinced of being alone in this world. They are convinced that their state of mind is something unique and that no one has ever experienced anything like it before. Their happiness surpasses all earthly wonders. It is a gift from the fairies, which happens to mortals no more than once in a hundred years. Their tragedy corresponds to the greatest tragedy a human can endure, quite similar to that endured by the pair whom God banished forever from Paradise into the tormenting life on Earth below. For us, too, that quarter of an hour felt like a miracle, unfathomable by human standards. We were fully aware of it as we sat there in silence, smiled, and looked at each other. Any word would have simply broken the charm of the moment. But the spell was soon shattered. The door suddenly opened, and my father showed up. He had been looking for me among the dancing couples and discovered I had disappeared. I had never before seen him so angry. He made an effort to control himself, mostly because of the guests who were not supposed to hear what he intended to tell me. In a muted tone of voice, he said, "I cannot but wonder at your inappropriate behaviour! You left others in order to indulge in your personal entertainment, instead of taking care of your guests like a good hostess. Go back immediately to your guests!"

With his hand, he pointed to the door. He did not even bother to look at Milko, nor give me a chance to explain myself. There was nothing else I could do but leave the room. Since the quadrille was about to start again, I felt obliged to join in and quickly found a dancing partner. I managed to catch a glimpse of Milko saying goodbye to my mother and leaving the house.

The following day, my father sternly announced that the flirtation with the lieutenant had to end. He did not wish to see him in his house anymore and forbade me from maintaining any contact with him altogether. There was no way a connection with that man could, according to my father, lead to anything of consequence. The man belonged to a milieu that had nothing at all to do with ours. Officers belonged to a world apart and suffered from exaggerated snobbery, while themselves living in miserable conditions of their own. As a Jew, and even more so according to the logic of his way of thinking, my father had nothing in common with that class of people and therefore did not want his daughter to make friends within those circles. He did not consider the lieutenant particularly likable once he had had the opportunity to meet him in person, although he had himself, unfortunately, drawn my attention to him at the beginning. The man was too much of a philosopher to make a good officer and, in order to become a good philosopher, he was too much of an officer. Father ordered me to return that same day all the books—all that degenerate literature, from Maeterlinck[308] to Ibsen—that I had received from Milko, no matter whether they were a gift or a loan, and no matter whether I had read them or not. The unfortunate incident of the day before had demonstrated, in his view, the extent of the corruptive effect of those books, how quickly they had made me lose my ability to make sound judgments and had ruined my sense of decency and good manners. He wanted this thing to end at once and for all! "That *Svengali*," as he called Milko, "practically hypnotized you. As your father, I will not have it. In future, you will not set foot out of this house on your own. Whenever you do go out, it will be from now on exclusively in the company of your mother!"

It was my father, the idol of my childhood, who was thus talking to me! I was not just distressed by the punishment, but also outraged by the manner he was treating me. It shattered my trust in his paternal authority. He was wrong, and not only in respect to the situation as such, but also in the inconsiderate way he dealt with it. He did not take my feelings into account, and what was worse, he ignored my motives—namely an entire attitude towards life, which had begun crystallizing within me ever so clearly, despite constant attempts at coercion by people around me. He had notably ignored my aspiration towards further intellectual growth and the search for higher spiritual and human values. In one gesture, it had all been dismissed as a sort of a child's play. It hurt deeply that he dismissed the fact that I wanted to study, that I simply had natural inclinations towards it. He ignored the fact that my interests extended beyond the limitations of women's lives, and that mere childbearing, cooking, and gossip would not satisfy me in life. The most intimate and essential part of me was the desire to do serious and useful work, but all this was characterized as an abnormal product of an exalted state of mind and needed to be suppressed by all available means. And while it hurt, it also confirmed my decision that, at least in my most intimate self, I would remain steadfast and not let anybody influence me. This experience was even more painful, because it caught me off guard. My relationship with my father so far had been close and based on trust. I respected his intelligence, and even more so, his true kind-heartedness, which I had never had reason to doubt. He was usually lenient and understanding as far as human weaknesses were concerned, always ready to help with a piece of advice or a good deed. His kindness was simply captivating, and particularly evident in his interactions with his subordinates and common people, and they all loved him. Where did all this intolerance and roughness come from, precisely when it concerned me, his daughter? It inevitably pushed me into a state of defiance. Mother suffered as well and would have gladly helped me, but it was unfortunately beyond her power. Each attempt in that direction ended with renewed outbursts of anger.

Indeed, I was for a while treated like a prisoner. My lessons with Professor Matić turned out to be my only connection with the outside world. I continued with my studies with the greatest of ardour, first, to take my mind off my misery, and second, to master the material required for the high school graduation before summer. Professor Matić convinced me that I could pass the graduation exam without any problem and was sure that I would be successful. This was my consolation and I began making renewed plans to ask my parents, once the exam was over, for permission to pursue my studies further. I also heard from Matić that Milko had been recently appointed a member of a recruitment commission and had been out of town for two months. That information, in a way, made me less upset on a daily basis. My parents must have heard the news as well, because, by the beginning of April, my quarantine was lifted, and I was dispatched to my aunt in Zagreb. They hoped that an extended absence would help me forget the "impossible" flirt with the lieutenant, who had evidently been holding me in his power with his *Svengali*-like magic.

This was my first visit to Zagreb. I found the city beautiful and interesting far above my expectations, and especially in comparison with Osijek, which now seemed like a really small town. Not that Zagreb, was a particularly big city, but it appeared so with its architecture and intensity of life. It was not only the political, but also the cultural heart of the country. It was all still limited in scale, but there was everywhere clear evidence of a latent energy warranting the potential for accelerated growth.

My relatives lived in the Pongratz Palace, built at the corner of Duga ulica (Long Street)[309] and Trg Bana Jelačića (Ban Jelačić Square), at the location presently occupied by the Central Pharmacy.[310] The apartment was spacious and elegant and consisted of five or six rooms. A big bay window at one corner of the building overlooked, on one side, the lively and busy Ban Jelačić Square, where people sold fruit and flowers under their red parasols. Across the street was the gloomy facade of the hospital run by the Order of the Knights of the Hospital of Saint John of Jerusalem.[311] Looking out in the other direction, one could see a stretch of the Long Street, the old city walls of the Upper Town, with lush gardens perched atop, and further away, have a potential glimpse of the mountain Sljeme.

Besides the well-furnished rooms for everyday accommodation, the apartment had an almost ten-metre-long reception hall. It was decorated with beautiful and undoubtedly expensive furniture in Renaissance style, with Indian-red velvet upholstering, a couple of paintings by Vlaho Bukovac[312] and Menci Clement Crnčić,[313] a tall Venetian mirror, and an enormous crystal chandelier. The space was used exclusively for special events. It was not heated in winter, and during the summer, everything was covered with unsightly grey cloth as protection from moths and dust. The covers were taken off only when visits by respectable guests were expected, which became more and more frequent with time. My uncle was a well-known art collector, Salamon Berger,[314] but the special attractions in the hall were the three glass display cases containing beautiful exhibits of our Croatian folklore embroidery and weaving, collected by my uncle over the years.

There was also a series of drawers in which he kept most wonderful folk costumes with gold and silk embroidery, of the kind worn by village women in the regions of Posavina, Pokuplje, and Podravina.[315] Those were examples of a gradually disappearing folk art, preserved in this way, thanks to my uncle's dedication. The indisputable value of those exhibits was confirmed by the fact that the three glass display cases provided the foundation of the Ethnographic Museum, which Salamon Berger launched a few years later. The museum's collection gained with time the international reputation as one of the richest and most interesting of its kind in Europe.

My uncle liked to talk about the origins of his collection. He was born in a Slovakian village, and, even as a child, was impressed by the colourful costumes of the village women around him. He came to Zagreb as a young man and found work in a textile shop, which sometimes kept on display samples of various folk costumes. In the backyard behind the shop stood a large container filled with bits and pieces of cloth discarded by shop employees. From there, he would dig out pieces that were woven or embroidered with colourful wool and carefully stored them away. In time, he began to collect such items in a more systematic way and was offering colourful kerchiefs to the peasant women from nearby villages, in exchange for their embroidery. After a while, he began handing out aprons and chintz textiles in order to obtain more valuable pieces. In the process, he gradually extended his knowledge and appreciation of various patterns and techniques. At the start, he was mostly motivated by business concerns and perceived it as a matter of personal interest, rather than serious ethnographic research. He was looking at the practical use of those patterns and the possibility of reproducing them and marketing them. While his collection grew, he developed an industrial enterprise providing employment for many people. He designed patterns and models himself and exported them abroad. More importantly, he brought public attention to the hidden treasures of local folk art and saved them from being lost for good. He may have lacked scientific knowledge, but he had a good instinct and a highly developed sense of organization. He understood the importance of his task and carried it out wholeheartedly. What started as a sideline interest gradually grew into his main occupation. At the beginning, there were barely three display cases in my aunt's salon, which he used to show with great pride and joy to his visitors. Twenty years later, he bequeathed his entire collection to the City of Zagreb. He founded the still existing Ethnographic Museum and became its first director. He was involved in its activities and its growth until his death in 1934.[316]

My aunt was a good and kind person, an exemplary housewife, and a gentle mother. Everything about her would have been just fine, had it not been for her extreme social-climbing aspirations, focused on the circle of Upper Town nobility. This was a caste already doomed for extinction, but she could still not acquire access to it, due to her own social standing and origins. It was interesting hearing her piously uttering the names of those "excellencies" with one or two aristocratic titles to their credit—how slowly those names melted on the tip of her tongue, and how she paid her respects to those admired role models, upon their rare social encounters. Those were the only occasions when one could have seen a smile on her usually stern face. The smile would make her thin lips even thinner. In the meantime, her eyes would not be smiling because that would have suggested an excess of familiarity! Her appearance also imitated those "excellencies" with residences in Visoka and Kapucinska (later renamed Matoševa) Streets. She usually wore only tightly fitting English dresses buttoned up to her neck, with a stiff white collar and small neckties, all of which was first-class and twice as expensive, precisely because it was so simple. On her sleek hair, pinned at the back, rested a round *Girardi* hat. She looked partly like an English lady and partly like a noble countess from a romance novel by Eugenie Marlitt.[317]

Her only daughter, a twelve-year-old girl called Tilda when I met her, was raised in that spirit of *noblesse oblige* so important to her mother. She wore the best dresses, had the best tutors, and was told from dawn to dusk to follow the rules of upper-class etiquette. She had to learn how those endowed with double noble titles walked, stood, sat, spoke, and smiled. Since she was five years old, she was consistently told that behaving naturally was actually commonplace and vulgar, that true sincerity was a sign of indiscretion, and that, in contact with other people, one should keep one's distance and never say what was really on one's mind.

Tilda was by nature a cheerful, impulsive girl, full of warmth and healthy instincts, which turned out to be difficult to restrain, notwithstanding my aunt's insistence. The growing protest within her made her eventually go astray in life and ended in an untimely death.

It was not just my aunt's house, but also other bourgeois houses I visited exhibited signs of social ambitions, in many ways beyond the standards still observed in Osijek. I would not consider those ambitions of the wealthier citizens of Zagreb an indication of their higher cultural standards and aspirations, because that was not necessarily the case. In comparison with Osijek, Zagreb had simply reached an economically more advanced stage of development—a different way of creating wealth and of maintaining its relationship with its environment.

Osijek's bourgeoisie had already experienced prosperity before the occupation of Bosnia[318] and its heyday lasted another few years—namely from the early eighteen sixties to some time in the mid-eighties. This was due to the lucrative exploitation and export of raw materials, mostly timber from the vast forests of the surrounding Slavonia. The city's geographic location was also important, situated as it was on both a navigable waterway and a direct roadway, which happened to be an indispensable transit corridor from Budapest to the Bosnian border, in the absence of an available railway line. Osijek was a traffic hub, while Zagreb was, so to say, on the sideline. Osijek families made money in the days when the bourgeoisie seemed cohesive, and the commercial and social interactions kept relying on certain fundamental virtues in business—diligence, efficiency, thriftiness and steadfastness of character. Some of those qualities had not been lost in later years either. There were no wholesale merchants nor daring entrepreneurs in Osijek. There were no money speculators nor people in search of quick profits. The people of Osijek were craftsmen, who had earned their money over the years of hard work, tradesmen with clean accounts, people of independent professions, as well as local landowners spending cold winter months in town. Some among them might have owned assets worth a few million but, on average, they formed a solid middle class, guided by a belief in the virtue of keeping one's debit and credit sheets in strict balance.

It was different in Zagreb. Wholesale businesses and entrepreneurship blossomed there. The town was full of bankers and directors of local and foreign shareholding companies, as well as skilful speculators, who made their money by purchasing empty plots of land, parcelling them up, and then selling them, with one hundred percent profit in return. There was a whole line of dealers involved in lucrative foreign stock markets and all kinds of undertakings, in which one could make a lot of money and lose just as much. The appeal of making money encouraged Zagreb's bourgeoisie to launch itself into affairs, which, at times, bordered on improvidence and even foolhardiness. At play was a different kind of calculation—not only in terms of profits to be made, but also, costs involved. The purpose was not to accumulate wealth, in the way those who had built their prosperity in the 1860s and 1870s would have appreciated it, but rather to be able to lead a life in a more upbeat style, by spending money and enjoying it.

Over time, the city's upper class—originally consisting exclusively of the hereditary nobility of the Upper Town—was extended to include a newly formed aristocracy, whose entitlement to that privilege relied on their fortune and on the lifestyle they could afford by surrounding themselves with things acquired with money and not through inheritance. They built the first apartment palaces along Ilica Street and the first villas in the city's green spaces of Josipovac and Tuškanac, all in the tasteless style of those days. The streets were full of horse-driven carriages, with coachmen dressed in livery and decorative footmen perched on the back seats. Spending summer holidays in Karlsbad and Bad Gastein, followed by an extensive stay in Semmering after the cure at the spas, became a permanent practice.[319] Gowns ordered from leading Viennese fashion houses and coats in Persian lamb or broadtail wool provided proof of financial solvency.

There was a constant desire to display one's worldly refinement and a penchant for things European, although, to be exact, it all centred on Vienna and its immediate surroundings. Vienna was the main criteria for all elegance, the forum of all cultural values, and the Mecca everyone turned to when looking for solutions. At the same time, no attention was paid to local residents—it was as if they did not exist. The locals were badly dressed clerks and their prematurely aged wives. They were dissatisfied and constantly arguing intellectuals capable of concocting God knows what, although their foolish ideas never got them anywhere. The locals who lived in the city's periphery were servants and so-called common folks with whom one talked condescendingly in their own dialect, provided one could master it. Common folks were, in the eyes of the privileged, something unspecified, some kind of a necessary evil, a world of wickedness, nasty germs, and criminal inclinations. They were considered sworn enemies of the good society, which would, however, be unfortunately unable to function on its own in their absence. After all, there had to be people available to fulfil all those menial jobs and attend to the comfort of the others. In that way, all was well organized and there was a fitting place for everybody.

It was evident that the bourgeoisie thrived under Ban Khuen's regime. Khuen liked satisfied people who were blowing his horn out of gratitude. He found it convenient to give to some, what he took from others. The bourgeoisie was guided by the maxims, "Everyone for himself!" and "Charity begins at home!" That was the opinion of all those fortunate enough to have plenty of food on the table, convinced that the Good Lord himself had thus decided in his great wisdom. They let the madmen protest and shout on the streets until they turned hoarse in the process, while they themselves kept safe and unharmed in their palaces. That was in accordance with the style of their class, within the spirit of the entire Francisco-Josephine era, identified by such social markers as middle-class self-confidence, prosperity, and a sense of security in the face of internal and external dangers. No wonder they were convinced, in their unwavering optimism, that everything they had built and acquired for themselves was protected by a higher power and that it would last forever!

Young girls I associated with in Zagreb greatly differed from my friends in Osijek. Almost without exception, they all attended the local lyceum for young women which could, in no way, be compared with the girl's high school in Osijek, not merely in terms of its extended curriculum but more so regarding its prevailing spirit and atmosphere.[320] The crucially formative role the lyceum played in the life of those young women could hardly be overestimated. Most of the teachers were well-educated women, such as Marija Jambrišak, Camilla Lucerna, and Jagoda Truhelka, who advocated women's equal rights to take part in the cultural and political affairs of the nation, and were very conscious of the pioneering nature of their teaching activities at the lyceum.[321] They endeavoured not only to give their students access to advanced knowledge, but also to inspire and enable them to pursue those endeavours in the future, guided by that same progressive spirit.

In those days, to be raising awareness meant revolting against the ruling social order and so the education received at the lyceum did have an effect on many of its students in their future lives. The teaching awoke latent creative powers in that generation of young women, mobilized their collective consciousness, diverted their attention from personal to social problems, and broadened the scope of their interests. That did not make them worse wives and mothers, as presumed by the older generations—quite the contrary in fact. Lyceum graduates were able to share common intellectual interests with their husbands and raise their children in a new and more liberal spirit.

Young women practising sport were yet another novelty in those days, which also had a liberating effect against prejudice. Girls started joining Sokol[322] training halls and practising gymnastics—even fencing. They began skating and playing tennis, and became quite good at it, as far as their fish-boned corsets, their long, heavy pleated skirts, and stiffened high collars would allow.

Many young girls also graduated from the conservatory, where they had acquired a remarkable musical education. A few lyceum graduates continued their studies at the university and took up mathematics, philology, or history as their area of specialization, with the view of pursuing a high school teaching career. They were no longer denied acquiring knowledge, and with talent and goodwill, they were up to the challenge—something that, in those days, was not merely a personal matter, but a clear breakthrough in the fight against social prejudice. Those young women were providing proof that, in intellectual matters, they were as capable as men, and were establishing a solid argument in support of their claim for equal rights.

I must add here that, despite various exciting diversions and countless new impressions and acquaintances, I still had not forgotten the main purpose of that trip to Zagreb. Soon after my arrival, I took steps to obtain permission to take the high school graduation exam as a private candidate. No one was supporting me in this attempt, and I had to face a multitude of obstacles. Truth be told, however, no matter how ashamed I am of it now, I had become rather indolent in those few weeks and invested insufficient energy in planning how to deal properly with the matter. I was distracted, always had something else to do that claimed my attention, and I eventually missed the right moment to act as I should have.

While developing a guilty conscience, I was also deceiving myself with all kinds of excuses. I did make some attempts, and initially sought advice from people who had nothing directly to do with the matter. At each attempt I was advised to talk to someone else, at a different level of authority. In the end, I was advised to address my application to the Croatian governor himself, attaching my birth certificate and the latest school report, both of which I had left at home in Osijek. The documents took a long time to arrive, because my parents tried to delay the application for as long as they could, and even prevent it entirely, if possible.

Over time, I had also lost my initial confidence. Having spoken with the director of the lyceum in person, who warned me, with best intentions, that the exam was particularly rigorous in the case of private candidates, I suddenly began doubting my own aptitude. After everything I had heard, it seemed to me I was not yet sufficiently prepared, and I concluded it would be best to postpone taking the exam for another year and avoid potential embarrassment. A complex mix of opposing states of mind was behind that hardly honourable retreat. In the first place, it was improvidence. I believed that, even if I missed out on something, I could always make up for it with a bit of goodwill. At the time, I was still unaware as to what extent mishandled situations could impact on one's life in the future. Secondly, it was apprehension. Suddenly it seemed impossible to confront all the obstacles piling up to obstruct my way forward. I preferred to take a bypass and postpone dealing with the matter in question for a while. Thirdly, my mind was absorbed by too many new experiences, which prevented me from staying focused. Everything I experienced at the time seemed extremely important to me. I did not want to miss any of it, and simply could not handle anything else with the adequate intensity.

I thus missed a unique opportunity that would have given me much broader, future avenues in life, not to mention the self-confidence I so badly needed. It might have been different if I had proved to myself and everyone else at the time that I was serious about going to university, and capable to carry through with success what I had set myself as a firm goal. Instead, I gave everyone a good reason to regard everything else I had set myself to do on other occasions, as mostly inconsequential.

I should mention here that, thirteen years later, as a married woman and mother of four, I did eventually pass the high school graduation exam. The year was 1912. I enrolled soon thereafter at the Faculty of Natural Sciences at the University of Munich. Two years later, World War I broke out and I was prevented from finishing my studies.

It is difficult not to resort to some theorizing while describing the last decade of the 1900s. It was characterized by a conflict between the older and the younger generations, which gradually turned into a proper clash of two worldviews.

This development has usually been referred to as the crisis of the fin de siècle (century's end). There was a tendency at the time to perceive the turn of the century as a breaking point in the previously undisturbed course of events. In cosmological terms, this was naturally nonsensical, because the turn of the century is an arbitrarily established date and the concerns with the fin de siècle were entirely psychological—something was about to end, something new was ahead. There were expectations, as well as anxiety. People were noticing a rising storm on the political horizon, saw the gathering of clouds and witnessed an occasional lightning strike. Some of it appeared dangerous, which increased their anxiety. The time had come. The sands of time had run out. People looked with wistfulness at the passing of the last decade of a dying century. The bourgeois world did well during that period and was thriving, thanks to technological advances it had brought in, which had made life so much more comfortable. In those years, riches were simply pouring in and were gladly accepted, without paying much attention to the reverse side of the coin.

And now the crucial moment had arrived. Some people suddenly felt caught up in a game with all their chips at stake. They worried about facing the future and imagined it somewhere out there, hindered by an as-yet undefined barrier. They felt tired and somehow detached from current developments, which did not seem part of their world anymore. With the passing of the old century, they felt as if they themselves had suddenly aged and were merely part of a past world.

Literature and art also reflected that fin de siècle mood. Artists and writers felt compelled to advance forms of artistic expression not previously attempted, resorting to paradoxes, exaggerations, contrasting tones, and random associations, no matter whether a particular artistic expression had a compelling form, but was devoid of content, or was rich in content, but lacked form. There was talk of mushiness, mediocrity, and hypocrisy of the bourgeois society. A whole generation was determined to break with everything still in place and be ready, with the crossing of the crucial threshold, to face the mysterious new century.

In that mood, previously long held worldviews began to be observed from a deliberately opposing standpoint. Conclusions were made that had nothing to do with logic. People adopted a way of thinking that was barely in touch with reality and resorted to finding explanations in dreams and symbolism instead. They found themselves floating in a semi-conscious state, in a foggy space with no clear outlines. They expressed their feelings in wordplays, paraphrases, and codes. Nothing was definitive. "Maybe" became an evasive answer to everything.

Thinking was confused. Problems accumulated during the course of the century continued to increase in number and remained unresolved. All that had heavy psychological consequences on everyday life. People were searching for something that was, in reality, before their very eyes. A mood full of misgivings and melancholy spread in the form of a wave across the English Channel and over to the continent. That was the time when Oscar Wilde published his *Portrait of Dorian Gray* and his "trial" was launched.[323] Maurice Maeterlinck wrote *Les aveugles* (The Sightless), Jules-André Barbey d'Aurevilly, *Les diaboliques* (The She-Devils) and Maurice Barrès, his *Du sang, de la volupté et de la mort* (Blood, Pleasure and Death).[324] In 1890, an independent scholar from Holstein, Julius Langbehn, published his *Rembrandt als Erzieher* (Rembrandt as Teacher), which, in a short time, went through thirty-seven successive editions.[325] He told the Germans they should be aware of the demoralizing influence of science on how humanity had progressed and reached a dead end, and was the first to advance in his arguments racially based theories, which made him the precursor of German Nazism.

A wild confusion reigned, and everybody claimed to be the authentic holder of the "truth". Friedrich Nietzsche contributed to the confusion in people's minds with his *Umwertung aller Werte* (The Revaluation of All Virtues)[326] and Arthur Schopenhauer,[327] and his numerous followers, by exposing the limitations of personal willpower. While Ibsen talked about the search of the Absolute, Schopenhauer found it to be, in his final analysis, an entirely impossible quest.

These philosophical theses, with their exalted intonations, were in Vienna scaled down. Nevertheless, Arthur Schnitzler wrote his *Liebelei* (Flirtation),[328] Hugo von Hofmannsthal his *Terzinen über Vergänglichheit* (Stanzas in Terza Rima—On Mutability),[329] and Peter Altenberg his stylish miniatures *Wie ich es sehe* (How I See It).[330] There was also evidence of a new style in visual arts, with abundant vegetal motives set in ornamental structures—colourless and twisted patterns of skeletal and sinuous tubular forms in elongated vertical arrangements floating in a vacuum. This was the typical decadent art of the fin de siècle called Secession. The name referred to the demonstrative withdrawal of a group of its proponents from the Austrian Association of Artists by building their own exhibition pavilion.[331] The president of the group was Rudolf von Alt and its members, people like Gustav Klimt, Alphonse Mucha, Wilhelm Bernatzik, Max Kurzweil, Otto Wagner, Joseph Maria Olbrich, Josef Hoffmann, Koloman Moser, and others.[332] The Secession Pavilion was actually the first modern building constructed in Vienna with a strictly designed motive and purpose in mind. The Viennese were partly outraged and partly amused at the sight of that "ridiculous building". Newspapers debated its impact from architectural as well as ideological points of view. Secession was not merely a new artistic theory, but also a philosophical outlook—one could almost say a new state of mind. And so, the Secession Pavilion with its four bare walls and the golden bay leaf-covered globe on the roof soon became the symbol of Vienna in the same vein as the spire of Saint Stephen Cathedral.

In Croatia, the extent of the revolt was, for a while, not as broad. It avoided cosmological or cosmopolitan issues, limiting itself to local concerns, which preoccupied many people in the troubled days of the Khuen

Héderváry's regime. This was chiefly evident in the protests organized by the young generations against the conservatism of the old—the triteness of romantic clichés they kept applying, the narrow scope of their ideas, and their dependency on traditional forms of expression, which had, with time, inevitably become stereotyped and sterile. At the same time, young people demanded creative freedom, with regard to the choice of both the subject and its aesthetic format, which would enable a more individualized literary expression. They did not want to be limited to exclusively patriotic topics, and were against heroic tirades and canzones, classical hexameters and *terza rima*. They wanted to promote representations of real events and texts with a visionary perspective through free associations and rhythm, without restricting rhymes and the tyranny of versification.

Following the burning of the Hungarian flag by a group of students on the occasion of the visit by Emperor Franz Joseph to Zagreb in 1895, many students left the University of Zagreb, partly through fear of persecution and partly in protest. They also wanted to escape the oppressive and confining atmosphere in the country and, once abroad, breathe the air of freedom. They enrolled in universities in Vienna and Prague, where they were exposed to a variety of new ideas and influences. Those who studied in Prague attended Masaryk's lectures and were inspired by his political, positivistic, purely humanistic views of an ideal democratic world of the future.[333] Won over by those ideas, they started their own progressive magazine *Hrvatska misao* (Croatian Opinion), announced as a literary magazine, but mostly dealing with political issues of Croatian national identity and South Slav collaboration.[334]

Students who left for Vienna soon fell under the influence of the *Jung-Wien* (Young Vienna) movement, and its modernist weekly newspaper *Die Zeit* (The Times), edited by Hermann Bahr.[335] Along with *Die Zeit*, there were also the highly radical *Neue Revue* (New Review), the *Wiener Rundschau* (Vienna Review) and the *Waage* (The Scales), with all four advancing progressive ideas in both literary and political spheres. The papers had a slightly socialist tone and occasionally sounded like preachers in the desert, as when they spoke with sympathy about oppressed Slavic "minorities" in the monarchy. Bahr undoubtedly went the furthest in the way he advocated in *Die Zeit* a wide range of worthy humanist ideas, but, on the other hand, had limited knowledge of the actual situation in the domain of minority relations. This was evident in his travel notes from Dalmatia. He was entirely unable to see what was hiding behind the decorative scenery, described everything in the form of entertaining anecdotes, hardly touched upon real problems, and provided a distorted portrait of local inhabitants.

Cultural movements of those times, such as the "Modern" movement, for instance, should not be assessed from today's perspective. One should instead imagine oneself back in the time they were launched and represented something genuinely revolutionary. The ideas they spawned could later be traced in various subsequent forms and manifestations. But in 1898, it was all still sensational, astounding, and came as a revelation. It was the novelty that counted, no matter whether in a good or a bad sense, in its cleverness or senselessness. We were clearly saying "no" before we had even found the suitable "yes" in exchange. All we knew was that things could not continue the way they had so far. We were grateful to whoever had mustered the courage to replace old spiritless forms with the new, even if those turned out to be, on closer examination, as spiritless as those just rejected. We enthusiastically saluted the "new", as a matter of life-changing significance, to be espoused and diversified. It offered the answer to our undefined dreams, provided a justification for our mental fretfulness, and an excuse to indulge in aberrations in life, literature, and art. However, this was not the aim in itself, as we believed at the time, but rather a means to make further worthwhile discoveries, improve explanations, and expand logical conclusions in the future. At the time, it meant breaking with traditionalism. We were lacking the prerequisites for anything more.

On 1 January 1898, a group of Croatian students in Vienna began publishing the magazine *Mladost* (The Youth). On the one hand, the magazine was relying on the ideas of the Viennese modernist movement and, on the other, the social-democratic ideology, as promoted by a few students associated with a group called *Sloga* (Unity). The two editors of *Mladost*, Dušan Plavšić and Guido Jeny, were both Osijek natives and I had known them from before.[336] I knew Plavšić personally, because his father was the

secretary of the Chamber of Crafts and Trade and therefore my father's friend and collaborator. We often used to meet, and I knew about his intellectual activities and the modernist direction he was taking. I knew Jeny, however, only by name. He was already a renowned connoisseur of art and a talented painter, with a great future predicted in that domain. However, he came from a family without financial means, and like most other students, needed a scholarship to continue his studies. Since he was interested in art above all else and had been constantly drawing and painting in high school, he decided to enrol in the Academy of Fine Arts in Vienna after his high school graduation and acquire the proper artistic formation. In search of a scholarship, he travelled to Zagreb and asked Isidor Kršnjavi,[337] minister responsible for culture and education, for help. Kršnjavi did admit that Jeny was talented but rejected the request. "We already have enough hungry painters around," he said. "What we need in this country today are people with a good technical specialization. You can get a scholarship, but only if you are willing to study mathematics. That is the only thing I can grant you. As for your paintings, hang them up on the wall and call it quits!"

What else could Jeny have done but accept the advice—go to Vienna, and enrol in the University of Technology? His interest in all forms of art remained unchanged and equally vivid. He went to exhibitions and museums, wrote articles about social issues (always following the line professed by the Social-Democratic Party, a member of which, he had meanwhile become), became an expert art commentator, and drew and painted as much as possible. Let me mention here that Guido Jeny became my tutor several years later, giving me lessons in freehand drawing and descriptive geometry at the time I was preparing for the high school graduation exam, at the age of thirty. He would linger after our lessons, despite being a quiet and introverted person, and reveal some aspects of his life, including the founding of *Mladost (Youth)*, which seemed to have represented the fulfilment of his greatest aspirations. His expectations were high, not only as far as he was personally concerned, but even more so in terms of its impact on Croatian youth.

Jeny explained to me, among other things, that the magazine had no programme, that its objective was exclusively literary and artistic, and strictly avoided day-to-day politics. The only exceptions were scholarly features, especially those with a progressive socio-political point of view. The idea was that *Mladost* become a forum open to everyone who had something to say. Indeed, the first issues already had an almost international, or at least a pan-Slavic, character. Besides numerous translations of foreign literary texts, there were contributions from Belgrade, Ljubljana, Prague, and even one article from Budapest on Hungarian literature, all clearly demonstrating the publishers' tolerant approach. Besides the critical reviews of artistic and theatrical life in Vienna, there was also an article about land reform, refuting the recent thesis by American publicist Henry George, whose book *Progress and Poverty* had generated much discussion and was widely read.[338] The question was re-examined from an opposing point of view in two subsequent articles, containing numerous citations from Marx and Engels. No wonder the magazine was quickly severely attacked from all sides, as if it were something of a coup d'état, rather than a purely literary undertaking. The insolence of the "young" made the "old" furious and they began vigorously assaulting the paper. The Croatian nationalistic Party of Rights scolded this new magazine for its lack of political engagement, and the editors of *Obzor* (Horizon) talked about "libertinage and pornography". *Katolički List* (Catholic Newspaper) was attacking *Mladost* for irreverence, godlessness, and immorality. Its atheism and scepticism, it argued, were poisoning the minds, not only of young people, but the population at large. *Narodna misao* (People's Opinion) thought that the publishers of *Mladost* were ensnared by foreign influences and kept promoting nothing but foreign intellectual interests, without taking into account our national needs. *Mladost* was, in a witty way, called "the Salon of Cast Outs". Ante Tresić Pavičić spoke about "bleating, secessionist sheep, bats who dwell in darkness, conceited dandies and fools".[339] His literary magazine, *Novi viek* (New Age) from Split, published a poisonous attack from the pen of Friar Kerubin Šegvić, who blamed the publishers of *Mladost* for dirty manipulation. Among other accusations, he questioned the source of the paper's financing, referring at the same time to certain dangerous people behind the scene, whose prime interest was to undermine the country to the point of destroying it.[340] The liberal unionist press also became involved. They looked with suspicion at the paper's socialist ideas, particularly, quotes from Marxist literature, because government circles were terrified by socialism as much as by nationalism promoted by the Party of Rights or *Obzor*.

It was a matter of course that a publication such as *Mladost* could not survive for long. The intention was good, and the overall programme executed with a youthful élan, but not under the right conditions. The publishing office was in Vienna and the printing house in Zagreb. This alone was untenable. Preliminary censorship was strict in such cases. Various texts in each issue were thus censored. The last of those was a lengthy article dedicated to the fiftieth anniversary of the 1848 revolution, where some misconceptions of those historic events were reviewed and corrected, and the role played by the Croats presented in a new light. These historical revisions were highly offensive to the authorities and the article in question was at the last minute banned from publication. However, by then, it was already in print, which meant that the whole seventh issue, and consequently the existence of the entire magazine, was in jeopardy. This marked the end of *Mladost*, but the storm in a teacup it had caused lasted for quite some time afterwards.

The ideological confrontation between "old" and "young" intensified, involving constant discussions, by not only referring to literature, but to all aspects of life. A select number of Croatian fine artists also became involved. Taking the example of the Vienna Secession, they formed a separate group of followers of an artistic trend called the *plein air* (outdoor) painting. That technique had already made its debut in Paris in the eighteen sixties and seventies, but it took a long time, not until the early eighties, for the Croatian public to accept it. Artists who studied mostly in Munich and Vienna took, however, another twenty years to abandon the practice of exclusively studio-produced art. This was part of the new cultural trend of generally turning away from the strict academic mannerism and Munich literary and artistic genre. Old techniques were replaced by a purity of artistic expression, a new range of colour tones and the approach of using light and bright colours as seen in nature. Above all, the new techniques served to disclose the experience of light with all its unexpected effects.

Following the Viennese example, our secessionists also founded their own association, *Društvo hrvatskih umjetnika* (Society of Croatian Artists), with Vlaho Bukovac[341] as its leader. Ten painters and two sculptors organized their first exhibition as a group at the new art pavilion on Zrinski Square in Zagreb, built on the occasion of the millennium celebrations of the Hungarian kingdom, two years earlier.[342]

The public in Zagreb was quite backward at that time in all matters of art and looked at the modern trend in art with prejudice. Biased, narrow-minded art critics did not help. People were greatly confused at the sight of the art on display in the new pavilion. For most of them, something was beautiful when it appealed to their senses at first sight. Those were usually either paintings, which they might wish to have as a decoration in their own salons, or colossal canvases, which, due to their historical themes, were exempt from all objective criticism. Everything else was stigmatized as an "artistic aberration", an abnormal and perverse manifestation, and a clear sign of disrespect for socially sanctioned good taste. Upright citizens became seriously upset. They might not have made much sense of the whole thing, but they had an inkling of what was hiding behind it all. All those revolutionary experiments on a piece of canvas with brush and paint as tools, were aimed against them—against their norms, morals, understanding of the so-called eternal beauty, and other firmly established ideals. As for portraits, the objection was that they did not provide enough resemblance to their models and were revealing not only external aspects of the models, but also their insides, as if observed with the help of X-rays. As for the landscapes, people were wondering, who had ever seen such colours in nature. Light effects clashing like the firing of rockets! Purple clouds and blue trees? How about those Elysian fields wrapped in garish green fog and sulphur-yellow mist and populated by ethereal forms dissolving themselves into nothingness? Some things were barely hinted at, others emphasized, even over-exaggerated and vertically elongated so that no sensible person could find any meaning in it. And that was supposed to be art?

Even Isidor Kršnjavi, who usually seemed to understand what art was all about, was initially angry at seeing the exhibition organized by the Society of Croatian Artists, perceiving it as a hidden attack on the government.[343]

But, notwithstanding his loyalty to Khuen and his pro-Hungarian politics, he was still sufficiently independent when it came to his appreciation of art. He therefore conceded to the modernists their right to exist. He went so far in these concessions as to put at the disposal of a few of our most prominent painters, several studios in the building behind the Institute for Deaf and Dumb People in Ilica Street, free of charge. This was why writer Antun Gustav Matoš,[344] for instance, was complaining several times in his *Ogledi* (Essays) about the difference in treatment between painters and writers in our country. While the authorities were bestowing upon paint-ers well-heated and illuminated quarters, free of charge, our poets had to freeze to death in their small attic rooms, with no one paying any attention to their existence. Moreover, they were forced to stop writing even before reaching their full artistic maturity and take office jobs, provided they had not already died of inherited tuberculosis or finished up in a madhouse.

The 1898 exhibition was accompanied by a luxuriously illustrated cata-logue—or more precisely, a commentary—published in four volumes and entitled *Hrvatski Salon* (Croatian Salon). It featured reproductions of some paintings, several photographs of the pavilion's interior, and a comprehen-sive written overview of the whole event. The central showpiece in one of the exhibition rooms was the model of a monument Robert Frangeš[345] created in Osijek in honour of General Josip Šokčević.[346] It was the rep-resentation of a soldier at the instant of being mortally hit by a bullet. Rudolf Valdec's *Genius* dominated another room.[347] The commentaries on the reproductions of paintings by Vlaho Bukovac,[348] Bela Čikoš Sesija,[349] Oton Iveković,[350] Ferdo Kovačević,[351] and Menci Clement Crnčić[352] were written by several local modernists, from Xeres de la Maraja[353] to Vladimir Nazor,[354] a recent arrival on the literary scene. Yet, what had been per-ceived, in 1898, as extreme and unacceptable, was, just a few years later, considered tame and an established artistic expression—the audience had simply become used to such supposed "outrages" and stopped getting overexcited about them.

Most prominent among the leading promoters of the modernist move-ment was Dr. Milivoj Dežman[355] who, under the pseudonym Ivanov, effectively undertook to define the programme of the new movement in a short manifesto[356] he published in the commemorative edition of *Croatian*

Salon. Among other things, he stated, "They called us traitors. Why traitors? Because, they say, we try to destroy all the things past, because we do not seem to honour our bygone warriors and folk heroes and have turned our backs on our people and our moral standards. Instead of following blindly the existing old formulas, however, we are acting the same way as our ancestors used to act before us. Where did Illyrian promoters get their ideas from?[357] Where did the romantics in the seventies and the realists in the eighties get their energy and inspiration from? Wasn't there a much broader movement around them fuelling their enthusiasm as well? And if we today look for inspirations not exclusively amid our own people, but also beyond the bounds of our homeland, does that make us traitors?"

By the time I arrived in Zagreb in May 1898, the exhibition had closed its doors. I was naturally sorry, and mentioned it to Frangeš, whose monument to General Šokčević had just been erected in Osijek, and I had made his acquaintance on that occasion. He replied that there was a potential remedy. He invited me to his studio to see a few plaster models of his older pieces, as well as the sketches and drafts of those still in the planning stage. I liked the drafted ideas for the monument dedicated to Šokčević far more than its final format, above all because it represented something entirely uncommon in those days. Instead of a victorious military commander parading on his horse, Frangeš chose an ordinary soldier to represent Šokčević's regiment. The soldier was in full charge when he was shot and was shouting out something while collapsing. His figure, as cast in bronze by Frangeš, was unfortunately not caught in the motion of charging, but rather as being in a spasm, with his limbs oddly bent, his head too small, and his face distorted in a grimace. That did not stop me from publishing a poem upon the unveiling of the monument, where I attempted to clarify the idea behind its conception.[358]

Frangeš was at that time not yet famous for his own dramatic handsomeness and aloofness, both of which became his hallmarks a few years later. He was a lively young man, attractive and talkative. He was so obliging that he took me to visit several other studios, where I was able to see some of the paintings exhibited a few months earlier in the pavilion.

We first went to see Vlaho Bukovac, whose studio was located on Franz Joseph Square (today known as King Tomislav Square). It was an important occasion for me because I was highly impressionable in those days, eagerly absorbing everything like a sponge. When it came to paintings, my understanding of the technical aspects was limited, but that did not mean that I was entirely incapable of a valid critical appreciation. I abhorred deception and was well equipped to recognize when something was faked or artificial. An honest intention enhanced, in my eyes, the value of the end product. I was able to recognize such honesty right away and instinctively discern in each case how much of himself the artist had put into it— whether the work was the product of a genuine ardour, mere conformity with the latest fashion or trend, or governed by entirely external motives.

I liked Bukovac. I liked the man just as much as I liked his works. He had pleasing features and bright, translucent eyes. He spoke French with a strong accent, but entirely effortlessly and so fast that I had difficulties following him, despite my good knowledge of the language itself. He was quickly switching from one subject to another—Paris, Dubrovnik, America, the account of how he was "discovered", the French school, studying in Alexandre Cabanel's class,[359] his relationship with nature and his homeland, and his first success at the Paris Salon of 1878. Then followed, year by year, new studies, new experiences, and new successes. The most significant artistic experience of them all was his discovery of the *"plein air"* technique, followed by an even more intense use of the palette, inspired, as he claimed, by colourful oriental carpets and all that light and sunshine he had learned to love while living by the sea in the south. He was not an impressionist in the real sense of the word—more likely a neoclassicist using pure colours, even surfaces, and clear outlines in the style of Ingres. He chatted along, was very friendly, and commented approvingly on my pretty light green dress and the expression of delight and amazement in my eyes. He told me, "You seem so happy that everyone else in your company must feel the same!" (He was wrong about that, because at that time I was far from happy!) Having recently painted portraits of my uncle, my aunt, and little Tilda, he suggested that I pose for him, too. He immediately drew a small sketch of me in pencil, with a few well-executed lines, and promised he would work on it later and give it to me as a present.

But that never happened, because that same week he left for Cavtat[360] and forgot all about it afterwards.

Bela Čikoš Sesija and Menci Clement Crnčić[361] worked in the small studios on Ilica Street, which Kršnjavi had secured for them and which later served as the foundation of the Fine Arts Academy. Čikoš welcomed me as his compatriot because he was also from Osijek. In his studio, I saw a few big compositions depicting fantastic figures and exotic motives, all highly colourful and enhanced by striking light effects. It was all too powerful for my taste and I frankly did not know what to say. Fortunately for me, no one really expected me to say anything of consequence. I knew close to nothing about the technical side of painting, and I was not hiding it. I neither wanted to seem snobbish nor ridiculous. I simply wanted to learn, and that meant learning how to observe and to understand art as a mere layperson. Even today, recalling those experiences, I am not trying to give a critical assessment, but an account of how I happened to visit our most famous painters in their studios, how I had the opportunity to watch them while they were working and how much that meant to me. While I was in Crnčić's studio, who only occasionally stayed in his Zagreb studio and preferred to live on the Adriatic Coast, I saw his usual marine vistas, but also several portfolios of his graphics and sketches, and those I liked a lot. They made a more immediate impression on me than any of his big canvases. The sketches, still unfinished and incomplete, revealed the process of creation far better than the finished works. The reason I reacted that way was entirely personal and due to my own incompleteness as a person, my immaturity. I had always been more interested in the process of the formation of phenomena than on phenomena themselves, in life just as much as in art.

One day, Frangeš invited me for a cup of coffee, which he prepared in a corner of his studio and served on a low elaborately carved Bosnian stool. A good friend of his, Srđan Tucić was also present.[362] Tucić had just finished writing the play *Truli dom* (Rotten Home) and asked me to translate it into German. He left the text for me to read and asked me to let him know whether I would be inclined to do the job. I read his drama that same evening, and since I was more knowledgeable in literature than in fine arts, I was immediately able to assess it. I noticed that in his realism,

Tucić paid less attention to the milieu than to individual characters, which was the usual approach in our naturalistic literature. Symptoms were exposed, but their social and psychological causes not substantiated—a typical approach of the entire literary production concerned with the rural subjects of the times. The explanation for unfortunate and tragic events relied on heredity, degeneration, and similar causes. Once it would be a tyrannical father who gave in to drinking and thus ruined the estate, at another time, a perverted son or a seduced daughter. Meanness, greed, inheritance, or boundary disputes—those were all external characteristics, while the real social root of evil always remained untouched. *Rotten Home* was written in the same vein. Nevertheless, I liked his consistent naturalistic procedure and told Tucić I was prepared to translate his drama, which I eventually did.

While in Zagreb, it turned out that I mostly moved in the Party of Rights circles.[363] Most intellectuals supported this political party and I knew quite a number of them, thanks to my work as a translator. I had been for a while engaged in correspondence with Ante Tresić-Pavičić,[364] as well as Milan Begović,[365] Mihovil Nikolić,[366] and a few others, and therefore did not hesitate to transform those written ties into personal contacts during my stay in Zagreb. I met Begović at a friend's house and paid a visit to old Đuro Arnold,[367] whose poem *Notturno,* I had also translated. I met most of these people at the home of journalist Jacques Frank, whose sons Edo and Leo had been my friends since childhood, especially Leo, who studied medicine in Vienna and often visited me while I was at the boarding school. The older Frank brothers—Josip, Simon, and Jacques—were Essekers. Simon and Jacques were in the newspaper business, the former as editor of Osijek's *Die Drau* and the latter, as a correspondent for Viennese and Budapest newspapers. Josip Frank[368] (sometimes referred to as Josef, also known as Pepi in the family) took over the leadership of the Party of Rights after its founder and leader Ante Starčević passed away. The party became later known as the Frank's Party and his followers as *frankovci* (Frankists). This party—oddly enough named after an "outsider"[369]—caused considerable trouble in the whole country forty years later.

I used to take part in heated debates in the Frank family home with Jacques Frank's sons Edo, Gusti, and Leo, and occasionally Ivica Frank,[370] Josip Frank's younger son. All four would come right at me and would not let me catch my breath. They would mock my naive idealism, my belief in certain ideas, and my enthusiasm for what they labelled as "lofty matters". In their opinion, all that was useless, and they tried to make me realize it. They were skilful talkers, especially Edo and Leo, while Gusti mostly stayed on the side, and Ivica kept disrupting the discussion with his loud intrusions. They had a sophisticated touch about them and were also great cynics, so I was no match for them in those debates. Everything they asserted appeared as incidental remarks, and I had the impression that they were mostly indifferent to it all anyway. Even when they were squabbling with me, it was more to provoke me and make me angry than because they truly cared. Their condescending smiles revealed their lack of appreciation of my ideas as well as me. They found it distasteful and pointless to get overexcited and emotional about something, be it in the form of love or hatred. If they did get excited, it was purely for art for art's sake—it had nothing to do with that particular something as such, but merely for the sake of dealing with it. Still, it was not mere attitude—it came from their blasé personalities, their nervous dispositions, as well as the generally depressive mood typical of the time. It was the influence of a snobbish outlook on life, a mixture of Russian nihilism of the Turgenev type, and English eccentricity of the Oscar Wilde style, to which was added a dose of French frivolity, especially when it came to the subject of women. There was also a considerable number of inferiority complex issues, which undeniably resulted from being of the Jewish race, notwithstanding the conversion to Christianity. The only things they took seriously were their paradoxical political engagements and aesthetic interests.

Jacques Frank's influential position in press circles facilitated his good relationships with our artistic community. He received many of their paintings for next to nothing—as a present, in exchange for publishing a favourable critique or intervening in order that an unfavourable review not be published. He owned a good selection of modern Croatian artwork, including the beautiful study of a semi-nude, remarkable for the glowing freshness of the youthful skin that Bukovac painted in 1895. Besides those homegrown originals, there were also purchases from abroad—beautiful and expensive copies of some famous Dutch artists, engravings on copper plates and wood, and old Viennese and Meissen china in glass cases—all in all, an entire museum. There were, in addition, expensive oriental carpets and a large library containing numerous monographs with high-quality reproductions. The Franks were acquainted with foreign literature, be it only partially, and were not burdened with small-town prejudice, which usually destroyed any attempt at progress from the start. To be an opponent worthy of their attention, I had to gather all my strength, coming as I did from the bleak Osijek atmosphere, straight into that ice-cold way of thinking, where a word conveying a witty point was of more importance than successfully refuting an erroneous argument. It seemed like a fencing match, where one was constantly on guard, changing position, crossing swords, and never showing weakness, because the opponent was not willing to grant you favours, but was rather looking for the best way to hurt you with a caustic, highly embarrassing and even humiliating remark. In order to avoid an unpleasant defeat, one was obliged to adopt similar tactics in return. I soon discovered the importance of thinking quickly and providing speedy repartee in a debate.

Although I was not yet seriously interested in politics at that time, it was inevitable, moving as I was in circles highly interested in that subject, that I acquired a certain understanding of the principles upon which the Party of Rights was founded. I learned what caused the split within the party between "original" and so-called "pure" party members, and the role played by Dr. Josip Frank. There were people who could not understand how he managed towards the end of Ante Starčević's life to win the old man over to the point that Starčević appointed him his successor as leader of the party. A simple assumption would be that the old and weary Starčević got caught in the web woven by an ambitious, shrewd, well organized, and obliging lawyer. This would reveal only one side of the story, however. What was it that made someone like Starčević—who had unrelentingly resisted so many other temptations in life—give in to Dr. Frank? Why did he choose him as his favourite disciple, and after the fall of Fran Folnegović,[371] as his successor? Was the insightful and strict judge suddenly blind to the mistakes he had judged elsewhere so sternly throughout his life? Or perhaps

Dr. Frank's ambitions did incorporate real devotion, loyalty, and understanding for the man who was far greater than he was? Where was the fine line between loyalty to an idea and opportunism, between honest dedication and purposeful calculation? It is highly possible that the line did not even exist and that everything happened in the sharp antitheses contained in the complex human nature. One thing is undeniable—once Dr. Frank was, due to the circumstances, brought into the position of party leader, he had to take part in certain, not always fully transparent, machinations and manoeuvres, in order to prove he was enterprising and capable. It was therefore understandable that he could not have strictly abided by the standards Starčević had mapped out. Frank was not apostolic in character, but he was a skilled lawyer, organizer, broker, and demagogue who did not hesitate to use his name in order to conclude a bad deal. At the end, the deceiver, which he was, turned out to be deceived himself several years later in the Ignác Strasnoff Affair.[372]

In private life, Dr. Frank's behaviour was that of a kind uncle, especially towards me. I met him when I was eighteen and was not yet able to form a psychological judgment of people of his makeup. I relied on external symptoms—his kind greetings, friendly facial expressions, funny and well-meaning remarks, and most of all, the fact that he was the leader of the opposition, and Ante Starčević's heir. As such, he worked against the existing regime, which alone served for me as a guarantee of his honourable nature. I could not know at the time what was taking place behind the scenes.

I used to visit the Frank family home quite often, although I did not find any company of my own age there, except his sister-in-law, Luisa von Martini, who was also engaged in translating poems from Croatian, and that alone provided something in common. There was also Ivica, with whom I was always arguing about things that I did not understand myself, and he did not know much more either. Dr. Frank's eldest son, Vladimir,[373] was married to the daughter of the original inventor of the zeppelin, David Schwarz.[374] There was also little Olga (Olgica), Frank's daughter from his second marriage, a pretty, quite shy, and introverted ten-year-old girl. She used to visit my aunt's house quite often because she was my cousin Tilda's friend, although Tilda was a little younger. Ten years later, at the age of twenty-one, Tilda committed suicide after an unhappy love affair. At the same time, Olga married a general staff officer of the Austrian-Hungarian army, Slavko Kvaternik,[375] who later became chief commander of the armed forces of the infamous Independent State of Croatia during World War II. After the war, he was brought to trial by the new government and executed as a war criminal. Even more tragic was Olga's destiny as a mother—she gave birth to a monster, Dido Kvaternik.[376] He hated the fact that his mother's half-Jewish, and his grandfather's purely Jewish blood had infected his own blood flow and he surpassed all records in the number of treacherous and cowardly murders ever committed because of it. He only had to say a word and a hecatomb would follow. He massacred the hated Jews and equally hated Serbs. He ordered that villages disappear in flames, hostages be hanged, and always more victims sent to concentration camps. He personally gloated over the suffering of the people he was slaughtering. One of his victims was his mother, who took her own life, stricken by grief at witnessing the evil deeds of her son, and for failing to influence him and prevent him from acting that way.

It was in the home of the Frank family that I met Eugen Kumičić,[377] one of the most intimate collaborators and most loyal supporters of Dr. Josip Frank. Both of those elderly gentlemen talked to me, but I must admit that my conversations with Kumičić were far more interesting and beneficial. To begin with, he explained to me some aspects of politics, an area about which I had known nothing or very little before. He also talked about his theoretical views on literature. I found this to be far more engaging than his fiction, which was an irreconcilable mixture of a naturalistic style borrowed from abroad and a strong dose of romanticism that was in his native blood. God knows why he gave me the impression of a nice old man—he was not even fifty yet! During my stay in Zagreb, he assumed the same fatherly and protective role that Franjo Ciraki used to perform in my life two years earlier. We would go for walks together and he would elaborate for me his understanding of the duty of writers to keep as close as possible to the truth and to choose social themes as subject matters of their works. He also argued that it was not up to a modern writer necessarily to find solutions to these problems, but at least draw attention to them by means of a frank rendition conceived to reveal the destructive cancer infecting today's society. His fiction did not reflect that theory, either deliberately or because he lacked the creative ability to produce something of that kind. Instead, in his widely popular books, he opted for a racy, rather than elucidative, treatment of each subject.

During our promenades, Kumičić kept drawing my attention to various noteworthy aspects of social life in Zagreb. He knew a great number of artists, writers, and politicians—in fact, almost anyone of any significance in the city. He used to season his anecdotes with a lot of humour and, in so doing, was able to describe not only an individual, but also a whole circle of people, even the entire society.

A good part of social life in Zagreb in those days took place around Zrinjevac,[378] which was simply bustling with people from noon until late afternoon. They would arrive in a solid stream all the way from the corner of Frankopanska Street and its newly opened coffee house Bauer (later Croatia)—renowned for being the ultimate gathering place for a rapidly growing circle of local bohemians. The stream would stroll along the commercial Ilica Street to Jelačić Square and the two popular coffee houses on its south side, the Velika Kavana (Grand Café) and the noisy Narodna Kavana (People's Café). The two cafés acted as a sort of a stock market, where foreign agents were habitually making business deals with local brokers over a cup of coffee. From there, the stream of people would turn right at the next corner, continue along Marie Valerie Street (today known as Praška Street), and reach Zrinjevac, where the proper promenade (the so-called *corso*) would then take place—namely crowds of people engaged in strolling, chatting, and laughing. Among them were students, officers, and young girls, who all wanted to see and be seen, as they walked under the slim, pale green plane trees encircling well-groomed lawns and colourful flower beds. Strollers were, at the same time, kept under the watchful eyes of representatives of the older generation, seated on park benches or in the fashionable Kavana Zagreb (Zagreb Café) across the street and leisurely savouring an ice cream or sipping a mocha coffee. A military band used to perform operetta medleys or Ziehrer's marches in the round pavilion in the middle of the square,[379] while a Romani band played schmaltzy

Hungarian melodies in Kavana Zagreb. A political demonstration would occasionally take place on the square too, accompanied by patriotic songs, slogans, booing, and antigovernment shouts. Police whistles would soon resound, followed by the sudden arrival of a mounted police patrol. Demonstrators would be hit with flat sabre blades. There would be bumps, bruises, and arrests and people would scatter in panic in all directions.

The large number of coffee houses in Zagreb was not only indicative of how fashionable the city had become, but also what a dynamic intellectual life it had. People were restless and sought company. They were keen to be abreast of news, felt the need to exchange viewpoints and new ideas, and share with others their misgivings of the regime. The largest group among the coffee house regulars—card players and business dealers excluded—were disgruntled intellectuals, poets without publishers, painters without a public, and philosophers preaching in the wilderness. Among them were also secondary school teaching assistants, who had passed their qualifying exams with distinction and had even written poetry in their youth. Now they were racking their brains for ways to feed their families with a monthly salary of forty guldens. There were also patriotic civil servants withering away for years at work in the archives, wearing their fingers to the bone with all the writing they had to do, and never making it beyond the fourteenth level on the salary scale. All those people drank more than they should have, because, while in an intoxicated state, they could indulge in dreaming about things they had been denied their entire lives. While intoxicated, the weak became bold and the meek found a new élan, until everything dissipated once again and turned into an endless hangover and depression.

Along with mistreated and poorly paid civil servants, regular patrons of the coffee houses were also out-of-town students—mostly starved wretches who earned a living by giving private lessons and barely managed to survive. Scholarships were granted only to those who supported the regime and were ready to sell their souls for a few guldens. For that reason, there was a lot of bitterness and frustration vented out in numerous public outbursts in those circles. The youth were the bearers of nationalistic feelings and argued for a regime change, without really having a clear idea of how to improve the situation.

At the same time, the cold-hearted, rational, and merciless Ban Khuen sat in the Ban's Palace in the Upper Town, quietly destroying the country and installing within its borders a graveyard-type of peaceful atmosphere. Notwithstanding the 1895 flag burning incident, he was convinced of being successful in keeping the peace in the country, arguing that three years had gone by without any new significant incidents. A few noisy troublemakers on the streets and on editorial boards of opposition newspapers seemed to have been easily dealt with by police and stricter censorship rules. Meanwhile, newspapers supporting the government continued, unhindered, with their smug reporting on the general progress, flourishing trade, and promising developments in "our new industry", as well as other symptoms of "our growing prosperity", all thanks to the successful reign of Ban Khuen Héderváry under the protective clout of the Crown of Saint Stephen.[380] Without fail, those who thought differently lost their jobs and their livelihoods. In more severe cases, one was pursued in court and imprisoned, even when entitled to the protection of parliamentary immunity.

One day, as we were passing by the palace, which is today home to the Modern Gallery, but was, at the time, the residence of Archduke Leopold Salvator,[381] the only member of the Habsburg royal family with whom Zagreb had the honour to have any association, Kumičić suddenly leaned over and whispered into my ear, "There goes Tresić![382] He has been pestering me for a while already to know who is the young lady I have been strolling around with on Zrinjevac. I have been discreet until now and he doesn't suspect that you are the person who has translated his poetry. He believes it to be an elderly, unmarried lady, who translates poetry in her leisure time. If you would like, I could make the introductions. But be aware, he is terribly conceited, and a dangerous seducer!"

He waved to Tresić to come over and introduced him. "This is the great author of *Simeon the Great!*" Then he put his hand on my shoulder and declared in a solemn tone of voice, "Here is the muse you have so much to be grateful for! This is the elderly lady who has the courage to translate your splendid verses into German. How about that?"

Tresić was evidently surprised to make my acquaintance in that manner. He immediately began walking along with us and started right away to boast. From the very first moment, he revealed his innate penchant for the highly emotional display of feelings, evident not only in his poems, but in private conversations as well, irrelevant of the content itself. I introduced him to my aunt, who was sitting with a couple of friends on the terrace of Kavana Zagreb, and she invited him to pay us a visit one day.

He came the very next day and again soon afterwards, until it turned out to be a daily occurrence, to the point that he occupied all of my time. We were promenading on Zrinjevac and went, a few times, to the theatre, as well. More specifically, my aunt held a theatre box and he would simply join us there. I thus saw *Hamlet* with Andrija Fijan in the title role. It was a beautiful performance and although I later saw *Hamlet* with Alexander Moissi and Josef Kainz in Vienna, I had never appreciated anyone as much as Fijan in this role. On another occasion, I watched Tolstoy's *The Power of Darkness* with the Borštniks and Milica Mihičić in the leading roles. Those were all excellent performances easily comparable with any in much bigger cities.[383]

Tresić had studied in Geneva and at the Sorbonne in Paris, and his visiting card identified him as "*Licencié en lettres*" (Bachelor of Arts). He was tall, slim, and altogether cut an elegant figure. But his face was arrogant and cold, with thin lips and grey eyes lurking from behind a pince-nez. The most striking thing was a big scar on his forehead, stretching from the hairline to the ridge of his nose. He was, without doubt, well educated, especially in the classics. His patriotism was less a matter of feelings and more an exaggerated and obsessive idea. He was one of those rare people who were methodical in their effusiveness and, although most of his phrasing sounded hollow due to the way it consistently pursued a definite objective, his poetry revealed a strong sense of form. Not only did he master rhyme and rhythm with an admirable skill, but he also knew how best to fit his poetic images into those structures. His sense of form was also evident in his everyday life. He was always dressed with a great deal of care, even when things were not going well for him. His manners were tactful and polite and his discourse, full of metaphors and hyperboles, streamed smoothly as he spoke. It was all done in such a way that his real personality never came to light, to the point that even several weeks after having made his acquaintance I had learned nothing further about him beyond what I had known from the start—that he was a Croatian poet who thought very highly of himself.

I have never encountered anybody else endowed with so much evident and unambiguous vanity. He was convinced of his outstanding qualities, of his right to aspire to whatever he wanted, and of his ability to obtain it all. He constantly talked about how brilliant he was and how there was no one in this country who could match him. He measured himself exclusively against some of the greatest names in the entire world of literature. Besides his role models from Greek and Roman antiquity (which he had spent long hours studying), he recognized only Giacomo Leopardi[384] and Giosuè Carducci,[385] the two great bards of the Italian national revival (*Risorgimento*), as worthy of his respect. He liked Leopardi for his rich style, and Carducci for his inspirational patriotic élan. He followed their lead and was inspired by their enthusiasm. His rendering of similar feelings, however, paled in comparison because, truth be told, he was less of a lyrical poet and more of a politician.

The only person he appreciated among his contemporaries was the firebrand Gabriele D'Annunzio, the verbose poet of *Primo vere* (In Early Spring), *Canto novo* (The New Song), and the notorious Poema paradisiaco e *Odi navali* (Paradisiacal Poem and Marine Odes).[386] D'Annunzio's true fascist and irredentist aspirations were already detectable from behind the flamboyant torrent of words in these works. Tresić saw something of himself in this Italian Phoenix, who, no matter what, always managed to recover his strength and arise from the ashes of his own all-consuming fire. Full of admiration, Tresić kept citing D'Annunzio's motto, "Will, Sensuality, Pride and Instinct".

But apart from vanity and self-centredness, something else possessed him, suffocated him, and occasionally emerged, from behind the steely calm of his poses, in the form of a sparkle in his eye, which gave him a changed, almost dangerous appearance. It was his boundless ambition, which extended to both his literary and political activities. Hence, all those superlatives, hyperboles, onomatopoeic exaggerations, and his tense and exalted nature. He did not just want to be more respected. He wanted to be something far more than he actually was. With such a plan in mind, his teachers were not just Leopardi and Carducci. He reached even deeper into the past, to the Renaissance and Machiavelli, whom he had designated as his hero, his patron saint and a role model in a brochure he wrote back in 1894. That very same Machiavelli, who had placed blood-drenched weapons in the hands of all tyrants, starting with Cesare Borgia and all the way through to modern autocrats in Russia, legitimizing their deeds under the motto that "the end justifies the means"! He openly admitted, "Everything is allowed as long as it contributes to the welfare of the home-land"! What a pliable definition and a welcome excuse for the already com-mitted and future misdeeds! Tresić's panegyric to this unusual Renaissance "saint" ended with "May Machiavelli's name be sacred to every nation which finds itself in a position similar to the one the Italians were in, and may his work provide a constant spiritual incentive!"

He was telling me with immense bitterness about his failure, three years earlier, to win the contest for the best drama organized under the auspices of the Croatian National Theatre. The choice was between Vojnović's *Ekvinocij* (Equinox)[387] and his own *Simeon Veliki* (Simeon the Great). He had to endure the fact that the award went to Ivo Vojnović and not him! Not even someone as influential as Stjepan Miletić[388] could console him with his article in *Hrvatsko glumište* (Croatian Stage), in which he wrote: "The idea behind Tresić's drama is in many ways far more exalting. If it were about awarding ideas, the poet Tresić would undoubtedly come out of this competition as a winner. But in awarding this prize, one should consider not only the literary quality, but also the dramatic conceptualiza-tion and stage effectiveness, and this is where Vojnović has exhibited the true craftsmanship!" There was no way Tresić could accept that. His eyes were flaring with anger and his forehead turned crimson, so that his large scar became even more visible. He was screaming, "It is pure barbarism to draw a parallel between my *Simeon* and the *Equinox*! It is the same as comparing a cathedral with an ordinary fishing hut!"

Even his criticism of the "Young Movement" was motivated by his personal resentment. He did not condemn the modernist and decadent literature merely out of principle, but in order to thwart the competition. He detested Milan Begović, a noteworthy "modernist", who also admired the ancient classics. In Begović's collections of poems, *Knjiga Boccadoro* (The Book of Bocca d'oro),[389] forest deities clearly exhibited human and carnal desires. While his nymphs were radiant and cheerful young women, Tresić made his dryads speak solemnly in hexameters and pentameters. Tresić also managed to ridicule Vladimir Nazor,[390] by comparing him in his magazine *Novi viek* (New Age) to Icarus, whose wings made of wax melted in the sun and he met his miserable end by crashing on the ground. In exchange, he praised all second-class authors, from whom he had nothing to fear, calling them "original, thoughtful, and talented". In one of his critiques, he wrote that Dinko Sirović's poetry was characterized by noble refinement and was taking giant steps towards perfection. He said that humanity could expect a lot from Anton Antonić in future! He dared to praise them, because he was fully aware that they were far inferior to himself, while Nazor was in fact overtaking him with giant steps!

There were occasions, however, when he provided an entirely different image of himself. It would happen as we sat alone in the living room, with twilight penetrating through the windows and making objects in the room barely visible. One could vaguely hear a mixture of sounds from Jelačić Square—of people shouting and streetcars ringing, bells announcing the hours from the cathedral tower, and pigeons cooing, providing additional melodious sounds in the background as they fluttered under the eaves. He would suddenly get carried away under the impact of the surrounding atmosphere and would descend into melancholy. The arrogant look on his face would disappear, he would turn gloomy, and spontaneously confess that he was feeling misunderstood and unappreciated. He thought that his best friends had betrayed him, and that he was standing on a wobbly springboard, unable to move either backwards or forward. He believed that he, Dr. Ante Tresić-Pavičić in person, with all his reliability and competence, had been taken advantage of by his political colleagues, whose only ambition was to achieve their own personal goals!

The tone of his voice revealed a true pain and an obvious dose of contempt for Dr. Frank, the party leader. He was determined to turn his back on him at the first opportunity. In fact, he was hardly in an enviable position within his party, being torn between two opposing trends—the opportunism promoted by a world-wise lawyer against the uncompromising radicalism of the fanatic monk, Friar Kerubin Šegvić. He felt politically akin with the latter, despite Šegvić's goals being related to the Church, while Tresić, although conservative in his soul, was himself a classicist, inspired by pagan antiquity. He was thus compelled to make concessions on both sides. At the same time, he was convinced that he was meant to be a leader himself, a conviction he had conveyed to me on many occasions.

Tresić was thirty-two years old at the time. I knew little about his past beyond what he had once told me in his style of onomatopoeic rhetoric. He had spent considerable time living in Paris, but had not absorbed any of its unique spirit found in Guy de Maupassant or Gustave Flaubert, or in the poetry of Paul Verlaine and Charles Baudelaire[391]—the two poets whom he considered in the depths of his soul to be cheap scribblers. He underlined the contrast between their bohemian manners and his aristocratic superiority, and their abandonment of poetic forms against his strict observance. He brought nothing back home with him but his classicism, reinforced by his indefatigable work in libraries during his stay there, his hatred of everything politically progressive that he identified with subversion, and a few spirited maxims he had borrowed from Duke de La Rochefoucauld.[392]

I had the impression that he had experienced some difficult moments while abroad but was too proud to talk about it. It often seemed to me that the vehemence of his pathetic speeches served as an attempt to stall potential disappointments and reaffirm his viewpoint. I had never managed to fathom, however, what kind of a true human being hid behind that torrent of words, whether in verse or prose. Therefore, even though we spent numerous weeks in each other's company on a daily basis, I did not establish any human closeness with him. In fact, he prevented it by turning everything emotional into abstractions. Even when he tried to impress me—and he actually did try on various occasions—he never managed to adopt a warmer, more frank tone, ignore Greek tragedy, and rejoin the realm of humans, where we could have shared something in common. During all that time, he never truly revealed himself and never allowed me to see something of his intimate self, which was astounding, considering that he talked about nothing else.

I was at the time translating Tresić's poem *Uranion*, quite literally by the sweat of my brow. Even today, I cannot help but wonder how much patience I had. Nine hundred and eighty-six verses consisting entirely of trochaic and dactylic hexameters! What a labour of Sisyphus it was! What a waste of time it was! Tresić himself thought highly of that poem and kept implying to me that it was a masterpiece, suggesting that by translating it into German, I would earn not just his personal gratitude, but that of the entire Croatian nation! He said that without a shred of irony or scepticism—something of which he was completely incapable anyway.

The translation was progressing slowly, due in many ways to the fact that Tresić himself occupied most of my time. He came by every day and read his poems to me. We would then spend another hour or two going out together for a walk. I noticed that all my former friends and acquaintances slowly began to avoid me. Even Kumičić, if we happened to meet him, would pass by with an insinuating smile and without stopping. Only Mrs. Frank still invited me occasionally for tea. On one such occasion, Edo and Leo greeted me with a reproachful expression on their faces. Without much introduction, they began talking about my dealings with Tresić. Edo was direct. "Do you have any idea who Tresić is, anyway? Are you familiar with his antecedents? Do you know how he earns his living? He is over his head in debt and allows our Uncle Josip Frank to support him. It is said that he lives on the party's money. It is only natural that, in such circumstances, he would chase after any girl who might bring along a dowry, which is why he is walking around with you with the intention of marrying you!"

Such indiscreet remarks were outrageous, and I replied with determination that there was no question of marriage between the two of us.

Edo continued. "Then why are you parading with him day after day, letting the whole Zrinjevac talk about a potential scandal?"

Now I was really taken aback. I had no idea what kind of a scandal it could turn out to be. I was strolling with Tresić as so many other couples did, while my aunt was sitting in Kavana Zagreb enjoying her ice cream.

Edo went on. "Except that other couples walk around in pairs, and you are strolling in a threesome! While Tresić is courting you, his last victim is shadowing the two of you close by! The person in question is Marta W., who happens to be, unfortunately I must say, our close relative. He compromised her in front of the whole city, as their relationship had been public knowledge for a while. He even got engaged to her, but then, right before the wedding, he stood her up because of some money-related affair!"

"I know nothing about it, for sure. But why are you talking to me instead of to your relative?"

"Because she is unhinged! Beside herself with despair. In one word, insane. And she still loves him. Now she has got it into her head that you have stolen him from her! She is therefore threatening to make it a public scandal!"

I felt awful to be mixed up in something of that kind. One thing was certain—I had no intention whatsoever of stealing Tresić from anyone. That is why I decided to clear the matter and had my chance the very next day during our excursion to Podsused,[393] together with a number of other people. I went ahead with Tresić, away from the others, and on a windy path climbing up to the fortress, I asked him if there had been any truth to the story. He got terribly angry at hearing my first few words. He kept silent for a moment and then started fumbling for excuses. At the end he said that it was not his fault if some crazy woman had nothing better to do than chase after him and threaten him with a scandal. Such women belonged in a madhouse!

To this I replied, "But you used to love her! You were even engaged! And now you are calling her a crazy woman!"

He explained to me that no man could be expected to marry every woman who chose to throw herself around his neck. Marta W. was one of those women who had plenty of experience in chasing after men, with quite a history in that domain too, and was in a hurry to get married to avoid further consequences. But why pick him as her victim when it had been quite a while since he had stopped loving her? He bent closer to me, put his hand on my shoulder, looked straight into my eyes, and said, "Think of it no more. Marta W. is ancient history for me!" Then, after a meaningful pause, he added, "There is only one woman in my life today, and that woman is you!"

That was the first time he had spoken to me in that manner, but I hardly paid attention to what he was saying. I found his behaviour despicable, especially the way he had avoided implicating himself and how he had even made fun of his victim. All the sympathy I had felt for him until that moment, because I respected his great knowledge and valued, if only to a certain point, his poetry, was now all gone. Worse things could be expected from a man capable of acting in that way. A man who betrayed a pledge to a young woman could also easily betray a friend in any circumstance. Guided by his motto, "The aim justifies the means", he would surely be capable of lying and deceiving as well, and not only in politics, but wherever and whenever it would be of use to him.

Tresić must have noticed that I was deep in thought and that I was holding back. He launched into a long monologue, explaining that he was a man who did not merely belong to himself, but to his homeland as well, and that his choice of a life companion had to be made with that consideration in mind. It would have to be a girl of noble qualities, capable of sharing his ideals and ambitions, someone who would stand by his side in those exalted spheres where the sun was the main element of life, way above vulgar human urges and instincts. And who was Marta W. anyway? A shrewd and calculating woman, who wanted to live a comfortable life and have jewellery and fancy dresses! He, on the contrary, yearned for a life that transcended all that, in which his poems would be the jewels, and the ideas he intended to put to work would provide brilliance and splendour! At stake was not just his own prestige, but the prestige of the entire homeland itself!

Words well spoken had always managed to leave a deep impression on me, but this time I was aware that it was all a mere veneer—just as those layers of gold and silk on the paintings of saints, in front of which people bow their heads in profound veneration, although there is nothing but a wooden plank underneath all that shiny coating. No matter how hard he went on trying, I remained cold and unapproachable.

Our friendship was nearing its end. He came back the next day unannounced and outside the usual visiting hours. My aunt was not at home and little Tilda was practising her piano in the room next door. He was in urgent need of clarifying certain things to me. He did it without any introduction, explaining that it had been me he had been referring to the day before as the ideal woman, fit to share with him the exalted life of a poet. He loved me and was willing to marry me. He was looking straight into my eyes as he spoke, and I must admit, his look was spellbinding. The only way to escape it was to direct my attention to other things and look ostentatiously the other way. And then, suddenly, I was reminded of Milko's image, which had been slowly fading with all the things happening to me on a daily basis. Nothing had reminded me of him for a whole month, and I had had no news concerning him. But in that particular moment, he was there, vividly and compellingly. I knew then that I loved him. Only him.

When Tresić noticed my reluctance, he became almost aggressive. Frightened, I said, "No!" He reacted in anger, "You don't want to share your destiny with a Croatian poet? You don't want to help him fulfil his mission? What is it that you want then? Money? Comfort? A four-storeyed palace? That is something I certainly cannot offer you! And you obviously have no understanding for my poetic endeavours! Yes, yes, I should have thought so!"

He was very close to starting to insult me. Nevertheless, he composed himself and applied himself to clarify the matter once more, this time with more honesty. He admitted that the life he had been leading so far no longer appealed to him. He felt the need for peace and a home of his own. He spoke about his mother. She was the love of his life. But the two of us could lead an ideal life and work together. He held my poetic soul in high esteem. Together we could reach all those heights his spirit was craving for!

I was unable to give him an answer. On the one hand, I did not want to hurt him, but I did not want to leave him with uncertainty concerning my real intentions either, so I just kept shaking my head vigorously at everything he said.

He was furious and turned pale. His lips tightened and he uttered, "You should think it over!" Then he grabbed his hat and left. I never saw him again after that most embarrassing scene. He stopped coming to the house, and a few days later, I left Zagreb in my mother's company for a holiday at Lake Bled, where, to my greatest of joys, I was to meet Sofie, my old schoolmate from the boarding school in Vienna.

This carefully planned journey was part of the "rehabilitation" therapy my parents subjected me to in order to make me forget all about Milko. The idea was that my stay in Bled would extend the period of our separation by another few weeks. I was supposed to meet new people and gather new impressions with the final effect that I would forget him for good.

While in Bled, I received from Tresić the latest issue of the magazine *Novi viek,* of which he was the publisher at the time. It contained his poem *Sokol i utva zlatokrila* (The Eagle and the Ruddy Shelduck), written with an evident reference to me. This ruddy shelduck lived in its swamp and, according to his interpretation, appeared to be an ordinary and plain duck, unfortunately perfectly content with its destiny. The eagle unsuccessfully tried to convince her to accompany him into the luminous realm of his dreams. The duck was hopelessly materialistic and afraid of flying up into the sky, finding no appeal in the atmosphere high above. In the end, the eagle left her waddling in her foul-smelling swamp and said, "Since you are not interested in my luminous heights, find yourself a fat drake for a companion instead!"

A few years later, I learned about a young woman who had taken her life in front of the locked door of Tresić's apartment in the staircase of the building where he lived in Zagreb (it was not Marta W.). Upon the young woman's death, her family published the letters he had written to her prior to her death, which revealed to the public the unpleasant side of his persona. Nevertheless, he continued to be successful in his political career, became a member of the Austrian parliament, and later, in the times of the Kingdom of Yugoslavia, served as ambassador to Spain and Argentina.

The reunion with Milko, after months of separation, made us both aware that we were in perfect accord on all matters of mutual concern and preoccupations, whether of mundane or, even more so, of broad intellectual significance. Most striking was my awareness of the impact his personality had on me, how obvious was his affection for me, and how much he admired me. This affection, evident from the first moment of our encounter, could only be understood in light of Milko's past, where the origins of his complex character resided. He had never succeeded in overcoming the multiple contrarieties of his family's past. Hundreds of years of the bondage his ancestors had had to endure burdened his soul and were at the root of his self-restraint. The consistent poverty of his people made him despise money and everything connected with it. The ancestral "blood and tears" stanza, which was part of his cultural heritage, affected his overall disposition. The evidence was detectable in his proud composure and facial expression. It provided the basis of the affinities that brought us together. There were actual similarities in both our situations. I was also a descendant of an oppressed nation, burdened with the traditions of a tragic past, in protest against the small-town atmosphere of the present, and fearful of an uncertain future. Similar causes had produced the same effects in us and made us sensitive, perturbed, and sceptical. I was aware of this from the very beginning of our relationship and that awareness enhanced my understanding of both the strong and the weak sides of Milko's personality.

In those days, we could only sporadically talk and exchange ideas, and even then, never alone, face to face, but always in the presence of other people. Since I was strictly forbidden to invite him to our house, or even talk to him in the street, we organized our meetings in the winter of 1899 at the homes of mutual friends, where we managed to see each other, if only in the company of others. No matter how many people were there, we felt as if we were alone and considered the presence of others as an inevitable inconvenience to be ignored. We would see nobody and nothing but each other, hear not a word of what was being said, and when we said something ourselves it contained hidden meanings, understandable only to us. Every gesture had its own assuring and delightful meaning that would remain unnoticed by others present but would provide comfort we had to rely upon during the long days ahead when we had to be apart again. We were soon deprived of those brief moments of joy as well, and I was no longer allowed to go to the houses frequented by Milko. Meanwhile, however, we had become formally engaged. Milko put on my finger the wedding ring his mother had been wearing until her death, and we made a vow that we would wait for each other for as long as it took. In the depths of my soul, I felt more decisively bound to him in this way than had we been legally married. It had a calming effect at that time of my life when the issue of my marriage became a matter of growing concern in my family. The first suitors began to appear, to the great satisfaction of my father. He beseeched me in any way he could not to be reckless and miss out on a good opportunity, just because of my silly, childish, and wild ideas about love which, according to him, derived from my sheer lack of life experience. Besides, what was love in a woman's life anyway? Something foggy that faded into nothingness in the clear daylight of reality. All a woman could wish for in her life was a secure existence without worries, by the side of an honest man. Everything beyond that belonged to the realm of novels and all those other unsound ideas young people relished.

Day after day, I had to listen to reproaches, pleadings, and bleak descriptions of the abyss of perdition I was heading towards. To make matters worse, my entire family joined in this campaign. Acquaintances and relatives found themselves invited to help me come to my senses, to protect me from going astray and failing in life. They were also encouraged to draw my attention to my daughterly duties and explain to me how badly and unreasonably I was behaving, not merely as far as it concerned me, but also my parents, our solidly built family traditions, and the customs of the entire town, where individual wishes and penchants were not appreciated!

Of course, there were people who watched my struggle with interest and curiosity. Some were even well-disposed people, who had nothing against me pulling the chestnuts out of the fire. But their discerning smiles were no less uncomfortable than the animosity of my opponents. The saddest thing about being the object of all this attention was the fact that Milko and I were constantly watched, and, if we happened to meet somewhere, it would be immediately reported to my parents. My mother, of course, would try to hush it up, but it would still find its way to my father's ears, because, to my surprise, even the most respectable gentlemen took part in spreading the gossip about us. My father's ensuing dramatic outbursts were highly upsetting.

Since personal contact became increasingly difficult, and eventually entirely impossible, we reached for the only means still available—we daily wrote each other long letters, even though we lived in the same town. Of course, I was sending mine directly to his address, but since I was not allowed to receive letters from him, he was writing to me *poste restante* under the poetic cover name of "Angela Donati". As a way to let me know there was a letter waiting for me at the post office, he would pass by my window at the same time every day and give me the eagerly expected sign by holding a white glove in his hand.

Our cook, Vicki, who had replaced the bad-mouthed Marija, and who had a great appreciation for her own and other people's love affairs, would then bring me the letter later in the afternoon, once she had finished her work. It often happened that I was too impatient to wait, and I would resort to begging, flattery, and all forms of bribery to make Vicki leave the stove in times of the biggest hustle in the kitchen to go to the post office. Meanwhile, I would be mixing sauces, peeling potatoes, washing vegetables, sometimes even kneading dough. In so doing, I learned more about cooking than ever before, when it had been forced upon me as part of my obligatory overall education. While I was thus toiling away in the kitchen, Vicki was fetching the cherished letter.

Here I need to add that these precious letters often made me shed bitter tears, because Milko had become overwrought and restless with impatience. He resented the life I was leading without him, of which he knew little and had no part in. He was jealous of every breath of wind that touched me. He was wary and would agonize at the thought of having to continue to suffer in that way for years to come, while at the same time, even less prepared to lose me or leave me. His unwarranted reproaches were always followed by new assertions of his great love, and then more reproaches after that. He was accusing God and the whole world with Him, and eventually even me for our misfortune.

My feelings for Milko rested foremost on the conviction that he needed love more than anyone else. His pessimistic predispositions, his sensitivity, his imaginative world, his wide intellectual interests, his emotionalism, the internal fire that consumed him, the poetic talent—all of that was incompatible with his unhappy status as an officer. He was subordinate to people far less cultured than he was, in the rough conditions of military service, with the distressing aspects of our relationship to top it all. I was imagining myself being able to compensate for all these troubles, if not right away, then in the course of a long life ahead, by offering him my love. What a delusion! What an untenable objective from the start! How conceited it was of me! I was attributing my feminine conception of love to a partner who was entirely unlike me. For him, love was supposed to bring a different kind of fulfilment and had a different appeal, and a different set of feelings, for which I had, at the time and for years to come, no means of providing the expected atonement. He was undoubtedly attached to me as I was to him, but I might have attributed to myself the role of Kundry or Senta, while he was neither Parsifal nor the Flying Dutchman.[394]

What were we supposed to do in the position in which we found ourselves? I was still a minor. Besides obtaining the parental consent, we were required to deposit a large monetary caution, necessary to get the army's official permission to marry. Only those in the rank of staff officers were allowed to marry without such a caution, and, in Milko's case, with his rank of first lieutenant, it would take him another fifteen years to rise to that level. Was he supposed to leave the service and become an ordinary post office clerk or an accountant? In that way, I would morally and financially cause his ruin. Because, notwithstanding claims to the opposite, despite the endless chicanery he had had to put up with in the service, despite the impositions of his arrogant superiors, despite Kant and Schopenhauer, he was proud of his uniform trimmed with gold braids and of his military status. That pride was one of the contradictions of his personality, which I have never fully understood. Still, I did not love him because of his colourful uniform, but rather in spite of it, and despite my undeniably anti-militaristic and pacifist convictions. The man I loved was unfortunately an officer. There was nothing to be done about it, and it could not be helped. I simply had to put up with this fact.

What would have happened if we had decided to run away from home and presented my parents with a *fait accompli*? I was prepared to go that far. In moments of solitude, I dreamt of an idyllic remote island, a hut with a palm leaves roof, a dreamland, where no one could disturb us. It was not for nothing that I read *Paul and Virginia* while at school in Vienna![395] Unfortunately, even in the most modest of huts, far from every civilization, we would have been forced to find something to eat. On the other hand, upon any such attempt, Milko would have been inevitably brought before the military disciplinary court, and most likely prosecuted in civil proceedings for the abduction of an underage girl. We could do nothing except break up or wait. Since we found the first option entirely out of the question, we chose the alternative. We decided to wait until circumstances changed in our favour, until something unexpected happened, until the hand of fate intervened. Despite my natural optimism, however shattered it had already become, I could still not count on the possibility that my father changes his mind. We simply had no choice. So, we wrote endlessly long letters to each other, which occasionally helped attenuate our mental strain, but more often contributed to its intensity. We indulged in constant affirmations of our love and in vivid depictions of the anticipated happiness the future had in store for us. Hundreds, thousands of times we talked of that happiness, that bliss and fulfilment we would be able to enjoy one day. We lived in an elated state of emotions expressed with passion on his part and with loving devotion by me. We were transferring on paper our kisses and embraces, which filled our hearts with pleasure, as much as bitterness.

Those letters—which we exchanged for years—contained no real observations, no descriptions of events, no word about our contacts with other people or things that we experienced, as if we were living in a vacuum, alone in this world, deaf and dumb to everything happening around us. Milko occasionally worked himself into a state of poetic trance, philosophical contemplations, metaphors, and other forms of abstract lyricism, which were all reflections of his personality and inner desires. That was his way to resist and keep at bay outside pressures, His personality was the product of an overcrowded and overwhelming imagination, manifested later in his literary work, which barely touched upon reality, and consisted basically of visionary accounts, sometimes approaching the demoniacal, sometimes revealing a surprising naivety, but always impregnated by an overriding eroticism.

While Milko was thus escaping into an imaginary world, I always remained personal, trying to pull him out of his melancholy, and, armed with my belief in a better future, to build his confidence. This exclusive focus on ourselves and our love for each other, evident in all those hundreds and thousands of letters we exchanged in the course of three years, showed the extent of our retreat from an unbearable reality. We were oblivious of the world around us. Neither were we capable of a critical look at the ironies of our situation. We were too closely involved to be objective about it. The only thing we cared about was our mutual affection in constantly new variations—nothing was grand and profound enough to compare with our love. We were looking ahead of time. We were husband and wife. We had children. They were part of our visionary love story. With the years, we grew old. We had to face further hardships, as did many other people. It was easy for us, because we were together. There were tears, too. Being together, we were able to overcome such sufferings too. How lucky we seemed to be. We were thus daily exchanging our declarations and assurances of love. I was prepared to keep writing to him for the rest of my life, idealizing and shedding tears while doing so, but Milko's attitude was unfortunately entirely different. For him, this was all extremely painful. His pride and his male dignity suffered badly. He went along with the inevitable, but he was no Abélard[396] and was not fit for soulful confessions, passivity, and years of asceticism. He was, during his entire life, at the mercy of his temptations. Plenty of girls and women in town felt ready to offer consolation and act in concrete and available ways—something I was unable to fulfil at the time. They did not limit themselves to love letters and kisses and embraces sent on paper. It was enough that Milko expressed his desire and they would come to his room. Our love story lost, in that way, its aura of purity and uniqueness. The steadfastness of our feelings would have inevitably been questioned, had they not retreated into some specific confines, pushing aside everything else and turning from love into something pathological.

Our situation was becoming increasingly unbearable. The pressure on behalf of my family intensified. I would simply shake my head as a response to it all, including well-intentioned remonstrances. They could do nothing to convince me. Under such conditions, I lost my youthful freshness, the true sense of *joie de vivre*, and all initiative. I gave up working on my translations. I stopped taking private lessons. I avoided whatever activities there were that could act as a distraction from what counted most for me. I entirely focused on only one thing—under no circumstances was I ready to lose Milko!

Every now and then, I received marriage proposals from people considered "good parties", as I was told, with respectable positions in society and solid incomes. People around me tried to talk me into it and warned me that I would gravely regret not being reasonable. I had never met those men before. I had nothing in common with them, no compatible ideas or interests, not to mention anything to do with love. So why would I, or how could I marry them? They told me love would come later in marriage. They also told me that other girls had got married in the same manner and found happiness in marriage. I kept shaking my head. They could never convince me of that!

Many of my friends were indeed already married, under the same conditions expected of me. Those were noisy weddings, beautiful presents for the bride, big dinners with solemn speeches exalting the future happiness of the young couple, who had merely met two or three times before, without exchanging a single intimate word between themselves, let alone sharing affection for each other. It was all a well-calculated matter, a matter of speculation even—the dowry, the income level, and family ties were all crucial factors in the decision to get married. There were cases where daughters married their mothers' former lovers, and no one saw anything odd in that!

A friend of mine had a suitor, whom she could naturally only meet in the company of a chaperone, who happened to be a pretty and still young governess. The three of them walked daily around the glacis together. He was courting the daughter and at the same time maintaining an affair with the governess. After the newlyweds returned home from their honeymoon in Venice, the governess was kept in the house as "support staff". Everyone knew what was going on. It was a topic of amusement at afternoon gatherings and conversations at the Casino and people had a good laugh. It was at best a "racy story" and no one blamed the man in question for his behaviour.

There were, of course, young women unhappy in love who accepted, under pressure from their families, to marry *par dépit* the first man who came along to propose. They simply did not care anymore. I had a friend, a lovely, attractive girl, full of life, who came from a family with many children and did not have a dowry. A young doctor fell in love with her. He was intelligent and ran a solid doctor's practice. My friend was lucky. But there was a catch—the man was divorced and marriage to a divorced man meant abandoning the Catholic Church and accepting some other confession, either Eastern Orthodox or Protestant. My friend's father would agree to none of that. He did not want a divorced man for a son-in-law, even if he were a respected doctor and his daughter loved him. The doctor's marriage proposal was rejected. Since my friend had four other unmarried sisters at home, the family focused on getting rid of them in the cheapest available way. In the case of my friend, a new suitor appeared shortly after. He came from somewhere out in the country, and was a grain merchant, past his prime. He looked sickly and worn out, and had sallow, flabby cheeks and heavy bags under his watery blue eyes. My friend found him repulsive, but she married him anyway, because she had no other option. On her wedding night, she was prepared to throw herself out of the hotel room window but was at the last minute prevented from doing it. Two years later, the husband was diagnosed with progressive paralysis and was hospitalized. He lived in the hospital for another ten years and would not let her divorce him. It also turned out that he was entirely without financial means and, filled with resentment and bitterness, she had to go back to her parents' house to rejoin her younger sisters.

I could give many more accounts of similar cases. On her wedding night, one of my cousins contracted a sexual disease from the husband the family had imposed on her. She remained ailing and childless for the rest of her life. An acquaintance of mine possessed a small dowry that her parents had painfully put together for her. She married a widower with three children. His late wife's mother continued to live in the same house with them, and he obviously maintained an affair with her. He used his new wife's dowry to pay his debts, and a few months after the wedding, sent her back home to her parents under a badly disguised excuse.

Of course, imposed and conventional marriages did not always end in such dramatic ways. On the contrary, in most cases they seemed like permanent and heavy yokes, by which both spouses were bound, and were forced to endure for the rest of their lives under the iron laws of the permanency of matrimony. There were women who grew old and grey-haired without ever experiencing love. They lost their liveliness and freshness in the course of the first few years of marriage. Due to their indifference towards their spouses, they gave up on expressing their femininity. Besides, a married woman was, by tradition, not supposed to express her real feelings. A reserved demeanour was seen by society as a virtue and in the husband's eyes, it was a guarantee of his spouse's preserved fidelity. A woman who maintained a passive attitude in her relationship with her husband, and, who in exercising her marital obligations, lacked enthusiasm and initiative, was never a cause for any concern outside the marriage bounds. Such patriarchal rules applied only to women, of course, while men had it free and easy. Woe to the woman caught by her husband for having committed or merely attempting to commit adultery. What a tragedy it turned out to be when those forcibly suppressed feelings eventually came to light, when the woman allowed herself to be carried away by her emotions and showed interest in someone else's compelling expressions of affection. Even more so, if she could not help but respond in return, mostly because she had looked for a way in which to escape the untenable conditions of a marriage imposed on her and wanted to experience some warmth and change in her life!

She was doomed! Whatever efforts were made to keep her infidelity a secret, small-town gossiping, family intrigues, and jealous friends would still bring everything out in the open. All the secrets would be revealed, and a big fuss made over the slightest of details. The offended husband would feel a moral obligation to defend his honour. If he was a reserve officer, a duel was inevitable. Otherwise, there would be squabbles, public insults, slaps in the face, sometimes even whip lashing, preferably in the presence of numerous eyewitnesses and in a public place. As for the sinful wife, she would be taken to court and dragged through a scandalous divorce process, would lose her home, children, and the right to alimony. Even the refund of her dowry would be called into question. In short, the life of such a woman would be ruined forever.

The period of my life between 1898 and 1900 was burdened with too many problems, which would have been hard to bear, had I not spent that time in systematic and intense reading, something that helped me eventually acquire a new world perspective. Until that time, and for quite a while, too, I had lacked access to good books, which had been finally, at least partially, resolved. Milko kept (secretly of course) supplying me with good reading material. He was buying books with his measly first lieutenant's wages, which compelled him for two years to go to bed without his supper, and still left him with a considerable debt all the same. Those books were far more than just a pastime, although that would have been significant in itself. They provided me with plenty of material for thought and considerably contributed to restoring my disturbed spiritual balance. Furthermore, Victor Frische's bookshop was experiencing a revival. The new manager was a young man called Trpinac, and we soon became friends. Since my parents' home was only a few houses away from the bookshop, I would run down to the shop after lunch, while my parents were having their afternoon rest, and since there were no customers in the shop at that time of the day, I would be able to chat with Trpinac. Even more importantly, he would let me browse around freely. On occasions, he would lay out on the counter books he thought might interest me, and, specifically, publications received most recently. Trpinac and Milko—surely one of his best customers—had been friends. If Trpinac noticed that I was particularly interested in a book and had a hard time leaving it behind, he would allow me to take it home for a few days, where I would hastily read it, sometimes the night through! Once I had returned it, he would readily let me have another.

He probably had no idea how much it all meant to me. My situation appeared impossible, everything seemed hopeless, and I greatly needed some sort of mental support. Since I could not get it from people close to me, I found solace in the world of books. In addition to providing access to new knowledge and new ideas, books strengthened my thinking and helped me better assess my own predicament. I soon realized that my case was not unique. It was a revolutionary epoch for some of us women striving to get rid of the centuries-old yoke imposed upon us and to cast away the myth about our inferiority. It was still just a battle waged on paper, with arguments and examples to provide proof of its legitimacy, but mostly it was a passive kind of resistance against the tyranny of one's family and the exalted rule of "marital obedience", which had been stylized into a life norm. I learned from those books that there was a movement abroad aimed at achieving the liberation of women. The goal was to win for women the right to study and work, the right to be able to vote and stand for election in the political sphere, equal rights in marriage, as well as the rights of unmarried single mothers and of children born out of wedlock. The narrow-minded, medieval rules and restrictions which made women's lives dependent on the will, first of their fathers, then of their husbands, definitely had to be abolished!

We found particular inspiration in the books written by Nordic authors, who were the first to tackle those issues. With Henrik Ibsen[397] being the most prominent among them, they wrote about prejudice, hidden depravities, and malicious insinuations of public opinion—so characteristic of a petit bourgeois milieu. We were facing the same restrictions imposed by public opinion in our parts of the world, too, and were forced to live the same lives against our nature and against our aspirations. It was a life wrapped in hypocrisy, especially as we lacked the strength for an open rebellion. The result was an array of inner contradictions, sometimes even neurotic states of mind. A woman was unable to be true to herself, and since she could not always adapt to prescribed rules, she was ultimately doomed.

In contrast, Nordic authors were sailing ahead under the motto, "Be yourself". Be who you are. Evolve in the direction that would allow you to succeed in that endeavour! Even Bjørnstjerne Bjørnson,[398] who was usually deeply rooted in his Christian conservatism, declared at one point, "Each person has a proper vocation and should follow it or be doomed to fail at everything else." Ibsen also argued for "subjectivity first and foremost". He created female characters such as Nora and Hedda Gabler, whose subconscious urges and impulses led them to strive for fundamental liberation. The title character of his play *Brand* professed the attitude of "all or nothing". None of these characters, however, found the way to a true liberation, but nonetheless, they outlined the way and undertook the first steps. By subverting long-standing preconceptions, they made it easier for all the others after them to reach new grounds upon which to build their lives, something their predecessors had been unable to do.

In those days thus spent in intense reading, I followed the long road that took me from Henrik Ibsen, Jens Peter Jakobsen,[399] August Strindberg,[400] and Gustaf af Geijerstam,[401] to my own liberation! It was not easy to get rid of an oppressive burden, overcome false presuppositions, appease my conscience and tell myself that justice was on my side. The road to complete spiritual freedom involved numerous misapprehensions, obstacles, diversions, and tragic relapses. There was so much to overcome, so many inevitable sacrifices to make, and long-established habits to do away with, no matter how cherished they might have been. Personal relationships had to be broken, long-time traditional precepts disavowed, and abandoned. All of this, of course, was not going smoothly, often progressing in a zigzag manner. One day something was inevitable, only to be refuted the following day. A certain goal, that presented itself in a wild fit of inspiration, would fade into the distance after more mature consideration. How was one supposed to get to the truth? Did it even exist? And so, in those days spent in reflection, with little action, I understood for the first time the very worthwhile nature of my quest. I realized that confronting and examining oneself was more important than reaching any concrete goal, no matter how questionable the whole effort sometimes seemed. "The path was ours to take," the saying went. And the path itself was supposed to explain our true selves and inner urges. There was no way to know where that path would be heading and at what point, after years of efforts and struggle, one would reach the chosen goal.

The path I followed led me at first to a heightened self-awareness. My reading provided me with an entire arsenal of catchwords, slogans, battle cries, and pathetic phrases that helped me pour new wine into old bottles. It was no coincidence that the first stimulus came from the Scandinavians. The literary work they produced contained far more substance than the German literary production. They talked about social issues that affected us as well, while the Germans simply stayed away from current trends and polemics, and kept being concerned with psychological refinements, which, in many instances, turned into a pure art-for-art exercise. There was another factor—Nordic writers were in vogue in Germany at the time. The important publishing houses in Germany issued them *en masse* and so they were much more accessible to us than French and Russian writers, whose works were translated rarely and on a selective basis. Nordic literary works would reach Osijek sooner than, for instance, those by Maupassant or Flaubert, even Tolstoy or Turgenev. They had more appeal to us, and not only through novels and plays, but also through their theoretical discussions. Young people read books on women's emancipation and child education written by the Swedish sociologist Ellen Key as if they were the Holy Scriptures themselves.[402]

Along those claims for one's self-realization, which, according to Ibsen, should lead to finding absolute truth, there were, naturally, in the case of women, further claims for equal rights and emancipation. The enhanced preoccupation with that subject opened vast new perspectives for us. The pursuit of equality and emancipation was not merely a personal claim but involved solidarity with other women and a struggle that would inevitably free us from our self-centred isolation. That new insight brought about another realization, namely that the liberation of women could only be achieved within the framework of a new and more liberal social order. That discovery led us automatically to the domain of social sciences and brought us in touch with socialism.

When it came to the subject of women's issues, there were two ways of approaching it and for a long time, I did not know which to adopt. One advocated the view that women should first acquire higher forms of education and culture before entering politics. In other words, start by giving women access to high schools and universities, and form a solid female cadre. Others, however, believed that, as a first step, women should gain the right to vote and be elected. This was the only way women could be in the position to work for the benefit of all women and achieve the passing of enabling laws to that effect. Access to higher education was still one of the top priorities. Both approaches found their foundations in everyday life experiences. The matter was evidently complex, and concerned everything from education, prostitution, politics, religion, and family, through to the labour market, and so many other issues. They were all intertwined and hard to separate one from the other, all hard to resolve by themselves, and all with many additional and yet unrevealed crucial aspects of their own. Among various written works by fighters for female rights trying to shed light on this issue with more or less objectivity, I came across August Bebel's *Die Frau und Sozialismus* (Woman and Socialism).[403] I was merely expecting to find some clear indications of what was the position that women held within, and in respect to, socialism. Unexpectedly, I received instead my first lesson in socialist theory. I was reading this book as if it were a fairy tale, initially in disbelief and excitement, soon replaced by an increasing interest. Beyond my conversations with Fritz and Vlado, I had never before heard anything about it. Now a whole new world opened up in front of me—not one of ambiguous symbolism and partial solutions that I had encountered until then in other pieces of literature, but a firm and convincing promise that everything was about to change and improve in a foreseeable future. There would be incredible possibilities in store—happiness for everyone, food, jobs, healthy living spaces, sports and games to toughen the body. There would be no need for women to beg for their rights or keep proving that they have them. In a world where equality was the ruling maxim, those rights would be taken for granted! Children would not go hungry and would not work in sweatshops any longer. They would instead be able to acquire adequate education, whether they were rich or poor, and always according to their talents. The simple disclosure of such perspectives ended all my previous psychological hesitations. A veil had been lifted and my emotional and intellectual meandering was over. There was no more going back to earlier positions, only going forward, slowly and step by step. Everything from that point has hinged on that vision, whether in a good or a bad sense. In the course of my whole life, I might have occasionally been wrong, done things that seemed attractive but were devoid of substance, overestimated things of ephemeral value, given credit to insignificant thoughts, and followed fashionable tendencies with false promises of being everlasting. I am fully aware of it, because making mistakes is part of life, but I have never changed my mind regarding the perspective I had made my own. Since the age of twenty, I have never deviated from that correct path, which meant always firmly abiding by the truths I had first learned from Bebel—not in a scientifically impeccable, but all the more convincing way.

As a result of my father's intervention, Milko was, on 1 May 1900, transferred to the town of Gospić in Lika.[404] The intention was clearly to separate the two of us for good. At the time, Gospić seemed to be at the far end of the world, or at least on another continent. There was still no railway in Lika, only a stagecoach slowly staggering across the valleys and hills. During periods of abundant winter snowfalls, there was no stagecoach either, which meant being cut off from the world, with no way to get out and no mail or newspaper deliveries. The transfer to Gospić was equal to a penal banishment, occasionally prescribed by Austrian courts as a sentence for political or administrative offences.

We were both extremely upset, especially as we were not even allowed to say farewell to each other. It seemed to be justified, in light of a rumour spread by certain irresponsible people, that Milko intended to shoot me first and then himself, while saying goodbye. I was immediately confined to a small room overlooking the courtyard and forbidden to leave it until his departure. He was for days waiting somewhere near our house, expecting in vain to catch me on one of my usual outings, or at least see me at the window one more time. All this waiting increased our agony. It lasted that way until my old grandmother, who by that time had only rarely gone out of the house, decided to visit Milko at his lodgings and asked him, for my sake, to leave town, for I was unable to endure the imposed misery any longer. She told him, "Go, for God's sake. Gospić is not the end of the world. There is always hope as long as one lives, and you will see each other again one day!" She kept crying and the tears of the old lady convinced Milko to leave town that same evening. My house arrest was over, but during those fourteen days of confinement, I had lost ten kilos and developed heart failings. I was so weak on my feet that I could hardly walk out of my cage, once they finally opened its door.

Still, all my energies and all my thoughts were from then on concentrated on finding a way to organize a meeting as soon as possible, before the imposed separation effectively tore us apart. I asked my parents to let me go to Zagreb, as I had learned from Milko that the Gospić battalion would participate in the regimental manoeuvres scheduled for the month of June in the town of Karlovac, south of Zagreb—a circumstance to be taken advantage of at all costs. With not much fuss, I obtained permission to go, but, much to my regret, it was to be in my father's company. He apparently had work to do in Zagreb—although it is more likely that he wanted to keep an eye on me—and the trip was not to take longer than eight days!

As soon as I arrived in Zagreb, Milko and I started exchanging *poste restante* letters and telegrams. Milko promised to come, but his leave was cancelled at the last minute. The permission for leave of absence, be it for a mere day or a few hours, was hard to obtain as long as the Big Spring manoeuvres lasted. Monday, Tuesday, Wednesday went by. He would announce his arrival and then had to cancel it an hour later by telegram. The situation was far too stressful for me. What had not happened in the course of those long years and recent difficult weeks finally came to pass during those few days of constant switching from hope to disappointment. Something in me snapped. I suddenly became weary of fighting to achieve something that was apparently impossible.

I was supposed to return home on Saturday. On Friday after lunch, I went to the post office one more time, with little hope of finding something there. Just as I was about to enter the building at the corner of Gajeva and Nikolićina streets, I saw Milko coming towards me. He had just arrived by train and, by sheer coincidence, we found ourselves in the same place at the same time! He had come without proper permission and had to return to Karlovac that same evening. I, too, had to go back to Osijek the next morning. Nevertheless, the few hours ahead of us before his departure were all ours.

The future course of our lives had thus been determined by pure chance. I had been going to the post office with keen impatience every day, but had I, on that day, 19 June 1900, been there just ten minutes later, I would not have met him and perhaps my whole life would have been entirely different. Overwhelmed by the hopelessness of our struggle, I would have probably resigned myself, while he would most likely have undergone a personal transformation under the influence of his new environment. His life would have taken a different turn. Other women would have appeared in his life (which did happen anyway). There was nothing concrete for both of us to hold on to. Our memories would have become nothing but dreams. Notwithstanding our heartfelt wishes and love, we would have been obliged to accept the stark reality. His transfer to Gospić would have meant the end of a beautiful dream.

But a miracle occurred! We found each other in the big city without any preliminary arrangement, in a street filled with strangers, some ten minutes after he had gotten off the train. This was so incredible that we just stood there frozen, unable to utter a word. I took his arm and we started walking side by side in silence. For the first time we were free and alone, although we were in the middle of a busy Gajeva Street. None of the passers-by knew us, and no one even cared to look at us at all. We were not in Osijek where we would have been followed around by indiscreet stares and remarks. No one could stop us here, nor disturb us. By the time we had reached the corner of Gajeva and Mihanovićeva Streets, we felt as if the oppressive burden that had weighed on us for years had suddenly lifted and we felt liberated. All the past gloom was behind us. For the first time, we were nothing more than two young people, happy to be together and to love each other.

It was a mild summer day. The sky was slightly cloudy. The smell of linden blossoms was in the air. There was a light mist in the distance. There was nobody in the Botanical Garden when we entered it. We passed by the little pond with its white-petalled water lilies floating on the surface, and we disappeared in the thick shadows of the surrounding trees.

The autumn of 1900 was marked by a true tragedy, when my father fell seriously ill. He was afflicted by a mental illness that had been dormant within him for a considerable time. My mother found herself forced to take over his business affairs, and I took over his personal care, which became my main occupation for the following two years. For the first few months, we looked after him at home, but since his condition kept deteriorating, we transferred him first to Vienna, and then, a few weeks later, to a clinic for neurological diseases in Priessnitztal, in the vicinity of the capital.[405]

Initially, my mother and I took turns in nursing him, but she then felt obliged to return home to take care of what was left of his business occupations and ensure that we had something to live on in the future. Father had never cared for accumulating wealth. He had focused his attention on public undertakings, and, first and foremost, on the activities of the Chamber of Trades and Crafts, where he had made important decisions, and, with an amazing energy and wasting no time, carried them through. He had been one of the founders of the Slavonian Shareholding Company—set up to provide funding for a regional railway network—and participated in the launching of its first railway line, as well as subsequent extensions. He had been involved in improving regulations regarding the waterways and the navigability of the River Drava. He had introduced significant innovations in the area of business and trade by-laws. All that had absorbed much of his time and had been of far greater personal interest than earning money for himself. We had essentially lived on his monthly income alone. There was some additional money available from what my father and mother had inherited from their parents, but those were not considerable sums.

My mother therefore had to leave my father's bedside and try, for the sake of the family, to save what could still be saved. It was not easy. Many of my father's former contacts were no longer accessible. A number of people, who had, until recently, claimed to be our friends, now turned their backs on us, trying to take advantage of the tragic situation that had cut short the multiple activities my father had been involved in for years. To begin with, my mother had to grasp the scope and intricacies of his multiple business concerns. She was entirely unfamiliar with the world of business. In fact, she had distanced herself from it all, preferring instead aesthetic subjects, such as literature, music, or languages—all the things she had already cultivated in her own parents' home. In addition, once married, she had confined herself to the realm of her household. Although my parents were a close and loving couple in marriage, my father avoided talking to her about "serious" things and never raised the subject of his business successes or failures in their conversations. That was entirely in accordance with the idea held at the time that women should not be concerned with serious business. They had no understanding of it and were not up to it. Burdening a woman with knowledge of the brutal reality of the business world was perceived as possibly harmful for her state of mind. A caring husband was supposed to spare his spouse any such experience, guided by the prevalent idea that even the most intelligent woman was partially still a child.

My mother was thus compelled to assume this new task with no prior preparation. At issue was not whether she would be in general capable of handling his business affairs, but whether, more specifically, for instance, she would be able to convince the management of the Franco-Hongroise Insurance Company in Budapest (whose representative for Croatia and

Slavonia my father had been until his illness) to transfer to her, in full confidence, her husband's role as their representative, with all its responsibilities and benefits. She successfully did so.

During her week-long absences, I was left alone with my seriously ill father. We had to save money so we could not hire a private nurse, which meant that everything depended on me. I was constantly bound to stay in his room, because I could not leave him alone for even a minute. The room was on the first floor, as small as a prison cell, with two iron beds, a table, two chairs, and a cupboard. The barred window overlooked a farmyard with stables and barns enclosing it. The only thing I could see of the charming surrounding landscape was a narrow stretch of a forest-covered mountain top, and, above it, a little bit of blue sky and fast-moving clouds, whose movements I would sometimes wistfully watch. There were, of course, other people in the clinic, which officially, accepted only light cases of nervous disorders, depressive conditions, and pathological degenerations. It was, nevertheless, breaking regulations and accepting, against a financial contribution, other kinds of patients. In official mental institutions, once admitted, patients were declared incompetent to make their own decisions. That was inconvenient. But with lots of money and a good recommendation, Priessnitztal could provide alternative assessments. There were cases of criminals admitted as patients of unsound mind and irresponsible for their actions, who were therefore able to count on judicial consideration of "mitigated circumstances". There were husbands who wanted to get rid of their troublesome wives, or, in reverse, women who had placed their husbands there to become free to live their lives according to their inclinations. Among the patients was a former mistress of Archduke Otto of Habsburg, with whom he had had a child. [406] The Habsburg household eventually stopped providing for her and her child's material well-being. The poor woman, in despair, turned to morphine, became addicted, and was interned in Priessnitztal. There was also the case of a well-known composer of popular song music from Vienna—an old man with white hair and a deformed spine. His infirmity did not hinder his sexual drive. He attacked women on the street and, after a few such incidences, was also interned in Priessnitztal.

Patients not deemed dangerous were allowed, more or less freely, to walk in the garden and nearby surroundings. During those short walks which I was sometimes able to take while my mother was there, I got to know some of them. I became used to their muddled speech, terrified screams, and occasional outbursts of anger. Among them were a few former poets and artists—mere derelicts of their former selves. They were too highly strung, oversensitive, bestowed with wild imagination, and, since they could not cope with real life, found escape in the world of dreams, accentuated by the help of alcohol or narcotics.

I was spending my time in laborious handicraft, and while my father was asleep, in reading. Hidden in the clinic's library, amid all kinds of trash, I discovered the collected works of Emile Zola in German. I took it upon myself to read it all, from the first volume of the Rougon-Macquart series, through to *Doctor Pascal*.[407] A complex life story of a family as depicted by Zola was unfolding before my eyes like a giant fresco. What impressed me most, having read the whole series in one breath, was his naturalism and meticulously detailed descriptions, his multifaceted presentations of the milieu, his large gallery of characters from all classes and layers of society, with their human weaknesses and vices, but also their hopes and pathetic expectations. My appreciation of it all was enhanced by the tragic reality I was experiencing myself at the time.

During those extremely difficult weeks, the only person I kept regularly in touch with was a young assistant doctor, Dr. Otto. He turned out to be not merely someone who helped and advised me, but a true friend as well. That friendship was enriching and remained cordial for almost forty years, until the day Dr. Otto became yet another victim of the Hitler regime and found death in one of the Nazi concentration camps.

He would come to see me in my father's room whenever he could spare some time. He would then chat with me, sometimes late into the night. He would bring me flowers, books, and fruit. If he noticed that I was too exhausted, especially after sleepless nights, when my father, haunted by horrifying visions, could not calm down, he would take me by the hand to his room and make me sleep for a few hours, while he kept himself watch on my father.

Before meeting Dr. Otto, I had never known a person capable of dedicating so much of his undivided attention to people around him. For him, there were no philosophical or psychological speculations, only the patient, who was suffering and who needed his help. In providing that help, he never limited himself to finding medical solutions, but viewed his patients essentially as being in the throes of various mental troubles, struggles, and weaknesses, blindly looking for guidance. In this sea of suffering, he was always trying to find the bright side of things and impart to people what they needed most—courage for the forlorn, self-confidence for the desperate, and new faith in themselves for the mortified. If nothing else, he brought a bit of light with him to break the shroud of deepest darkness, a bit of relief, a kind word, encouragement, and hope that a better future was still possible. In the Priessnitztal clinic, that was more valuable than any medicine. Patients who had either fully or partially retained their consciousness, simply idolized him. And in tragic cases, where there was little that could be done to help, they were grateful for his care and comfort.

As a medical doctor, he approached each case analytically and tried to get to the root of the problem. He involved patients' family members in the process. He sometimes managed to solve some apparently hopeless cases and restore a patient to his familiar surroundings. He was doing this with his body and soul fully engaged in the effort. He had even become engaged to a young patient to save her from committing suicide. At the time, she was nothing more than a patient, but he made the sacrifice of his own life to save hers.

During the evenings we spent together, I was able to get a glimpse of his inner self and realize that whatever I was doing there, was insignificant in comparison with his dedication. I also came to understand that love felt for other human beings is an incomparable human value, without which we cannot and should not exist. It contains the solution to all problems. There is no need to be a Christian to recognize it and act in that spirit.

Upon her return, my mother found me run down. That is when we acquired a nurse and I was able to get out, and also move freely inside and outside the sanatorium. I began to travel every now and then to Vienna, where I looked up my old friend Sophie H., and visited my old boarding school. It had been relocated to an extremely comfortable new building in

Ober Donaustrasse and endowed with bright classrooms and a bathroom. Mrs. Szanto was by then close to eighty years old and our former director, Dr. Max, was in charge of the institute. I was met with great enthusiasm. It turned out that I had been considered a legend at the school. Stories about me had been told to new pupils and I found myself encircled by young girls who all wanted to meet me. They must have been pretty disappointed as a result, as God knows what their expectations had amounted to before that encounter. Sophie had been married by then. Her husband, Carl Nähr, turned out to be a pleasant, down-to-earth engineer by profession, who later became a professor at the Vienna University of Technology. He demonstrated a great understanding and leniency as far as Sophie's inclinations and wishes were concerned, including her desire to go on the stage. She was taking acting classes at the time and was hoping for a role on stage the following year. She told me confidentially that she had married Nähr, because her petit-bourgeois parents were firmly against the idea of a career in theatre, while he was helping her achieve it.

I visited the new Secession Pavilion that had been built only two years earlier and saw, in Sophie's company, the ongoing exhibitions of works by Gustav Klimt, Max Klinger, Max Slevogt, and Max Liebermann, and project designs by Josef Hoffmann and Koloman Moser.[408]

We also went to the theatre a couple of times. We refrained from seeing tragedies this time, as it had been obligatory during our boarding school days. We went instead to the Raimund Theatre, where I had the great pleasure of seeing and hearing Girardi[409] in *Der Verschwender* (The Spendthrift) and Nestroy's play *Der böse Geist Lumpacivagabundus oder Das liederliche Kleeblatt* (The Evil Spirit of Lumpacivagabundus or The Messy Cloverleaf).[410]

I also attended one of Karl Kraus's famous lectures.[411] He had by then launched his newspaper *Fackel* (The Torch) and was vigorously denouncing what he called the "petit-bourgeois narrow-mindedness" of the press, and specifically that of the newspaper *Neue Freie Presse*, which had never before been the object of any such criticism. Karl Kraus's attacks consisted of a series of caustic jokes about the paper being a typical case of the tyrannical nature of the press. He garnished his lecture with carefully sampled quotes from its columns—so absurd in themselves that they provoked genuine outbursts of laughter in the audience. His humour was clever and fearless, but clearly lacking in objectivity. He was malicious and personal in his attacks, allowing himself to be guided by his own egotistical motives, wounded vanity and forthright megalomaniac ambitions. However, he was an extraordinary and impressive speaker, capable, with incredible facility, to bring out clever punch lines, funny stories, *bon mots*, maxims, aphorisms, and asides, which somehow always sounded unintentional, random, and spontaneous, although entirely calculated in both content and style. All put together, Karl Kraus and his amused audience needed each other and were a perfect fit.

Two of my former young friends from Osijek, Rudi and Fritz, paid me a visit one day while I was in Priessnitztal. They had finished their medical studies and were, at the time, completing their internships in a general hospital. They had matured since I had last seen them. They had lost much of their youthful energy and interest in their former ideals, which they now considered not only merely trivial, but of no concern whatsoever. They viewed them as the childish products of an adolescent crisis. The realities of life, they argued, forced one to give up on such things. Rudi's face was still round and childlike, the only difference being a blond walrus moustache, which hardly succeeded in making him look any older anyway. He informed me of his excellent career expectations as, by being in possession of personal income, he was not forced to accept whatever job there was available. He also had chosen to specialize in surgery and worked as an assistant to the renowned Professor Albert—a useful patronage, it appeared, which could warrant him a promising future.

Fritz, on the other hand, had been, until four years earlier, an enthusiastic member of the Social-Democratic Student Association called *Sloga (Unity)*—a gathering of all progressively oriented South Slav students. He was no longer interested in ideological issues, which now seemed to him nothing more than battles with windmills, he told me, and of no consequence whatsoever. Life itself was a burden, and one should concentrate on personal matters and leave the settling of earth-shattering public concerns to those specifically trained and assigned to deal with such tasks. He immediately added that he neither believed in the possibility that those concerns could be effectively settled, nor in the capacity of the ruling class to do anything to that effect. History was full of repetitive demonstrations of people's stupidity, and he could not imagine why it would be any different in our time.

His arguments naturally led to an extended and engaging discussion. I had a few things to say in response to his arguments, although I was no longer as abrupt and forceful as four years earlier, having, in the meantime, learned that it was not easy to convince people by words alone. Fritz was embittered. In contrast to Rudi, his prospects for an equally successful future were limited. He would have liked to be able to choose a medical specialization—something he had always hoped for—but his father had died, and he could not expect any more financial help from home. He had to find a job as soon as possible, particularly as he had been engaged for the past four years to my friend Lida and she wanted to get married. He had been offered a position as the district medical officer in Slavonia and the fact of being forced to become a country doctor had cut short his intellectual aspirations.

I began by saying, "You once told me specifically not to get married and you tried to convince me to become a socialist activist. Do you remember? It was in Lida's garden. We were sitting and eating watermelon together."

He laughed. "That was then. You were sixteen and I was twenty. Times have changed. By the way, I was told that you are still flirting with your learned lieutenant! Are you going to marry him?"

I nodded.

"That is nonsensical! You intend to marry him, and you hardly know him!"

"I have known him for a full four years!"

"From a distance! Do you call that knowing someone?"

"You do not know him either!"

"No, but I know you! You must keep your freedom to learn, study, and write."

"Does marriage impede on all that?"

"Naturally! Particularly marriage to such a man and, on top of that, founded on such a premise as yours! Your exalted ideas regarding love and marriage have already destroyed what is most praiseworthy in you, most of all your urge for independence, knowledge, and free thinking. You will get entangled in the web of your own feelings. You will naturally have a couple of children right away and it will be then, in any case, all over!"

I argued back, "But that is exactly what I want. What you have just mentioned is exactly what will make me happy! No life on one's own but living in someone's company. Sharing thoughts and aspirations—that is exactly what I have in mind."

"What you have in mind! That is a pious wish, but totally unrealistic."

"But why, if I may ask?"

"Because you are energetic and strong. Your view of the world is large. You will wither away in marriage, and that would be a real pity! By the way, that will happen to us all. Life is no child's play. I am going down that same route myself now, and luckily for me, Lida will join me. If you ever come to pay us a visit in ten years' time, you will be able to see what life has done to us. You must be aware that my future domain will be a rich Slavonian village where fat sausages, so to say, grow in your mouth. I will develop a nice round and protruding stomach, and even Lida will quickly lose her perfect body shape, once she has settled in the prolific future home of ours. All those antiquated ideas of ours that we might still hold at present will quickly become things of the past."

The summer went by and my father's condition worsened. It was agonizing to see him in such a state. Milko was also sending me letters full of despair, unfounded reproaches, and suicide threats. Instead of providing comfort, his words felt like heavy drops of bitterness in that overall atmosphere of darkness. Quite often, I did not dare to open a newly arrived letter and carried it around unopened and unread in my pocket into the evening. The stress I was experiencing was so great that I was on the verge of a nervous breakdown. I lost all optimism and suffered from severe insomnia, which was not surprising, considering that, not only my father was often restlessly moving around the room throughout the night, but there were also restless patients in the rooms next door. Their groaning and sudden shrieks would pierce the night. Fearing that I would not be able to fall asleep anyway, or that I would soon be woken again, I got into the habit of reading for long hours by the faint candlelight. It was not merely that I suffered from insomnia. I also lost all desire to sleep. I was afraid to fall asleep, and in a half-conscious state, lose control of myself and, then and there, sink into nothingness. The stress was equally unbearable at the sight of all those other patients around me during the day. I was exhausted and close to suffering a complete physical and mental collapse. My mother became aware of it as well. Since there was no more hope for any real improvement in my father's condition, she finally decided to release me from my unbearable position. Without letting me know, she sent Milko a letter and asked him to come.

And so, one morning on my way down to the park, I saw him standing in front of me. We were both speechless with joy! This was the official recognition of our relationship. We did not have to hide anymore, resort to secret schemes and be afraid of causing a scandal, as had been the case so far. On the rare occasions when we had been able to spend time together while still in Osijek, we would walk for kilometres out of town, passing through fields, vineyards, and meadows, to find refuge at some obscure turn of the river or the marshes across the bridge. This misery was over. We were allowed to walk arm in arm around the park or wander into the nearby forest in its full autumn colours. We could finally lean against one another and give a sigh of relief for being free from anxiety. We were able to confide in each other things we had been suppressing for years, and we could get to know each other better. We were both weary of the many years of uncertainty and exhausted from fighting for so long. The wild and youthful élan of our feelings was gone, instead becoming intimate and deep, more mature and composed, just like the colourful autumn, pouring its warm and golden light on us. Everything was suddenly all right, as we were sure that we had a future together. There was a new cheerfulness in our relationship, and we were delighted about it. We were able to joke—something we had refrained from in the past. Our youth, with all its suppressed instincts, had found its free expression. The awareness dawned on us that a long life together was ahead for us. No more self-denials and renunciations! No more suicidal thoughts either! Only confidence in our future happiness. We had long conversations about our expectations regarding a future together, with far more certainty than ever before, as now we knew that we had a future!

Milko stayed in Priessnitztal for more than a month. Then came the time when we had to take our patient back home. This happened on 1 November 1901. Nine more months went by, however, before we could remove the final obstacles that stood in the way of our wedding. To begin with, we had to secure the money for the caution required by the Austrian military authorities to issue an officer permission to marry. For that purpose, a house was bought to serve as collateral. There was also the question of religion, as my mother was firmly against my converting to Christianity and there were no civil marriages permitted in Croatia at the time. Therefore, we had to arrange that our permanent residence be registered in nearby Darda (under direct Hungarian administrative rule, at the time), which took another few months to obtain.[412] Then it turned out that the Hungarian War Ministry, Milko's superior authority, recognized only church marriages. That required finding a priest who would—once the civil marriage procedure according to Hungarian law had been performed at the registry office—give us the blessing of the church, notwithstanding our different religious affiliations. He would then be able to provide us with an official marriage certificate. Then there was yet another matter. I was legally considered a minor until the age of twenty-four and needed my father's written consent to get married. Out of reverence, my mother did not want to declare officially that my father was mentally incompetent, so she had to sign the consent herself. It was an illegal procedure and she felt most uncomfortable about it. It was a difficult thing for her to do, but she did it for my sake.

By the summer of 1902, things were sorted out and we thought we could finally marry. But then, yet another obstacle caused a further delay. Milko received the order to report to his new assignment in the remote town of Csíkszereda in Transylvania. It was a small place high up in the Carpathian Mountains on the border of Bukovina, a forty-hour train ride from Osijek, thirty from Budapest, and six from the nearest large town called Brassó, close to the Romanian border.[413] The army was preparing its big autumn manoeuvres, making it almost impossible for Milko to be granted a leave of absence—certainly not long enough to allow him to travel such distances and get married. For us, however, each additional day being apart was torture. We so badly wanted to be together after five long years of waiting! On 17 July, however, arrived a telegram from Milko to say his brother, Vlatko, was dying and Milko was recalled to his deathbed. Milko decided that on his way to Zlatar,[414] where Vlatko and his family lived at the time, he would make a stop in Osijek, get married, and then, with me at his side, proceed to see his brother.

What followed was carried out in the utmost hurry, in only five days. Wedding banns had not yet been properly called out and a special dispensation from the Archbishop of Pécs was therefore required. There were suitcases and trunks to be packed and it all left me with barely enough time to make the most important farewell calls. Milko arrived on 20 July, and two days later, we were married in Darda—first in the registry office and then with the blessing of the local minister of the Reformed Church. I vowed obedience and he protection. I swore I would follow him wherever the future may take him. I vowed to be faithful to him in suffering and in happiness, and he promised he would stay by my side until death would us part. We then exchanged rings. Everything we had been awaiting for years was thus accomplished in merely five minutes. We were husband and wife.

The dream was over, and the emerging reality turned out to be very different from the world we had imagined. Until then—and for a long time, too—we had imagined everything in advance and elaborated upon it in our thoughts and our numerous letters. We were now ecstatic, saw everything in bright colours of hope, and expected that our most secret wishes, along with all our corresponding expectations, aspirations, and emotions, would finally be able to come out in the open, and be part of our newly shared reality.

How much can someone expect from real life, anyway? Can one person really embody all things to another person, as we had believed? There are, right from the start, hundreds of disturbing details, insignificant in themselves, but still apt to cast some early shadows over an all too brightly preconceived picture. Practical issues of life have to be faced. They might produce an immediate cooling effect, and take the form of an encounter with people totally indifferent to one's excitement, or of a missed train, a hotel room overlooking a noisy yard, a lost piece of luggage, an unexpected price miscalculation, a sudden rain shower interrupting a promenade, and one of the newly married couple falling ill with a head cold. Mere trifles in comparison with the bliss of finally being together. But there is this tiny expression of annoyance, an almost imperceptible hesitation, a faltering voice never noticed before. No less fateful was that our marriage began under the cloud of death. Vlatko, who was dying of tuberculosis at the age of thirty, entrusted his young wife and their two children, three-year-old Sasha and one-year-old Danica, to Milko's care. And we did take care of them. But at the time, at the very beginning at least, that obligation cast a shadow over our mood, although neither of us ever talked about it.

We spent ten days in the Slovenian mountains, where the happiness and love we felt prevailed over the gloom of the circumstances. Then we took off on a forty-hour train ride to our new home. On 1 August, Milko reported for duty at Csikczereda and I had some time to put myself together and reflect on everything that had just happened. The little settlement, slightly bigger than a mere village, but hardly comparable to a market town, was high up in the Carpathians. It was the last Hungarian outpost close to the Romanian border. Its inhabitants were indigenous ethnic Hungarians. There were, however, more soldiers than actual townsfolk. The place was dirty and dusty but situated amid a beautiful countryside. Unfortunately, there was no local inhabitant around who spoke any other language but Hungarian. As a result, I could not understand what people were saying and they could not understand me. This situation created a series of major problems as we tried to set the household in motion. I had to buy groceries, find a carpenter or a locksmith, but to my great regret, no one understood what I was saying.

There was one additional comfort besides the beautiful landscape, which was, from our perspective, an absolute blessing—it was the low cost of living. One could buy whatever one needed, and not just foodstuffs, for practically nothing. As a young couple, we had to acquire a number of things for our new home. A local village carpenter made us a chest with three drawers. Back at home, a simple kitchen table would have cost more to put together than the chest in question. True, it was not painted so I had to step in and use my skills. At roughly the same time, we had a new sofa made as well. I had brought from Osijek a pretty material for upholstery—pink with red flowers and green entwining foliage. To our misfortune, it rained heavily the day the finished sofa was delivered. Instead of waiting for the weather to improve, it was delivered drenched. Two fellows brought it into the house on their heads, most likely to protect themselves from getting wet. The colourful upholstery was entirely washed out. The pink background had turned dirty brown and the flowers and green foliage were indistinguishable. It took eight days for the sofa to dry out, before we could sit on it.

Our first home was in incredibly bad shape, full of cute little mice that kept hopping up on our bed. On Milko's suggestion, I set a trap each night, and next morning let go one or sometimes even several of those trapped little animals into the yard, making sure there was no cat lurking nearby. By the evening, they were all back running up and down our bed.

Milko kept reassuring me that we would soon find another place to live. This turned out to be indeed the case as we changed our dwellings every six months in the course of the following two years—six times altogether. We changed garrison three times. During the first year itself, Milko was transferred from Csikczereda to Brassó. Next, it was Barót, and finally Budapest. His appointment to the Ludovica Military Academy in Budapest effectively implied a promotion. It also meant that from then onwards, his military service consisted of teaching in various cadet schools, altogether better suited to his abilities and predilections. As a teacher, he specialized in general history, warfare history, and the Croatian language.

Each new change of residence entailed the usual arduous packing and unpacking of boxes. It also meant damaged furniture, broken dishes, and the loss of various objects. Every now and then, we would sit down at the table, face to face, and assess our financial situation. It turned out that Milko still had debts incurred in his bachelor days to pay for his uniform and books, or his trips to Osijek and back. There were also promissory notes he had undersigned to help his supposed friends who, as it had turned out, were not settling their bills and we, as guarantors, had to take over the obligation of payment. All of it had to be sorted out and settled before we had children. Our furniture was partially bought on loan, which had to be reimbursed in monthly instalments. There was the option of writing home for money. So soon after the wedding! I wanted at all costs to avoid that. Had it not been everybody's prediction from the start? No, that was not an option. My mother had already made a big sacrifice by covering the considerable cost of our marriage licence. In addition, the care of her ill husband was costly, and she had to look after my sister, who was about to turn eighteen, would soon want to marry, and would need similar help.

I was struggling to keep us afloat and found myself closely examining every kreuzer before spending it. We could not afford anything much beyond bare necessities and remained in dire straits for two years. Those days were not easy for a young married couple. Milko had never doubted my intellectual abilities, but he frequently questioned my skills in handling finances. He simply could not understand that it was much easier to incur debts than to settle them. And yet, on 1 August 1904, fully according to my calculations, we settled the last of our financial obligations. Our account was in the black, and we could finally avail ourselves of Milko's full income from then on. On the fifteenth of the same month, I gave birth to my first son, Branko.

The Ludovica Academy, where we lived at the time, was on the periphery of Budapest, surrounded by one of the city's most beautiful parks, the Orczy Garden—endowed with shady groves, quiet ponds, flower beds, and well-kept pathways. While expecting the forthcoming moment of great happiness, I used to go there for long relaxing walks. That time in our lives was marked by the *de facto* end of our romance, as such, for Milko, and the beginning of a whole new chapter for me, rich in content and deep in meaning.

Those sunny spring days and weeks all burgeoning with life were uplifting and filled me with a new energy and hope. I had developed a vivid connection with my child—that being inside me that was mine, exclusively mine for the time being. It was an entirely new feeling of empowerment and my happiness was overwhelming. June came, and with it, the sweet scent of linden trees. The roses blossomed in their full splendour. The sky had never been so blue, the green grass never so glistening and bright. I was absorbing it all—colours, smells, sensations. Not by a simple instinct, but deliberately, because I was harbouring within me a new living being. I wanted to pass over to him, through my blood, all those thrilling sensations and make an impact on him, although he was still merely in the stage of formation. I wanted him to become big and strong, but most of all I wished him happiness. Overwhelmed with love, I wanted this gently beating heart to be aware of that love of mine from the very early moments of its existence. I loved him so much even before he was born! More than anything!

I returned to Osijek in July to spend there the last few weeks before his birth. I was impatient and beside myself with joy. In the night between the fourteenth and fifteenth of August, I felt his gentle heartbeats become louder and agitated, and my whole body was in upheaval. I felt the first contractions and realized that the moment had arrived. Still, it took seventeen long hours to happen, and I invested all the strength I had during that time to help him. Pain and bliss blended into one single feeling that I had no words to describe, but which countless mothers had experienced before and would experience after me. It is an ecstatic condition full of extremes—not merely a sensation of pain or exhilaration, but something additional revealed only to female creatures in the moments of their ultimate fulfilment.

The growing tension became hardly bearable. And then it happened! The muscles, nerves, senses—everything suddenly relaxed, and, entirely without a transition, sank into a state of sweet weakness and calm. In that same moment, a cry could be heard. It was a voice I had never heard before. A child was born—my son, my Branko. An hour has passed and here he is lying in my arms. I am watching his face by the faint light of the night lamp. His eyes are blue, unfocused, and turned inwards. I am holding him in my arms. I am pressing my cheek against his fluffy little head. Tears start welling in my eyes. I am seized by a wave of hard-to-describe languid sadness. No! I do not want to know what the future has in store for him or for me. I am wiping away the wet traces of my tears lingering on his face. Closely snuggled against each other, we are falling asleep.

Zagreb, December 1954

The map of Croatia today

Osijek—the view of the city

River Drava

Osijek—The Upper Town's main square—late nineteenth century

Osijek's horse-driven omnibus

The road connecting the Upper and the Lower Towns over the old moats

*Rabbi Judah Loew ben Bezalel
of Prague*

Sabbatai Zevi

The Osijek synagogue (destroyed in 1941)

Sophie Weiss (née Ullman)   *Solomon Weiss*

*Osijek's Lower Town—the main square where Vilma's grandparents
owned a building*

Young Charlotte Weiss

Young Julius Miskolczy

Josephine Miskolczy (née Rosenbaum)

Županijska Street, with Max Miskolczy's house and store (the dark facade on the left), Grand Hotel with the Casino further to the right, and the synagogue at the far end of the row

Vilma's annual visits to the photographer

A kindergarten applying Fröbel's method of pre-school education

The Long Courtyard today

Julius Miskolczy with his two daughters, Vilma and Anny

Setting the table for the afternoon tea party at the Miskolczys

High school for boys (on the left) and Vilma's school for girls across the street (on the right)

Klotilda Cvetišić, Vilma's beloved teacher

Vilma (top) and her classmates

A late nineteenth-century anti-Semitic cartoon:

Top line: "The University once and now"; Bottom line: "So it was … and so it is now"

The Dreyfus Affair　　　　　　　*Theodor Herzl*

Karól Khuen Héderváry
Governor (Ban) of Croatia

Josip Juraj Strossmayer
Bishop of Đakovo

Vilma with her younger sister Anny

Vienna—New Market Square

Vienna—Prater Street

Charlotte Wolter

Fritz Krastel

Bernhard Baumeister

Georg Reimers

Vienna—The Burgtheater

Vienna—Kunstmuseum (Museum of Art History)

Osijek—Jaeger Street at the time Vilma lived there

Osijek—Café Corso at the corner of Kapucinska Street where Vilma saw Milivoj for the first time

Milivoj (far right) with his fellow officers

Young Milivoj

Young Vilma

Charlotte Miskolczy

Julius Miskolczy

Literary Flowers by Lavoslav Vukelić (Vilma's father-in-law)

Vilma's German translation of "At Solferino" by Lavoslav Vukelić, as it appeared in the local newspaper Die Drau

Henrik Ibsen

August Strindberg

August Bebel and his Die Frau und Sozialismus (Woman and Socialism)

Tilda Berger (Vilma's cousin), in a painting by Vlaho Bukovac

*Zagreb—Ban Jelačić Square—Pongratz Palace where the Berger family lived
(demolished in 1937)*

Ilica—the main commercial street in Zagreb—late nineteenth century

Zagreb—Zrinski Square (popularly called Zrinjevac)

Ante Tresić-Pavičić   *Eugen Kumičić*

Vilma and Milivoj—on their wedding day (22 July 1902)

Vilma with her two sons, Branko (standing) and Slavko

A POSTSCRIPT

By Ivana Caccia

Vilma's memoirs end with the birth of her first child, her son Branko. As she held him in her arms for the first time and watched his face by the faint light of the night lamp, she felt overwhelmed by the uniqueness of that experience in her life. In that blissful moment, she refused to think what the future had in store, both for him and her.

The future, in fact, had much in store for them both.

Vilma gave birth to three more children—Slavko, Ljiljana, and the youngest, Elinor, my mother, born in 1911. Through the years of being a good mother and an officer's wife, moving from one small town to another within the Austro-Hungarian Empire as the military postings of Milivoj Vukelić changed, she never abandoned her interest in literature, nor her ambitions to improve her education. While still nursing her youngest child, she enrolled in 1913 at the University of Munich to study biochemistry. German universities were, at that time, still mainly closed to women. She was one of the first women allowed to take up natural sciences as the subject of her studies. The outbreak of World War I in 1914 cut that ambitious project short. She did not give up. She was a devoted mother, but she refused to be exclusively bound to hearth and family for the rest of her life. Vilma kept writing (exclusively in German), and, as in her youth, translating Croatian poetry into German, to make it known to foreign readers. Her first novel *Die Heimatlosen* (People Without a Homeland) was published in Leipzig in 1923, her only literary work to be published in her lifetime.

Milivoj was also writing in his spare time. He used a pseudonym, Milkan Lovinac, and managed to have a few of his short literary works published, although with limited success. By the end of World War I, Milivoj and Vilma grew apart. Their intellectual interests began to diverge. His lifelong traditionalism and conservatism prevented him from being in sync with the new trends in art and literature. Vilma, instead, inspired by her reading of contemporary literature and political pamphlets, was convinced that change was inevitable and meaningful. While her husband, for instance, saw in the 1905 revolution in Russia (the setting of his collection of novellas called *Purpurne noći (Purple Nights)* nothing but mindless terror and savagery, Vilma discerned in the revolutionary developments of their times a clear promise of great social transformations and the dawn of a new age.

Through her parenting and examples of her actions and literary interests, she transferred that political worldview to her children, specifically her sons. The brothers were close, but different in character. Branko was an extrovert, an enthusiast and an artist. By contrast, Slavko was withdrawn and quiet, endowed with an excellent technical instinct. The boys pursued their high school and early university studies in Zagreb. Branko's attempt to study painting quickly failed, due to his need to express his political beliefs in his drawings, which profoundly displeased the instructor. His adolescent fascination with the October 1917 Revolution and the establishment of the "first socialist country in the world", the Soviet Union, was soon followed by more serious involvements in Communist illegal and conspiratorial activism, leading to arrests, short imprisonments, and house inspections by the police in search of illegal literature. Vilma decided to take the family to Paris to give the children the best possible education, and most of all, rescue Branko from police persecution and, hopefully, also from the influence of his radicalized Zagreb friends. Vilma and the four Vukelić children moved to Paris in 1926. Milivoj stayed behind.

In Paris, Branko and Slavko finished their studies—Branko in law at the Sorbonne, Slavko in engineering. They also both married—Branko to Edith Ohlssen, a Danish gymnastic instructor (with whom he soon had a son, Paul), and Slavko to Evgeniya (Zhenya), daughter of Iliya Kovarsky, a former Russian politician forced into exile by the Communists after the

October Revolution of 1917. Their sister Ljiljana married a French count and, for a while, settled in the south of France. The youngest, Elinor, was a ballet dancer, with promising opportunities in film and theatre, until tuberculosis cut short all her dreams, and she was, for years, confined in various sanatoriums.

The move to Paris did not remove the two young men from the influence of radicalized friends. On the contrary, both Branko and Slavko were immediately in touch with Yugoslav political exiles, many with strong Communist ties and commitments. All, including Branko and Slavko, genuinely believed it a truly honourable thing to fight for the rights of oppressed working-class people and to be engaged in the struggle for social justice, equality, and a better future for humanity. They also believed that engaging in Communist activities masterminded by the Soviet Union was the only effective way available to them to fight against the rising menace of fascism. Before long, Branko and Slavko were co-opted into the network of the Communist International (Comintern) and recruited to work for the secret service of the Soviet government itself.

Slavko, a skilled electro-engineer, had access, through his work, to important industrial innovative projects in France, and he provided a few espionage services for the Soviets. In 1934, he felt obliged to leave Paris in a hurry to avoid arrest and deportation. He went to the Soviet Union. His wife Zhenya soon followed him. They spent their first two years in the "land of socialism" in Kharkov, in Ukraine. Kharkov was an industrial hub surrounded by a devastated countryside, destroyed by collectivization of agriculture, expropriation of private farmland, confiscation of crops, and the ensuing catastrophic famine in 1932-33. As an operative of the central military intelligence agency (GRU), Slavko was, in 1936, sent to Spain, where a civil war had just broken out, and where the Soviets intended to play a commanding role and help pro-Soviet Communists assume control of the left-oriented, democratically elected Spanish government. Slavko's role consisted of setting up a well-functioning shortwave radio connection between Soviet agents in Spain and their Moscow headquarters. He returned to Moscow in August 1937, and quickly discovered a new and devastating reality of life in the Soviet Union—general terror of an incredible magnitude and violent purges in Communist circles, involving nightly arrests, imprisonments, and executions or exiles to Siberia of many friends and acquaintances. Slavko and Zhenya were also arrested and imprisoned in 1938. They spent a terrifying year in separate prisons and were eventually released in the summer of 1939. That is when they learned that their two daughters, Zora and Maya, had been, immediately after their parents' arrests, dispatched to an orphanage for "children of enemies of the people". With his family reunited, an exhausted and disillusioned, thirty-four-year-old Slavko died in a Moscow hospital on 20 August 1940, and was buried under his conspiratorial name, Andrei Markovich.

Branko, under instructions from the same Soviet military intelligence agency (GRU), accepted to travel to Japan and, under the guise of a journalist, also act as a Soviet agent. He became an active participant in one of the most famous espionage operations of the World War II years, carried out under the strategic leadership of Richard Sorge—a journalist of German origin, born in Baku (Azerbaijan), with good Communist credentials and a well polished, but fake reputation as a Nazi sympathizer. Sorge was a skilful spy, who quickly managed to befriend the German ambassador to Tokyo, Eugen Ott, and receive from him, in full confidence, information contained in military, and other communications, sent from Berlin. At the same time, as a staff member of the Tokyo office of the French Havas Press Agency, Branko was collecting information circulated in international press circles. On the personal front, his marriage to Edith had collapsed and he soon married the young Japanese, Yoshiko Yamasaki, and had a second son, Hiroshi.

The task of Sorge's five-member group was to provide intelligence on Japan's military and political plans regarding its Asian neighbours and, specifically, the USSR. The group's espionage operations lasted eight years, but in 1941, the group dispatched its most important pieces of information, which changed the course of World War II. Sorge learned at the German Embassy of Hitler's plan to launch a surprise attack on the USSR in June 1941, and he sent that information to Moscow. The Soviets at first refused to believe it. They took seriously the group's next communication that Japan had no intention of attacking the USSR on its eastern borders. That knowledge provided them with enough time to reorganize their troops, concentrate them around Moscow, and save their capital from falling into Nazi hands.

In October 1941, the Japanese counterespionage service uncovered the group's operation and arrested all five members. Sorge was sentenced to death and executed in 1944. Branko was sentenced to life imprisonment and died of exhaustion and illness in Abashiri Prison in northern Japan in January 1945, only a few months before the end of the war.

Meanwhile, Vilma and daughter Elinor returned to Zagreb in 1934. Elder daughter, Ljiljana, subsequently also returned to Zagreb. In 1938, Elinor married Ive Mihovilović, a journalist by profession and, at the time, director of the Zagreb daily newspaper *Novosti (The News)*. The new family, with Vilma as its integral part, spent the World War II years in Zagreb, facing constant danger.

The first devastating shock the Mihovilović family had to overcome in the upcoming decade of terror, tragedy, and insanity, in the name of racial purity, ethnic pride, communist ideology, and politically motivated retributions, took place in April 1941. Ive was removed at gun point from his job as director of *Novosti,* the same day that the Croatian national-ists, the *Ustashe,* took power in Croatia following the Nazi invasion of Yugoslavia. The Independent State of Croatia they created turned out to be a fascist, anti-Semitic, and anti-Serbian political entity carved out of the former Yugoslavia. Vilma was Jewish, but somehow, due mainly to her late husband's Slav surname (Milivoj had died in 1938), and his reputation as a Croat nationalist, she escaped arrest and deportation. During the four years of a raging war, Ive was an active and effective member of an urban resistance group, secretly operating in Zagreb, until his arrest and brutal imprisonment in December 1944.

In May 1945, with the liberation army advancing rapidly towards Zagreb, *Ustasha* army contingents and government officials of all ranks undertook a hasty retreat in the direction of the Austrian border. Among the hostages they took along as potential bargaining material with the Allies were several of their most prominent prisoners, including Ive. They were intercepted by the partisan forces and thousands of those retreating were mercilessly massacred in the valley near the Austrian border cross-ing at Bleiburg. Ive and several other hostages managed to escape the indiscriminate carnage and were free to go home. By that time, World War II was over, Zagreb was liberated on 8 May, and a new government was put in place.

Six days after his return home, Ive was arrested by the Communist-run political police (OZNA), savagely tortured, and, with no explanation, kept in a secret prison for three long months until August 1945. He was then, still with no explanation, abruptly released. Judging from questions asked under torture, his interrogators wanted him to admit (falsely) that he was an agent of a Western power.

Vilma's first concerns after the end of World War II were to find out what had happened to her sons, their wives, and their children in the distant countries. She learned, in late 1945, about Slavko's tragic end in Moscow in 1940, and, in early 1947, about Branko's activities and his untimely death in Japan in January 1945. She was heartbroken, but at the same time proud of her sons. As she said in her memoirs, she had always been "inclined to worship all those who had remained faithful to their convictions and died for them", and she understood the driving idealism and the motivation behind her sons' sacrifice. Silently grieving, she concentrated on her writing. She wrote her memoirs and eight novels (all in German) and, at the time of her death on 24 March 1956, left her manuscripts at different stages of final editing. They are currently stored at the State Archives of Zagreb.

Vilma had seven grandchildren. With most of them scattered around the world (in the Soviet Union, Japan and Australia), she devoted her last years—when not absorbed by her writing—to her three grandchildren of the Mihovilović family, with whom she shared life in Zagreb. I was one of them.

We adored her.

ENDNOTES

1 The Upper Town (Gornji grad) and the Fortress (Tvrđa) each received the status of a separate municipality in 1702. In 1704, the Lower Town (Donji grad) also became a separate municipality. They were unified in a single municipality in 1786.

2 The town of Osijek (name derived from "oseka" or "ebb tide" in Croatian) was known through history under its German name Esseg (or Essek, in Hungarian), and its inhabitants as Essekers.

3 The fortified seat of the Ottoman rule in southern Hungary in the seventeenth century.

4 Today's Karlovy Vary, a spa town in the Czech Republic.

5 Bad Ischl, a spa town in Upper Austria.

6 The Hermann-Weiss store was one of the best-known shops in the Lower Town. It was continually in business until World War II, and members of the Hermann family still live in Osijek today. The building was demolished in 1978 and the modern department store called *Doma* was built in its place.

7 The two wardrobes are still in the family's possession.

8 Johann Christoph Friedrich von Schiller (1759–1805), German poet, playwright, and philosopher, author of *Wilhelm Tell, Maria Stuart, Don Carlos,* the *Wallenstein Trilogy* and many others.

9 Ferdinand Raimund (1790–1836) and Johann Nestroy (1801–1862), wrote highly popular light comedies and are considered the founders of the typical Vienna *Volkstheater* style of shows. See also endnotes 169 and 410.

10 Alexandre Dumas (1802–1870), French novelist, famous for his historical novels *Count of Monte Cristo, The Three Musketeers,* and *Twenty Years After.*

11 Eugène Sue (1804–1857), French novelist, best known for his *Les Mystères de Paris* (Mysteries of Paris), serialized in 1842–1843.

12 August von Kotzebue (1761–1819), German playwright.

13 Heinrich Zschokke (1771–1848), German writer.

14 Mór Jókai (1825–1904), Hungarian playwright and novelist.

15 Sándor Petőfi (1823–1849), hero of the 1848 Hungarian Revolution, and acclaimed Hungarian national poet.

16 Today's Czech Republic.

17 Sabbatai Zevi (also known as Shabbetai Tzvi) was born in 1626 in Smyrna (today known as Izmir, in Turkey) and died in the Albanian town of Ulcinj (today in Montenegro) in 1676. He was a Sephardic rabbi with compelling messianic pretensions since the age of 22 (in 1648), inspiring multitudes of

followers wherever he appeared. His activities in Cairo, Salonica (Thessaloniki) and Smyrna alerted the Ottoman authorities and he was arrested. To avoid execution, Zevi converted to Islam. Some of his followers joined him in that conversion and were known as Dönmeh, or crypto-Jews. He was denounced as a false Messiah already in his lifetime, and he died in isolation.

18 Nathan Ghazzati, commonly known as Nathan of Gaza (1643–1680), was born in Jerusalem of Ashkenazi origins, and gained fame for his prophetic announcements of the imminent arrival of a new Messiah.

19 Joseph Escapa (1572–1662) served as rabbi in Salonica (Thessaloniki) and Smyrna (Izmir) and was the teacher of Sabbatai Zevi, whom he, eventually, excommunicated and banished from Smyrna, because of his disturbing and false messianic pretences.

20 Present-day Thessaloniki in Greece.

21 Present-day Bratislava in Slovakia.

22 One of the constitutive parts of present-day Budapest.

23 The Battle of Mohács took place in 1526 and is considered the most consequential battle between Hungarian forces and the Ottoman Empire.

24 Today in Montenegro.

25 Mihály Vörösmarty (1800–1855), Hungarian romantic poet, playwright and supporter of the 1848 Hungarian Revolution.

26 Heinrich Heine (1797–1856), German poet, journalist, and literary critic, was a member of the radical movement called Young Germany, highly critical of the political situation in the country. He spent most of his adult life in exile in Paris. Born in a Jewish family, he converted to Christianity in 1825. His books were attacked by authorities and banned in Germany during his lifetime, and, with a particular vehemence, during the Nazi regime when his books were demonstratively burned on a public square in Berlin. There is today, on the site of the burning, a memorial plaque with the inscription of one of his famous predictions, "That was but a prelude. Where they burn books, they will ultimately also burn people."

27 Karl Ludwig Börne (1786–1837) was a German-Jewish political writer, journalist, and a brilliant satirist. Born in Frankfurt am Main in Germany as Loeb Baruch, of Jewish faith, he converted to Lutheranism in 1818. He was admired for his highly critical writings about the political situation in Germany. Along with Heine, he was one of the members of the radical Young Germany movement. He spent his last years of life in exile in Paris.

28 Lajos Kossuth (1802–1894), Hungarian national hero of the 1848 Revolution, known for his patriotic speeches and revolutionary fervour. He was Governor-President of the unilaterally proclaimed independent Kingdom of Hungary in 1848–1849 and spent the rest of his life in exile after the collapse of the uprising.

29 Ferenc Deák (1803–1876), Hungarian politician, who served as Minister of Justice in the revolutionary government in 1848. He supported the 1867

Austro-Hungarian Compromise (see endnote 62) and was later known as "The Wise Man of the Nation".

30 Integral part of today's Budapest.

31 Today a town in Serbia.

32 Reference to the surrender of Hungarian troops at Világos (today called Siria, in Romania) on 19 August 1849, which marked the end of the Hungarian Revolution.

33 The "Thirteen Martyrs of Arad" were thirteen generals of the Hungarian revolutionary army executed by Austrians in the city of Arad (today in Romania) at the end of the unsuccessful Hungarian independence war in 1849.

34 A kreuzer was a silver coin and the unit of currency in the Austrian-Hungarian Empire at the time. A gulden was 100 kreuzers.

35 A dynasty of princes and kings, which ruled Hungary from the ninth to the fourteenth century.

36 At the time, it was called Schanzelgasse (Entrenchment Street).

37 The geographic area surrounding the River Drava.

38 A town in southern Hungary on the right bank of the River Danube.

39 Pécs was known in German language as Fünfkirchen (Five Churches).

40 Today's Bratislava, capital of Slovakia.

41 Indicating their origins in Frankfurt, Cracow, Dessau, Vienna and Mannheim.

42 Shoemaker, tailor, butcher, son of a rabbi, in that order.

43 Walnut tree, deer, bear, grapevine, boot, in that order.

44 "At the Sign of the Red Shield". The word "rothen" in the sign *Zum Rothen Schild* was an old German spelling of "roten" (red).

45 Today's Karlovy Vary in the Czech Republic.

46 The largest synagogue in the Prague Jewish ghetto built in the Baroque style, the Klausen Synagogue has survived numerous city fires, demolitions of the ghetto area for urbanistic purposes in the early twentieth century, and the World War II holocaust tragedy. It still houses today the Jewish Museum and the Jewish community archives.

47 Judah (Yehuda) Loew ben Bezalel (1520–1609) was Rabbi of Prague and Poznań, who, with his Talmudic scholarship, compassion and wisdom, had a remarkable impact on Jewish communities of Eastern Europe and is still considered one of the most important figures in Jewish history. He is sometimes referred to as "The Maharal", a condensed derivative of the Hebrew saying, "Our Teacher, Rabbi Loew."

48 Today's Poznań in Poland.

49 A young student of the Talmud.

50 Known as Popovac in today's Croatia. The village is situated some 10 kilometres from Beli Manastir, close to the Hungarian-Croatian border, in the Baranya region (the area between the rivers Danube and Drava).

51 The reference is to Archduke Karl of Teschen, Emperor Franz Joseph's brother, who led the Austrian army to victory against Napoleon's forces at the Battle of Aspern-Essling in 1809.

52 Inhabitants of Baranya of ethnic Croatian origin.

53 Both villages are situated in the surrounding Baranya region, Darda in today's Croatia, Villány in Hungary.

54 The house (today known as Županijska ulica No. 1) has undergone only minor changes since this description. It was built in 1867 and its first owner was the wholesale merchant Leopold Hiller.

55 The manor was built between 1796 and 1801 by Count Sigismund (Žigmund) Pejačević on his estate called Retfala near Osijek. Several members of the Pejačević family played a considerable role in the history of Croatia through-out the nineteenth and early twentieth centuries, notably as provincial Bans (Governors) of Croatia (see endnote 246).

56 In those days, women wore dresses falling flat from throat to toe in front, with the skirt volume piled into folds and topped with garniture in the back, resulting in an extremely big backside, known as *cul de Paris* (Paris bottom), which was supported and shaped by an underskirt device named *tournure* or bustle.

57 Established in 1750, this park occupied 42,500 square metres and was arranged in the French garden style. It was a favourite site for strolling, public performances, concerts, and flower shows. The site is today a soccer stadium.

58 The park attached to the Schönbrunn Palace, the elegant summer residence of the Habsburg royal family, located in the outskirts of Vienna. It was created in the eighteenth century in a typical French style.

59 Pierre-Joseph Proudhon (1809–1865), French politician, "father of anar-chism", promoter of cooperative ownership, famous for his arguments that "property is theft" or "anarchism is order without power".

60 David Ricardo (1772–1823), British economist.

61 Adam Smith (1723–1790), Scottish economist, laid down foundations of the free-market theory in economics elaborated in his ground-breaking work, *The Wealth of Nations,* published in 1776.

62 The Austro-Hungarian Compromise of 1867 established the dual monarchy of Austria and Hungary with the same head of state at the top of both entities, the Austrian Empire and the Kingdom of Hungary, each with its own govern-ment and Prime Minister.

63 Siebenbürgen (Seven Castles) was the German name for Transylvania, a mountainous region of Romania.

64 Today's Cisnadie in Romania.

65 Today's Sibiu in Transylvania, whose founders were mainly of German (Saxon) origin.

66 A coarse homespun woollen fabric.

67 Ethnic group of Ukrainian origin, also known as Huzulen, settled in Eastern Carpathian Mountains in southern Ukraine and northern Romania.

68 A Hungarian subgroup settled in southern Hungary in the surroundings of the village of Csikeria.

69 Székelys, sometimes also referred to as Szeklers, form a subgroup of the Hungarian people living mostly in the Székely Land, in the Eastern Carpathian Mountain region of Transylvania.

70 Alphonse de Lamartine (1790–1869), French romantic poet and politician, who briefly served as Minister of Foreign Affairs during the Second Republic established following the 1848 Revolution.

71 Wilhelm von Humboldt (1767–1835), German philosopher, linguist, diplomat and promoter of educational reforms. He founded, among other initiatives, the University of Berlin in 1811 (today's Humboldt University of Berlin). His younger brother was Alexander von Humboldt, a renowned naturalist and geographer (see endnote 105).

72 Brothers Jacob (1785–1863) and Wilhelm (1786–1859) Grimm were German philologists, known for their work in recording and collecting German folklore literature, and for popularizing such folk fairy tales as *The Sleeping Beauty, Cinderella, The Frog Prince, and Hansel and Gretel*.

73 Ludwig Bechstein (1801–1860), German writer and collector of folk fairy tales.

74 Friedrich Fröbel (1782–1852) was a German pedagogue, who founded the first kindergartens. He considered playing with such objects as soft balls, wooden blocks, sticks, rings, and beads (collectively referred to as the "Fröbel Gifts") to be the best means of developing children's creative abilities.

75 Today's Zadarska Street.

76 Today's Strossmayerova Street.

77 Bouquets made of dried flowers, twigs, and grass deemed indispensable in a respectable middle-class drawing room. They were named after the Austrian painter Hans Makart (1840–1884), who had been considered, since the 1870s, to be the ultimate expert in matters of good taste.

78 The Long Courtyard still exists today. However, its exit into Zadarska Street (No. 19) has been blocked, while the entrance at Županijska Street (near the post office) is still used by around ten families who all live within the yard. A few workshops, sheds, small gardens, and the indispensable water well are all still there, along with a few ground floor and shabby apartments.

79 The street has changed its name twice since the nineteenth century. Until 1945, it was called Desatičina (Dessaty Street) after the Osijek benefactor Adela Dessaty. It was renamed ulica Republike (Republic Street) in 1945, and finally, ulica Republike Hrvatske (Republic of Croatia Street), its current appellation.

80 A whip made of several braided and very sturdy leather strips.

81 A specially shaped container for storing water.

82 This is the Croatian version of the German word *Shandkerl*, a man who is the cause of embarrassment for another person.

83 The Esseker dialect was still in use by 10,000 German-speaking people (30% of the town's population) prior to World War II. Their exile and persecution after 1945 resulted in its disappearance.

84 A salesperson who sells his fare from door to door, a pedlar.

85 Today Olomouc, the second-largest town in Moravia.

86 Known in German-speaking parts of Europe as "*Himmel und Hölle*" (Heaven and Hell) and in Croatia as "*škola*" (school).

87 A wooden structure, either standalone or as an added feature of an existing building, in the form of a covered balcony or terrace, providing a secluded and shady space for airing. It is common in the Balkan region as a remnant of the Ottoman housing style.

88 A master sample of the pattern to be followed while knitting or crocheting.

89 *Gartenlaube* (Garden Arbour) was the earliest example of a mass-circulation, family-oriented magazine, addressing a German-speaking middle-class public with a series of reports on current events, short stories, essays, poetry and full-page illustrations. First published in 1853, it ran for 91 years, until 1944.

90 Hair curlers made of pieces of parchment.

91 The *Kronenwerk* (Crown Fortress) was a fortress located on the Baranya side of the River Drava and was used to protect the bridge. Its remains are still visible today.

92 For the changing names of Wilderman Street throughout the twentieth century, see endnote 79.

93 From the poem *Dvije Ptice* (Two Birds, 1845) by Croatian poet Petar Preradović (see endnote 190).

94 The Croatian anthem begins with the words "*Lijepa naša domovina…*" ("Our beautiful homeland…"). It was recognized as the Croatian people's anthem long before it was officially and constitutionally confirmed as such in the second half of the twentieth century. Poet Ivan Mažuranić wrote the original lyrics in 1835, and Josip Runjanin put it to music in 1861. For Mažuranić, see endnote 96.

95 Nikola Šubić Zrinski (1508–1566), also known under his Hungarian name Zrínyi Miklós, was Ban (Governor) of Croatia, and most of all, a famous military commander in the service of the Habsburg monarchy. He participated in several crucial battles against the Ottomans, who, led by Sultan Suleiman the Magnificent, made serious attempts to invade the totality of Hungarian and Croatian territories and to penetrate further north into Europe. Zrinski's death in 1566 during a heroic, but finally unsuccessful, defence of the fortress of Szigetvár is legendary. Both Croatia and Hungary claim him as their national hero.

96 Ivan Mažuranić (1814–1890) left a significant mark on Croatian literature as the author of the epic *Smrt Smail age Čengića* (The Death of Smail-aga Čengić) written in 1845 (see endnote 293), as well as the words of the future Croatian anthem, *Lijepa naša domovina (see endnote 94)*. He was active in politics and served as the Croatian Ban (Governor) from 1873 to 1880.

97 Henrik Ibsen (1828–1906), Norwegian playwright, author of such plays as *Hedda Gaber* and *A Doll's House,* dealing with issues of a woman's place in the bourgeois social setting.

98 August Strindberg (1849–1912), Swedish novelist and playwright, best known for his play *Miss Julie.*

99 Count Josip Jelačić, Ban (Governor) of Croatia from 1848 to 1859, stood loyally by the Austrian Emperor during the Hungarian Revolution of 1848 and organized a military campaign into the Hungarian territory, against the revolutionary forces who were fighting for Hungarian independence and a responsible government of their own. Jelačić hoped for a favourable reaction by the imperial authorities to benefit Croatia after the conflict and to extract the province from being under direct Hungarian administration. He is today considered a Croatian national hero.

100 Today known under its Czech name of Mariánské Lázně, a spa in the Czech Republic, which used to be a popular destination for the rich and famous.

101 A suburb of Osijek.

102 Kálmán (Koloman) Tisza was an influential Hungarian politician during the second half of the nineteenth century. He was the founder of the Hungarian Liberal Party in 1875 and the longest sitting Prime Minister in Hungarian history (from 1875 to 1890). He was credited for crucial economic reforms that saved the country from bankruptcy as well as for successfully strengthening the Hungarian government in its relationship with the Austrian imperial authorities within the Austro-Hungarian Empire.

103 See endnote 26.

104 See endnote 27.

105 Alexander von Humboldt (1769–1859), famous German geographer, naturalist and explorer (in Latin America, North America and Russia). His acclaimed *Cosmos*, a five-volume treatise on science and nature, summed up his understanding of the world as he perceived it—an orderly and harmonious system. The treatise was based on his Berlin lectures given in 1827–1828 and took years to be written (1845–1862), with the last volume published posthumously. For his brother Wilhelm von Humboldt, see endnote 71.

106 Karl Julius Weber (1767–1832), German writer, best known for his *Demokritos, oder hinterlassene Papiere eines lachenden Philosophen (Demokritos, or the Literary Remains of a Laughing Philosopher)*, a series of satires on the subject of human follies.

107 The highly influential German philosopher Arthur Schopenhauer (1788–1860), wrote the *Parerga and Paralipomena* (Appendices and Omissions) in 1851 as a collection of philosophical reflections, further elaborating on his previous philosophical treatise on the role of Will, on the world as a representation, on morality, aesthetics, etc.

108 Friedrich von Spielhagen (1829–1911), Friedrich Gerstäcker (1816–1872), Georg Moritz Ebers (1837–1898) and Gustav Freytag (1816–1895), as well as Eugenie Marlitt (1825–1887) and Wilhelmine Heimburg (1848–1912), were all authors of highly popular, easy-reading novels of the time.

109 August Šenoa (1838–1881) was an important cultural figure in the nineteenth-century Croatia. As the author of a considerable number of historic novels and tales written in verse, he is considered the founder of modern Croatian literature and, most of all, of the modern Croatian literary language. From 1874 until his death, he was editor-in-chief of the biweekly magazine *Vienac* (The Wreath), later spelled *Vijenac,* devoted to the promotion of cultural issues of all kinds, specifically, the newly awakened Croatian literary production. Several poems written by Lavoslav Vukelić, Vilma Vukelić's future father-in-law were first published in *Vienac.*

110 Heinrich der Finkler (Henry the Fowler), Duke of Saxony, was the founder of the Ottonian Dynasty of German kings and emperors when he was chosen king of East Francia in 919. The dynasty was in power until 1024.

111 "Der Alte Fritz" (Old Fritz) was the nickname of Frederick the Great, King of Prussia (1740–1786).

112 Kaiser Wilhelm was Emperor of Germany from 1888 to the end of World War I in 1918.

113 Thekla von Gumbert (1810–1897) was a prolific German writer of books for children and youth in the second half of the nineteenth century. In 1855, she launched a highly popular magazine for young women, *Töchteralbum* (Daughters' Album). More than forty annual volumes of the album were eventually issued. As suggested by von Gumbert, the editor, the album provided entertaining material to be read in the comfort of the home for the edification and enjoyment of young women as they grew up.

114 Franz Grillparzer (1791–1872) was a well-known Austrian dramatist. *Die Ahnfrau* (The Ancestress), a gruesome and violent drama of fate and vengeance performed for the first time in 1819, made him famous.

115 This is the reference to a theatrical adaptation of Sir Walter Scott's *The Bride of Lammermoor* and not Donizetti's opera of the same name.

116 *Der Müller und sein Kind* (The Miller and His Child) was written by the German playwright Ernst Raupach (1754–1852), and first performed in 1830. This melodrama about doomed lovers, birds of death and graveyard ghosts, was extremely popular and repeatedly performed on Hallowe'en well into the twentieth century.

117 Today known as Popovac (See endnote 50).

118 Johann Ludwig Uhland (1787–1862), Emmanuel Geibel (1815–1884), and Ferdinand Freiligrath (1810–1876) were all well-known German romantic poets, politically liberal and nationalistic. Uhland's poem *Ich hatt' einen Kameraden* (I Once Had a Comrade), a lament for a dead soldier, was put to music and is still played in Germany and Austria at military funerals and on Remembrance Days.

119 Wilhelm von Kaulbach (1805–1874) was a German painter known for his romantic renditions of historic spectacles. Unless the reference is to his son Hermann von Kaulbach (1846–1909), German painter and illustrator, known for his drawings of children. Adrian Ludwig Richter (1803–1884) was a German painter of landscapes and a beloved illustrator of fairy tales.

120 Bad Gleichenberg is one of several thermal spas and health centres situated in Styria, southeast of the city of Graz in Austria.

121 His name was Attila Uray and he served as a parish priest in Baan between 1870 and 1905.

122 This is a reference to Gotthold Ephraim Lessing's last play, *Nathan der Weise (Nathan the Wise)*, which uses the "Ring Parable" of three rings to discuss which is effectively the true faith—Judaism, Christianity, or Islam. It also deals with the question of religious tolerance and common values found in all three. Gotthold Ephraim Lessing (1729–1781) was a renowned writer, playwright and philosopher of the German Enlightenment era.

123 An Austrian confection consisting of a cone or a tube of pastry, filled with whipped cream or meringue.

124 A vanilla and custard cream cake.

125 Marienbad (see endnote 100) and Karlsbad (see endnote 45) were both the most celebrated spas in the Austro-Hungarian monarchy.

126 Loosely woven and lightweight fabric made of wool, silk and cotton, named after the French town of Barèges.

127 Today's Nazorova ulica (Vladimir Nazor Street).

128 Salamon Berger (1858–1934), industrialist, businessman, passionate collector of ethnographic artifacts (samples of homespun textiles, embroideries and full folklore costumes), founder and first director, from 1919 to 1925, of the rich Ethnographic Museum in Zagreb.

129 Three- to five-month-old, specially fattened poultry.

130 See endnote 74.

131 A garden with rocks and sandy soil for alpine plants needing well-drained and cool environment.

132 A straw *hat w*ith a flat crown and brim named after the popular Austrian actor and tenor singer Alexander Girardi (the Girardi hat is also known as a "boater"). On Girardi, the actor, see endnote 409.

133 A popular card game in central Europe, also known as Ferbel, resembling the game of poker.

134 Robert Hamerling (1830–1889), popular Austrian poet.

135 See endnote 89.

136 *Vom Fels zum Meer* (From the Cliffs to the Sea) was a German illustrated home and garden magazine published from 1881 until 1917, when it merged with *Die Gartenlaube* (see endnote 89). "*Vom Fels zum Meer*" was the motto of the ruling Royal House of Hohenzollern.

137 The shepherd Celadon was the ultimate, unhappy lover as portrayed in pastoral poetry of the seventeenth and eighteenth centuries and became the symbol for a particularly remarkable and desperate love. Celadon is the hero of the pastoral romance *Astrée,* written by Honoré d'Urfé (1568–1625) depicting in four vast volumes the love and loyalty Celadon and Astrée, the two love-stricken shepherds, felt for each other. The novel was an immense literary success in seventeenth-century France. In one of the classics of

English literature, the pastoral poem *The Seasons* (1726) by James Thomson (1700–1748), Celadon appears in the section dedicated to Summer—amid a spectacular summer thunderstorm, his beautiful lover Amelia is stricken by lightning and dies in his arms.

138 In German, *"der Dompfaff"* stands both for a priest and a bird species in the finch family, called bullfinch, turning the whole text into a play on words.

139 Arthur, comte de Gobineau (1816–1882) was a French aristocrat, diplomat and traveller, who, in his 1848 *Essai sur l'inégalité des races humaines (An Essay on the Inequality of the Human Races)*, developed the theory of the Aryan master race.

140 Houston Stewart Chamberlain (1855–1927), British-German philosopher, author of *The Foundations of the Nineteenth Century,* first published in German in 1899, in which he elaborated a pseudo-scientific racial history of Western Aryan society. His father-in-law was composer Richard Wagner.

141 Karl Lueger (1844–1910), Austrian politician and Mayor of Vienna, known for his populist and anti-Semitic politics, as well as for his significant endeavours to make Vienna a modern city.

142 Adolf Waldinger (1843–1904), born in Osijek, received his education as a landscape painter at the Art Academy in Vienna.

143 *Hermann and Dorothea* is an epic poem written by German writer Johann Wolfgang von Goethe between 1796 and 1797. Originally a Swiss legend, *Wilhelm Tell* is a play written by Friedrich von Schiller in 1804.

144 This is a reverse reference to Goethe's autobiography *Dichtung und Wahrheit* (Poetry and Reality).

145 Károly (Dragutin) Khuen Héderváry (1849–1918) was a Hungarian politician appointed in 1883 as Ban (Viceroy or Governor) of the Kingdom of Croatia and Slavonia. His strong policy of Magyarization in Croatia (transforming Croatia into a fully Hungarian province, economically, politically and culturally) was highly unpopular and he eventually left office in 1903 to become Prime Minister of Hungary.

146 Head of the governing body of a county (županija).

147 "Long live (the Governor)!"

148 The Party of Rights (*Stranka prava*) was founded in 1861 by Ante Starčević (see endnote 289) with the message that the rights of Croatians as sovereign people should be recognized and defended. The party held strong anti-Hungarian and anti-Serbian views, but did not necessarily argue for full independence from the monarchy.

149 *Obzor* (Horizon) was a daily newspaper with strong Croatian nationalistic views. It was published, on and off, from 1860 until 1941.

150 In other words, approving and encouraging Hungarian (Magyar) political and administrative authority over Croatia.

151 Croatian parliament.

152 Bishop Juraj Strossmayer (1815–1905), was a politician and benefactor, born in Osijek, and instated as bishop of Đakovo in 1850. He promoted the use of Croatian language in public institutions, and founded, in 1867, the Yugoslav Academy of Arts and Sciences (today's Croatian Academy of Arts and Sciences), the University of Zagreb in 1874 and the Strossmayer Gallery of Old Masters in 1884, all three established in Zagreb.

153 An ideology promoting the advantages of a political and cultural union of south Slavs (Yugo-Slavs), namely Slovenians, Croats and Serbs (sometimes also including Bulgarians).

154 The ecclesiastical title in the Serbian Eastern Orthodox Church, translatable as "bishop", was used here derogatively to highlight Strossmayer's promotion of a south Slav unity and a Croatian and Serbian rapprochement—an idea highly unpopular in Osijek.

155 Term used in reference to the greatly unpopular rule of Ban Khuen Héderváry from 1883 to 1903, marked by the sweeping measures of Magyarization directed at crushing Croatian aspirations for autonomy and self-expression. See also endnote 145.

156 Appointed parish priest in 1886 at the old church of St. Peter and Paul on Županijska Street, Josip Horvat presided over its demolition, and supervised and brought to the conclusion the construction of the new cathedral in its place, with the moral and financial support of Bishop Strossmayer, who performed its dedication in 1900. Politically active, Horvat supported the Croatian cause against Magyarization and in 1902 launched the first Croatian newspaper in Osijek, *Narodna odbrana* (National Defence).

157 Benjamin Disraeli, 1st Earl of Beaconsfield (1804–1881), British politician of Jewish origin, leader of the Conservative Party and twice Prime Minister of the United Kingdom during the reign of Queen Victoria, in 1868 and 1874–1880.

158 Sir Moses Montefiore (1784–1885) was a British banker and philanthropist of Jewish origin, originally from Italy.

159 Adolphe Crémieux (1796–1880), French politician of Jewish origin, responsible for the 1870 Crémieux Decree, securing French citizenship rights for Jews of Algeria, but not for its Muslim population.

160 Gerson von Bleichröder (1822–1893), German banker of Jewish origin, was chief personal banker of German Chancellor Otto von Bismarck and of the Prussian State as a whole.

161 Maurice de Hirsch (1831–1896), banker and philanthropist of Jewish origin.

162 Theodor Herzl (1860–1904), Austrian journalist and promoter of Zionism, a Jewish movement advocating the re-establishment of a Jewish homeland in the territory defined as the historic lands of Israel. His pamphlet *The Jewish State,* published in 1896, presented the creation of a Jewish State in Palestine as a modern solution to the Jewish question.

163 Until 1918, the term "virilists" indicated a category of members of the Croatian parliamentary assembly (Sabor) by right of their aristocratic status or function, i.e., they had the personal right to exercise legislative duties (*votum virile*), instead of being elected as representatives of a constituency (*votum curiale*). By extension, the term also applied to supporters of that right.

164 *"Judenschwamm"* (Jewish sponge) was the folklore name for *Boletus luridus*, a spongy edible mushroom. It is here an implication that medieval rulers sponged everything out of Jews before letting the masses massacre them.

165 "Census suffrage" meant that votes cast by those eligible to vote were weighed according to the person's rank in the census (people with high income had more votes than those with a small income).

166 The term "Biedermeier" refers to a style in art. It also refers to a typically middle-class, everyday style of living in comfort and peace, prevalent in central Europe in the period between the end of the Napoleonic Wars in 1815 and the 1848 revolutionary year.

167 See endnote 9.

168 A famous public park in Vienna.

169 Built in 1893, the Raimund Theatre was named after the celebrated playwright, Ferdinand Raimund (see endnotes 9 and 410). Its repertoire has consistently focused, from its early days, on lighthearted plays, operettas, and more recently, American-style musicals.

170 Arthur Schnitzler (1862–1931) was an Austrian playwright of Jewish origin, known for writing plays that openly talked about sexuality and its impact on human psychology, bourgeois understanding of morality and prostitution. His plays were censored for being pornographic and their production in German-speaking theatres banned for decades.

171 The heroine of Schiller's *Wallenstein Trilogy*.

172 The main heroine of Schiller's play *The Robbers*.

173 The villain character in Schiller's *Wallenstein Trilogy*.

174 The villain character in Schiller's play *The Robbers*.

175 See endnote 118.

176 See endnote 118.

177 Adelbert von Chamisso (1781–1838) was a German botanist and poet, known for his romantic poetry.

178 See endnote 97.

179 Frank Wedekind (1864–1918), German playwright, known for his criticism of bourgeois morality. His play *Frühlings Erwachen* (Spring Awakening) *written in* 1891 dealt with such subjects as adolescent sexual awakening, rape, child abuse, homosexuality, abortion, and suicide. His *Erdgeist* (Earth Spirit) *written in* 1895 served as the basis for the acclaimed modern-style opera *Lulu* by Alban Berg, premiered in 1937.

180 See endnote 98.

181 Eugène Marcel Prévost (1862–1941), prolific French writer and member of the Académie française. His book *Les demi-vièrges* (The Half-Virgins) was a literary sensation in 1894. The subject was the modern education of adolescent girls, who, while remarkably advanced in their knowledge of how the world turned, were still inexperienced in everyday ways of life.

182 Charles Baudelaire (1821–1867), French modernist poet inspired by sensual and aesthetic fulfilments experienced in a modern urban setting.

183 Pierre Corneille (1606–1684), great French author of classical tragedies, such as *Le Cid*.

184 Jean Racine (1639–1699), Corneille's contemporary and a great author of classical tragedies, such as *Phèdre*.

185 Eugène Scribe (1791–1861), French playwright and librettist, known for his light comedies and vaudeville-type plays.

186 Germaine de Staël (1766–1817), French-Swiss essayist and novelist, was engaged in contemporary political discussions of the tumultuous times in which she lived, marked by the French Revolution and the Napoleonic wars.

187 George Sand was the pen name of Amantine-Lucile-Aurore Dupin (1804–1876), French novelist of the romantic era. *La Petite Fadette (Little Fadette)*, written in 1849, is one of her most popular novels. Her private life was intense, and her lovers included Alfred de Musset, the poet, and Frédéric Chopin, the famous composer. She was known for wearing men's clothing in public, as a matter of convenience.

188 Jean-Baptiste Poquelin, known as Molière (1622–1673), was a French playwright of comedies displaying great insight into the frailty of human nature.

189 Gerhart Hauptmann (1862–1946), German dramatist and novelist, 1912 Nobel Prize winner in literature.

190 See endnote 94.

191 Petar Preradović (1818–1872), Croatian poet and professional soldier, who reached the rank of general in the Austro-Hungarian army. His poetry was inspired by romantic nationalism.

192 See endnote 28.

193 *See endnote 25.*

194 See endnote 15.

195 See endnote 14.

196 See endnote 95.

197 King Koloman (1102–1116) and King Bela IV (1210–1270) were rulers of Hungary and Croatia and belonged both to the Hungarian Árpád Dynasty.

198 King Lajos (Louis) II of Hungary (1506–1526) drowned in the River Mohács during the crucial battle against the Ottomans in 1526.

199 Austrian Queen and Empress Maria Theresa (Theresia) of the Habsburg dynasty (1717–1780) was allowed to ascend to the throne of Austria in 1740—and become an absolute sovereign with extensive powers and influence—thanks to her father's exceptional proclamation in 1713, called the Pragmatic Sanction, by which he had affirmed that Habsburg hereditary possessions could be lawfully inherited by a daughter in the absence of a legitimate male heir.

200 During the War of the Austrian Succession (1742–1748), Baron Franz von der Trenck and his paramilitary formation of *pandurs*, mostly ethnic Croats from Slavonia, enlisted in the service of Empress Maria Theresa and became famous for their guerrilla-style tactics, characterized by excessive violence and bravado.

201 See endnote 29.

202 See endnote 152.

203 Ernst Haeckel (1834–1919), German biologist, philosopher, artist, and promoter of Darwin's theory of evolution.

204 "Hep-Hep" was the anti-Semitic rallying cry during the violent pogroms targeting Jewish urban communities across German lands in 1819, triggered by heightened political, economic and social difficulties in the aftermath of the Napoleonic era.

205 Pieter Brueghel the Younger (1564–1638), Flemish painter and son of the even more famous Pieter Brueghel the Elder (1525–1569), was sometimes referred to as "Hell Brueghel" because of a series of depictions of hell and grotesque imagery, which were, for a long time, attributed to him. It has only recently been determined that the author of these paintings was rather his brother Jan Brueghel the Elder (1568–1625).

206 The Baroque fountain in the middle of the New Market Square is sometimes identified as Donnerbrunnen after its creator, sculptor Georg Raphael Donner (1693–1741).

207 Charlotte Wolter (1834–1897) was a famous Viennese actress. In 1862, she triumphed for the first time on the Burgtheater stage in the title role of *Iphigenia in Tauris* (a play by Johann Wolfgang von Goethe) and, upon her death in 1897, was, at her request, buried in the costume of Iphigenia.

208 The title character in *Maria Stuart (Mary Stuart),* the drama in verse by Friedrich Schiller, premiered in 1800.

209 *Götz von Berlichingen,* a play written by Goethe in 1773, was based on the legendary life of a German historical figure of the same name from the fifteenth century.

210 Adolf von Sonnenthal (1834–1909), famous Viennese actor.

211 The title character in the play *Nathan the Wise.* For the play, see endnote 122.

212 Friedrich Mitterwurzer (1844–1897), famous Viennese actor.

213 Main character in Schiller's three plays, known under the common title of *Wallenstein Trilogy.*

214 Bernhard Baumeister (1827–1917), famous Viennese actor.

215 Josef Lewinsky (1837–1907), famous Viennese actor.

216 Friedrich (Fritz) Krastel (1839–1908), famous Viennese actor.

217 Count Dunois, character in Friedrich Schiller's play *Jungfrau von Orleans* (The Maid of Orleans), retelling the story of Joan of Arc.

218 Main character in Heinrich von Kleist's play *Das Käthchen von Heilbronn oder Die Feuerprobe (Katie of Heilbronn or the Trial by Fire) written in* 1807–1808.

219 Georg Reimers (1860–1936), famous Viennese actor.

220 A character in Lessing's *Nathan the Wise. For* the play, see endnote 122.

221 The English soldier in Schiller's play *The Maid of Orleans.*

222 In Greek mythology, Cerberus is a monstrous multi-headed dog who guards the gates of the Underworld in order to prevent the dead from escaping.

223 Meaning the early 1950s, when the memoir was written.

224 Max von Gruber (1853–1927) was not a sociologist, but a well-known bacteriologist specializing in problems of public health and hygiene.

225 Published in 1794, as a reaction to the events surrounding the French Revolution, it deals with the role of aesthetics in one's attitudes to life.

226 Published in 1767. For Gottfried Ephraim Lessing, see endnote 122.

227 Christian Oeser was the pseudonym used by the high school professor Tobias Gottfried Schröer (1791–1850).

228 Namely, the final stages of one's soul in life and afterlife—Death, Judgment, Heaven and Hell.

229 At the time of Friar Luka Ibrišimović's activities as a pious friar and sword-wielding warrior against the Ottomans in the second half of the seventeenth century, Slavonia was still under the Ottoman occupation and Luka Ibrišimović's victorious battle with Ottoman troops at Sokolovac near Požega in 1689 had historical consequences for the liberation of the area. His family name is sometimes spelt in literature as Imbrišimović.

230 Ottoman title for a military officer.

231 Franjo Ciraki (1847–1912), poet and politician, mayor of the town of Požega from 1881 to 1904, and simultaneously town representative in the Croatian Parliament as a supporter of the government pro-Hungarian party. His best-known work, a collection of poems about his impressions of Florence and Tuscany, was published in 1872 in the magazine *Vienac*, under the title of *Florentinske elegije* (Florentine Elegies).

232 Official authorization to start practising law under the Austrian monarchical legal system.

233 Meaning, to have the capability to endure or to persevere in an activity.

234 Alexander Sergeyevich Pushkin (1799–1837), Russian romantic poet, playwright and novelist, author of *Eugene Onegin*.

235 Adam Mickiewicz (1798–1855), Polish romantic poet, born in Vilnius (today in Lithuania), whose inspirational patriotic poetry had an equally powerful and parallel effect on Polish, Lithuanian, Belarussian, and Ukrainian aspirations for a national independence of their own.

236 The literary supplement of *Die Drau's* No. 92, published in 1897, contains an article on that subject printed on ten of its columns. The article is unsigned.

237 Ancient Greek poet of the sixth century BCE.

238 *See endnote 187.*

239 Sofya Vasilyevna Kovalevskaya (1850–1891) was a major Russian mathematician and the first woman to hold the position of tenure university professor in Sweden where she taught mathematics. She is also known in literature as Sonya Kovalevskaya and Sophie Kowalevski.

240 Mirko Bogović (1816–1893), Hugo Badalić (1851–1900), Tugomir Alaupović (1870–1958), Djuro Arnold (1853–1941), August Šenoa (1838–1881), editor-in-chief of *Vienac* (The Wreath) (see endnote 109), Ante Tresić-Pavičić (1867–1949), playwright and politician (see endnote 382), Silvije

Strahimir Kranjčević (1865–1908) and the noteworthy dramaturg Milan Begović (1876–1948) (see endnotes 353 and 389), were well-known Croatian writers and poets in the second half of the nineteenth century, some of them appreciated for their efforts to introduce in their poetry fashionable modernist elements, but most of them, for their patriotic feelings as Croats.

241 See endnote 96.

242 Maxim Gorky (born Alexei Maximovich Peshkov, 1868–1936) Russian novelist and short story writer, known for his realistic accounts of lives of the downtrodden and homeless in the Tsarist Russia.

243 Vladimir Jelovšek (1879–1934), physician and poet in the modernist style, born in Osijek.

244 "To preach to stones" implies preaching to whatever is around, however seemingly unresponsive, until it can hear you. The expression derives from the discussion by Martin Luther of the meaning of the words "all creation" in the passage in Mark 16:15, quoting Jesus: "Go into all the world and preach the gospel to all creation". Should one preach the gospel to "trees and stones, mountains and waters" and include them in the meaning of "all the world" and "all creation", Luther asked.

245 Anker Stone Building Set (*Anker Spielbaukasten*) was a highly popular pedagogical toy for children and adults alike. It consisted of red, yellow and blue construction blocks of various weights, shapes and sizes, with a distinct stone quality, made of a compressed and baked mixture of sand, whiting and linseed oil.

246 Count Teodor Pejačević (1855–1928), member of the powerful Pejačević family considered one of the wealthiest landowners in Croatia. His father was the Croatian Ban (Governor) from 1880 to 1883. He was himself a politician and served as *Veliki Župan* (county prefect) for Slavonia from 1886 to 1901, and as Governor of Croatia from 1903 to 1907.

247 On the Party of Rights, see endnote 148.

248 A stiff, cylindrical military dress hat with a metal plate in front, a short visor, and a plume.

249 *Die Ahnfrau* (The Ancestress) was first performed in 1819. See also endnote 114.

250 The operetta *Die Lustige Witwe* (The Merry Widow) by Franz Lehár (1870–1948) was actually composed ten years later, in 1905. It was based on the comic play *L'attaché d'ambassade* (The Embassy Attaché) by French playwright Henri Meilhac (1830–1897), first performed on stage in 1861, and the reference here is most likely to the play and not the operetta.

251 City in Vojvodina, in today's Serbia.

252 *Trilby* was a popular British-American play, first performed in 1895, as a stage adaptation of a novel by the same name written by George du Maurier. It tells the story of how the hypnotist Svengali transforms a young uneducated launderess called Trilby into a celebrated opera singer. *Die schöne Galathée* (The Beautiful Galatea) was a popular operetta by the Austrian composer

Franz von Suppé (1819–1895), first performed in 1863, based on the myth of Pygmalion and the statue of Galatea he loved.

253 *Heimat* (Homeland) by Hermann Sudermann (1857–1928) was premiered in Berlin in 1893, *Hanneles Himmelfahrt* (Hannele's Assumption) by Gerhart Hauptmann (1862–1946) also in 1893 and Die *Mütter* (The Mothers) by Jewish playwright Georg Hirschfeld (1873–1942) in 1896.

254 Victorien Sardou (1831–1908) wrote his play *Fédora* for the celebrated actress Sarah Bernhardt in 1882. The main character, Fedora Romanoff, wears a type of a soft felt hat, which, promptly named fedora after the play, soon became a popular headwear item for both men and women.

255 Georges Ohnet (1848–1918) was a popular French novelist and playwright best known for his novel *Le Maître de Forges* (The Ironmaster) written in 1882, which he himself turned into a popular play of the same name.

256 Oscar Blumenthal (1852–1917) and Gustav Kadelburg (1851–1925) collaborated on several popular plays.

257 City in Moravia (Czech Republic) known today as Olomouc.

258 City in the Czech Republic known today as Žatec.

259 Small town in Austria.

260 City in the Czech Republic known today as Valašské-Mezeřičí or Valmez.

261 Men-only clubs in German-speaking communities, whose members pledged friendship, art and humour, and no discussion of politics whatsoever.

262 An Austrian traditional event during the carnival period.

263 Black and yellow were the colours of the Austrian army.

264 In southeastern Poland.

265 In Austria.

266 Plzeň, in today's Czech Republic.

267 In Austria.

268 The idea of an Austrian national unity of the ethnically diverse Austro-Hungarian Empire.

269 The Royal Croatian Home Guard was created in 1868 with the military training conducted in Croatian. It was only in 1912 that the Guard was ranked with the rest of the Austro-Hungarian Army, as the so-called joint army.

270 The Military Frontier was a distinct territory along the border with the Ottoman Empire under the direct imperial military and administrative jurisdiction. From the seventeenth century until 1881, its main purpose was to provide a well armed and always on-full-alert cordon of protection along the border against Ottoman armed incursions northward. Generation after generation of its male inhabitants pledged their lifelong military service to the monarchy in exchange for land grants and a few other specific privileges (such as free education for male offspring).

271 Alexander Roda Roda was born as Šandor Friedrich Rosenfeld (1872–1945) in Moravia (The Czech Republic). His family moved to Slavonia, notably Osijek, where he lived for a full thirty years, including seven years of military service as an officer in the local garrison, both in the artillery and the cavalry.

He launched his literary career as Alexander Roda Roda, writing spoofs on the city life for local newspapers. His subsequent stories and comedies with themes from military life earned him a reputation as one of the best humorists in Austrian literature.

272 Adele Sandrock (1863–1937) was a German, Dutch-born theatre (later also cinema) actress, of some renown for her performances in theatres in Berlin and Vienna. She was at one time engaged to Alexander Roda Roda.

273 Pan-Slavism was a political movement centred on the idea of cooperation and unity of all Slavic peoples.

274 Russian writer Ivan Sergeyevich Turgenev (1818–1883) wrote his acclaimed novel *Fathers and Sons* in 1862. It is a depiction of the tense inter-generational confrontation between the old, traditionalist outlooks of "fathers" and the new, nihilistic approach to life professed by their "sons".

275 Mikhail Petrovich Artsybashev (1878–1927) was a proponent of a naturalist literary style in Russian literature on the eve of World War I. His *Sanin* (1907) was censored by both Russian and Soviet authorities for its frank sensuality, "individualist anarchism" and the depiction of sexually liberated behaviour by its main protagonists.

276 See endnote 98.

277 See endnote 97.

278 Friedrich Nietzsche (1844–1900) was an influential German philosopher preoccupied with questions of morality, nihilism, will to power, and dominant Judeo-Christian values.

279 Mikhail Alexandrovich Bakunin (1814–1876), prominent Russian anarchist.

280 The social hygiene movement involved a series of public initiatives designed to protect and improve the family as a social institution, aiming specifically at the elimination of venereal disease and prostitution.

281 Meaning a Croatia which would include all the territories inhabited by Croats within the monarchy, notably Croatia, Slavonia, Vojvodina, Istria, Dalmatia and parts of Bosnia.

282 Unity among the South Slav peoples of the Balkan region (the Yugo-Slavs)—Serbs, Croats, Slovenes and Bulgarians.

283 Reisner House belonged to the most important industrialist family in town, the Reisners, most notably Adam Reisner (1855–1939), owner of the highly successful match factory.

284 See endnote 107.

285 Eugen Rolfes (1852–1932) German philosopher who specialized in the study of Aristotle's *Metaphysics*.

286 Immanuel Kant (1724–1804), highly influential German philosopher of the Enlightenment era.

287 Lavoslav Vukelić (1840–1879), Croatian poet, whose poignant, pacifist poem, *Kod Solferina* (At Solferino) (1879)—with its poetic denunciation of the human cost of wars—is considered by literary critics as one of the best Croatian lyrical works of the nineteenth century.

288 Bude Budisavljević (1843–1919), civil servant, writer, and a close friend of Lavoslav Vukelić since their school days in Senj and their training years at the military academy in Vienna. After Vukelić's premature death at the age of 39, Budisavljević took it upon himself to publicize his friend's literary work and provide moral and financial support to his young family.

289 Ante Starčević (1823–1896), Croatian politician and writer, a fervent Croatian nationalist and founder, in 1861, of the Croatian Party of Rights (see endnote 148). Largely celebrated today as one of the fathers of the homeland, he is also criticized for his racism and anti-Semitism.

290 A small town on the Adriatic coast, where Lavoslav's parents, Petar and Antonija Vukelić lived after Petar's retirement from active military service, and where Lavoslav attended school.

291 Dante Alighieri (1265–1321) and Torquato Tasso (1544–1595) were Italian Renaissance poets, William Shakespeare wrote in English, Johann Wolfgang von Goethe (1749–1832) in German, and Adam Mickiewicz (1798–1855) in Polish (see endnote 235). For more on Goethe, see endnotes 143, 144, 207 and 209.

292 Friar Andrija Kačić-Miošić (1704–1760), Croatian Franciscan monk and poet, whose *Razgovori ugodni naroda slovinskog* (Pleasant Conversations of Slavic People) (1756) describes in poetic language the history of various Slavic people from the Baltic Sea to the Adriatic, and contains full texts of folk songs and other material drawn from the South Slav oral folk literature.

293 The epic poem *The Death of Smail-aga Čengić* consists of five sections and altogether some 1000 verses. For details on his author, see endnote 96.

294 See endnote 270.

295 See endnote 191.

296 The translation was published on 1 January 1898, on the front page of *Die Drau*'s literary section.

297 Milko was a familiar form of the name Milivoj.

298 *Die Gesellschaft* (The Society) was a literary magazine published between 1885 and 1902, known for its vigorous promotion of new naturalistic and realistic trends in German literature and art. The renowned poet Ludwig Jacobowski (1868–1900) was its editor from 1898 to 1900.

299 Richard Dehmel (1863–1920), Baron Detlev von Liliencron (1844–1909) and Arno Holz (1863–1929) were all eminent German poets in the modernist style of that period.

300 Emile Zola (1840–1902) wrote in French, Oskar Ivar Levertin (1862–1906) in Swedish, Arne Garborg (1851–1924) in Norwegian, Henryk Sienkiewicz (1846–1916) in Polish and Maxim Gorky (1868–1936) in Russian.

301 See endnote 108.

302 Emmanuel Geibel (1815–1884), Ludwig Christoph Heinrich Holty (1748–1776) and Count Anton Alexander von Auersperg (known as Anastasius Grün) (1806–1876) were highly popular German romantic poets.

303 Lika is a region of Croatia situated between the mountain range of Velebit along the Adriatic coast and the mountainous border with Bosnia, in the north-east. The region is known for its rugged natural environment and the remarkably resolute and resilient people who live there.

304 Arne Garborg (1851–1924), Gustaf af Geijerstam (1858–1909) and Jonas Lauritz Idemil Lie (1833–1908) were, along with their contemporaries, playwrights Henrik Ibsen (1828–1906) and August Strindberg (1849–1912), Scandinavian writers of considerable renown.

305 Dušan Plavšić Nikolajev (1875–1965) was the central figure of the Osijek circle in Vienna. He was a fine arts and theatre critic. After World War I, he turned to politics and became an official of the Yugoslav government. Guido Jeny (1875–1952) was the initiator of the Croatian-language magazine *Mladost* (Youth) briefly published in Vienna. He returned to Osijek in 1899 and worked as a high school teacher, painter and fine arts critic. Otto Kraus (1875–1923) was a versatile journalist and art and theatre critic, both in Vienna and Osijek. Vlado Jugović (1876–1939), also known as Vlado Schmidt, was a pharmacist by profession. He left Osijek for the small town of Petrovaradin (today an integral part of the city of Novi Sad in Serbia) and indulged in writing local histories in his spare time.

306 *Jugend* (Youth) was an influential art magazine, published between 1896 and 1940. The highly ornamental style of its illustrations in the early years of its publication, created by such artists as Thomas Theodor Heine, Hans Thoma or Ephraim Moses Lilien gave birth to the distinctive German decorative and graphic style of the 1890s and early 1900s, named after the magazine as *Jugendstil,* contemporary of *Art Nouveau* in France and Liberty Style in England.

307 *Simplicissimus* was a satirical weekly magazine published in Munich, with some interruptions, from 1896 until 1967.

308 Maurice Maeterlinck (1862–1949) was a Belgian playwright, poet, and 1911 Nobel Prize winner in literature, known for the mysticism and symbolism of his plays, notably *L'oiseau bleu* (The Blue Bird) written in 1908 and *Pelléas et Mélisande* (1893), later adapted as an opera of the same name by Claude Debussy. See also endnote 324.

309 Today's Stjepan Radić Street.

310 The Pongratz Palace was an elegant apartment building owned by the prominent businessman, industrialist, real-estate owner and supporter of fine arts and public cultural institutions, Guido Pongratz. It was designed and built in 1885–1886 by the renowned architect Herman Bollé, and was demolished in 1937 to provide space for a modern structure still standing in its place today.

311 The Merciful Brothers of the Order of the Knights of the Hospital of Saint John of Jerusalem ran the operations of the only publicly owned hospital in town, founded in the early nineteenth century. They were in constant land disputes with the public authorities over the coveted prime real-estate location their hospital occupied in the centre of the city. The hospital building was finally demolished in 1935.

312 Vlaho Bukovac (1855–1922) was born as Biagio Faggioni in the small town of Cavtat near Dubrovnik. He travelled extensively and learned his art in the United States, Great Britain, Zagreb and Prague, and, most of all, Paris. He was considered the pre-eminent Croatian artist of his time, best known for his female portraits and nudes and his painting of the Croatian National Revival (1895) on the ceremonial curtain of the Croatian National Theatre in Zagreb.

313 Menci Clement (Klement) Crnčić (1865–1930) Croatian painter, best known for his marine scenery.

314 See endnote 128.

315 Agricultural lands along the rivers Sava, Kupa, and Drava, respectively.

316 Salamon Berger was the full-time director of the Ethnographic Museum only until 1925. He was then named honorary director and continued his involvement with the museum until his death in 1934. For more on Salamon Berger, see endnote 128.

317 See endnote 108.

318 Austria took over the control of Bosnia from the Ottoman Empire in 1878.

319 Karlsbad (today's Karlovy Vary spa resort in the Czech Republic), Bad Gestein (spa and ski resort south of Salzburg in Austria) and the summer resort Semmering in Austria were all popular holiday destinations for wealthy families in the Austro-Hungarian Empire at the turn of the nineteenth to the twentieth centuries.

320 The lyceum for the education of young women opened its doors in Zagreb in 1892, as one of the earliest public high school institutions for girls in the Austro-Hungarian monarchy.

321 Marija Jambrišak (1847–1937), Camilla Lucerna (1868–1960) and Jagoda Truhelka (1864–1957) were all accomplished teachers, writers and advocates of women's rights to education and meaningful social integration.

322 The Sokol movement, founded in Prague in 1862, had, as its objective, to promote a healthy lifestyle, specifically through physical exercise (gymnastics) and education, under the motto "a strong mind in a sound body". The movement was highly popular in most Slavic countries of central Europe and its training and lecture halls existed in many parts of the Austro-Hungarian Empire. Although officially apolitical, it became nationalistic in spirit, made evident in various public events in the course of the twentieth century.

323 Oscar Wilde (1854–1900), Irish poet and playwright, whose only novel *The Picture of Dorian Gray* was published in 1891. This highly controversial novel dealt with questions of beauty, morality, hedonism, and the hypocrisy of British high society. Wilde was publicly denounced for his homosexuality, tried in court for gross indecency and sentenced in 1894 to two years of hard labour.

324 Maurice Maeterlinck's (1860–1949) one-act play *Les aveugles* (The Sightless) was first performed in 1890. The play, written in a symbolist style, shows blindfolded protagonists trying to make sense of, and find hope, in their lives. For Maeterlinck, see also endnote 308. The six heroines of Jules-André Barbey d'Aurevilly's (1808–1889) *Les diaboliques* (The She-Devils), published in 1874, commit acts of violence and revenge driven by passion and boredom. The book met with a vast public uproar as immoral. Maurice Barrès (1862–1923), a French novelist associated with the symbolism movement and a fervent nationalist, published in 1894 his impressions of Spain and Italy in a book entitled *Du sang, de la volupté et de la mort* (Blood, Pleasure and Death).

325 Julius Langbehn (1851–1907) wrote this tract against modern rationalism, liberalism, materialism and mass culture by using Rembrandt as the quintessential example of a perfect product of the pure German race.

326 The book in question is a critical analysis of Christianity, calling it the religion of suffering. Nietzsche criticizes it for the conception of the original sin and its overall negative attitudes towards purely natural manifestations of human life. See also, endnote 278.

327 See endnote 107.

328 Arthur Schnitzler's *Liebelei* (Flirtation) was written in 1895. See also endnote 170.

329 Hugo von Hofmannsthal (1874–1929) was a celebrated Viennese poet and playwright. As a librettist, he collaborated with composer Richard Strauss on several of his famous operas, e.g. *Elektra, Der Rosenkavalier (The Knight with the Rose), Ariadne on Naxos.* His poem entitled T*erzinen über Vergänglichkeit* (Stanzas in *Terza Rima—on Mutability)* was published in 1894.

330 Peter Altenberg (1859–1919), known for his impressionistic and poetic short stories published in 1896 as a collection entitled *Wie ich es sehe* (How I See It).

331 The pavilion opened its doors in 1897.

332 Among the founders of the Austrian Secession group were, most notably, Gustav Klimt (1862–1918), a symbolist painter, de facto the group's first president while Rudolf von Alt was its honorary president; Alphonse Mucha (1860–1939) painter and decorative artist famous for his posters; Wilhelm Bernatzik (1853–1906) known for his impressionist landscapes; Max Kurzweil (1867–1916), painter and graphic artist; Otto Wagner (1841–1918), architect and urban planner; Joseph Maria Olbrich (1867–1908) the architect who, in collaboration with Joseph Hoffmann (1870–1956) designed the exterior and the interior of the Secession Pavilion; and Koloman Moser (1868–1918), known, along with Josef Hoffmann, for their innovative designs in furniture, tapestry and household goods (glassware, flatware, silverware and textiles).

333 Tomáš (Thomas) Garrigue Masaryk (1850–1937) was a Czech intellectual, philosopher and professor at the University of Prague, whose teaching inspired the Czechs to seek independence at the end of World War I. He was the first president of an independent Czechoslovakia from 1918 to 1935.

334 *Hrvatska misao* (Croatian Opinion) was a monthly magazine with a progressive outlook on literature, politics and social issues. Altogether only eight issues appeared, all in the course of 1897 and all published in Prague.

335 *"Jung Wien"* (Young Vienna) was a broad movement, including writers, visual artists and intellectuals who abandoned the naturalist trend in arts and literature and called themselves "modernists." The group included Peter Altenberg (see endnote 330), Hugo von Hofmannsthal (see endnote 329) and Arthur Schnitzler (see endnote 170), among others. The weekly newspaper *Die Zeit* (The Times) appeared between 1902 and 1904, preceded in influence by *Wiener Rundschau* (Vienna Review) published from 1895 to 1901. Hermann Bahr (1863–1934) was a highly influential member of the *Young Vienna movement*, active as a writer, playwright, and most of all as the art critic who was the first to use such terms as "modernism", "symbolism" and "impressionism" in his critical writings.

336 See endnote 305.

337 Isidor (Izidor) Kršnjavi (1845–1927) was an art historian, painter and politician. After joining Ban Khuen's National Party, he entered the government and held the position identifiable in today's terms as the Minister of Education. This was why Jeny turned to him for help, and all the more so because Kršnjavi was from Slavonia. He was born in Našice (a small town south of Osijek) and had worked as a high school teacher and journalist in Osijek before becoming a politician.

338 The book was subtitled "An Inquiry into the Cause of Industrial Depressions and of Increase of Want with Increase of Wealth".

339 See endnote 382.

340 Friar Kerubin Šegvić (1867–1945) was a Catholic priest, professor of philosophy, literary critic and a convinced promoter of the theory that Croats were not of Slav but of Gothic origin, akin to German and Nordic people.

341 See endnote 312.

342 This is only partially correct. The pavilion was, in fact, originally built in Budapest during the celebration of the Millennium of the Hungarian kingdom in 1896, to provide a temporary exhibition hall for Croatian art. Its metal-frame structure was subsequently transported to Zagreb to be used for the construction of a permanent Art Pavilion, which opened its doors in January 1898.

343 As a member of the Khuen Héderváry's government, Isidor Kršnjavi was responsible for matters concerning both education and culture. See also endnote 337.

344 Antun Gustav Matoš (1873–1914) was a Croatian writer, poet and essayist, significant for being an early and successful proponent of modernism in Croatian literature.

345 Robert Frangeš Mihanović (1872–1940) was a prominent Croatian sculptor, teacher and one of the founders of the Society of Croatian Artists. His best-known work is the equestrian monument to the ninth-century Croatian King Tomislav erected in front of the Central Railway Station in Zagreb.

346 Josip Šokčević (1811–1896), born in Vinkovci (Slavonia), was a celebrated general in the Austrian army and Ban (Croatian governor) from 1860 to 1867.

347 Rudolf Valdec (1872–1929) was, along with Robert Frangeš, one of the founders of the Society of Croatian Artists and the Croatian school of sculptors.

348 See endnote 312.

349 Bela Čikoš Sesija (1864–1931), painter in a symbolist style, known for his historical themes.

350 Oton Iveković (1869–1939), painter of historical motives.

351 Ferdo Kovačević (1870–1927), painter.

352 Menci Clement (Klement) Crnčić (1865–1930), modernist painter of marine vistas.

353 Xeres de la Maraja was one of many pseudonyms of Milan Begović, poet and dramaturg. For more on Begović, see endnote 389.

354 Vladimir Nazor (1876–1949), poet and short story writer, member of the "modernist" movement. He was politically active in the Yugoslav resistance movement during World War II and served as the first president of the People's Republic of Croatia from 1946 to 1949.

355 Dr. Milivoj Dežman Ivanov (1873–1940) was a renowned medical doctor specializing in tuberculosis, as well as an active member of the "modernist" movement and an important figure in Zagreb cultural circles, as essayist, dramaturg, art critic and journalist.

356 *Naše težnje* (Our Objectives) published in *Hrvatski Salon* (Croatian Salon) in 1898.

357 The Illyrian movement (circa 1830–1848) was a significant Croatian cultural and political movement with the objective of revitalizing and standardizing the Croatian language, promoting Croatian cultural unity and establishing a respectable place for the Croatian nation in the community of Slavic nations within the Habsburg monarchy.

358 The ceremony of the unveiling of the monument took place on 17 July 1898, followed by a big party attended by representatives of military circles and all municipal institutions. Several days later, on 24 July, the German-language newspaper *Die Drau* published the mentioned poem by Vilma Miskolczy.

359 Alexandre Cabanel (1823–1889), French painter of historic scenes and portraits.

360 A small coastal town near Dubrovnik, Bukovac's birthplace.

361 For Bela Čikoš Sesija, see endnote 349. For Menci Clement Crnčić, see endnote 352.

362 Srđan Tucić (1873–1940), Croatian dramaturg and playwright.

363 See endnote 148.

364 See endnote 382.

365 See endnote 389.

366 Mihovil Nikolić (1878–1951), Croatian lyrical poet.

367 See endnote 240.

368 Josip (Josef) Frank (1844–1911), lawyer and politician, led a strongly nationalist faction within the Ante Starčević's Party of Rights (see endnote 148), labelled *Čista stranka prava* (Pure Party of Rights) following the dramatic split within the party in 1896 (see endnote 371). The faction eventually became a party of its own, known as Frank's Party and its followers as *frankovci* (Frankists). The Party was known in subsequent years for its strong anti-Serbian and anti-Yugoslav stand.

369 A hint that Josip Frank was of Jewish origin.

370 Ivica (Ivo) Frank (1877–1939) participated in the burning of the Hungarian flag in Zagreb in 1895 and was politically active in the defence of Croatian sovereign rights, particularly as a member of his father's Pure Party of Rights. As such, he was elected a member of the Croatian representative assembly (Sabor). Firmly opposing the Yugoslav project of the unification of South Slavs and a political collaboration with Serbia, he was disillusioned with politics after the 1918 peace agreement and the foundation of Yugoslavia as a new state. He was equally disillusioned with the ultranationalist turn of some followers of his father's party, and he went into exile. He settled in Budapest where he died in 1939.

371 Fran Folnegović (1848–1903) was next in command of the original Party of Rights, until he criticized the burning of the Hungarian flag in Zagreb in 1895 by young Croatian nationalists. As a consequence, the party split into two factions in 1896—on the one side, the Pure Party of Rights, with Ante Starčević and Josip Frank as leaders, also known as *pravaši* (rights defenders), and, on the other, the Party of Rights, with Folnegović and the newspaper *Hrvatska domovina* (Croatian Homeland), known as *domovinaši* (homelanders). For more on the original Party of Rights, see endnote 148. For more on the Pure Party of Rights under Josip Frank's leadership, see endnote 368.

372 Ignác Strasnoff (Strasznof) was a first-class swindler from Hungary, who pretended to be of noble origin and capable of obtaining favours from the imperial court. He was eventually caught in 1906 and sentenced to eight years of prison for fraud and extortion of money from several high-level members of the Catholic Church in Croatia, with Dr. Josip Frank being unwittingly implicated in those fraudulent transactions.

373 Vladimir Frank (1873–1916), Josip Frank's eldest son was also a politician and lawyer. He was an active member of the Pure Party of Rights, and, as such, elected in 1906 to the Croatian representative assembly (*Sabor*).

374 David Schwarz (1850–1897), Croatian-Hungarian aviation pioneer, who built the first airship with a rigid hull, which served as the prototype for the famous Zeppelin dirigibles.

375 Slavko Kvaternik (1878–1947) was a high-level officer in the Austrian-Hungarian Army during World War I and one of the founders of the *Ustaša* Croatian nationalist movement in the late 1920s. Immediately upon the arrival of German troops in Yugoslavia, on 10 April 1941, he announced over the radio the creation of the Independent State of Croatia and became its first Chief Commander of the Armed Forces and Minister of Defence. He held those positions until early 1942, when he fell out of favour with Ante Pavelić, the head of the Croatian State. Accompanied by his family, he then left the country and spent the rest of the war in Slovakia. In 1945, Allied troops delivered Slavko Kvaternik to the new communist government of Yugoslavia. He was tried as a war criminal and executed in 1947.

376 Eugen (Dido) Kvaternik (1910–1962), son of Slavko Kvaternik and Olga Frank (daughter of Josip Frank), was, from an early age, involved in the extreme Croatian nationalist *Ustaša* movement. At the creation of the Independent State of Croatia, he was appointed Chief of Internal Security Services, responsible for ethnic cleansing and elimination of all Jews and Serbs in the territory of the State. Although always extremely loyal to Ante Pavelić, the Head of State, he found himself, in early 1942, in a serious disagreement with his leader, and went into exile with his father Slavko Kvaternik (see endnote 375) and the rest of the entire family, first in Slovakia, and later in Argentina, where he died in a car accident in 1962.

377 Eugen Kumičić (1850–1904) was a well-known author of novels with historical and social themes and an essayist. He was also a politician, a member of the Party of Rights and an elected member of the Croatian parliamentary assembly (*Sabor*).

378 The popular name of Nikola Šubić Zrinski Square in downtown Zagreb.

379 Carl Michael Ziehrer (1843–1922) was an Austrian composer and military band conductor, competing his entire life with the Strauss family members for popular appreciation.

380 Namely, the Holy Crown of Hungary, signifying here the monarchical rule as such. The Croatian territory was, at the time, part of the Kingdom of Hungary within the Austrian-Hungarian Empire.

381 Archduke Leopold Salvator of Austria (1863–1931), Prince of Tuscany, member of the House of Habsburg-Lorraine royal family.

382 Ante Tresić-Pavičić (1867–1949), a Croatian poet born on the island of Hvar, known for his epic poetry and poetic dramas with historic themes, among them *Simeon Veliki* (Simeon the Great) published in 1897. Tresić-Pavičić was actively involved in politics (as a member of the nationalistic Party of Rights) and served between 1919 and 1927 as ambassador to Spain and the USA on behalf of the Kingdom of Yugoslavia.

383 Andrija Fijan (1851–1911) was an acclaimed Croatian actor and director, best known for his rendering of Shakespearean characters. Alexander Moissi (Aleksandër Moisiu) (1879–1935), Austrian actor of Albanian origin and Josef Gottfried Ignaz Kainz (1858–1910), Austrian actor of Hungarian origin, were both highly acclaimed theatre performers in Vienna. Ignjat (Ignacij) Borštnik (1858–1919) and his wife Zofija (Sofija) Zvonarjeva-Borštnik (1868–1948) were Slovenian theatre actors who performed with a remarkable success both

in Zagreb and Ljubljana (Slovenia). Milica Mihičić (1864–1950) had a 50-year career as an actress in Zagreb.

384 Giacomo Leopardi (1798–1837), Italian poet, philosopher and essayist.

385 Giosuè Carducci (1835–1907) is considered the most important Italian national poet of the nineteenth century and was awarded the Nobel Prize in Literature in 1906.

386 Gabriele d'Annunzio (1863–1938) was a celebrated Italian poet and playwright, renowned for his aestheticism and flamboyance, both in life and his literary output. He was a precursor in style and ideology to Mussolini's fascism, due to his political and nationalist activities, particularly his irredentism—the belief that Italy should regain power over all the territories controlled by the Roman Empire centuries earlier. He became famous for his resolve, at the end of World War I, to extend Italy's control of the Adriatic Sea by occupying Istria, Hrvatsko Primorje, and notably, the port of Rijeka. That led him, among his other famous theatrics, to undertake spectacular military airplane exhibitions flying over Trieste and Rijeka (Fiume), scattering propaganda leaflets from the air.

387 Ivo Vojnović (1857–1929), a native of Dubrovnik, of Serbian origin, was a renowned playwright, best known for his *Ekvinocij* (Equinox) (1898) and *Dubrovačka trilogija* (Dubrovnik Trilogy) (1903).

388 Stjepan Miletić (1868–1908), playwright and theatre critic, is best known for his immense impact on the theatrical culture in Zagreb by founding the first actors' school in the city. He provided generous financial support for, and innovative leadership at, the National Theatre, whose new building opened in 1895 during his tenure as its director. *Hrvatsko glumište* (Croatian Stage) was a collection of his critical essays and reminiscences, put together and published in one volume in 1904.

389 Milan Begović (1876–1948) was a prolific and versatile Croatian novelist, poet and playwright. *Knjiga Boccadoro* (The Book of Bocca d'oro) was published in 1900 under the pseudonym Xeres de la Maraja. It was a pure lyrical expression of aesthetic hedonism and a typical example of modernist literary style.

390 See endnote 354.

391 Guy de Maupassant (1850–1893), author of numerous short stories, belonged to the naturalist movement of French writers, as was Gustave Flaubert (1821–1880), the French novelist best known for his portrait of *Madame Bovary* (1857), as well as symbolist poets Paul-Marie Verlaine (1844–1896) and Charles Baudelaire (1821–1867). For Baudelaire, see also endnote 182.

392 François, Duke de La Rochefoucauld (1613–1680) published in 1665 a slim collection of moral philosophy maxims, which made him famous.

393 Podsused is a small settlement at the foot of the remnants of a medieval fortress called Sused Grad, located on the slopes of the Medved Mountain (Medvednica) near Zagreb. The settlement is today a suburb of Zagreb.

394 Kundry and Senta were romantic heroines of Richard Wagner's operas *Parsifal* (1882) and *The Flying Dutchman* (1843), respectively.

395 *Paul and Virginia* is a novel written in 1788 by Jacques-Henri Bernardin de Saint-Pierre about the innocent childhood of two young people who fell in love on the distant island of Ile de France (today's Mauritius) and were tragically separated.

396 The twelfth-century philosopher and monk, Pierre Abélard, and lively and intelligent Héloïse, his pupil, were deeply in love. They were forbidden to see each other by her uncle and guardian and so spent most of their lives in their respective convents, writing each other letters containing expressions of their passionate physical love, and maintaining keen theological discussions.

397 See endnote 97.

398 Bjørnstjerne Bjørnson (1832–1910) was a Norwegian poet and playwright, awarded the Nobel Prize in Literature in 1903. A strong nationalist, he authored the patriotic lyrics of a song first produced publicly in 1864 which still serves as an unofficial Norwegian anthem.

399 Jens Peter Jakobsen (1847–1885) was a Danish novelist, poet and scientist (botanist). His depiction of women driven by their sexual desires had a major influence on English writer D. H. Lawrence, among others.

400 See endnote 98.

401 See endnote 304.

402 Ellen Karolina Sofia Key (1849–1926) was a Swedish feminist writer, renowned since the 1870s for her commentaries on family life, child education and ethical questions concerning women's lives.

403 August Bebel (1840–1913) was the founder and leader of the Socialist Democratic Workers' Party of Germany. He was an uncompromising advocate for the workers' movement, for peace and understanding among nations, as well as for an all-encompassing female emancipation.

404 Gospić is a small town in central Lika, one of the least economically developed regions of Croatia in those days. See also endnote 303.

405 Priessnitztal sanatorium was located on the outskirts of Mödling, a small town at the edge of the celebrated Vienna Woods, the forest-covered hills near Vienna, in Lower Austria.

406 Archduke Otto of Austria (1865–1906) was a member of the imperial Habsburg family, nephew of Emperor Franz Joseph of Austria and father of Charles I, the last Austrian Emperor (1916–1918). Otto was known for his libertine life.

407 Emile Zola (1840–1902), French author in the naturalist style. His series of novels about the Rougon-Macquart family consisted of 20 volumes written between 1871 and 1893 and carried the subtitle "The Natural and Social History of a Family under the Second Empire".

408 Max Klinger (1857–1920) was a German painter, sculptor and graphic artist. Max Slevgot (1868–1932) and Max Liebermann (1847–1935), both

German, were known for their impressionist landscapes. Regarding Gustav Klimt, Joseph Hoffmann and Koloman Moser, see endnote 332.

409 Alexander Girardi (1850–1918) was an extremely popular Viennese actor and operatic singer, still remembered today for his favourite boater hat, the "Girardi hat", named after him. See also endnote 132.

410 *Der Verschwender* (The Spendthrift) was written and first performed by Ferdinand Raimund (1790–1836) in 1833. *Der böse Geist Lumpaczivagabundus oder Das liederliche Kleeblatt* (The Evil Spirit of Lumpazivagabundus or The Messy Cloverleaf) was a play written by Johann Nestroy (1801-1862) in 1835. The two Viennese playwrights wrote and performed a number of highly popular comedic plays in a very successful style of theatrical farces and parodies of the Viennese bourgeois society that are still performed today in the Raimund Theatre. See also endnotes 9 and 169.

411 Karl Kraus (1874–1936), Austrian writer, journalist, satirist and playwright.

412 Darda is a small Croatian municipality located north of Osijek, across the River Drava, in the region called Baranya. Until World War I, the entire Baranya region was under the direct administrative rule of the Kingdom of Hungary and not part of Croatia.

413 Csíkszereda is a small town known today as Miercurea Ciuc in a largely Hungarian-speaking ethnocultural region of Transylvania in western Romania. Between 1876 and 1918, Csíkszereda was a county seat in the historically defined administrative region of Bukovina on the eastern borders of the Kingdom of Hungary. Bukovina disappeared as a distinct region with a distinct history, following its incorporation into Romania after World War I. Its northern part was occupied by the Soviets in 1940 and has since remained part of Ukraine.

414 A small town in the Krapina-Zagorje region, in northern Croatia.

CPSIA information can be obtained
at www.ICGtesting.com
Printed in the USA
BVHW071542190920
589122BV00003B/10

9 781525 556296